DØ285900

The publisher gratefully acknowledges the generous support
of the Anne G. Lipow Endowment Fund for Social Justice and
Human Rights of the University of California Press Foundation,
which was established by Stephen M. Silberstein.

Interrupted Life

Interrupted Life

*Experiences of Incarcerated Women
in the United States*

———

Edited by

Rickie Solinger, Paula C. Johnson,
Martha L. Raimon, Tina Reynolds,
and Ruby C. Tapia

UNIVERSITY OF CALIFORNIA PRESS

Berkeley   Los Angeles   London

University of California Press, one of the most distinguished university presses in the United States, enriches lives around the world by advancing scholarship in the humanities, social sciences, and natural sciences. Its activities are supported by the UC Press Foundation and by philanthropic contributions from individuals and institutions. For more information, visit www.ucpress.edu.

University of California Press
Berkeley and Los Angeles, California

University of California Press, Ltd.
London, England

Library of Congress Cataloging-in-Publication Data

Interrupted life : experiences of incarcerated women in the United States / edited by Rickie Solinger . . . [et al.].
   p. cm.
  Includes bibliographical references and index.
   ISBN 978-0-520-25249-3 (cloth : alk. paper)—ISBN 978-0-520-25889-1 (pbk. : alk. paper)
   1. Women prisoners—United States.   2. Female offenders—United States.   3. Women prisoners—Abuse of—United States.   4. Children of women prisoners—Services for—United States.   5. Women prisoners—Family relationships—United States.   I. Solinger, Rickie, 1947–
HV9471.I63   2010
365'.430973—dc22   2009023612

Manufactured in the United States of America

19   18   17   16   15   14   13   12   11   10
10   9   8   7   6   5   4   3   2   1

This book is printed on Cascades Enviro 100, a 100% post consumer waste, recycled, de-inked fiber. FSC recycled certified and processed chlorine free. It is acid free, Ecologo certified, and manufactured by BioGas energy.

CONTENTS

Certain Failures

Representing the Experiences of Incarcerated Women in the United States

Ruby C. Tapia

The politics of representing the experiences of incarcerated women play out on a landscape of necessity and violence. To turn away from the need to understand and reveal the mechanisms and circumstances of dehumanization that mark the women's prison is unconscionable in any political or intellectual sphere that makes a claim to feminism in the twenty-first century. To believe that any of us can fully render this picture for ourselves or for anyone else is equally so. For the past three years, the editors of this volume have been compiling writings that seek to illuminate the environment and experiences of incarcerated women in the United States. The book is necessary but will inevitably fail this mission—substantially. Publishing personal, academic, and artistic testimonies to the tools and intricacies of the prison machine is essential if we are ever to dismantle it, but we must also recognize that we cannot sufficiently know the complex reality of the prison system. In representing and reading the experiences of women-not-ourselves who have been institutionally erased from the category of human beings, we have to know that failure is certain, and we have to try to determine why.

Since 1977, the population of women prisoners in the United States has increased by over 700 percent. These women are without access to proper health care, without their children, whom many of them will lose permanently; they are without. These stark details are obscene in their materiality. They are facts, but they are only a piece of the picture. The picture is impossible. Indeed, the picture is the problem.

If pictures give us "windows" or "inside looks," if they provide "rare glimpses" into brutal experiences not our own, enabling us to see ourselves "there," then we recruit them to play central roles in what Saidiya Hartman aptly indicts as "the violence of identification." If we set out to *make*—or take with us—these pictures, then we do far worse: we orchestrate this violence. We must consistently interrogate and disrupt this relationship between pictures of "others" and what we imagine and want them to do for "us." This is the aim of this book, the context in which it struggles, perhaps achieves some success, and yet fails in important ways. But this context not only carries the risk of creating unproductive, even violent, relations of representation and interpretation, it is also, significantly, produced by an institution of trauma. The trauma of the prison is characterized by both unspeakability and ubiquity, so the failure of figuring this trauma is as inevitable as the attempt to define it is urgent.

This volume is not and cannot be a full picture of women's incarceration: it is a researched, multivocal struggle to highlight the gender-specific technologies of dehumanization within the prison system. It stages a variety of testimonies to the daily violations of the rights, the bodies, the very *lives* of women afflicted by the misguided, ineffectual, discriminatory, and deadly practices of criminal "justice" as they pertain to women. The testimonies are different, their foci vary, and the remedies they suggest sometimes diverge. Through the voices of more than fifty incarcerated and formerly incarcerated women, and the writings of activists, policy makers, scholars and other experts, this collection renders a dialogue *about* women's experiences of and struggles against incarceration, not—as a whole—the experiences themselves. Each piece, in its own way, treats the violence perpetrated by the notion of rehabilitating people in and through human cages and renders a specific struggle to end this violence. Real women's real experiences are at stake, but these experiences are not meant to be processed, assimilated, left on the page as understood. They are meant—as we frame them here—to inform and to incite movement—toward the pursuit of more information, toward change.

Beyond combating the erasure and silencing of incarcerated and formerly incarcerated women, this volume launches a multidisciplinary and systematic critique not only of institutional definitions and treatments of "criminality" but also of traditional notions of activism, resistance, and community. It walks a thin and fraught line between rendering the prison as a machine of dehumanization and filling in the gaps in discourses about the prison with representations of the fighting, living, and loving that women practice and redefine in the face of this dehumanization. At the same time that it interrogates the pervasive intricacies of gender, racial, and sexual violence within the prison system, this book illuminates the creative and dynamic practices of expression, activism, and stringent social critique among incarcerated women, formerly incarcerated women, and their allies.

Together, the contributors to this book offer an unprecedented dialogue on the complexities of the prison as institution, the circumstances of death upon which it capitalizes, and the strategies of incarcerated women's daily struggles, resistance, and survival. Lawyers, scholars, artists, activists—many of them with firsthand, lived experience of the prison—render images of the prison that, together, train our vision toward what, exactly, it systematically interrupts: justice, humanity, life. The many voices here, often testifying to the same mechanisms of dehumanization, depict the reach of the prison's violence and the imperative to work against it within every sphere it touches.

This book is a call to action, a demand that we examine and uproot common-sense notions of right and wrong, justice and injustice, action and inaction, and life and death as they pertain to women's imprisonment and the social conditions that produce it. Here you will find (at least) two philosophically different approaches to addressing the iniquities of the prison: reform and abolition. Reforming the prison entails changing its existing practices to make the system a better one. Abolishing the prison entails dismantling it wholesale. Reformers object to how the prison is administered. Abolitionists object to the prison's very existence. We have approached this project as abolitionists who seek to participate in the current swell of activism inside and outside the prison that focuses on its dismantling. Not every piece in this volume shares this agenda, but we have selected each piece for its insights into information and strategy, the debates in which it participates, and the stakes of its approaches and conclusions. We invite readers to take issue and to keep taking issue. The debates and disagreements here are urgent; the gaps and seams are the maps to follow and ponder.

The United States incarcerates a larger percentage of its population than any nation in the world. This society's commitment to mandatory minimum sentences, to three-strikes laws, to broad and harsh practices of criminalization based on race and class yields a staggering picture of prisons today:

- Nearly 70 percent of women in prison are African American or Latina; female imprisonment in the United States has increased 757 percent since 1977.
- The majority of women incarcerated by the criminal justice system are poor and lacking in economic support systems.
- The majority of women in prison are there because of nonviolent offenses or low-level drug offenses.
- Most women in prison are not well educated and have few employment opportunities and skills.
- High percentages of incarcerated women have been victims of physical and/ or sexual abuse, often before the age of eighteen.
- As a result of childhood trauma, many women in prison experience physical and mental health problems and have histories of substance abuse.
- The vast majority of women in prison are mothers, and before incarceration, mothers were more likely than fathers to have been supporting and/or caring for their children.

This volume focuses on a world it can never fully represent: the realities of women's experiences inside prison. Toward that end, it presents narratives, essays, poetry, and reports that approach the social, material, and emotional complexities of being incarcerated. We have organized the testimonies of its contributors under topics that highlight the lived experiences of struggle, family, community, and creativity within the intricate, locked system of racism, sexism, classism, and homophobia that pervades U.S. prisons.

The first section, "Defining the Problem," provides an overview of and orientation to the origins, impacts, and experiences of women's incarceration, framing the prison system as both a unique institution of specific gendered violence and an index of broader social inequalities. The section that follows, "Being a Mother from the Inside," revises the notion that motherhood in the United States is "sacred," or even a *right,* when the mothers in question are poor, of color, and incarcerated. Indeed, families targeted for separation are overwhelmingly families of color, which underscores the racial qualification for motherhood established in popular discourse and by the language and actions of many politicians and policy makers. Due to the siting of prisons and other logistical obstacles, half of all incarcerated mothers do not get visits from their children, and many permanently lose custody of their children as a result. The writings in this section explore what motherhood means behind bars and the prison's effective and violent perpetuation of the idea that "legitimate" mothers are white and middle or upper class.

Forced separation and institutional policies also disrupt women's relationships with spouses, partners, and others who are significant in their lives. "Intimacy, Sexuality, and Gender Identity Inside" focuses on the ways that incarcerated women address their needs for closeness, community, and self-definition, particularly how they express their gender and sexual identities. As the essays in this section reveal, self-love and loving and affectionate relationships between women under the most oppressive circumstances are important acts of resistance to the state's systematic attempts to dehumanize them. Yet women pursuing intimacy inside prison are subject to the same prejudices and dangers they would face outside.

The essays in "Creating and Maintaining Intellectual, Spiritual, and Creative Life Inside" demonstrate how incarcerated women, often with the support of scholar- and artist-activist volunteers, maintain and fortify their lives inside. Through reading, writing poems and memoirs, praying, making spiritual life and art, and participating in critical discourse, incarcerated women practice a way of living that is complex, creative, and forward looking in the face of daily violence and systematically produced hopelessness. The contributors to this section illumine the profound intellectual, spiritual, and creative productions and experiences of words and art pushing against the prison. Women inside read and write, discuss and create, absorb and connect. They make language, images, and objects. We do not offer these creations to bring the reader comfort or to romanticize the resistance and survival of incarcerated women. They appear here because the life-affirming practices they represent constitute basic connections to self and community, the significance and stakes of which are far greater than they would be in any other context. We want this difference to register.

When Americans engage today in a national conversation about the right to adequate health care, few mention the abysmal standards of health care for the incarcerated. "Struggling for Health Care" calls attention to the effects of inferior or absent health care on women behind bars, many of whom are harmed by this neglect and some of whom die. The particular health care needs of women inside prison are not only unmet, they are used—by virtue of their denial—as further punishment. Refusing women the ability and resources to care for their bodies and psyches, the prison's health care system further dehumanizes incarcerated women. Inside, women's basic needs become liabilities; their individual circumstances of health or sickness assume a valence and materiality that can be deadly. The pieces in this section view health care as a basic human right and explore the pervasiveness and circumstances of its denial to incarcerated women.

"Serving Time, Sentenced and Unsentenced" renders the arbitrary, unchecked, and far-reaching injustice of incarceration as a system. Institutions of law enforcement, the courts, sentencing practices, and the geography and architecture of prisons all work together to produce a neoslavery system. The arbitrariness and ad hoc nature of sentencing—while illogical and unjust—serves to devalue life based on gender, race, class, and sexuality, mirroring the historical social landscape of the United States. Each essay in this section offers perspective on the inconsistent politics of sentencing at different levels and institutions within the system. At the same time that these institutions often contradict one another, they collaborate in spirit and ultimate effect to treat the lives of incarcerated women as worthless. As sentences grow more strict and parole boards assume the charge of "resentencing," women accused of violent crimes are kept locked up for periods far in excess of their minimum sentences. These longer sentences are producing both an institutional crisis as the population of incarcerated women ages and a crisis for the women themselves, who represent no threat to society and whose incarceration does no more than prolong the denial of their human dignity. This section also reveals the targeting of other "special" populations: with no trials and often no formal sentencing, immigrants and political refugees have even less protection than U.S. citizens do. And for women who are sentenced to death, erasure and invisibility mark their experience from the moment they are convicted. Their impending murder frames their existence, and the ability to account for these women's humanity is utterly absent within the system.

The next section, "Struggling for Rights," brings into relief the simple, basic, ugly contradiction between humanity and the prison. The pieces in this section raise the question of whether incarceration is a justifiable enterprise and document efforts to fight against the degradation and inhumane policies of the prison. How, given such profound limitations, do activists inside organize to be heard? Who on the outside is listening? The voices in this section frame the violences perpetuated inside and through the prison as systematic arms of dehumanization. They ask readers to consider how the system both devalues the basic human rights and experiences of motherhood, family, and work and recruits them as technologies of punishment for incarcerated women.

The final section, "Being Out," considers critical questions about life after incarceration. All formerly incarcerated women face an enormously complex array of issues involving family, work, housing, education, and other basic matters of life. Poor women of color are especially hard hit by structural obstacles when they leave prison, because not only do they face laws that discriminate against formerly incarcerated persons, but they are also likely to encounter racism and sexism among employers, landlords, institutions, and individuals whose relative power threatens the livelihoods of formerly incarcerated women. These women are victims of time violently lost and served. Their vulnerabilities are unique and extreme.

The explosive growth of the female population in jails and prisons reflects pervasive gender mandates in U.S. society and women's continuing subordinate social and economic status. The overrepresentation of people of color and poor people within the prison system reflects the deeply entrenched forces of institutional racism and class prejudice in the society. U.S. politicians and policy makers turn away from the needs of millions of women for education, employment, physical and mental health services, substance abuse treatment, and economic security. Too many politicians, policy makers, and many ordinary Americans see no problem responding to the crises brought on by this negligence by building more prisons and by locking up more women.

The perspectives of incarcerated women and their allies in this volume offer an elaborate dialogue on women's incarceration as a specific arm of state violence, one with its own refined technologies of social and material death. They also reveal the prison to be a microcosm of larger U.S. society, which devalues women and poor people and people of color so as to make hideous lies of the "American" ideals of equality and democracy. In addition to offering readers a multidimensional rendering of these lies and their deadly manifestations, the book offers testimonies that "illuminate past, present, and future possibilities for the reinvention of democracy," as scholar-activist Joy James has said. Toward this end, we encourage readers to engage with the dialogues here. We invite you to decipher the mission and practices that inspired the collection and to ally with the growing movement to dismantle systems of imprisonment and oppression through solidarity, collaboration, and action.

PART ONE

Defining the Problem

WHY IS THE UNITED STATES ENGAGING IN—gripped by—a crisis of mass incarceration today? What national and international factors are feeding this development, and whose lives are at stake? This volume begins with a series of pieces that lay out basic principles and analyses, gather and introduce voices of recently and currently incarcerated women, and consider dilemmas and strategies confronting individuals and groups working in the interests of incarcerated women and their families. Looking at the phenomenon in the largest terms, internationally renowned prison abolitionist Julia Sudbury explains the socioeconomic roots of mass incarceration in the United States in the context of the war on drugs and patterns of global migration and the criminalization of migrants. These developments, Sudbury explains, have underwritten the emergence of a poisonous prison-industrial complex in late twentieth-century America, a construct that justifies removing resources from poor communities of color to beef up law enforcement and prison construction.

Whereas the rampant growth of the prison-industrial complex is naturalized to the point of invisibility for many Americans, a recent United Nations report on violence against women in U.S. prisons, excerpts of which appear in this introductory section, demonstrates that in some quarters, the world is paying attention to the U.S. crisis of mass incarceration.

Still, the question remains, if many Americans are unaware of the prison-industrial complex, and unaware of the community crises generated by the policies and politics of mass incarceration, who can hear the voices of individual incarcerated

Prison Family, 1991. Photograph by Melissa Springer

women? Beginning in this section and continuing throughout the volume, we privilege this voice above all, offering poems, stories, essays, and autobiographical statements from women who have been—and are—inside. Joanne Archibald's prison autobiography is divided in half: the first part appears in this section, and the second part is in the final section. Kinnari Jivani, a poet whose work appears throughout the volume, considers life constrained by "the heavy six digit chain," and poet Elizabeth Leslie asks, "How long should the pain last?"

Formerly incarcerated editor Tina Reynolds lays down some basic principles about the politics of vocabulary, "in opposition to the language that society has adopted to unidentify people who have been in conflict with the law." Reynolds looks at the most commonly and unconsciously used locutions—"reentry," for example, and "inmate"—explaining why and how these word choices justify degradation and mass incarceration. She considers why other words and expressions can serve us better.

Because this book focuses on the experiences of incarcerated *women* in the United States, the subject of their children—and the real lives of these children—is a shadow topic that fights at every turn for air. Thus, we have placed "Children of Incarcerated Parents: A Bill of Rights" at the front of the volume to point to some of the crucial needs in this domain. This document also exemplifies a potent and popular form of claims making among populations stuck in prisons, venues where authorities depend on maintaining near rights-free vacuums.

Finally, demonstrating the complexities of *both* being an ally *and* embracing prison-abolition politics, Kay Whitlock risks opprobrium of various kinds as she lays down her very personal account of joining the struggle.

Overall, the pieces in this section lay down key perspectives on U.S. prisons as sites for violating human rights. In doing so, they underscore the importance of choosing and using language deliberately in the interests of human dignity for incarcerated and formerly incarcerated persons.

Unpacking the Crisis

Women of Color, Globalization, and the Prison-Industrial Complex

Julia Sudbury

The emergence of a vibrant antiprison movement has brought attention to the crisis of mass incarceration in the United States. This crisis is a direct outgrowth of tough-on-crime policies that have lengthened prison sentences and widened the net of activities that U.S. society deals with through imprisonment. As more and more people have received longer sentences, federal and state governments have responded to the ensuing overcrowding by building more prisons and contracting with private prison firms for additional prison beds. Low-income women and girls of color have particularly felt the impacts of the exponential growth in the use of prisons and jails.[1] Since the 1980s, governments have withdrawn resources from community infrastructure and economic supports for low-income families, in part to fund costly law enforcement and prison budgets.[2] This shift in public spending priorities is one manifestation of a global process of economic restructuring. Faced with ever-shrinking options amid these social and economic transformations, women turn to survival strategies that are increasingly criminalized. Poverty, racism, gender violence, and sometimes addiction intersect to create a cycle of survival, criminalization, and repeated incarceration. At the same time, as mothers, grandmothers, and community activists, women in low-income communities of color bear the burden of supporting and advocating for loved ones who have been locked up and caring for their dependents.

To address the cycle of mass incarceration, activists, academics, and policy makers need to understand the socioeconomic conditions that lie at its root. Unpacking these root causes allows us to identify meaningful transformative possibilities for long-lasting change. Connecting these phenomena with global transformations enables us to identify commonalties with women's struggles for justice in other parts of the world and thus strengthen transnational feminist solidarities. This essay examines four interlocking factors that underlie the prison crisis. First, I examine the impacts of globalization and economic restructuring on low-income communities in the United States. The rise in low-waged casual labor and cutbacks in welfare, education, health care, and social provision all contribute to women's economic insecurity, leading to the use of criminalized survival strategies. Second, I explore the war on drugs, a set of policies and practices that are U.S. led but global in nature and that have led to an exponential rise in domestic and international imprisonment. Third, I explore the role of globalization in fueling migration from the global South, the criminalization of migration, and the growth in immigrant incarceration in the United States. Finally, I describe the emergence of the prison-industrial complex, a symbiotic relationship between corporate and governmental interests that has fueled prison expansion in the United States and increasingly around the world. As an activist-scholar, my writing aims to encourage the reader to live in the solution rather than simply dissect the problem. The second part of the essay discusses the antiprison movement. I explore the antiracist and feminist abolitionist visions developed by antiprison activists and describe steps toward a world without prisons. This section includes examples of contemporary abolitionist work in the United States and Canada. I hope that these examples may dismantle the apparent omnipotence of the prison-industrial complex and help inspire grassroots action.

THE PROBLEM
Economic Restructuring and the War on the Poor

The introduction of Reaganomics in the 1980s signaled the beginning of a lasting shift in U.S. economic policy.[3] Arguing that "small government"—a combination of reduced spending on social provision, reduced government restrictions on corporate profit-making, and tax cuts—was necessary to stimulate economic growth and stem unemployment, the Reagan administration gradually rolled back the supports and protections on which many working families relied. Despite the rhetoric of small government, Reagan dramatically increased government spending on the military and imprisonment. During the 1980s, both federal and state criminal justice budgets grew exponentially as prison populations swelled due to tough-on-crime legislation and the war on drugs.[4] This shift from welfare state to law-and-order state was not unique to the United States. In Britain, for example, Thatcherism pushed a laissez-faire government, the ascendance of the free market, privatization, union busting, and cutbacks to the welfare state. And like Reagan, Thatcher pursued a racialized war on crime that targeted low-income communities of color for surveillance and punishment.[5]

At a global level, these strategies can be seen as political responses to corporate economic restructuring. Since the 1970s, corporations have begun to separate their manufacturing and administrative components. By using new technological developments, corporate headquarters in advanced capitalist nations could manage manufacturing operations in locations where land and labor were cheaper. Corporations headquartered in the United States and Europe were quick to capitalize on the low-waged, nonunionized women workers in nations in Asia, Latin America, and the Caribbean, many of which were still struggling with the legacies of colonialism and underdevelopment. As manufacturing moved overseas, economies in advanced industrialized countries began to shift toward service industries and specialized management and technology. A segmented labor market emerged, consisting of highly paid, high-tech positions for highly educated workers and more numerous low-waged, nonunionized, and casual positions.[6] With well-paying unionized skilled trade jobs in decline, women and men in urban communities faced unemployment or dead-end jobs that did not pay enough to support a family. Cutbacks and trickle-down economics were a double-pronged tool that governments in advanced industrialized nations used to reduce the potential economic burden of a growing population that was surplus to the needs of global capital. And criminalization and warehousing were the weapons of choice for minimizing the potential for social unrest and dissent.[7]

During her reign, Thatcher coined the acronym TINA, There Is No Alternative, to describe the lasting shift in economic policy signaled by free trade and economic liberalization. Since the 1980s, even left-leaning parties have been unwilling or unable to turn the tide of neoliberalism.[8] The impact on low-income women and girls of color of three decades of neoliberal policies has been severe. A key aspect of the move toward "small government" has been the radical transformation of welfare. Welfare reform has targeted women of color, depicting them as "welfare queens," overly dependent on state handouts, and as irresponsible mothers. Although the rhetoric of welfare-to-work programs emphasized "tough love" to wean poor women, in particular mothers, off dependency and push them to build economic independence, the reality has been the ejection of numerous families from the welfare rolls into minimum-wage jobs.[9] Because economic restructuring has involved the creation of numerous casual, low-waged jobs that often lack health insurance and seldom pay enough to cover adequate child care as well as living expenses, the welfare-to-work policy has largely furthered the sedimentation of poor women of color into a permanent poverty trap.[10]

With social expenditure decreasing, criminalization has become the primary response to growing poverty. Women's poverty is criminalized in numerous ways. Women who turn to the street economy, sex work, petty theft, welfare "fraud," or other economic survival strategies in the face of declining incomes and few economic opportunities are frequently caught up in the revolving door of initially short and then lengthier jail times.[11] For poor young women of color, especially those who have escaped abusive homes, the courts have become the state's alternative to adequate social services, youth programming, and educational opportunities. Queer and transgendered youth and young people of color who have been in foster or institutional care are particularly likely to spend time in the juvenile-justice system and to "graduate" to adult prisons and jails.[12] The criminalization of poverty also occurs when women with mental illness, including many who live with post-traumatic symptoms from childhood and adult sexual trauma, come in conflict with the law, either through antisocial or violent behavior or through self-medication with illegal drugs.[13] The next section examines the primacy of the war on drugs in the prison boom of the past three decades.

Making Addiction a Crime: The War on Drugs

In 1973, the state of New York's Rockefeller drug laws ushered in a new era of punitive antidrug measures and a shift toward determinate sentencing, with fixed sentences related to the quantity of drugs involved, regardless of the individual's history or circumstances.[14] By the early 1980s, Reagan had formally announced the "war on drugs" as a government priority, and throughout the 1980s, the federal government pumped billions of dollars into combating the newly identified "enemy."[15] With federal initiatives led by the "drug czar" and dramatic media representations fueling public fears, states soon began introducing mandatory sentencing. As judges were compelled to hand down lengthy sentences, even when they believed that the defendant posed little threat to public safety, the number of women in prison and the length of time they spent inside grew exponentially throughout the 1980s and 1990s.

The war on drugs has been a major contributor to the U.S. imprisonment binge. It has also expanded the criminalization of people by race and gender, leading to sharp increases in the numbers of incarcerated African American women and Latinas.[16] Women come into contact with the war on drugs both as consumers of criminalized drugs and as low-level dealers and couriers or family members of participants in the drug industry. The war on drugs has coincided with the retrenchment of health services in general, and drug treatment facilities in particular. Increasingly, women of color who are struggling with drug addiction are processed through the criminal punishment system rather than through drug rehabilitation programs or services that offer support for underlying issues, such as mental illness and trauma. Rather than viewing a rise in drug use as a public health crisis requiring generous public funding of treatment centers, education programs, mental health facilities, and clean-and-sober living arrangements, the war on drugs identifies drug use as a threat to public safety and pumps funds into the arrest and incarceration of both users and suppliers of criminalized drugs.

In the 1990s, low-income African American communities were particularly hurt by the moral panic about crack cocaine, a cheaper, more accessible form of the drug than the powder form. The media presented the "crack epidemic" as a crisis that posed a far greater threat to public safety than did the drugs more commonly used by middle-class users, such as powder cocaine, heroin, and methamphetamine. In addition, although the majority of crack users are white, the use and retail marketing of the drug was depicted as a black phenomenon.[17] Thus, policing operations focused on low-income urban black communities, sweeping up female family members and users as well as women and men working as low-level dealers and distributors. In addition, defendants in trials involving crack continue to be subject to discriminatory sentencing practices whereby the penalty ratio for crack versus powder cocaine is one hundred to one. Thus, a woman in possession of only five grams of crack cocaine receives the same sentence as one who possesses five hundred grams of powder cocaine.[18] Kemba Smith's case (see chapter 68 in this volume) demonstrates the intersection of racial targeting, gender violence, and punitive drug laws. A young mother and college student, Kemba neither used nor dealt in drugs, yet she was punished for "conspiring" with her abusive boyfriend and sentenced to a 23.5-year mandatory minimum sentence. Kemba was subsequently granted clemency by President Clinton in his final days in office and has dedicated her life to working for the women sentenced in the war on drugs.

The war on drugs has also disproportionately affected Latino/a communities. In 1997, Latinas/os comprised 33 percent of people held for drug offenses in federal prisons.[19] Latino/a communities in the United States and in Latin American countries have been stereotyped by the media and government initiatives as "narco-traffickers."[20] Whereas African American communities are stereotyped as dealers and distributors, Latinos/as are largely depicted as traffickers who bring drugs across the border or as "illegal aliens" who live outside the law. Both sets of controlling images lead to disproportionate policing, arrests, and incarceration rates. Latinos/as are subject to overpolicing, random stops for suspected insurance and immigration violations, inadequate and inaccessible legal representation, and language barriers at every level of the criminal justice system. For Latinas, racial discrepancies and cultural barriers are exacerbated by gendered vulnerabilities. As Juanita Díaz-Cotto demonstrates in her study of Chicana "pintas," Latinas are likely to self-medicate with drugs and alcohol to deal with childhood and adult gender violence and abuse. Once arrested, Latinas are disadvantaged by their low status in patriarchally structured drug networks; they often lack the valuable information necessary for plea bargaining. Finally, Latinas are sometimes caught in law enforcement efforts to intercept their male family members and may be encouraged to take full responsibility for a crime in order to protect their menfolk.[21]

Latin American women are also vulnerable to criminalization and incarceration within the United States. The federal government wages a war on drugs both within and outside its borders. The U.S. strategy of destroying agricultural land to eradicate the coca crop, while failing to address demand for illegal drugs, promotes economic insecurity among rural communities, which are simultaneously suffering from the impact of free-trade agreements in the region.[22] In the context of foreign debt, structural adjustment, civil unrest, and U.S. interventions in Latin America, women face increasingly limited survival options. With the unabated demand for illegal drugs in the United States, acting as a courier or "mula" is one option available to women struggling to make ends meet. Once they cross into the United States and are interdicted at the border or in the airport, these women are treated as "traffickers" and consequently receive lengthy sentences disproportionate to their low-level involvement in the illegal drug industry. On completing their prison time, these women are deported to their countries of origin, with few resources to survive, and are thus forced back into the cycle of poverty and criminalization.

If we look only at the racial and ethnic makeup of women's prison populations, we overlook the impact of immigrant status. Latinas in U.S. prisons include women arrested when crossing the border, women who were living in the United States either as documented or undocumented immigrants before their arrest, and women who were born in the United States. The next section turns to the criminalization of migration and argues that Latina immigrants are the overlooked face of women's imprisonment in the United States.

Criminalizing Migration

Globalization creates the structural conditions for mass movements of women and men around the globe, leading immigrant rights activists to label migrants "the refugees of globalization."[23] In 2005, approximately 185 million, or one in thirty-three of the world's population were migrants, and nearly half that number were women.[24] Globalization and neoliberal economic policies drive women's migration in multiple ways. Women are particularly vulnerable to structural adjustment policies, often imposed on debt-laden developing nations by the International Monetary Fund. Like economic reforms in the United States, structural adjustment policies involve cutbacks in government spending on education, health care, and social provision. As women struggle to pay more for basics such as education, health care, water, and food, migration becomes a realistic alternative to extreme poverty and offers the opportunity to provide remittances that can support dependents. Women are also affected by food insecurity caused by free trade and the global integration of food production, processing, and sales.[25] With less access to growing their own food, women must work for transnational corporations or migrate if they are to meet family nutritional needs. Women who migrate to work in export-processing zones are also more likely to continue their migration journeys into the global North.

A key aspect of globalization is the selective control of national borders. Although free-trade agreements open borders to the flow of capital and enable free movement of a highly educated capitalist elite, they call for much stricter control of the movement of workers. As socioeconomic conditions at home drive outmigration from countries in Latin America, the Caribbean, Asia, and the Philippines, labor needs in U.S. agriculture and service industries draw workers across the border. Many women rely on family reunification provisions in immigration legislation or come on temporary work visas, but those who are ineligible are forced to rely on migrant "traffickers" who facilitate illegal entry into the country. Once these women are in the United States, racism, xenophobia, and anti-immigrant sentiment combine with lack of documentation to ensure that they are restricted to low-waged, casual, and nonunionized labor in the service sector, jobs as domestic caregivers, or work in the sex industry.

During the past three decades, the budget of the U.S. Citizenship and Immigration Services (USCIS, formerly the Immigration and Naturalization Service, or INS) has grown exponentially as U.S. immigration policy has become more punitive. Although the USCIS is also tasked with providing information and services to "new Americans," budget increases over the years have focused on enforcement and interdiction, with an emphasis on the U.S.-Mexico border. Increasingly, the goal of controlling migration has been conflated with that of controlling drug importation and crime, and it has been classified as a national security concern rather than a matter for economic policy. This emphasis in turn has led to closer integration of the USCIS, the Border Patrol, the Drug Enforcement Agency, the military, and the police.[26] Enforcement activities on the U.S.-Mexico border have become militarized operations, involving military technology, surveillance equipment, and tactics to trap undocumented migrants. Women are particularly affected by the militarization of the border because they are vulnerable to the sexual assault and harassment that is a documented characteristic of war zones.[27] These operations clearly demonstrate the racialization of immigration policy, with Latinos/as making up 90 percent of deportations.[28] The surveillance and policing of Latinos/as, who are racially profiled as potential "illegal aliens," ensures that a disproportionate number of Latino/a immigrants are picked up for other infractions, from drug possession to driving without a license. These frequent interactions with law enforcement lead to higher rates of arrest and incarceration.

Noncitizen immigrant women who are convicted of offenses other than immigration-related charges are labeled "criminal aliens" by the state. These women make up 27 percent of the federal prison population. In the state prison system, 80 percent of noncitizens are imprisoned in five states: Arizona, California, Florida, New York, and Texas.[29] The policing and criminalization of immigrant Latinas has therefore been an important factor in U.S. prison expansion in the past three decades and has become a feature of life in the border states in particular. The majority (over 60 percent) of incarcerated noncitizens are from Mexico, with women and men from Colombia, the Dominican Republic, Jamaica, and Cuba making up about one-fifth of the federal noncitizen population. When globalization, free trade, and neoliberalism in Latin America and the Caribbean intersect with xenophobic and racialized law enforcement in the United States, the result is the criminalization of migration and the growth of globalized prison populations.

Profiting from Punishment:
The Rise of the Transnational Prison-Industrial Complex

Since the late 1990s, antiprison activists and scholars have adopted the concept of the "prison-industrial complex" to explain the complex web of overlapping interests that together have driven three decades of prison expansion. The concept derives from the "military-industrial complex," a term coined by President Dwight D. Eisenhower to describe the "conjunction of an immense military establishment and a large arms industry."[30] Making visible the corporate interests behind the Cold War arms buildup, Eisenhower called on "an alert and knowledgeable citizenry" to prevent this complex from exerting "unwarranted influence" over national policy. The term *prison-industrial complex* was first used by urban theorist Mike Davis in 1995 to describe a multibillion-dollar prison-building boom in California that, he argued, "rivals agribusiness as the dominant force in the life of rural California and competes with land developers as the chief seducer of legislators in Sacramento."[31] Conceptualizing prison expansion as the result of interlocking economic and political forces has enabled radical intellectuals to explain the apparently illogical willingness of politicians to continue to spend billions of dollars on a failed social policy despite evidence that the prison buildup has had no positive impact on public safety or the fear of crime.

The concept captures two related processes. The first is the transformation of prisoners into profits. In private prisons, criminalized and processed bodies are bought, sold, and traded. Federal and state governments pay private corporations a fee per prisoner per day, thus transforming the deprivation of a human being's freedom into a transaction that can be traded on the stock market. The majority of private prisons are designed, constructed, managed, and financed by multinational corporations. Thus, this form of private enterprise has integrated low-income communities of color into the global economy. Warehoused in megaprisons designed for economies of scale rather than rehabilitation, prisoners have become a commodity that is sold to governments, and ultimately to taxpayers, under the guise of "keeping us safe." And the corporations and their stakeholders that profit from these transactions in turn benefit from and actively promote criminal justice policies that guarantee rising rates of incarceration.[32]

The dramatic increase in the number of people sentenced to time behind bars has led to a prison-building boom in the United States, Canada, Latin America, parts of Europe, Australia, and elsewhere. Prison construction has also become denationalized. Today a prison in South Africa is likely to have been built by a U.S.-headquartered multinational corporation, or a prison in Chile may be constructed by a Chilean subsidiary of a French-headquartered multinational corporation. Prison expansion has generated a host of profit-making opportunities for both multinational and local construction firms, architecture firms, and manufacturers of security and telecommunications equipment, as well as for service industries, including real estate agents, banks, and restaurants. These profits flow whether the prison is ultimately operated by the state or by a private company. Imprisonment transforms immense sums of public money into private profits. These funds are then unavailable for expenditure on the public workers and facilities—from schools to rehabilitation centers—that support families and individuals in crisis before they can come into conflict with the law.

The second process that scholars have drawn to our attention is the cementing of the prison into local economies. For rural towns devastated by economic restructuring and free-trade competition, prisons seem to be a panacea for economic stagnation and population loss.[33] Amid the farm bankruptcies and factory closures caused by the rise of corporate agribusiness and the influx of foreign products, the jobs and construction contracts offered by new public or private prisons have pitted small towns against each other in bids to offer the most attractive package of tax breaks, cheap land, and other incentives. Politicians and business elites in rural towns in the United States and Canada have promoted prison construction as a form of economic development, touting prisons as a recession-proof and non-polluting industry.[34] Ultimately, however, prison towns fail to reap the promised benefits and instead suffer from inflated real estate prices, high unemployment, and environmental degradation.[35]

Although the prison-industrial complex emerged in the United States, the past two decades have seen it become a transnational phenomenon. Punitive U.S. measures—including tough sentencing for troubled youth, three strikes, truth-in-sentencing policies, and mandatory minimums—have spread internationally.[36] As politicians around the world have pushed their own versions of U.S.-style tough-on-crime strategies, global prison populations have begun to rise inexorably. As a result, countries have again turned to the United States for an answer to the dilemma of how to lock more people away while minimizing the cost of growing prison populations. Mass warehousing in "no frills" superjails that may house over a thousand prisoners has increasingly become politicians' solution, fueling the growth of a transnational prison-industrial complex.

ENVISIONING A SOLUTION:
WOMEN IMAGINE A WORLD WITHOUT PRISONS

The brutal impact of the prison-industrial complex on families and communities has led to the creation of a strong grassroots antiprison movement. This movement is made up of a plethora of organizations, campaign and lobby groups, activist collectives, nonprofits, prisoner associations, and student groups. These groups focus on a range of intertwined issues, including the war on drugs, police accountability, incarcerated women, LGBT (lesbian-gay-bisexual-transsexual) prisoners, political prisoners, private prisons, prison expansion, prison financing, the death penalty, juvenile justice, human rights violations in prisons, access to health care, control units, deaths in custody, post-9/11 harassment and detention of Muslims and Arab Americans, detentions in the war on terror, and the rights of undocumented and incarcerated immigrants.[37]

Although men make up over 90 percent of prison populations in the United States and globally, women, particularly women of color, play critical roles in antiprison movements. In the United States, activist-intellectuals and former prisoners such as Angela Y. Davis, Ruth Wilson Gilmore, Ramona Africa, Linda Evans, and Kemba Smith have played key roles in analyzing the prison-industrial complex, popularizing understanding of this analysis, and mobilizing opposition. As activists and mothers, women do much of the hard work of community organizing and providing support to prisoners and their families. Women activists have ensured the visibility of women prisoners and their issues through organizations such as the National Network for Women in Prison, the California Coalition for Women Prisoners, Justice Now, Free Battered Women, Legal Services for Prisoners with Children, and the Out of Control Lesbian Committee to Support Women Political Prisoners.

For diverse groups to become part of a collective movement, they must be unified by a common understanding of the problem and share a vision of the possible solutions. These radicalizing and life-affirming visions move us beyond a combative dualism, whereby we know only what we are against, to a place of constructive imagination, where we can begin to build the world we want to live in. For the antiprison movement, abolition is the key to a radical and profoundly transformative vision of social change. A number of organizations are promoting dialogue about abolition, discussing what it means and how it can translate into concrete action.[38] Justice Now is an Oakland, California–based organization that provides legal services for women prisoners and campaigns against women's imprisonment. The organization's Building a World Without Prisons campaign provides a forum for women in and out of prison to share abolitionist ideas and strategies. Informed by women's experiences of interpersonal violation and state violence, Justice Now's politics is feminist and abolitionist:

> As an organization that works with women in prison, we see that prisons are a form of violence against women, and that locking up men is not a solution to interpersonal violence in our communities. We are interested not only in challenging what we see happening in prisons, but also in building a different world—a world where all of us have affordable housing, food, healthcare, economic opportunity and freedom from both individual and state violence. This vision includes creating new ways to respond when people hurt each other, ways that no longer rely on violence and control.[39]

This feminist abolitionism grows out of the deep belief that a world without prisons can also be a world in which women are safe from interpersonal violence. It resists the antiviolence movement's tendency to assume that policing and prisons are an effective tool against male violence, but it also holds the antiprison movement accountable for finding alternative strategies to end violence and build safety.

For an abolitionist vision to offer anything meaningful to communities and individuals suffering from overpolicing, criminalization, and incarceration, it must be accompanied by practical actions that promise short- and medium-term successes as well as long-term transformation. Critical Resistance, founded in 1998 by a group of Bay Area activists including Angela Y. Davis, has played a critical role in coordinating gatherings where diverse organizations can generate alternatives to the prison-industrial complex. Critical Resistance describe abolition as:

> [a] political vision that seeks to eliminate the need for prisons, policing, and surveillance by creating sustainable alternatives to punishment and imprisonment. . . . An abolitionist vision means that we must build models today that can represent how we want to live in the future. It means developing practical strategies for taking small steps that move us toward making our dreams real and that lead the average person to believe that things really could be different. It means living this vision in our daily lives.[40]

In this sense, prison abolitionists shoulder a dual burden of first, transforming people's consciousness so that they can believe that their own visions of a different world are possible; and second, taking practical steps to oppose the prison-industrial complex. Abolitionist work involves three steps that build on one another with the ultimate goal of "shrink[ing] the system into non-existence."[41] The first is a moratorium: ending prison expansion. This step may call for raising public awareness of the cost of prisons to reduce public support for prison constriction and laws that increase prison populations. It may also require campaigns to prevent the construction of specific prisons or jails. For example, the Prisoner Justice Action Committee's 81 Reasons 2005 campaign asked Ontario residents to think of alternative ways of spending the $81.1 million (Canadian) that the provincial government planned to spend on a new youth "superjail" in Brampton, a suburb of Toronto.[42] The campaigners mobilized public concerns about spending cuts in other areas, including education, to create pressure on the provincial government to explore less expensive and punitive alternatives to incarceration for youth.

The second step is decarceration: shrinking the prison population. The most common approach is to target a specific prison population that the public sees as low risk and argue for an end to imprisonment of this population. For example, California's passage of Proposition 36, the Substance Abuse and Crime Prevention Act, in 2000 allows first and second-time nonviolent drug offenders charged with possession to receive substance abuse treatment instead of prison, and this measure channels approximately thirty-five thousand people into treatment annually.[43]

Free Battered Women's (FBW's) campaign for the release of incarcerated survivors is another example of decarceration. The organization supports women imprisoned for killing an abuser, challenging their convictions by demonstrating how the battering led to the killing. In addition, FBW draws attention to the large proportion of women prisoners who have a history of intimate violence and challenges the state's use of imprisonment as its response to women's victimization. By revealing the connection between women incarcerated for defending themselves against a violent partner and the majority of women in prison, FBW promotes the decarceration of women at a massive scale.

The third strategy is abolition: building a world without prisons. As a strategy, abolition moves from opposition to construction. It aims to build "a world where all people have access to the material, educational, emotional, and spiritual resources necessary to be safe and thrive in our communities."[44] For Critical Resistance South, located in New Orleans, abolition means working in coalition with grassroots economic and racial justice organizations to build community empowerment and representation in the reconstruction of the city.[45] Because the war on drugs has played such a huge role in the boom in imprisonment, strategies to tackle substance abuse and addiction must play a critical role in any abolitionist vision. The recovery movement, a user-led mental health and addiction movement, offers an important alternative to the criminalization of drug and alcohol abuse.[46] Divesting of prisons and investing in sober-living houses, recovery programs, treatment centers, and women's wellness and mental health programs designed and run by and for women and men in recovery would promote healing from addiction and self-determination for affected individuals and communities. Promoting community recovery would also stem the demand for criminalized drugs, undermining the transnational drug industry and creating economic crises for rural communities around the world that cultivate coca and opium. Transforming the war on drugs through an abolitionist politics must therefore involve a commitment to global economic justice and the creation of alternative economic development opportunities for all communities involved in the drug trade.

Abolition also requires alternative strategies for dealing with interpersonal harms that threaten the safety of individuals from oppressed groups. For Justice Now, abolition means facilitating community conversations about collective strategies for tackling violence against women that do not rely on criminal punishment. For INCITE! Women of Color Against Violence, abolition means developing and disseminating "community accountability" politics and practices for progressive organizations run by people of color, so that gender abuse and violence in activist settings is neither brushed under the carpet nor dealt with using the criminal punishment model.[47] Through their activities, these organizations become a reflection of the world we want to live in, providing real safety based on justice and focusing on healing and transformation rather than punishment and imprisonment.

NOTES

1. See Arthur T. Denzau's *Fiscal Policy Convergence from Reagan to Blair* (New York: Routledge, 2003) for a detailed overview of, and the legacies bequeathed by, Reaganomics and Thatcherism.

2. Although fewer women are imprisoned than men, women's imprisonment has grown at a faster rate than men's since the 1980s. Between 1986 and 1991, the number of people in state women's prisons increased 75 percent, versus a 53 percent increase for men. The trend continues, with women's prison populations increasing 4.8 percent in the twelve months to midyear 2006, versus a 2.7 percent increase for men. U.S. Department of Justice, Bureau of Justice Statistics, *Special Report: Women in Prison* (Washington, DC, 1994); U.S Department of Justice, Bureau of Justice Statistics, *Prison and Jail Inmates at Midyear 2006* (Washington, DC, 2007). African American women and Latinas are imprisoned at four times and twice the rate of white women, respectively, indicating that the prison boom has disproportionately affected women of color (U.S. Department of Justice, *Prison and Jail Inmates.*)

3. Rebecca Bohrman and Naomi Murakawa, "Remaking Big Government: Immigration and Crime Control in the United States," in *Global Lockdown: Race, Gender, and the Prison-Industrial Complex*, ed. J. Sudbury, 109–26. (New York: Routledge, 2005). The other major shift of public spending priorities has been from the welfare state to the global war on terror.

4. Ibid.

5. Julia Sudbury, "Transatlantic Visions: Resisting the Globalization of Mass Incarceration," *Social Justice* 27, no. 3 (Fall 2000): 133.

6. Saskia Sassen, *The Global City: New York, London, Tokyo* (Princeton, NJ: Princeton University Press, 2001).

7. Angela Y. Davis, "Race and Criminalization: Black Americans and the Punishment Industry," In *The Angela Y. Davis Reader*, ed. James Joy, 61–73 (Oxford: Blackwell Publishers, 1998).

8. Neoliberalism is a philosophy that views the unfettered market as the key to economic and social progress. Neoliberal policies include government cutbacks, privatization of state services, reduced governmental protection of workers and the environment, and the removal of trade barriers, in particular through international trade agreements such as the North American Free Trade Agreement and the Free Trade Area of the Americas. Antiglobalization activists and scholars view these developments as a recipe for corporate profit at the expense of marginalized communities. See Noam Chomsky, *Profit Over People: Neoliberalism and Global Order* (New York: Seven Stories, 1998).

9. National Women's Law Center, "Welfare Reform Should Help Women Striving to Support Their Families, Not Hold Them Back" (Washington, D.C.: National Women's Law Center, February 2003); www.nwlc.org.

10. Judith Goode, "From New Deal to Bad Deal: Racial and Political Implications of U.S. Welfare Reform," in *Western Welfare in Decline: Globalization and Women's Poverty*, ed. Catherine Kingfisher, 65–89 (Philadelphia: University of Pennsylvania Press, 2003).

11. Beth Richie, *Compelled to Crime: The Gender Entrapment of Battered Black Women* (New York: Routledge, 1995).

12. Beth Richie, "Queering Antiprison Work," in Sudbury, *Global Lockdown*; Dorothy Roberts, *Shattered Bonds: The Color of Child Welfare* (New York: Basic Civitas Books, 2002), 201–7.

13. Terry Kupers, *Prison Madness: The Mental Health Crisis Behind Bars and What We Must Do About It* (San Francisco: Jossey-Bass, 1999).

14. For example, anyone convicted of selling two ounces or possessing four ounces of narcotics would receive a sentence of fifteen years. Marc Mauer, "The Causes and Consequences of Prison Growth in the United States," in *Mass Imprisonment: Social Causes and Consequences*, ed. David Garland (London, Thousand Oaks: Sage Publications, 2001), 6.

15. The federal budget for the war on drugs grew from $1.5 billion in 1981 at the beginning of Reagan's term to $6.6 billion in 1989, and it hit $17 billion ten years later; ibid.

16. Stephanie Bush-Baskette, "The War on Drugs as a War on Black Women," in *Crime Control and Women*, ed. Susan Miller, 113–29 (Thousand Oaks, CA: Sage Publications, 1998); Juanita Díaz-Cotto, *Chicana Lives and Criminal Justice: Voices from El Barrio* (Austin: University of Texas Press, 2006).

17. Although the majority of crack users are white, nearly 90 percent of those convicted in federal court for crack-cocaine distribution are African American. U.S. Sentencing Commission, *Special Report to Congress: Cocaine and Federal Sentencing Policy* (Washington, DC, April 2007), 8.

18. Drug Policy Alliance 2001, "Crack/Cocaine Disparity"; www.drugpolicy.org.

19. Díaz-Cotto, *Chicana Lives and Criminal Justice*, 20.

20. Ibid.

21. Ibid.

22. Julia Sudbury, "Women of Color, Globalization, and the Politics of Incarceration," in *The Criminal Justice System and Women: Offenders, Prisoners, Victims, & Workers*, ed. Barbara Raffel Price and Natalie J. Sokoloff, 219–33 (New York: McGraw Hill, 2003).

23. National Network for Immigrant and Refugee Rights, "Excerpts from the Mexico City Report: Globalization, Immigration, and Militarization: A Dialogue between NGOs"; www.nnirr.org.

24. Estimate by United Nations Population Division, International Organization for Migration, *World Migration 2005: Costs and Benefits of International Migration*; www.iom.int.

25. Food and Agriculture Organization of the United Nations, *The State of Food Insecurity in the World 2004*; www.fao.org.

26. Bohrman and Murakawa, "Remaking Big Government."

27. Sylvanna Falcón, " 'National Security' and the Violation of Women: Militarized Border Rape at the U.S.-Mexico Border," in *Color of Violence: The Incite! Anthology*, ed. Incite! Women of Color Against Violence (Boston: South End Press, 2006).

28. Bohrman and Murakawa, "Remaking Big Government," 112.

29. U.S. Government Accountability Office, *Information on Criminal Aliens Incarcerated in Federal and State Prisons and Local Jails* (Washington, DC, April 7, 2005); www.gao.gov.

30. Dwight D. Eisenhower, "Military-Industrial Complex Speech," Public Papers of the Presidents, Eisenhower 1961(Washington, DC: Office of the Federal Register), 1035–40.

31. Mike Davis, "Hell Factories in the Field: A Prison-Industrial Complex," *Nation*, February 20, 1995, 260.

32. For example, the Institute on Money in State Politics report identified evidence that legislators were introducing or voting favorably on bills that would benefit the private prison companies that had donated to their campaigns in Mississippi, Georgia, Florida, Oklahoma, and North Carolina during the 2000 election cycle. Edwin Bender, *A Contributing Influence: The Private-Prison Industry and Political Giving in the South* (Helena, MT: Institute on Money in State Politics, 2002), 4.

33. Ruthie Gilmore, *Golden Gulag: Prisons, Surplus, Crisis, and Opposition in Globalizing California* (Berkeley: University of California Press, 2007).

34. Geert Dhondt, "Big Prisons and Small Towns" (Amherst, MA: Center for Popular Economics, 2002).

35. Gilmore, *Golden Gulag*.

36. Sudbury, "Transatlantic Visions."

37. For an excellent list of over one hundred organizations, see the Prison Activist Resource Center's links page: www.prisonactivist.org.

38. These organizations include Critical Resistance, the Prison Moratorium Project, the Prison Activist Resource Center, Justice Now, the Prison Justice Action Committee (Toronto, Canada), and the International Conference on Penal Abolition.

39. Justice Now, "The VoicesProject: Building a World Without Prisons"; www.jnow.org.

40. Critical Resistance. "What Is Prison Abolition All About?" as reprinted in "Abolitionism: A British Perspective," www.alternatives2prison.ik.com/p_What_is_Abolition.ikml.

41. Ibid.

42. Prisoner Justice Action Committee, "The 81 Reasons Campaign Statement"; www.pjac.org.

43. Drug Policy Alliance, "California Proposition 36: Substance Abuse and Crime Prevention Act of 2000"; www.prop36.org.

44. Free Battered Women, "What We Believe: Our Vision & Guiding Principles"; http://freebatteredwomen.org.

45. Critical Resistance, "Hurricane Katrina Rebuilding and Relief"; www.criticalresistance.org.

46. The recovery movement includes twelve-step programs such as Alcoholics Anonymous and Narcotics Anonymous and a range of community-based recovery facilities. These programs are peer led and run, nonhierarchical and noncommercial.

47. INCITE! Women of Color Against Violence, *Gender Oppression, Abuse, Violence: Community Accountability within the People of Color Progressive Movement* (Seattle, WA, July 2005); www.incite-national.org.

2

Glossary of Terms

Tina Reynolds

Not every essay in this volume avoids the language described here, but many of the authors share our commitment to the power and politics of words.

I developed this glossary of terms in opposition to the language that society has adopted to unidentify people who have been in conflict with the law. These examples of oppressive terminology show how language harms people, deepening their invisibility as human beings and undermining their eligibility for forgiveness and redemption. Derogatory, dehumanizing, and oppressive, this language is passed down to innocent family members, including children, further complicating the acceptance of incarcerated and formerly incarcerated people into social circles and society.

Reentry   A broad term loosely used by government officials and academics to describe the process a formerly incarcerated person faces upon release from prison. The term does not refer to or embrace the complexities, challenges, and barriers a person faces upon release. *Reentry* does not appropriately address how the person who has been in conflict with the law is perceived by society. Most important, *reentry* does not acknowledge this truth: a person needs to know that she is welcomed and invited in order to reenter successfully.

Inmate   A label or definition attached to men, women, and children who are sentenced to jail or prison. Wholly dehumanizing, this label underscores the invisibility of the human being. It undermines the self-esteem and sense of self-worth of people as individuals, parents, and family members. Preferred terms: *incarcerated person, person in jail (or prison).*

Offender	A label usually applied to a person before he or she is convicted of and sentenced for a crime. *Offender* connotes that the person has *offended* family, community, and society. This term, used during court proceedings, before conviction, immediately effaces the person's human status. Preferred term: *person who is in conflict with the law.*
Convict	A label that connotes "once a convict always a convict." (A *convict* necessarily evolves into an *ex-convict*; see below.) In the United States, a person who is a "convict" no longer has access to person status. A "convict" has been "convicted" of a "crime." Convicts often become "prisoners" after a conviction. Persons convicted and sentenced to noncustodial sentences usually are not termed *convicts*. See *ex-convict*: Preferred terms: *incarcerated person, imprisoned person.*
Ex-con or ex-convict	Dehumanizing label for people who have completed their sentences. Using this term suggests that once a person has been identified as a convict, he or she will always occupy that category, even after serving time. Preferred terms: *person on parole (or probation), formerly incarcerated person, person who has been in prison.*
Rehabilitation	A term that refers to the beneficial effects of imprisonment, counter to widespread knowledge that time in prison and most available prison programs do not restore people to good health or to useful life. People who have been incarcerated are generally responsible for "rehabilitating" themselves.
These women, *these* men, *these* children, and *these* people	Terminology to describe people who have fallen from grace; "these" connotes the "other" identity of women and men who have been in conflict with the law and separates them from so-called upstanding citizens of society. Society also defines the children of incarcerated parents as "othered," at risk of criminal behavior because of the choices of their parents. Academics, policy makers, and service providers describe children in this situation as "these children," typically neglecting the impacts on young people of racism, poverty, poor education, and lack of community resources. Preferred terms: *children of incarcerated (or formerly incarcerated) parents, families of incarcerated (or formerly incarcerated) people, formerly incarcerated people, incarcerated people, people in conflict with the law.*

3

The Long Shadow of Prison

My Messy Journey through Fear,
Silence, and Racism toward Abolition

Kay Whitlock

Abolition of the U.S. prison system is not only a political and economic imperative for those concerned about the meaning of justice. It is also a spiritual necessity in a society that has turned the imprisonment of massive numbers of human beings, two-thirds of whom are people of color, into a brutal growth industry.

My path to this conclusion has not been a simple one of ideological certainty. The journey to abolition is intensely human; it is a volatile, complicated journey into the nature of relationships at the intersections of race, gender and gender identity, culture, class, and sexuality. It's about the interdependent nature of our day-to-day social, economic, political, and spiritual relationships with one another. The journey takes us straight into the heart of the inhumanity inherent in declaring vast numbers of people to be expendable—overwhelmingly people of color, poor people, women, youth, and people with mental illness. It is a journey not only into the violence individuals do to one another but also into the systemic violence of the state.

It is a painful journey that strips away self-delusion by requiring us to look critically not only at others but also at ourselves. In a polarized political climate that feeds on the creation and demonization of enemies, the journey to abolition is about as popular as the plague.

It is also one of the most spiritually illuminating journeys we can take—individually and as a society.

. . .

My journey began more than thirty years ago, with a rude personal awakening to the depth of my own racially charged fear of "criminals." I was sitting in Denver

County Jail on a sweltering August day, serving a thirty-day sentence for conspiracy and nonviolent civil disobedience against the war in Vietnam.

All of my fellow (white) female protesters had received shorter sentences and had just been released. Despite the presence of other prisoners, some of whom I liked, and with all of whom I believed myself to be in solidarity, I felt unexpectedly alone, off-kilter, and anxious.

That's when Wilma arrived.

I have no idea how old Wilma really was, probably not as old as she looked. Word was, she'd been a hooker and was now charged with murder. "Don't mess with Wilma," people said, and you could see why. She was little, but she was ropy. A jagged scar with big, Frankenstein-style stitches ran from under one ear all the way across her throat. Her front teeth were knocked out, and her seriously thinning hair was wrapped into a little topknot. She dumped her bedding on the cot next to mine and said, "I scare you, don't I, white girl?" Then she laughed and laughed while I remained mute, praying that I would dissolve into atoms.

A day or two later, she came up to me, eyes gleaming, punched me softly on the shoulder, and said, "What's your mama think about you being in here with all us nasty, evil, bad people?" She threw back her head, laughed, and walked away.

I adopted a strategy of avoidance, focusing instead on my personal jail witness.

From the moment I entered jail, I'd cooked up ways to protest the countless degradations: the unnecessarily painful gynecological exams by contemptuous health providers, the matrons' jokes about the prisoner who had committed suicide, the ways in which particular guards, both male and female, drunk on their little shards of power, felt us up. I tried to sabotage every sleazy job I was given, one of which was sewing together pieces of cheap, thin, denim material to make the three-armhole dresses we all wore. By screwing up the tension on the sewing machine, I produced stitches that, on cursory examination, looked fine. But once the dresses had been washed two or three times, they started to unravel.

Imagine my shock, then, when Wilma stormed up to me one morning, clutching a handful of her dress—which was, literally coming apart at the seams—and hissed, "Just what the fuck do you think you're doing? Who you think has to wear this thing?"

Never have I had a more shattering lesson about the nature of justice and interdependence. What I'd intended as a principled response to injustice was an affront to Wilma, an act that took away one of the shreds of human dignity—a decent piece of clothing—that she possessed.

I had voluntarily gone to jail because I believed myself to be one of the "good guys." In my view, somebody else was always the problem—the oppressive, violent, bigoted, ignorant "other." But Wilma pulled the rug of smugness out from under me, and as my self-righteousness hit the floor, I realized, *Ohmigod. It's not always just somebody else. It's me, too. Sometimes my own actions create injustice or do harm.* I had, wrongly, assumed that my good intentions would always translate into justice—not only for me but also for everyone else.

Wilma was a difficult teacher. The more I tried to avoid her, the closer she came. The more I didn't want to look at my fear, the more she threw it in my face. By demanding that I stop treating her as nonexistent, Wilma forever changed the space we both occupied.

No longer allowed access to the sewing machines, I could not repair Wilma's unraveling dress. I could only stop running away.

"Yes, ma'am," I finally blurted out to Wilma one evening. "You scare me to death." And I said, "My mama, who is a funny, decent woman who works her fingers to the bone, thinks you are the dregs of the earth, and she is afraid that you will rape and kill me, and she believes I have brought shame down upon our whole family by being here."

We talked, then, about whether I shared my mama's views, and what role race played in those views. I tried desperately to explain myself in a hundred ways. No, the people here were obviously not the dregs of the earth. A lot of the women were smart and funny and often kind in small ways that took my breath away. But, yes, despite my egalitarian political convictions, my subconscious image of "criminals" was largely an image of black and Chicano rapists and murderers. Yes, God help me, I had come in feeling at some emotional level that I was not only different from the other but better.

I hated hearing myself blurt out that dirty little secret, but the moment was strangely cathartic. If I really cared about justice, I had to own up to and divest from my secret, unexamined stash of white supremacy, not just protest somebody else's. But while it came clear to me that I was no better than my fellow prisoners, I also had to face the fact that I *was* different from most of them in certain respects.

I may have grown up working class, but I am also white, and was then in college. Most of the other prisoners were women of color, particularly African American and Chicana. Virtually all, whatever their race, were poorer than I had ever been. Few had finished high school. Many were mothers, struggling to maintain a meaningful connection with their children.

Several prisoners struggled with serious health concerns, for which they received little or no appropriate medical care. For example, one woman running a 104-degree temperature was simply placed in "red tag lockup," an isolation cell, without treatment. Another could scarcely walk because of a serious foot injury but had to make do with flip-flops. Many viewed physical and sexual abuse as a routine part of their lives. Most of my fellow prisoners were there for bounced checks, petty theft, prostitution, and drug use. Only two or three were in for assault, which, in at least one case, was directed against an abusive man. Wilma bore the most serious charge; she had shot and killed a man, whom she described to me merely as "a real snake."

Later, the only friendly matron at the jail told me that the guy Wilma shot was white—and he had shot her first.

Most of the women had been in jail for several weeks to several months, awaiting trial, doing "dead time" that wouldn't count toward their sentences, and having no idea when they would go to trial. They were not out on bail because they didn't have the necessary money or social standing. Their overworked public defenders or cut-rate defense lawyers seldom had much time for them.

By contrast, I had been released on personal recognizance before entering jail and was serving a short, definite sentence. Moreover, my legal advisors were from the National Lawyers Guild and the American Civil Liberties Union.

. . .

At first, I felt scraped raw; appalled by the ease with which my heartfelt political convictions were betrayed by my unconscious, habitual responses. But Wilma and I went on to talk about many things (our lives, popular music, jail conditions). My connections with other prisoners deepened as well.

I've spent the rest of my life trying to convey through my work the profound change that began to take place in me when Wilma and the other prisoners steamrollered into my fear, insisted on being fully human, and demanded that I do the same.

. . .

An idea began to stir my imagination: the idea that justice is not about punishment but about accountability to one another, and that accountability is rooted in just social, political, economic, and spiritual relationships. Still, I was not an abolitionist; if an abolitionist movement even existed then, I did not know about it and could not imagine it on my own.

I, like so many others, assumed the inevitability of jails and prisons, so I worked for the reform of dehumanizing conditions and for law enforcement training that would reduce racism and misogyny. I advocated for sentencing reform and for more educational and rehabilitation programs for prisoners. I fought against police brutality, for the expansion of legal aid for poor people, and for the human and civil rights of prisoners. I also cofounded a rape and sexual assault crisis center and worked to eliminate community violence directed against people of color and queers.

Such change seemed within reach. After all, at this time, in the late 1960s and early 1970s, the political atmosphere fairly crackled with new possibility. The antiwar effort and many justice movements held the life-affirming potential for reshaping the social, political, and economic landscape.

But on the cusp of significant social and economic change in the United States during this period, a powerful political backlash of staggering magnitude, organized by the right, was already well under way. One significant part of this backlash has been the "get tough on crime" crusade that started in the 1970s and continues today, a strategic policy shift emphasizing harsher sentences and use of imprisonment as the preferred civic response not only to acts of violence by individuals but also to a host of complex social and economic tensions, including drug use, poverty, crumbling public-school infrastructure, mental illness, and more.

Despite stable or falling rates of violent crime, the number of people imprisoned in the United States exploded from 326,000 in 1970 to 2.1 million in 2003. Today, 1 in every 140 U.S. residents is in jail or prison. The rate of women's imprisonment is now growing at double that of men. Another 4 million people or so, also overwhelmingly people of color, are also on probation or parole.

During the same period, calls for reform to end indeterminate sentencing abuses morphed into harsher sentences—mandatory minimums, penalty enhancements, three-strikes laws, and the like. Funding for legal services for poor people was slashed. Police brutality has been further institutionalized through the creation of "supermax" prisons and the increasing use of control units within general prisons, both of which employ physical and mental methods of control that are considered torture under international law. Educational and rehabilitation initiatives have been gutted.

The response to school-based bullying and other disciplinary infractions has been the explosive proliferation of so-called zero-tolerance policies, which have become a school-to-prison pipeline primarily for poor youth of color. With the closing of public health hospitals and clinics, jails and prisons are now the primary institutions housing people with mental illness. Most states have made it easier to try minors as adults in court and to send youth convicted of certain offenses to adult prisons. Private companies dedicated to building, administering, and providing services to prisons are now listed on the stock exchange. Jail bed space is an interstate commodity, bought and sold in the marketplace. Poor, primarily rural communities reeling from the loss of family farms and the closure of plants as businesses relocate elsewhere to obtain a cheaper labor supply now compete for new jails and prisons and the low-waged jobs that accompany them. The exploitation of prison labor for private profit, long a staple of the criminal justice system, has expanded.

In one thirty-year period, the long shadow of the prison has fallen over almost every aspect of civic life, driven by right-wing insistence that safety and security can be purchased only with more policing, more prisons, and more people in them.

What possible meaning can the word *reform* have in this context?

How on earth did we come to accept this nightmare and call it "justice"?

· · ·

The key word is *fear*, fear of a brutal, violent, racially coded criminal stereotype that is manipulated by politicians, lobbyists, and corporate executives with a clear stake in prison expansion. Never mind the fact that the overwhelming majority of people in prison are not there for major crimes of violence, and never mind that physical and mental abuse is endemic within prisons. This strategic manipulation of fear effectively silences serious public discussion about the meaning of justice, and about who is in jail and why.

As I began to write and speak publicly about the ways in which this explosive prison expansion intensifies rather than diminishes violence and injustice, my work took me into conversations with groups of people who were often openly hostile. This response is not surprising in a society that doesn't know how to think about justice in terms other than policing and prison. Moreover, because many of us fear that we, too, are being left out, left behind, and hurt by others in an uncaring society, we can easily project our own resentment, rage, and fear onto "criminals."

It's one thing to face the barrage of withering contempt, sarcasm, and ridicule from right-wing ideologues; polarizing and demonizing invective is their stock-in-trade. But the harder challenge has been closer to home as "get tough" crime rhetoric has shaped even liberal responses to violence and injustice.

Throughout the 1980s and into the 2000s, many civil rights and advocacy groups that championed justice for people of color, queers, women, immigrants, and others endorsed more policing and harsher sentencing for domestic violence and hate crimes. A few of these groups went far beyond disagreeing with those of us who argued that these approaches produced unintended harmful consequences; they actively joined the silencing attack.

The angry accusations are always the same, whether from conservatives or liberals: 1) you care more about the criminals than the victims; 2) you want to let vicious rapists, thugs, and murderers loose on the streets; and 3) you have nothing to take the place of prisons and jails.

It's no use pretending that these accusations don't resonate with many ordinary folks; they do. I have struggled with them myself. Rather than avoid them, I move directly into the rage, reframing the accusations into questions that should concern all of us who work for justice:

- How can we create a system of justice that stops violence perpetrated not only by individuals but also by public and private institutions?
- How can we create community capacity to address not only the short- and long-term impacts of violence but also the social and economic conditions that produce poverty, injustice, and violence?
- How can we address the question of extreme violence done to others? Within an unshakable framework of universal human rights, how can we hold those who harm others accountable for their actions, stop them from doing further harm, and protect the safety of those they have harmed?
- Do prisons really create a less violent, more just society? How can communities take greater responsibility for the creation of justice?

I don't pretend to have the answers to these questions; nobody does. Community by community, we will have to work together over the long term to create them. But some promising community-based work, led largely by women of color active in various kinds of antiviolence movements—the same women who have been so influential in creating and shaping the new abolition movement—has already begun.

. . .

In the end, the chilling national silence about what happens inside prisons, and about why prisons are expanding so rapidly, was what persuaded me to declare for abolition—particularly the silence about the history of imprisonment in this country, which is largely a history of the imprisonment and disenfranchisement of poor people of color. This reality is at the heart of our national inability to think about and work in fresh ways toward a new, transformative vision of justice.

What would real justice look like? That's the question politicians and prison profiteers don't want us to ask. Yet no society can create authentic justice without the creative capacity to imagine what is possible.

By shattering that silence, the abolition movement storms into our fear and opens up crucial new space in our civic imaginations. Here, we can begin to reenvision justice as the positive creation and strengthening of just relationships rather than as an endless series of increasingly harsh punishments for an ever-expanding list of crimes.

. . .

The journey toward abolition is the most challenging of any justice struggle I have embraced, but it is also the most life affirming. As I look back over the years, it is always Wilma's face I see. I was not permitted to visit or write to her when she was sent to the state penitentiary. There, two or three years later, in obscurity, she died.

4
———

Unpeeling the Mask

Elizabeth Leslie

Could you believe unpeeling my mask was such a difficult task?
Yeah . . . Because there were numerous questions to be asked.
I can't even begin to discuss the well-kept secrets from my past!
How long should the pain last?
It isn't easy unpeeling this mask . . .
I've got secrets to conceal
They are too unique to be revealed
This mask can't be unpeeled!!!
It's my best disguise
To cover all my lies . . .
And lies . . .
And lies . . .
I told you it isn't easy to unpeel!!
I mean unveil. . . .
Then I'll begin to feel
And feel . . .
And feel . . .
I don't want the real me to be exposed!!!
I don't want anyone to know
So, I keep the mask on and don't allow myself to grow
I'm afraid to say, I don't even know which way to go
Which way should I go?
Should I go up or down?
Should I smile or frown?

This mask is my protection
To gain your acceptance
To hide my puzzling reactions
To conceal the realism of expression
To cover the real me
The person I'm afraid to see
The person God made me to be
The mask is my tool to hide
What's really going on inside
Masking what's inside of me
My true identity
I have some questions to be asked
Do you want to live? Do you want to die?
Do you want to laugh? Do you want to cry?
The simplest question is:
To be or Not to be!!!

5

Children of Incarcerated Parents

A Bill of Rights

San Francisco Children of Incarcerated Parents Partnership

Two point four million American children have a parent behind bars today. Seven million, or one in ten of the nation's children, have a parent under criminal justice supervision—in jail or prison, on probation, or on parole.

Little is known about what becomes of children when their parents are incarcerated. There is no requirement that the various institutions charged with dealing with those accused of breaking the law—police, courts, jails and prisons, probation departments—inquire about children's existence, much less concern themselves with children's care. Conversely, there is no requirement that systems serving children—schools, child welfare, juvenile justice—address parental incarceration.

Children of prisoners have a daunting array of needs. They need a safe place to live and people to care for them in their parents' absence, as well as everything else a parent might be expected to provide: food, clothing, and medical care.

But beyond these material requirements, young people themselves identify less tangible, but equally compelling, needs. They need to be told the truth about their parents' situation. They need someone to listen without judging, so that their parents' status need not remain a secret. They need the companionship of others who share their experience, so they can know they are not alone. They need contact with their parents—to have that relationship recognized and valued even under adverse circumstances. And—rather than being stigmatized for their parents' actions or status—they need to be treated with respect, offered opportunity, and recognized as having potential.

The children of prisoners are guaranteed nothing. They have committed no crime, but the penalty they are required to pay is steep. They forfeit, too often, much of what matters to them: their homes, their safety, their public status and private self-image, their primary source of comfort and affection. Their lives and prospects are profoundly affected by the multiple institutions that lay claim to their parents—police, courts, jails and prisons, probation and parole—but they have no rights, explicit or implicit, within any of these jurisdictions.

A criminal justice model that took as its constituency not just individuals charged with breaking the law, but also families and communities within which their lives are embedded—one that respected the rights and needs of children—might become one that inspired the confidence and respect of those families and communities, and so played a part in stemming, rather than perpetuating, the cycle of crime and incarceration.

CHILDREN'S BILL OF RIGHTS

1. I have the right to be safe and informed at the time of my parent's arrest.

Many children are introduced to the criminal justice system when their parent is arrested and they see her taken away in handcuffs. Most police departments do not have protocols for addressing the needs of children when a parent is arrested. The resulting experience can be terrifying and confusing for the children left behind. Some wind up in the back of a police car themselves, on the way to the first in a series of temporary placements. Others are left behind in, or return home to, empty apartments. Arrested parents often prefer not to involve public agencies in the lives of their children, out of fear of losing custody. Many children share this fear, but at the same time long for someone to notice and attend to the family vulnerabilities that can both lead to and result from a parent's arrest.

Parental arrest is by definition a traumatic event for children. But if children's well-being is made a priority, it can also become an opportunity—to assess a child's needs, offer aid in what will likely be a difficult period, and connect with and support vulnerable families.

Rights to Realities

- Develop arrest protocols that support and protect children . . .
- Offer children and/or their caregivers basic information about the postarrest process: where the arrestee likely will be held, how long it may take for him to be processed, and visiting hours and procedures. . . .

When I was seven, a lady knocked on the door, and the police came. They said, "We're going to the park and we'll be back." At that time, I really did think I was going to the park. I sure didn't think I was going to the shelter, where they ended up putting me.

I don't think I really had an understanding about it. It was just, "My mom is gone and I'm here with these people. But I want to be with my mom right now."

What would have helped me is talking about it. When you don't know where your mom is, it's really scary for a child. And no one was talking about it. Just, "Here's a placement for you until she gets herself together." You don't know when she's coming to pick you up—if she ever is going to come.

It would help to have someone there for the child who would continue to be with the child through the process. There should be some kind of task force that specializes in dealing with kids whose parents have been incarcerated. It's all about consistency. Someone there who they can call on, and continue to grow a relationship."

Rochelle, 25

2. I have the right to be heard when decisions are made about me.

When a parent is arrested, children whose lives may already have left them with little sense of control often feel even more alienated from the events that swirl around them.

There are aspects of children's lives that must inevitably remain beyond their control. Children cannot choose whether or when their parents will be taken from them, nor how long their parents will be gone. But when young people are offered a voice within the system and institutions that come to dominate their lives, they are more likely to respect those institutions and find some sense of control and optimism in their own lives.

Rights to Realities

· Train staff at institutions whose constituency includes children of incarcerated parents to recognize and address these children's needs and concerns. . . .
· Tell the truth. . . .
· Listen. . . .

When I was about five years old, my mother and her boyfriend and my uncle were all arrested. I was with them. I can recall, as I sat in the police car, one officer saying, "What are we going to do with this kid?" The other guy said, "Well, we'll just take her to the children's shelter."

I said, "I'm not going to the children's shelter. You need to take me to my grandmother's house, or put me in a cab." I was already living with my grandmother at that time, but they never bothered to ask me, or ask my mother where did she want them to take me.

I was very young at that time, but, generally, as children, we do not know what is happening.

I was terrified of the police at that time, but generally, as children, we do know what is happening. I was very terrified of what I had seen, what happened to family members, what happened to my mother. I felt I hadn't done anything wrong. It was a very frightening experience.

Marie, 38

3. I have the right to be considered when decisions are made about my parent.

Increasingly tough sentencing laws, which have caused the U.S. prison population to increase fivefold over the past three decades, have also had a tremendous impact on children. But as it stands, sentencing law not only does not require judges to consider children when they make decisions that will affect their lives profoundly; in some cases, it actively forbids them from doing so. A more sensible and humane policy would take into account the fact that sentencing decisions will inevitably affect family members—especially children—and strive to protect their interests as much as possible without compromising public safety.

Rights to Realities

- Review current sentencing law in terms of its impact on children and families. . . .
- Turn arrest into an opportunity for family preservation. . . .
- Include a family impact statement in presentence investigation reports. . . .

When I was 16, the police came. They kicked the door in and took my mom to jail. They told me, "Call somebody to come watch you." They were so busy trying to take her out, they didn't care about me.

At first, I didn't know when she would be coming back. Then she called and said she was in jail for possession for sale. She told me to be good and strong. Keep going. After that I just did what she said.

I had to take care of myself for almost six months while she was in jail. I cooked, cleaned, went to school. Stayed out of trouble. I never liked being in my house by myself all the time. It got lonely and it got scary. I had 56 dollars in a piggy bank. I cracked out some money and bought some food. When the groceries got low, I did some work washing cars in the neighborhood, sold newspapers door to door. That's what I did to survive. The electricity got cut off, but I still had water. Then everything got cut off. I was sitting around in the dark. I had my friends come over and we'd sit around and talk. Go to sleep together. Wake up and go to school. . . .

My mom, they just put her in jail. Let her do her time. Kick her out. She's still the same person. She didn't learn.

I think they shouldn't have took my mama to jail that first time. Just gave her a ticket or something, and made her go to court, and give her some community service. Some type of alternative, where she can go to the program down the street, or they can come check on her at the house. Give her the opportunity to make up for what she did.

Using drugs, she's hurting herself. Take her away from me and now you're hurting me.

Terrence, 24

4. I have the right to be well cared for in my parent's absence.

When a child loses a single parent to incarceration, he also loses a home. In the most extreme cases, children may wind up fending for themselves in a parent's absence.

Rights to Realities

- Support children by supporting their caretakers. . . .
- Offer subsidized guardianship. . . .
- Consider differential response when a parent is arrested. . . .

All my life my mom's been in and out of jail for stealing, drug possession, forgery. I never met my father. He's been in and out of prison, too.

Since I was four, I've pretty much lived with my grandma. I used to always cry when my mom would leave. She's been in and out so many times that my heart doesn't allow me to cry any more.

I don't like telling my friends that my mom's locked up because then they're like, "Oh, well, that family's all bad. They're low class." They'll talk behind your back.

When they see that children don't have fathers and the mothers are incarcerated, they need to give the grandmothers more financial support. My grandmother gets SSI [Supplemental Security Income] and welfare gives her 140 dollars a month for four children. I don't know if she's going to have any money for next month's rent. My mom's always calling from prison. My grandma's phone bill is like 500-something right now. My grandma takes the calls 'cause she says it's her daughter.

Besides financially, I think my grandma also needs someone there for her, because it's not right that she's always stuck inside the house taking care of us. She needs to get out.

Amanda, 16

5. I have the right to speak with, see, and touch my parent.

Visiting an incarcerated parent can be difficult and confusing for children, but research suggests that contact between prisoners and their children benefits both, reducing the chance of parents returning to prison and improving the emotional life of children. Because increasing numbers of incarcerated parents are held at prohibitive distances from their children, too many children are denied the opportunity for contact with their parents. In 1978, only 8 percent of women prisoners had never received a visit from their children. By 1999, 54 percent had not received a single visit.

Rights to Realities

- Provide access to visiting rooms that are child centered, nonintimidating, and conducive to bonding. . . .
- Consider proximity to family when siting prisons and assigning prisoners. . . .
- Encourage child welfare departments to facilitate contact. . . .

I remember one time, when I was 10 or 11, my father came to pick me up so I could meet my mom on Mother's Day. He took me to a prison. I remember the prisoners were sitting at tables on one side, and we were sitting on the other, and there was a gate in between all the way down. I threw a rose over the gate.

It really messed my head up, 'cause you can only see your mom through a gate, and that's supposed to be your blood relative. The last thing I remember is I had to turn my back to her and leave. It was hard.

That was the last time I saw her until I was 13 or 14. If there had been some time set up where I could talk to my mom consistently on a one-to-one basis, I think my life would be completely different. Just knowing I had a mother that cared. You're living life solo, but there's a mother out there that you came from.

Danny, 18

6. I have the right to support as I face my parent's incarceration.

Children whose parents are imprisoned carry tremendous burdens. Not only do they lose the company and care of a parent, they also must deal with the stigma of parental incarceration and fear for their parent's safety and well-being. Researchers who have interviewed children who have experienced parental incarceration have found them vulnerable to depression, anger, and shame. One study found many showed symptoms of posttraumatic stress reaction—difficulty sleeping and concentrating, depression, and flashbacks to their parents' crimes or arrests. In the face of these difficulties, many young people will tell you that they rarely receive the support they need as they "do time" along with their parents.

Rights to Realities

· Train adults who work with young people to recognize the needs and concerns of children whose parents are incarcerated. . . .
· Provide access to specially trained therapists, counselors, and/or mentors. . . .
· Save 5 percent for families. . . .

When I was seven years old, I was taken away from my mother because she was addicted to crack cocaine. My father was never in the picture. He was in and out of jail.

Before I was taken away, my mom would get arrested sometimes and my brothers and I would be on our own. I didn't really understand what was going on, but I knew it wasn't right. Eventually, our lights, our phone, our water were all turned off. I know it's not the teachers' responsibility, but I wish they would have come by just to see how we were living. Just to see that we were on our own, in a dark room sometimes, with candles.

Finally, my older brother said, "I have to tell. I can't wash clothes. I can't cook every day. I can't do all that by myself. It's getting too hard for me." He went to my aunt and uncle and told them the situation, and they just took me out of the house. My oldest brother went to another aunt's, and my other brother stayed with my grandmother.

I think there should be a program to help kids cope with the fact that their mother is arrested. Therapy to see how the child is feeling and let them know what's going on. I know I needed something.

Shana, 19

7. *I have the right not to be judged, blamed, or labeled because my parent is incarcerated.*
Incarceration carries with it a tremendous stigma. Because young children identify with their parents, they are likely to internalize this stigma, associating themselves with the labels placed on their parents or blaming themselves for their parents' absence. As they grow older, many report feeling blamed or stigmatized by others—neighbors, peers, teachers and other authority figures, even family members—because of their parents' situation. Some try to keep a parent's incarceration secret. Many describe the shame and stigma they have experienced as the heaviest burden they carry, lasting long after a parent is released or a child grows up.

Rights to Realities

- Create opportunities for children of incarcerated parents to communicate with and support each other. . . .
- Create a truth fit to tell. . . .

I grew up with other kids whose moms used drugs, so I knew I wasn't the only one. I have a couple friends now, their moms use drugs, and we can sit down and have a conversation about it. It helps just to realize that we're not alone, and that we can still do what we're put here to do, 'cause I feel everyone was put here for a reason.

I think for young people in my situation, talking amongst each other would be really good. Have an adult present in the room to help guide the conversation, but I notice that it's better if young people talk about things amongst each other. If you and I both told a kid not to go touch that stove, it's hot, he most likely might listen to me, 'cause I got burned by that stove.

Richard, 18

8. *I have the right to a lifelong relationship with my parent.*
Abiding family bonds are the strongest predictor there is of successful prisoner reentry. For children, sustained attachments form the building blocks for successful development. But changes in child welfare law—specifically, accelerated timetables for termination of parental rights—have increased the odds that even a relatively short sentence will lead to the permanent severance of family bonds. When this happens, children are forced to forfeit the most fundamental right of all—the right to remain part of their families.

Rights to Realities

- Reexamination of the Adoption and Safe Families Act. . . .
- Designate a family services coordinator at prisons and jails. . . .
- Support incarcerated parents upon reentry. . . .
- Focus on rehabilitation and alternatives to incarceration. . . .

I met a couple people that were in foster care. I always had that over my head—like if they say my grandma is too old to take care of us, we might be going to foster care. Whatever the parent may have done, you shouldn't demonize or punish the child by taking the child away from everybody that he or she has loved and tearing away all values, all sense of family. That's a crime in itself to me, and is very saddening to me when I hear it. I have some friends from the visiting room and they were shipped away, taken away from all their loved ones. I know someone who is from the Bay Area and his younger sisters and brothers got moved all the way to Texas, 'cause they were adopted. The older one was over 18, so he wasn't adopted.

I didn't expect my mother to get out till I was 26, but she was paroled when I was 13. Because the contact I'd had with my mother was only for a couple of hours at a time, it wasn't easy when she moved back in with us. We had to get used to each other. One thing I'd really missed was her walking me to school. I remember one day when she first got out, she walked me to school. A lot of kids are ashamed that their mom's walking them to school. I was so happy for her to be in my presence, and for the first time in my life for my mom to even come to my school, that I couldn't care less what people thought.

Malcolm, 17

6

United Nations Report on Violence against Women in U.S. Prisons

The following report was prepared in 1999 for the United Nations Human Rights Commission as part of an investigation of rights violations around the world. The special investigator for violence against women, Radhika Coomaraswamy, a lawyer from Sri Lanka, visited state and federal prisons in six U.S. states and the District of Columbia, taking testimony from many incarcerated women and prison employees. Ms. Coomaraswamy's report highlights the fact that incarcerated women in the United States are disproportionately poor and black and many of them are there because they were unwittingly involved in drug trafficking. It also describes the unacceptable use of shackles on refugees and asylum seekers at the airport and on women in labor. The report calls for minimum standards of treatment to conform with U.S. obligations under international human rights treaties.

United Nations
Economic and Social Council
Commission on Human Rights
55th Session

Integration of the Special Rapporteur on violence against women, its causes and consequences, Ms. Radhika Coomaraswamy, in accordance with Commission on Human Rights resolution 1997/44

Addendum
Report of the mission to the United States of America on the issue
of violence against women in state and federal prisons (excerpts)

THE POLICY FRAMEWORK

Wherever the Special Rapporteur went, officials asked her why she decided to visit the United States. She explained that based on information received from diverse sources, she was convinced that there were serious issues of custodial sexual misconduct in United States prisons that had to be investigated. Many felt nevertheless that special rapporteurs should concentrate on crisis situations around the world rather than focus on countries where human rights protection is more or less ensured. The Special Rapporteur maintains that . . . human rights protections are not only applicable during emergencies, but are also required in societies perceived to be crisis-free. Although the United States has a comparatively high level of political freedom, some aspects of its criminal justice system pose fundamental human rights questions. . . .

Legal Framework for the Treatment of Prisoners

International standards with regard to the treatment of prisoners are set out in the Standard Minimum Rules for the Treatment of Prisoners adopted by the First United Nations Congress on the Prevention of Crime and the Treatment of Prisoners in 1955 and approved by the Economic and Social Council by its resolutions 663C (XXIV) of 31 July 1957 and 2076 (LXII) of 13 May 1977. Although the Rules are not binding, they set out international standards for the treatment of prisoners based on consensus and practice.

The basic principle of the Rules is non-discrimination. According to rule 6, all rules "shall be applied impartially. There shall be no discrimination on grounds of race, colour, sex, language, religion, political or other opinion, national or social origin, property, birth or other status . . . "

With regard to the treatment of women, the Rules are very clear. Rule 8 (a) states that "[m]en and women shall so far as possible be detained in separate institutions; in an institution which receives both men and women the whole of the premises allocated to women shall be entirely separate . . . " Rule 53 . . . states that "[n]o male member of the staff shall enter the part of the institution set aside for women unless accompanied by a woman officer" . . . [and that] "[w]omen prisoners shall be attended and supervised only by women officers. This does not, however, preclude male members of the staff, particularly doctors and teachers, from carrying out their professional duties. . . . " Rule 9 (1) . . . states "[w]here sleeping accommodation is in individual cells or rooms, each prisoner shall occupy by night a cell or room by himself. If for special reasons, such as temporary overcrowding, it becomes necessary for the central prison administration to make an exception to this rule, it is not desirable to have two prisoners in a cell or a room . . . "

With regard to health services, it is stated in rule 22 (1) that "[a]t every institution there shall be available the services of at least one qualified medical officer who should have some knowledge of psychiatry." According to rule 23 (1), "[i]n women's institutions there shall be special accommodation for all necessary prenatal and post-natal care and treatment. Arrangements shall be made wherever practicable for children to be born in a hospital outside the institution. If a child is born in prison, this fact shall not be mentioned in the birth certificate." Rule 23 (2) states that "[w]here nursing infants are allowed to remain in the institutions with their mothers, provision shall be made for a nursery staffed by qualified persons. . . . "

Rule 33 states that [i]nstruments of restraint, "such as handcuffs, chains, irons and straightjackets, shall never be applied as a punishment. Furthermore, chains or irons shall not be used as restraints. . . . "

Rule 35 recognizes the right of prisoners to be informed about their rights and grievance procedures and to make a request or complaint without censorship to the central prison administration, the judicial authority or other proper authorities. Rule 46 sets out guidelines for the hiring of corrections officers and calls for a "careful selection" and proper training of the personnel not only when they join, but also during their service. The Rules also suggest that prisoners be given work, but that the "organization and methods of work in the institutions shall resemble as closely as possible those of similar work outside institutions, so as to prepare prisoners for the conditions of normal occupational life" (rule 72 (i)). Also, rule 77 provides for setting up education programmes for inmates integrated, so far as practicable, with the education system of the country.

The Rules also stipulate that "[p]ersons who are found to be insane shall not be detained in prison" and that "those who suffer from other mental diseases or abnormalities shall be observed and treated in specialized institutions under medical management" (rule 82).

The Standard Minimum Rules for the Treatment of Prisoners is augmented by the Basic Principles for the Treatment of Prisoners, adopted by the General Assembly in its resolution 45/111 of 14 December 1996. The Principles are based on the premise that "[a]ll prisoners shall be treated with respect due to their inherent dignity and value as human beings." They also point out that all prisoners retain their fundamental rights under the Universal Declaration of Human Rights as well as all other rights as spelled out in international conventions and declarations. In addition to the Standard Minimum Rules and the Basic Principles for the Treatment of Prisoners, the General Assembly also adopted, in its resolution 43/173 of 9 December 1988, the Body of Principles for the Protection of All Persons under Any Form of Detention or Imprisonment.

Additionally, the United States has ratified the International Covenant on Civil and Political Rights as well as the Convention against Torture and Other Cruel, Inhuman or Degrading Treatment or Punishment. It has, however, claimed that the provisions of the conventions are "non-self-executing." This means that, unless there is enabling legislation, no one can bring an action in the United States courts. The

Human Rights Committee, in its General Comment 16 on article 17 (right to privacy), argued that "[s]o far as personal and body search is concerned, effective measures should ensure that such searches are carried out in a manner consistent with the dignity of the person who is being searched. Persons being subjected to body search by State officials, or medical personnel acting at the request of the State, should only be examined by persons of the same sex" (see HRI/GEN/l/Rev.3, part I).

Under United States law, the constitutional provisions that are invoked to vindicate prisoners' rights are the Eighth Amendment and the Fourth Amendment. Although the Eighth Amendment prohibits "cruel and inhuman punishment," it has been interpreted quite narrowly by United States courts. To prove a violation, one must not only prove the injury, but also the intent of the person inflicting such injury. With regard to women prisoners, a 1994 Supreme Court decision held that the Eighth Amendment is violated when an officer with deliberate indifference exposes an inmate to a substantial risk of sexual assault. In a decision of the ninth circuit federal court, it was held that subjecting women with a history of sexual abuse to pat searches by men could constitute cruel and inhuman punishment.

The question whether prisoners have a right to privacy under the United States Constitution has not been clearly decided. In *Hudson v. Palmer,* the Supreme Court held that prisoners do not have reasonable expectation of privacy, but in another case, the Court argued that convicted prisoners do not forfeit constitutional protections merely because they are prisoners. So while the international standards clearly state that a prisoner does not give up his/her civil liberties, including the right to privacy, upon conviction, the United States courts have not made a final determination on this matter.

The United States is a federal system and the states are responsible for their own criminal laws, prisons and prisoner legislation. It is seen as an affair of government devolved upon state authorities. However, the United States Department of Justice can enforce national standards based on statutory authority. Under Title 18, sections 241 and 242, of the United States Code, they can proceed under the criminal law for violating a prisoner's right and convict individual officers. They have to prove beyond reasonable doubt that a right has been violated and that there was a specific intent on the part of the official to deny the person his rights. It is extremely rare that prosecutions take place under this law.

The more popular civil provision is the Civil Rights of Individual Persons Act. This law, passed in 1980, allows the Federal Government to bring suit against state institutions for violating constitutional rights. The standards for intervention are quite high. The Department of Justice must have reasonable cause to believe that the state is involved in a set of practices where there are "egregious or flagrant conditions" that violate constitutional provisions. The Department of Justice receives information from diverse sources and when it deems that it has a sufficient body of information, it begins investigations. According to the briefing paper prepared by the Department, it investigated 246 jails, prisons, juvenile correctional facilities, mental health facilities and nursing homes from 1980 to September 1996. Currently they are investigating women's prisons in Arizona and Michigan. Even though the Michigan State government refused them access, the Department is going ahead. When the Department investigates, its attorneys and consultants visit the establishments, conduct interviews with the inmates, tour the facilities and, if conditions are "egregious or flagrant," it will write to the state, summarizing its findings and setting out the steps that need to be taken. If there is no action by the State within 49 days, they may institute legal action against the State for constitutional violations. In their discussions with the Special Rapporteur, members of the Department of Justice said that, owing to limited resources, the Department could not be as active as it would like to.

GENERAL FINDINGS

Diversity and the Lack of Minimum Standards

The first finding that the Special Rapporteur would like to highlight is the extraordinary diversity of conditions in United States prisons. The Special Rapporteur was astonished that the prisons that she saw on video in Michigan and the prison that she toured in Minnesota were in the same country. Diversity is an important part of federalism in the United States context; however, there is diversity even within the states. . . .

There is a need to develop minimum standards with regard to state practices in women's prisons, especially in the area of sexual misconduct.

Use of Instruments of Restraint

Rule 33 [of the Standard Minimum Rules on the Treatment of Prisoners] states clearly that instruments of restraint should not be used as punishment and that chains or irons should never be used as restraints. The Special Rapporteur was informed that there were large-scale violations of this provision in United States prisons. Reportedly, women refugees and asylum seekers coming into the United States are, in many cases, shackled at the airport even when there is no criminal sanction against them. In INS [Immigration and Naturalization Service] detention centres, prisoners are taken to their interviews in leg-irons.

. . . Amnesty International reports that mentally disturbed prisoners have been bound, spreadeagled on boards for prolonged periods without proper medical authorization . . .

Women in labour are also shackled during transport to hospital and soon after the baby is born. The Special Rapporteur heard of one case where shackles were kept on even during delivery.

The use of these instruments violates international standards and may be said to constitute cruel and unusual practices. Some States, such as Minnesota, have abandoned the use of four-point restraints and instead use a "chair" with a straight-jacket. . . . The chair can be abused and Amnesty International has chronicled these abuses in detail. The use of gas . . . chemical sprays, and electroshock devices is also widespread in the United States. . . . The use of restraints without medical supervision and for prolonged periods is a clear violation of international standards.

Sexual Misconduct

The Special Rapporteur interviewed women who had been subjected to some form of sexual abuse in practically all the facilities except in Minnesota. Sexual misconduct covers a whole range of abusive sexual practices in the context of custody. Rape does occur, but it is a fairly rare phenomenon. The more common types of sexual misconduct are sex in return for favours or consensual sex. Given the power imbalance inherent in prison/prisoner relationships and the hierarchy within the prison, relationships between prison guards and prisoners corrupt the prison environment and tend to exploit the women. Sanctioned sexual harassment, i.e. women being pat-frisked by men and monitored in their rooms and in the showers by male corrections officers, is also prevalent . . .

[S]exual misconduct by male corrections officers against women inmates is widespread. . . . Although the Standard Minimum Rules for the Treatment of Prisoners requires that women prisoners be supervised only by women officers, the Supreme Court has deemed such a standard as unconstitutional under Title VII of the Civil Rights Act of 1964, the equal employment opportunity statute. Accordingly, it was found that the employment and career opportunities of female corrections officers would be curtailed if such a standard were implemented since there are only a small number of women's prisons. As a result, the United States continues to have male corrections officers supervising women prisoners. The United Nations Human Rights Committee has also expressed concern about male prison officers guarding women in United States prisons.

The presence of male corrections officers in housing units and elsewhere creates a situation in which sexual misconduct is more pervasive than if women were guarded by female officers. Although there have been cases of sexual misconduct on the part of female corrections officers, such cases were the exception rather than the rule. Corrections officers told the Special Rapporteur that men were necessary in women's prisons because they provided positive male role models. They argued that the key to success was in the professionalism of the officers and not their gender. They also said that the presence of women in male correctional institutions has a calming effect on the men. They argued that the prison should be seen as a microcosm of society, with both males and females providing good role models. In response, the Special Rapporteur would point to the prevalence in United States society of violence against women generally, and sexual violence specifically, which raises particular worries about the use of male guards in female facilities . . .

Though sexual misconduct remains a serious problem in United States women's prisons, recent court cases and awareness-raising campaigns have resulted in some encouraging changes, especially in the State of Georgia ... Under Title 18 of United States Code, section 2241, sexual intercourse by the use or threatened use of force is a felony with the maximum penalty being life imprisonment. Section 2243 prohibits consensual sexual contact between a person in custodial, supervisory or disciplinary authority and the person supervised. According to Human Rights Watch, 27 states and the District of Columbia have expressly criminalized sexual intercourse with, or sexual touching of a prisoner by prison staff ...

The State of Georgia has set up procedures to deal with sexual misconduct which may be relevant elsewhere. The development of these procedures was a response to the *Cason v. Seckinaer* case in which 10 women, identified only as Jane Does, brought a class-action suit complaining of rape, sexual assault, coerced sexual activity, involuntary abortions and retaliation. The shocking revelations forced the court and the Department of Corrections to make sweeping changes ...

Corrections officers have to sign statements that they agree with the *Cason* conditions. Staff failing to report sexual misconduct may also be punished. A special unit has been set up in the Georgia Department of Corrections to deal exclusively with allegations of sexual misconduct. All inmates in Georgia prisons interviewed by the Special Rapporteur told her that after *Cason*, they had seen a welcome change with regard to the attitude of corrections officers ...

[N]o figures in respect to the number of individuals terminated or prosecuted could be provided to the Special Rapporteur. The NGOs [nongovernmental organizations] welcomed the reforms instituted after *Cason*; they reported, however, that although the framework was now in place, action was not being taken. Women rarely come forward since they fear retaliation; further, women ask, who would believe a felon? Nevertheless, the reorganization in Georgia as a direct result of the *Cason* class action suit was unique.

Though the *Cason* provisions address unwanted sexual advances, there remains the problem of the right of women prisoners to privacy. . . . [T]he presence of male corrections officers in women's housing units is a direct violation of the right to privacy. . . . Women complained to the Special Rapporteur that they were watched in the toilet, in the showers and while they were undressing. They reported that the male presence was extremely intrusive. . . . In Connecticut, women inmates reported that they don't go to the cafeteria to avoid being pat-frisked by male guards. Many inmates reported that they felt that pat-frisks by men were very intrusive.

Health Care

Women prisoners in many cases have distinct health-care needs, particularly in light of the high levels of pre-incarceration violence experienced by many of them. . . . [U]nlike young men, women in the age group 18–40 clearly have special medical

needs. The mere replication of health services provided for male prisoners is therefore not adequate.

Violence against women, especially sexual violence, has numerous short- and
long-term reproductive health consequences for women. As such, women prisoners represent a high-risk group for reproductive health problems. Practically all the
women interviewed complained of deficiencies in obstetrical and gynaecological
services.... [W]omen's prisons may require a gender-specific framework for health
care which emphasizes reproductive health, mental illness, substance abuse and
counselling for victims of physical and sexual abuse.

Except for Bedford Hills in New York, none of the prisons was equipped to deal
with large-scale mental health problems. In light of recent trends towards deinsti-
tutionalization, women with mental illnesses are increasingly being found in prisons.... [M]entally ill women are at high risk of sexual abuse in custodial settings....

The Special Rapporteur heard complaints, especially in the State of California,
about unequal treatment of patients with terminal illnesses. Professor Chavkin's paper documents cases of AIDS victims being shackled to their infirmary beds or their
wheelchairs. In Chowchilla, no autopsies are performed on AIDS victims.

Parenting

Despite the fact that the overwhelming number of women in prisons are mothers,
there is no consistency among the states and even within institutions in dealing with
this issue ...

One of the most difficult problems attendant upon putting mothers in jail is
the destruction of the family unit. The foster care option may lead to the permanent break-up of the family. For many inmates, children are a life-sustaining force.
To break that bond is punishment of the worst kind. The location of many prisons in some cases prevents visitation by children who cannot afford to visit at regular intervals.

... The effect of large-scale incarceration of African American women *is* having a major impact on the African American family. Research and analysis in this
regard should be pursued ...

Grievance Procedures

... With the exceptions of Minnesota and Georgia (after *Cason*), no states have grievance procedures that rely on outside monitoring. Most grievances are addressed
within the institution, with a great deal of discretion vested in the warden. Many
grievances are dealt with through informal procedures.... [I]n situations of a captive population, the need for outside review cannot be underestimated.

Most of the inmates said that they had no faith in internal grievance procedures ... [and] were also afraid of retaliation.... [O]utside review should be an essential part of the monitoring of inmates' complaints.

Impunity and Corrections Officers

Corrections officers and officials are reported to enjoy a high level of impunity. The Special Rapporteur *was* informed that in all the states visited, except for Minnesota, corrections officers had a very strong trade union with important political connections. Prisoners, on the other hand, are not a voting constituency. This situation creates a climate of impunity and may help to explain why officers who transgress rules are more often transferred than terminated.

The training of corrections officers is an essential part of any strategy to combat impunity. . . . Perhaps the Federal Government can provide some sort of incentive to states to request training of their staff, especially in the area of sexual misconduct.

. . . [I]n many states there is no pre-screening and corrections officers are hired with only minimum qualifications. . . . [T]hey should be pre-screened, especially with regard to histories of violence.

Private Industry

In all the federal prisons and some of the state prisons, labour is performed by the prison population . . . [Prisoners'] salaries are far below the minimum wage and it has implications for economic and social rights, particularly of women. Such activity also affects the comparative advantage of those industries that do not rely on prison labour. If private industry is to use prison labour it should conform to minimum wage requirements and ensure that the wages are received by the inmates themselves.

Privatization of Prisons

The privatization of prisons raises particular concerns for the safety and well-being of prisoners in general, and of women prisoners in particular. The only private facility visited by the Special Rapporteur was the INS facility in Elizabeth, New Jersey. The emphasis of the facility seemed to be on security more than anything else, despite the fact that many inmates were not violent offenders. Rather, many of the inmates were immigrants in the country illegally and awaiting deportation. There were no projects for the women and no programmes. Most of the women spent their time sleeping, since there was very little activity. . . . If privatization is to be allowed, there must be strict guidelines and oversight so that the profit motive does not interfere with health and medical services, education, training and cultural programmes for inmates.

RECOMMENDATIONS
Federal Level

The United States should ratify the Convention on the Elimination of All Forms of Discrimination against Women and remove its reservations to important international treaties like the International Covenant on Civil and Political Rights and the Convention against Torture and Other Cruel, Inhuman or Degrading Treatment or Punishment. It should enact implementing legislation so that these international treaties have a legal *basis* with regard to the national legal system.

The President's Inter-Agency Council on Women, the working group of women in prisons as well as the Violence against Women Office of the Department of Justice should be given resources to study key policy areas such as:

1. Drug laws and their severe impact on women;
2. A national mental health policy and the imprisonment of women with mental health problems;
3. Race policy in light of the intersection of race, poverty and gender and the increase in the incarceration of African American women, the causes of this increase and the consequences for the African American family; and
4. Domestic violence and women in prisons.
5. Federal funding for state correctional facilities should require the following minimum conditions:
   a. The states should criminalize all forms of sexual violence and sexual misconduct between staff and inmates, whether it occurs with the consent of the inmate or without;
   b. There should be a prescreening of the backgrounds of those who apply to be corrections officers and any history of violence against women should disqualify individuals from being hired;
   c. All corrections officers should be trained with regard to sexual misconduct issues as part of the mainstream training programme;
   d. There should be external monitoring of prison management either by review boards, ombudsmen and/or special investigative units in corrections departments;
   e. In consultation with the psychiatric, medical and human rights community, certain methods of restraint should be prohibited;
   f. Minimum standards with regard to health care should be spelt out, including the presence of a qualified doctor on 24-hour call and easy access to gynaecologists;
   g. All facilities, whether public or private, should have a minimum number of programmes, especially on parenting and vocational training;
   h. Certain posts, such as corrections officers in housing units, and procedures, such as pat-frisks and body-searches should be based on same-sex guarding.

The Civil Rights Division of the Department of Justice should be strengthened and given adequate resources to pursue cases with regard to the Civil Rights of Institutionalized Persons Act. Data-gathering should be systematic and the establishment of a hotline would be welcome.

The National Institute of Corrections should develop national guidelines based on the United Nations Standard Minimum Rules for the Treatment of Prisoners. Training on sexual misconduct should be a high priority of the Institute's programmes with the states. Finally, the Institute should attempt to formulate a model grievance procedure that is more effective in dealing with prisoners' grievances.

With regard to the Immigration and Naturalization Services, the Special Rapporteur has the following recommendations:

The INS should have a gender policy that systematically deals with gender issues, including detention of pregnant women, provision of services and cross-gender guarding in the facilities;

There should be a uniform policy enforced in all districts. The lack of uniformity appears to promote the view that the INS is arbitrary in dealing with detainees;

Detainees should not be mixed with the criminal population either at detention centres or in jails. Instead of sending detainees to jail, more resources should be allocated for detention facilities run by the INS;

At no time should detainees be kept with leg irons and other types of restraints;

Even though the United States Supreme Court has held that detainees have no constitutional rights, they retain international human rights and therefore their due process rights should be protected. They should have full access to lawyers and translators. Families should have visitation rights;

All staff working at INS facilities and INS-sponsored facilities should have training with respect to sexual misconduct and how to address complaints of sexual misconduct;

As far as possible, family units should not be separated. Minor children especially should not be separated from their parents;

As far as possible, those seeking asylum should not be detained, but dealt with through other mechanisms.

State Level

All states should enact laws that criminalize sexual misconduct between staff and prisoners and those who violate these laws should be criminally prosecuted. All administrative codes should include detailed guidelines with regard to sexual misconduct.

Grievance procedures within state correctional institutions should ensure due process. External monitoring of prison conditions is a necessity. Ombudsmen, hotlines, external review boards, etc., should be established.

State correctional institutions should adopt the Georgia model with a special investigative unit within the Department of Corrections dedicated to the issue of sexual misconduct, its investigation and prosecution.

All states should include prohibition of sexual abuse and sexual misconduct as part of their mainstream training and core curriculum.

All staff, including corrections officers, should be subject to prescreening and no person with a history of abuse should be hired.

Inmates who bring grievances should be protected against retaliation. They should only be sent to administrative segregation at their request and those accused of misconduct should be suspended or placed in a position that does not allow them to come into contact with the inmates. The Special Rapporteur is particularly concerned at the situation in Michigan State prisons.

Inmates should have a limited right to privacy. Certain posts within women's prisons should be gender-specific. There should be same-sex guarding in the housing units and pat-frisks and body-searches should only be conducted by same-sex corrections officers.

There should be minimum standards with regard to health care. A qualified doctor should be on the premises for 24 hours. There should be timely referrals and easy access to gynaecologists. Women's reproductive health concerns should not be neglected. Given the fact that many of the women in prisons are mentally ill, special concern should be given to their cases and they should not be ignored or overmedicated. Special programmes should be available for women who have been physically and sexually abused. The Bridge Programme in Danbury is a model programme that should be followed in other jurisdictions.

More resources should be given to parenting programmes in women's prisons. Transportation of children to visit their mothers should be encouraged and qualified professionals and counsellors should help the women deal with their parenting problems. Special care should be taken when children visit their mothers and there should be occasions when some of the women can spend time with their children in a special unit. In this regard, Bedford Hills has a model programme for parenting that could be developed elsewhere.

The states should assist NGOs to set up halfway houses for women about to be released so that they can better integrate into the community once they are released. Minnesota's programme in this regard is worthy of emulation. Former detainees should be allowed to counsel women prisoners about returning to the community.

Alternative justice programmes should be explored for women. Given their parenting problems, home monitoring as used in certain cases in Minnesota may help resolve some of the more difficult concerns, especially in the case of non-violent offenders of victimless crimes.

7

Being in Prison

Joanne Archibald

I was sentenced to a year and a day in federal prison when I was three months pregnant. My court case took a long time, so I was able to give birth to my son outside. He was seven months old when I went in. That day is so clear in my mind, driving up to the gate in my sister's little Volkswagen bug, with my sister, my friend Joan, who was going to take care of David, and David and me. Then leaving him there and walking through that gate. And even though it was real then, it wasn't really real 'til I walked through those doors. And I barely stopped crying the whole first day. They sent me to the medical unit where I just sat and waited all day. They give you a physical and ask you questions, give you a pillow and a blanket and stuff, and then they assign you to a cell. That whole day when I was there crying and waiting to be processed at the medical unit, people saw me sitting there crying, and it was really kind of touching how many people came over and talked to me through the glass. They would say, "It's going to be okay." And, you know, ask a few questions. They couldn't really stay and talk long because you weren't supposed to. It kind of reassured me, and that helped.

The intake was probably a couple of weeks. While you're on intake, they give you a job. You go out in the morning and sweep up cigarette butts off the sidewalks, and you go to a lot of little presentations, and mostly you're basically just sitting around, and they tell you what goes on and what the rules are and what you can do and can't do. My roommate during that time was a woman from New Orleans, and she had cashed somebody's checks. I guess it was public-aid checks or social security checks, because it was federal. And she really, really had some mental health issues. We stayed friends during the whole time, and she actually ended up getting raped by one of the guards.

After the orientation, you're assigned a room and a regular job. My roommate then was a woman who was probably in her late fifties, a Spanish woman from Southern California whose husband beat her and forced her to cash these checks that he had stolen, because they were in a woman's name. She was actually relieved in a lot of ways, she said, to be there and be away from him. And she was a good roommate. We got along really well. Our room was small, like a small dorm room. There were bunk beds, little desks on each side, and then up near the door was a kind of divider. It didn't really block, but it blocked a little. And on the other side of that was our toilet, and there was a sink in there too. We gave each other space to have some time in the room by ourselves. There was a little glass rectangle in the door, and you weren't allowed to cover that up. We did have something that looked like a little potholder, and you were allowed to put it up just for a few minutes at a time while you were using the toilet. If they thought you had it on too long, they would come in your room.

I think I had more visits than anybody else in the prison, so I was really lucky. I was kind of aware of it at that time, but not really that much because I was so unhappy with the whole situation. I guess I couldn't really appreciate it. I mean, every time my son came, I still had to say good-bye and give him to somebody else, who would walk out with him, and it never got any less wrenching to do the good-byes. I cried every time, and I can't even count how many times I was yelled at by officers for crying: "What are you crying for, you get visits, a lot of people don't." That was true, and I was grateful for it. But it didn't make it any less difficult when he left.

When the visit ended, you had to get strip-searched. So I couldn't just go back to my cell and be by myself and think about the visit. You very seldom got strip-searched right away. There was just one officer doing it, and if it was near the end of visitation, everybody is leaving at the same time, so there's a line. It was always so awful in that line. You didn't chitchat or ask, "How was your visit?" Mostly we were so into the pain of seeing our people walk away again, that it was usually really quiet. And you didn't even look in anybody's eyes, you just kind of closed off. We had to stand in this line, but we were leaning against the wall, and everybody was in their own pain. And then going in this little closet-size room with an officer and stripping totally, shaking your hair, opening your mouth, showing them the bottom of your feet, bending over, squatting, and coughing. It was so degrading, and I will say that for a lot of the officers, it was degrading for them too. If they knew who you were and knew there wasn't a lot of risk, they would kind of go through it quickly, in a kind of cursory way, still doing every step. But then, some almost seemed to enjoy the degradation they were putting you through, and that made it even more difficult.

In the visiting room, a big high-ceilinged room, gray walls, gray tables, gray carpet, you were expected to just sit at the table and visit, which was not very realistic with an infant—expecting him to sit for three or four hours at a table. But, the Children's Center was great, like a nice day care place. My son could get dropped off, and then it would just be him and me visiting together, which was nice for us. It was also really nice for his caregiver because it gave her a little break. She had gone from being a single person to a full-time caregiver of an infant in a town where she didn't know anybody except me in the prison. I was really happy about the care that she gave him, but it was still awkward sometimes because he was so attached to her. I remember one time in the visiting room: he was crawling under the table, and he bumped his knee on the base of the table. He started crying, and he looked at me, then he looked at her, then he looked at me. He looked back and forth several times, like he was thinking, "Who's supposed to take care of me?" That was really hard. As much as I knew that it was important for him to be attached to her and really care for her, it still was difficult because it made me feel like I wasn't taking care of him, like I wasn't his mother anymore. That was hard to deal with.

I worked in the kitchen, which was really the drudge job. Pretty much everybody, when they first came in, got put in the kitchen. I made the mistake of doing too good a job, so I ended up as a cook there the whole time, because they didn't want me to leave. I was into cooking before I went there, so the way they cooked was just so offensive to my sensibility. They always put a lot of cornstarch in the sauces to thicken them up, make them go further. It really was not good food. Although I will say that when you worked there you ate better because you got to eat the food when it was first made instead of after it had been sitting for hours.

It was hard working there because . . . well, one, it was just hard; but it was coed, and I cooked with this guy who was constantly rubbing up against me and stuff. At the time I didn't even know the words "sexual harassment," but that's totally what it was. I just knew that he was really bothering me. A few times I complained about it, and the officer would talk to him about it, but then he would be so mean. It was almost easier to deal with him making comments and rubbing up against me than to tell on him. And after seven months, I talked to someone who could get me transferred out.

But, I would say, really, I had so few negative interactions with other people there. Most of the negative stuff was with staff and administration. It was much more, "We're all in this together, and we need to deal with it." The people who ran the Children's Center did classes on parenting—I took one on "your child's self-esteem." They had training programs that prepared inmates to work in the Children's Center, and I took those to keep myself busy. (I also took a course in yoga that women organized and one in miracles, participated in a stress reduction group, and other groups.)

For the most part, I just lived for my visits. I had some friends that I hung out with, but I kept to myself a lot and kept attached to the outside. I didn't have that long a sentence, and I kind of made friends with certain people that had longer sentences. And for their own self-preservation, they didn't want to get close to somebody who has a year. So, you end up making better friends with people with similar sentences, especially if you have a short time. It wasn't that hard and fast—there was somebody in my yoga group who was doing a really long time and we got really close—but I was aware that it was hard for them.

Mostly, I lived for when I would get out and could be with my baby again. And I lived for letters and the pictures of my son that my friends sent. Now there are more restrictions on how many pictures you can have, but there weren't any then, so I had lots of pictures, and that was really nice.

8

Wearing Blues

Kinnari Jivani

Wearing Blues
while our roots are grounded on the barren land
branches spread wider than wings
in hope that the wind-god will bring
the footwear for the roots
and free them from the heavy six digit chain

Wearing Blues
over the limbs that had ridden the ship of battles
out of desperation or need or want or
out of fear of the shadows crawling over our bodies

Wearing Blues
for the tears that never could bleed but dry and turn into scabs,
coarse tears scabs
that peel away slowly

Wearing Blues
brings somber burden, taboo and
the grief that cry the silent roar
the memoir introspection speaks that
underneath the ganglion and layers of wrinkled-skin-experiences
grow the layers of wisdom

Wearing Blues
takes the dare to survive the unknown
strength to stand the degradation and pain
courage to stand gracefully tall
faith to drink the love that rain drops shower

Wearing Blues
'cause in the limbo
notes of rock, jazz and rap
sounds like blues
and we are living the blues
with simper

PART TWO

Being a Mother from Inside

THIS SECTION EXPLORES THE DEEPLY EMOTIONAL REALITY of separation, loss, and grief that characterizes the experiences of so many mothers behind bars. It also looks at policies and programs that aim to respond to maternal incarceration, including some that facilitate the end of maternity and others that open spaces for honoring it.

A number of currently and formerly incarcerated mothers write in this section about the ways that tragic personal mistakes—along with the institution itself, institutional staff, and harmful applications of law and policy—threaten and degrade the possibilities of maternity from inside. For example, Kimberly Burke describes in searing detail a child's-eye view of parental authority while at a visiting center. Carole E. and others write about losing their children to foster care and adoption. Some women write about losing the opportunity even to have *memories* of their children's lives. A mother yearns, "I wish I was there to put you to sleep."

Sometimes prison authorities permit programs on the premises that help parents create and maintain bonds with their children. (Often these programs are developed by outsiders and staffed by volunteers.) For example, four women describe the Story Book Project at Bedford Hills prison in New York, which encourages incarcerated mothers to record good-night stories on tape, allowing children to hear their mothers' voices reading them to sleep. Small groups of women in Washington State, Nebraska, and California describe other projects that refuse to treat "prisoner" and "mother" as incompatible roles.

John and Mom, 2002. Women's Community Correctional Center, Kailua, Hawaii. Photograph by Cindy Ellen Russell

One chapter offers an excerpt of *Out of Sight, Not Out of Mind,* a manual written by staff at the Administration for Children Services, the child protective agency in New York City, which provides tips to incarcerated parents about how to retain legal custody of their children. In a chapter on the impact of the Adoption and Safe Families Act, Philip Genty and his coauthors show how easily parents can lose custody of children who are in foster care because of federal and state laws that shorten the time frame within which the state can permanently sever parental ties without taking incarceration into account.

Kathy Boudin and other women locked away from their children write in this section about how being a mother, even under these circumstances, can be a way of envisioning freedom, imagining the deep companionship of relation, dreaming about the dignities of being a beloved guide, and conjuring up the possible meanings of "guidance." Mothers writing in this section speak a great deal about their horror and shame about what they have lost but also about what they still hope to find.

9

Get on the Bus

Mobilizing Communities across California to Unite Children with Their Parents in Prison

Suzanne Jabro and Kelly Kester-Smith

I got to see my Mom today and I adore her.
There is no one in the world I have like my Mom.
CHRIS, AGE 14, GET ON THE BUS PARTICIPANT

The prison system was designed to punish men. Its activities, policies, and regulations were developed in response to male models of behavior, morality, and rehabilitation. When mandatory drug sentencing laws were passed in the 1970s and 1980s, the number of women serving prison sentences doubled. Despite increased female representation in the prison population, the system did not evolve to address the family crises that resulted when the laws changed. No one seemed to comprehend that more women in prison would result in the abandonment of more children to foster care or out-of-home kinship-care placements. No one predicted that deconstructing families would result in higher rates of recidivism for female offenders and higher rates of juvenile delinquency for their children. *No one considered the children.*

Women and Criminal Justice, a group of activists concerned about the plight of women in prison, was well aware that incarcerated women defined their greatest source of sadness and anxiety as the separation from their children. Most incarcerated women reported that they had not seen their children since their sentencing. Some had not seen their children for over five years: five years of missed birthdays; five years of growth and change; five years of children living without their mothers. All relevant research shows that regular contact between incarcerated mothers and their children is crucial to the mental health and development of both groups. Yet no programs existed to make this contact possible.

Chowchilla is five hours one way by car from Los Angeles, three hours from the

San Francisco Bay Area, and nine hours from San Diego. Unfortunately, "by car" is not an option for the families participating in the program. The vast majority of the children identified for a visit live with maternal grandmothers, who are struggling with poverty, poor health, and transportation difficulties. The cost of three bus tickets (one grandmother and two children) from Los Angeles to Chowchilla is over one hundred fifty dollars and entails eighteen hours of travel time. This amount does not include the cost of meals or the overnight accommodations necessitated by the length of the trip. The situation represents the classic "double whammy" so often encountered by the economically poor: mom is sentenced to a prison more than one hundred fifty miles away; the cost of a visit is more than the family's food budget for an entire month. The leaders of Women and Criminal Justice realized they needed to find some wheels.

Beginning in 1998, Women and Criminal Justice worked with prison officials and families to develop a program for bringing children to visit their parents in prison. The first bus left Los Angeles for Chowchilla prison the next year, carrying fifteen children. Today, Get on the Bus fills more than thirty buses with six hundred children from all over California to visit their mothers on the Friday before Mother's Day. In 2006, the program also brought children to visit their fathers in prison for Father's Day. The event unites families and informs the public of the devastation that occurs when a parent, particularly a mother, is sent to prison. A mother is still a mother to her children, even when she is separated from them by miles and prison walls.

> *I am in prison for 14 years. My family can't afford to come up and see me.*
> *This is a beautiful experience! I look forward to the next visit.*
> STAR, CENTRAL CALIFORNIA WOMEN'S PRISON, CHOWCHILLA

Every moment of the Get on the Bus program is tailored to the needs of children. Each child receives a brightly colored T-shirt and a goody bag filled with games and toys to make the long drive entertaining. Children are accompanied by their guardian, or if their guardian is unable to attend, they are assigned their own Child Companion, who ensures that they feel safe and attended to. Volunteers bring breakfast, and during the visit, families enjoy a special barbecue prepared just for them. Children receive free meals during the day. While at the prison, families enjoy a four-hour visit that includes family portraits taken by volunteer photographers. The photos are on instant film so that the children can take them home that day. Each mother and each child receives a photo, which becomes the most cherished keepsake of the day. Children often hold onto their photos all the way home—even while eating dinner. After the visit and back on the bus, children receive teddy bears and letters from their mothers. Volunteer counselors walk the aisles to provide comfort to children who have had difficulty saying good-bye. Anyone who has been on the bus will tell you that the day is immensely emotional, starting with the thrill of anticipation, proceeding to the sheer joy of the hugs and smiles of reunion, and ending with a quiet and somber ride home.

> *Mom, it was so great seeing you. We have enough joy and happiness*
> *to share with the whole world. We slept in our Get on the Bus*
> *T-shirts you signed, just to be close to you.*
> TAYLOR AND PARIS, LOS ANGELES

A mother whose children came on one of our buses wrote,

> I would like to take this time to thank you and your organization. This is the second
> year that my family and I have participated. We look forward to our annual visit.
>
> Being away from my family is very hard. There is not a day that goes by that my
> children and I don't suffer. I truly regret what I have put my children through. Through
> your efforts, I have the opportunity to reunite with my seven-year-old daughter Ash-
> ley, and my Mother. It is a very emotional time for Ashley and Me. Just the feeling of
> holding her and kissing her and seeing that smile brings peace of mind.
> *Vivian, Valley State Prison for Women*

A grandmother wrote,

> Please express my gratitude to all the ladies who put together the meals and activities
> for kids, and for those who coordinated this effort and served us so extensively. If there
> is anything I can do to assist with your program next year, please let me know. My
> daughter will be released from CCWF [Central California Women's Facility] in July,
> so we won't be "getting on the bus" next year!

While many prisoners' rights issues can be "hard sells" to the media, most people cannot ignore the pain of children who are separated from their mothers. By appealing to the basic human understanding that children need their mothers, Get on the Bus can open hearts and minds to the larger issue of reform—the need to prevent society from punishing children along with their parents.

Get on the Bus continues to explore ways to bring families together. Thanks to a successful legislative campaign, the organization will be initiating the Chowchilla Family Express, free monthly transportation for children and members of their extended families. The Chowchilla Family Express is a historic undertaking because it is funded by the first-ever contract granted by the State of California to provide transportation for children of prisoners. Seeds of systemic change are being planted and carefully tended by many caring people throughout the state who have become aware of the plight of children with parents in prison through their participation in or support of Get on the Bus.

Where will the bus go next? Communities in Washington State, Arizona, and Florida have expressed interest in replicating the program. Our vision is that no child anywhere in our country should endure the pain of parental incarceration. Providing transportation is an important service to alleviate separation, but we would prefer changes in sentencing laws to eliminate mandatory minimum sentences for nonviolent offenses and create community-based alternatives to incarceration for women with dependent children. By demonstrating the devastating social and economic impact on families when they are torn apart by incarceration, Get on the Bus serves as a key point of entry for education, activism, and collaboration. If hundreds of individuals can work together to fund and fill buses with children, then they can also be inspired and empowered to work together to create a powerful voice for reform.

> *It's so great just to spend some time with my babies (12 & 14)*
> *I am missing out on so much of their lives that it's a gift,*
> *this time we spend together.*

DIERDRE, VALLEY STATE PRISON FOR WOMEN

10

Do I Have to Stand for This?

Kimberly Burke
Riverside Unit, TX, 2002

Slowly my eyes blink open to the sound of my alarm. Because it's my day off, I shouldn't even be getting up, especially since I just went to sleep a few hours ago. I was so excited last night that it was hard for me to fall asleep. You see, today is my first visit with my seven-year-old son since I was first incarcerated three years ago.

My mother and son flew to Texas from Utah just to see me. I've been waiting for this for so long just so I could hug my son. The day has finally arrived. I spend the next two hours getting ready. A hot shower and plenty of baby powder later, I'm smelling sweet. I painstakingly apply just the right amount of makeup and curl my hair. I want to look extra special when they arrive. Each time the phone rings, I watch the guard's eyes to see if they fall on me. And finally they do, and she calls my name for a visit.

I jump up, dressed in crisp, creased state-issued whites, with my black state boots shining like new money. My heart is racing ninety miles an hour as I walk the hundred feet to the visitation room.

The door opens, and I see this beautiful set of green eyes that look so much like the child I left three years before, yet he is so tall, and all his baby fat is gone. His face lights up, but not as bright as mine, and we embrace in a hug strong enough to bend steel. I see my mother and hug her too. This is the moment I've waited so long for.

My eyes float over to the guard, and I recognize a glimmer of the hatred that fills so many in her position. Angry prison guards who feel their only mission in life is to make us feel less than human. I notice only one other visit in progress, and the visitors smile our way. They too realize how special a visit is to a prisoner.

As the visit goes on and I get reacquainted with my son, I comment to my mother that she's doing a wonderful job with him. He's polite, quiet, well mannered, and very well behaved. I can't help but notice the guard continually spewing hatred with her eyes.

My son gets up to get some children's books that are there for children on visits. The guard points her index finger at my son and motions for him to come to her. He hangs his head, and shyly walks over to her. In a rough voice she spits, "You need to stay in your seat, or I will end your visit. Do you understand?" He replies, "Yes ma'am" and sulks back to our table. I am shocked that this guard spoke so harshly to my child, when all he was doing was getting a book to read. Humiliation creeps over me as I realize I can do nothing about it. If I cause a scene, my visit will be canceled. Yet my hurt is strong. I decide to wait until after my visit and then speak to a ranking officer.

A while later my son becomes excited at seeing a large grasshopper on the window screen. He jumps up to get a closer look but only takes one step before the guard yells with venom in her voice, "I told you once already to stay in your seat and not get up, or I will end your visit, and you won't be able to see your mom anymore!" He falls back in his chair, lays his head on the table, and cries. I am furious. Who does she think she is? She can't speak to my child that way. I begin to console and calm my son. I tell my mother that the guard is not allowed to speak to him that way. I am an inmate and belong to the State of Texas for the next five years, but he doesn't. He is an innocent little seven-year-old boy, who has now been traumatized by this guard during the only visit he's had with his mom.

This incident happened to me on July 7. I'm still hurt, angry, and humiliated because I wasn't able to protect my child from the hate within these walls. It is understandable if a guard speaks to an inmate in such a manner, but not to an innocent child.

When I asked my son if he wanted to come again to visit me, he hung his head and said no. This incident will remain in his memory every time he thinks of our visit. It's hard enough being incarcerated and dealing with abuse by prison guards. On top of that, we have to deal with their abuse of our families when they visit us. It's no wonder over half the prison population never receives a visit during their incarceration.

Even though this situation is currently being investigated, I doubt if the prison officials take this as seriously as I do. In the end, it's still only an inmate's word against the word of an officer.

It is now 2008 and since this incident I still haven't seen my son, who is now thirteen. The prison guard was ultimately put on extensive probation and soon after fired for her treatment of my son. It rekindles my faith in the grievance procedure and shows others that doing the right thing is still the best thing.

If you'd like to write me about this incident, feel free. Write to Kimberly Burke #938449, 1401 State School Rd., Gatesville, TX 76599.

11

Out of Sight, NOT Out of Mind

Important Information for Incarcerated Parents
Whose Children Are in Foster Care

Children of Incarcerated Parents Program
NYC Administration for Children's Services

If you are incarcerated and your child is in foster care, this section is for you. It will provide you with important information about the child welfare system and your rights and responsibilities towards your child in foster care. Your child may have already been in foster care before your incarceration or may have entered foster care as a result of your arrest and incarceration, or during your incarceration. No matter what, your situation now may feel very difficult and frustrating. You may worry about your children, miss them, and wonder if and how you can parent under these difficult circumstances. While it will be difficult and not the same as before—*you can parent from inside* and it is so important that you make every effort to do so.

Even though you are incarcerated, it is very important that you actively plan for your child's future. When your child is in foster care, actively planning means being involved in their ACS [Administration for Children's Services] case and being in contact with the caseworker. In order for you to reunite with your child upon your release (if your sentence is not too long), you have to show that you are a responsible parent, are involved in your child's life, and are addressing the issues that led to your child being placed in foster care. All of this must be done within specific time frames.

PARENTAL RIGHTS AND RESPONSIBILITIES

As a parent with a child in foster care, you have certain rights and responsibilities. Your caseworker can answer many questions that you have. You should also speak with your Family Court lawyer as soon as possible to let her know where you are and to develop a plan for your case during your incarceration.

In order for you to receive the services that you have a right to, and to show your caseworker that you are fulfilling your parental responsibilities, it is very important that you develop a relationship with your caseworker—he/she is now an important person in your family's life, and both your child and you will benefit if you and your caseworker work together as a team. This is not always an easy thing to do, but it is very important.

YOUR RIGHTS AS A PARENT

- You have the right to know why your child is placed in foster care, which foster care agency your child is placed with, and what you need to do to reunify with him/her.
- You have the right to identify a family member or other resource person who you would like your children to live with, either as an alternative to foster care or to become foster parents. ACS should explore this choice with you.
- You have the right to know who your ACS caseworker is, and how to contact him/her and his/her supervisor with questions or concerns about your child. If your child's caseworker changes, you have a right to be notified of this change in a timely manner.
- You have the right to be assigned an attorney to represent you in any Family Court proceedings involving your foster care/ACS case, even between adjourn (court) dates.
- You have the right to receive available services to help you address the issues that led to your child's placement in foster care (for example, parenting classes, substance abuse treatment, etc.).
- You have the right to know your child's permanency goal and service plan, as well as to know the services and programs with which you are required to cooperate, and the goals you are expected to achieve. You also have the right to receive written notification of the date of your family's Service Plan Review (SPR) 14 days in advance of this conference. An SPR occurs every 6 months.
- You have a right to participate in the Service Plan Review although this may be difficult while incarcerated. In some cases (depending on where you are incarcerated), it may be possible to hold the SPR at your facility. If this is not possible, you can participate via phone conference arranged through your correctional counselor and caseworker. No matter what, you have the right to receive a copy of the service plan that has been discussed and developed at the conference. This should be mailed to you within 10 days of the meeting.
- You have the right to visits with your child. Unless the court has ordered otherwise, your agency/ACS must make efforts to facilitate at least monthly visits to you if you are incarcerated in the tri-state area (NY, NJ, CT). If the distance or the facility's rules make monthly visits difficult, you have a right to have

other forms of contact with your child such as phone calls and letters. At least monthly visits should be facilitated when you are transferred closer or the visit rules change to allow visits. If you are not receiving regular visits or are not satisfied with your visits, you should contact your caseworker or his/her supervisor. You can also call the ACS Office of Advocacy's Parents' and Children's Rights Helpline collect at (212)619–1309.

- You have the right to be notified of upcoming Family Court dates and to be produced for these proceedings. If you know of an upcoming court date, you should talk to your lawyer, caseworker, and Correctional Counselor to request that you be produced. You can also write to your Family Court Judge requesting that you be present at all proceedings involving your child.
- You have the right to be kept up to date on your child's health and development, behavior, and progress in school, including being given copies of your child's report cards. You have the right to consent for (most of) the medical care your child receives (unless your parental rights have been terminated).

YOUR RESPONSIBILITIES AS A PARENT

Planning

- In order to regain custody of your child, you must be able to show that you are involved in his/her life and are planning for his/her future. This includes making arrangements for a permanent home for your child during your incarceration, as well as planning for him/her upon your release, especially if you will be released soon. This plan can be for your child to live with a relative or friend during your incarceration who has agreed to care for him/her and who has been screened and approved by ACS, or some other legal arrangement.
- If you cannot arrange for a permanent place for your child to live, your child will be placed with a non-kinship foster parent who would be willing to adopt him/her if reunification will not be possible. You should keep in mind that foster care is a temporary placement not meant to last more than 15 months, with some exceptions.
- The agency/ACS is responsible for working with you, and you are responsible for working and cooperating with the agency. This includes communicating with them and agreeing to follow the service plan (you should have input into what the service plan is and can also voice your needs and disagreement). If you refuse to work with the agency, the agency may go to Court and report that you have "failed to plan" for your child's future and, as a result, they may ask that your parental rights be terminated.
- If you feel the agency is not working with you or that they are misrepresenting

you, you should speak with your lawyer, or call the ACS Office of Advocacy's Parent's and Children's Rights Helpline collect at (212) 619–1309 (Monday–Thursday, 9:00 A.M.–5:00 P.M.).

Staying in Contact

- You are expected to make efforts to stay in contact with your child. Keep copies of papers and document every contact and attempted contact. Keep a list of every visit scheduled (even if it didn't happen); of every phone call you make to the caseworker, your child, and your child's caretaker (even if you left a message or no one answered the phone); and of every letter, birthday card, or other mail you send (even if you don't get a reply).
- Be sure to keep every letter and document you receive that has to do with your ACS case. This will help you show your caseworker and the judge that you have made efforts to stay in contact with your child and the agency.
- You are legally responsible for maintaining contact (through visits, letters, or phone calls) with your child and your caseworker, and for notifying him/her of your whereabouts. If you do not plan for your child and maintain regular contact, your parental rights could be terminated. If a period of 6 months goes by and you have not had contact with your child, your caseworker, or the foster care agency, this can be considered abandonment of your child, and your agency can use this as grounds to terminate your parental rights.
- You are responsible for notifying your caseworker whenever you are transferred to a different facility or your address changes. You must notify him/her as soon as possible after a location change.

12

The Impact of the Adoption and Safe Families Act on Children of Incarcerated Parents

Arlene F. Lee, Philip M. Genty, and Mimi Laver
Child Welfare League of America

INTRODUCTION

On November 9, 1997, President Clinton signed the Adoption and Safe Families Act of 1997 (ASFA) to improve the safety of children, to promote adoption and other permanent homes for children, and to support families. The changes in ASFA are important to ensure the safety of children and increase their likelihood of placement in permanent homes. The change that requires close examination is the timeline for initiating termination of parental rights (TPR) proceedings. Under ASFA, TPR proceedings must be brought if:

- the child has been in foster care for fifteen of the most recent twenty-two months, or
- the court has determined that the child is "an abandoned infant."

Exceptions can be made to these requirements if a child is being cared for by a relative, the state agency documents a compelling reason why filing is not in the best interest of the child, or the state agency has not provided the child's family with the services deemed necessary to return the child to a safe home.

Many people have questioned whether these changes, if applied in their strictest terms, have had a detrimental effect on children of prisoners, because a large percentage of incarcerated parents are sentenced to longer than two years in prison. This section examines the potential effect of ASFA's TPR requirements on children of prisoners. It considers four questions:

- At what rate are children of incarcerated parents becoming the subjects of TPR hearings?

- Are these hearings triggered by the timelines delineated in ASFA?
- Has there been an increase in the rate of TPR for children of prisoners since ASFA's inception?
- Are children of prisoners becoming the subjects of TPR at a higher rate than other children in foster care, despite the potential for reunification, as an unintended consequence of ASFA?

To answer these questions, the Child Welfare League of America's (CWLA's) Federal Resource Center for Children of Prisoners, the American Bar Association's (ABA's) Center on Children and the Law, and Columbia University's School of Law joined forces to examine available information. Data collection involved gathering information about both state laws regarding TPR and the frequency of TPR of incarcerated parents and conducting a case review of sample cases.

As a result of parental incarceration—and the criminal behaviors that prompt it—thousands of children have endured traumatic and often lengthy separations from their parents.

ASFA was the first major legislation addressing the issues of permanence since the Adoption Assistance and Child Welfare Act (Public Law [P.L.] 96–272) in 1980. P.L. 96–272 was the first law to focus attention on the large number of children in out-of-home care and the importance of stability, continuity, and family connectedness to a child's healthy growth and development. To assist the states in achieving more timely permanence for children, P.L. 96–272 introduced new requirements for judicial oversight and clear timetables for decision making in child welfare cases.

Between 1979 and 1985, the number of children in out-of-home care significantly decreased, from about 500,000 to 270,000 (U.S. House of Representatives 2004). Due to family stressors such as HIV/AIDS, drug addiction, poverty, and violence, however, the number of children in out-of-home placements increased by 74 percent between 1986 and 1995 (U.S. House of Representatives 2004). The system struggled to provide the level of service each case needed to be successfully resolved. Large caseloads created an erosion in the capacity of child welfare agencies to achieve permanence for children in foster care.

The incarceration of women has important implications for child welfare agencies because most female inmates are mothers of minor children, and many are single parents. The question has been raised many times, and is supported by anecdotal evidence, although some have contended that incarcerated mothers have historically been neglected by the child welfare system:

The ideology of family reunifications . . . never has been applied with enthusiasm to prisoner mothers. This is in part due to the distance foster care workers must travel to provide visits for children with mothers in prison, and caseworkers' unfamiliar-ity with prison regulations, resources, programming and staff. It is also due in large part to a widespread bias against reuniting children with a mother in prison. . . . ASFA has exacerbated the plight of women prisoners and their children. (Smith 2000)

In December 2001, the ABA's Center on Children and the Law published an article in its *Child Law Practice* examining some of the early ASFA cases focusing on incarcerated parents and providing practice tips for judges and lawyers who represent parents, children, and the child welfare agency in abuse and neglect cases. The article discussed several topics, including the right of the parent to participate in hearings, reasonable efforts, the decision to not provide a parent with reasonable efforts toward reunification, and TPR. The case law and practice tips all point to the need for courts, attorneys, and other child welfare practitioners to seek a balance between protecting the incarcerated parent's rights and ensuring that agencies meet ASFA's permanency timelines and goals (including reunification, adoption, and guardianship, or placement with kin) for the child (Laver 2001).

The importance of maintaining family relationships while parents are incarcerated and the difficulties of doing so have been documented in numerous articles and studies (see, e.g., Genty 2003, and sources cited therein). Despite all of the research that practitioners have done on these issues, public policy aimed at preserving family relationships during and after incarceration is still severely lacking.

One reason for this is the absence of meaningful coordination between criminal justice and child welfare agencies. These two systems make decisions that, with respect to family relationships, may conflict.

It is, therefore, essential that the criminal justice and child welfare systems work together to develop coordinated policies for incarcerated parents and their families. It is impossible to do this, however, without reliable data. The importance of determining what portion of the child welfare caseload involves parental incarceration seems obvious, but state agencies do not track this information. The assessment of the needs of the children of incarcerated parents (as well as children whose parents were previously incarcerated) and the development of sound policies to address these needs require that agencies develop ways of collecting these data.

As a result of the questions raised and the lack of empirical evidence, the Vera Institute conducted one of the first large-scale studies of this issue, examining cases in New York City involving incarcerated women and children in foster care. Ehrensaft, Khashu, Ross, and Wamsley (2003) found that:

Most of the incarcerations occurred in the year after the child's placement, a pattern similar to that found for arrests leading to incarceration . . . The timing of arrest, conviction and placement suggests that children are removed in the midst of a downward spiral in the mother's life that continues after the removal. (p. 2)

Although Ehrensaft et al.'s work identified the link between foster care placement and maternal substance abuse preceding incarceration, it did not reach the question of how parental rights are ultimately affected . . .

The researchers' theory was that by identifying several different but related data points, they could begin to construct a picture of how children of incarcerated parents are affected by the changes in child welfare laws. What emerged was a picture of how children are affected by the intersection of three different trends: shorter timelines under ASFA, extended sentencing timelines, and the increase in the number of parents incarcerated for drug-related criminal offenses.

FINDINGS

ASFA was enacted in 1997, and all states enacted conforming legislation in the following years. At present thirty-six states have TPR statutes that deal explicitly with parental incarceration. Of these, twenty-five have statutes that are primarily time driven, such as permitting rights to be terminated based on the length of incarceration.

In reviewing reported TPR cases, the significant overall increase in the number of termination cases involving incarcerated parents that were filed from 1997 to 2002 suggests that ASFA has had an important effect. The results from the surveys of judges, attorneys, and child welfare representatives were:

- judges, attorneys, and to some extent, child welfare agency representatives believe that ASFA affects children of incarcerated parents differently than other children;
- most child welfare agency representatives feel that incarceration does not affect the likelihood of TPR or change the manner in which the agency handles children since ADFA was enacted;
- a high percentage of judges believe that parental rights are more likely to be terminated as a result of incarceration of parents in child abuse and neglect cases compared with those who are not incarcerated;
- judges believe incarceration expedites TPRs in cases of children of incarcerated parents, whereas child welfare agency representatives feel timeliness is not affected; and
- disagreement exists among judges and attorneys with regard to whether incarceration may be grounds for TPR, with a high percentage of attorneys responding positively to this but only a very small number of judges agreeing.

The results obtained in the case file reviews highlight the following:

- TPR was granted in 81.5 percent of the cases involving parents incarcerated due to drug-related offenses.
- The most common reason for incarceration was a drug-related charge.
- TPR was granted in 92.9 percent of the cases in which the mother was incarcerated.
- TPR was granted for 91.4 percent of the incarcerated fathers.
- When both parents were incarcerated, TPR was granted in 100 percent of the cases.
- The parental rights were terminated 94.4 percent of the cases with custodial parents and 100 percent of the cases with noncustodial parents.

It is urgent to develop improved programs, policies, and practices for children of incarcerated parents. The field should pay particular attention to the need for family-based and community-based substance abuse treatment programs, the lack of which appears to influence the frequency of TPR in cases involving incarcerated parents and their children. Another recommendation is the basic application of the principles and elements of good child welfare practice to the children and families affected by parental incarceration.

. . . This work provides structure and direction for future research, most particularly examining the intersection of ASFA, mandated sentencing policies for drug-related crimes, and the lack of available community-based substance abuse treatment programs.

. . . The current study generates several questions that researchers could use to expand the current research agenda on children of incarcerated parents. A few possible research questions are:

- What is the relationship between the lack of community-based substance abuse treatment programs, drug sentencing policies, and ASFA?
- Is the lack of available treatment and enhanced sentences resulting in higher rates of TPR for parents incarcerated for drug-related offenses?
- Does ASFA affect the rate of TPR and adoption for children of incarcerated parents in more recent case filings?

REFERENCES

Miriam, Ehrensaft, Ajay Khashu, Timothy Ross, and Mark Wamsley. 2003. Patterns of Critical Conviction and Incarceration among Mothers of Children in Foster Care in New York City. New York: Vera Institute of Justice.

Philip M. Genty. 2003. Damage to Family Relationships as a Collateral Consequence of Parental Incarceration. *Fordham Urban Law Journal* 30, no. 6:1671–84; and sources cited therein.

House Committee on Ways and Means. 2004. Green Book. Washington, DC: House Ways and Means Committee Prints; www.acf.hhs.gov/programs/cb/dis/tables/secIIgb/secIIgb .pdf.

Mimi Laver. 2001. Incarcerated Parents: What You Should Know When Handling an Abuse or Neglect Case. *Child Law Practice* 20, no. 10:145, 146, 155–59.

Gail T. Smith. 2000. The Adoption and Safe Families Act of 1997: Its Impact on Prisoner Mothers and Their Children. *Women, Girls & Criminal Justice* 1, no. 1.

13

ASFA, TPR, My Life,
My Children, My Motherhood

Carole E.

In 1997, as a thirty-seven-year-old single mother, I was arrested for the sale of ten dollars worth of crack to an undercover detective, and I'd just given birth to my fourth child. My brother picked up the new baby from the hospital, presumably to care for her until I was released six months later, but upon release I returned to drug use. My other children had been distributed among relatives; two of them had tested positive for drugs at birth.

Though I was on Rikers Island for five months, I was only allowed two visits with my children. The ACS [Administration for Children's Services] worker told me that she did not relish bringing the children for visits because the procedures were so difficult. For five months, I fought my case and the 3½ to 7-year sentence I was being offered as a plea bargain. Eventually, I wrote a letter to the judge and district attorney requesting an opportunity to attend treatment and get my life together. They relented, and I was sentenced to eighteen to twenty-four months of residential treatment; I spent six and thirteen months respectively at the Daytop and Phoenix House therapeutic communities.

Five months after I began treatment, my cousin and his wife, who now had a toddler of their own, asked me to allow them to care for my now one-year-old son until I completed treatment. I acquiesced and continued to have visits with my son on a regular basis. My cousin and his wife became the foster parents. My brother had already begun proceedings to adopt my five-year-old daughter. After nineteen months of treatment upstate, I returned to the city to complete six months of rehab treatment at the Crossroads Program for Women.

When I went to the agency to visit my son, I was told that my cousin and his wife wanted to adopt my son and that, due to the provisions of the Adoption and Safe Families Act (ASFA), my parental rights were being terminated.

I challenged the termination of parental rights (TPR) and fought in court, but as time went on, I was told by the foster parents, the caseworker, and the law guardian that removing my now 3½ year-old son from the foster parents would harm him. The experts believed that due to my drug use while pregnant, my son had delayed development.

Intimidated by ACS and the long court process, and believing that ultimately I would lose my son and not be allowed to see him again, I agreed to an open adoption. My cousin and I agreed on visits at the convenience of both parties, which would include holidays and summer vacations. But soon after the adoption went through, my cousins moved to Virginia, so I see my son much less frequently than the agreement provided. Most of those visits have taken place at his home in Virginia.

My son is now ten years old and knows that I'm his mother, but we see one another only two to three times a year, which is all that the uncontestable adoption agreement allows, and the adoptive parents do not see my visits as a priority. However, all my other children are in my life, and I'm raising my second-eldest daughter in my home.

Today I resent ASFA and the child welfare system, the coercion of the law guardian, the ACS attorney, and the cousins who adopted my son. My resentment has fueled my work as an advocate for other mothers who may not know their rights or know how to interpret the ASFA laws. If I had had the information then that I now have, and/or had a parent advocate, I would never have consented to my son's adoption.

In my studies at John Jay College of Criminal Justice, I learned that judges rarely terminate the rights of parents who have continually planned for and maintained ties with their children, as I had. I believe that the opposition used illegal tactics to addle me: they didn't really have a case.

The ASFA law states that if a child has been in the system for fifteen of the most recent twenty-two months, he or she can be freed up for adoption by termination of the parental rights. But this same law enables the foster care agency to abstain from filing the TPR if there are compelling reasons not to. The caseworker and supervisor agency knew that I was attending therapy and the Narcotics Anonymous Program to maintain my sobriety and that I was in computer school as well as living in a shelter as part of the process to secure permanent housing. They also knew that I had obtained a job immediately after completing training. My actions showed that I was planning for my son's return; they qualified as "compelling reasons" to halt the TPR filing in my case. A number of factors, including staff inexperience with the new law and the fact that state agencies know that the state earns federal monies by expediting adoptions, explain why the TPR filing went ahead in my case despite my explicit attempts to reunify my family.

ASFA was enacted to deal with problems in the foster care system and to move children out of an overburdened system. It was designed to promote permanency planning rather than multiple and long-term foster placements, as well as to encourage "reasonable efforts" toward reunification of the family. Since the term *reasonable efforts* was never explicitly defined by ASFA, ACS and the State of New York were allowed to define what was reasonable for my family. The state was empowered to ignore questions about my son's emotional well-being, the benefit that would come from being raised by his mother.

ASFA's fifteen-month time frame for the TPR is too brief a period for initiating termination proceedings, especially for women like me who enter into treatment or may be incarcerated. When a mother is removed from the home, if no secondary relative or friend is available to care for children in her absence, these children are relegated to the state's care. Many mothers who are in treatment or incarcerated have no means of maintaining regular contact with their children, so some children may enter the foster care system without the mother's knowledge.

ASFA's time clock starts ticking the moment a child enters the system, placing children at risk for termination from their mothers and their whole family, and perhaps at elevated risk of incarceration themselves, as a result. When mothers are released, they may find that they no longer have their children. Faced with this loss, many mothers like me find it difficult to maintain the positive state of mind that promotes a healthy reentry and helps thwart recidivism. I was fortunate to have support and resources.

Presently, I am a single mother who has been drug free for over nine years. I have been employed for that time as well. Last year, I graduated from John Jay College as an honors student with my bachelor's and master's degrees in forensic psychology. The daughter who I raised is an honor student as well and on her way to Pomona College in the fall.

My son is now ten years old, and he is visiting with me this week. I saw him at a family funeral three months ago in South Carolina, and he wants to come back to visit for the winter holidays this year. In the seven years since the adoption, I've spent three holidays with my son, but never Christmas. Most of our visits lasted only a few days, but we've had a weeklong visit twice. Knowing about the changes in open-adoption laws, I have considered going back to court time and time again, but I don't want to put my son through a custody battle. Also, I loathe riling the adoptive parents, which might mean seeing him even less. So I'm patient and humble, and I wait. He recently started calling me Mom instead of Carole. Yesterday, he asked me if he could come live with me in New York. I told him maybe someday.

14

The Birthing Program in Washington State

Tabitha and Christy Hall

This is no place for a pregnant mom to come.
TABITHA

Christy

Most people who think about an expectant mother behind bars probably jump to blame the woman and label her a bad or unfit mother. How could she let herself end up in jail? Surely such a woman behaved in selfish and careless ways. But if you spend time with mothers who are in prison, and listen, you find a much more complicated reality. As a prison doula, a birth attendant for incarcerated women, I've learned that incarcerated women love their children as much as any other mother does.

One of the recurring themes in the stories I have heard from incarcerated mothers is the damaging effect on mothers and their children once they get caught in the criminal justice system or child protective services (CPS). Breaking free from the hold of these entities is very difficult. Two incarcerated women in Washington State Correction Center for Women, Delessia and Tabitha, are working very hard against daunting odds to keep their families together. Delessia's struggle with addiction has been compounded by a forced separation from her children while she is in prison and beyond. Despite having been a wonderful mother to her children for many years of clean living, she slipped back into addiction, and now her whole life seems to have been easily taken away, piece by piece. She says, "I am trying to prove that I am not just a deadbeat mom. I love my babies."

Tabitha

Tabitha gave birth to her second child during her current prison term and continues to participate in the doula program for postpartum support.

When I came into the institution I was four months pregnant. I haven't seen my [first] baby since she was four months old. I missed out on my first child. She got taken from me when she was four months. I wanted to see all that. It took me eleven months to get pictures of my first daughter. Are you serious?! It took me calling my paralegal to get pictures. . . . My attorney isn't doing anything to represent me. It's sad how they can do this to you. How do they have that right? I have to show the state that I can be a better parent to my children. [Seeing my kids] is gonna be one beautiful thing. That's what keeps me strivin'. I'm ready.

Tabitha asked to have a doula at her birth, but when the prison paged the doula and she arrived, the hospital staff did not grant her access. This is an example of the many ways that a pregnant woman's sentence can be made more extreme by the actions of nonstate actors. In this case, the hospital took it upon itself to deny Tabitha the doula care that she had requested prior to her labor. This is one of her many concerns about the circumstances of the labor and birth of her child while in prison.

At 7 in the morning I lost my mucous plug. Before I left [the institution] I was already on the [fetal] monitor. I was only eight and a half months [pregnant]. I'm like, "Why are you making me have my baby?" The doctor said, "We need to speed this up." But she wasn't ready to come out. This is what happened. As I was taking my pants down, my water broke and I started bawling and crying because I wasn't ready to have her. I said, "I want to wait until [the doulas] get here." But then he started the Pitocin and I started having more contractions.

   I requested the doulas to be there, and they weren't. I didn't appreciate that. I didn't feel that was right. When the nurse saw the doulas, she told them to leave or they would be arrested. I didn't know about the breathing. . . . It was just me, the doctor, the officer, and the nurse. . . . I at least got to spend twenty-four hours with her and breastfeed her. I needed that extra time to bond with my baby. I don't feel right being away from her.

Tabitha, like other women in prison, voices concern that she was not able to choose her own provider and birth setting. "The lady who delivered my [first] daughter was nice and gentle, but the male doctor was real rough. I didn't feel right. When he sewed me up . . . having a man all down there . . . it was nasty. That hospital, from my experience, it was poor. I just went with it, but I was mad. I was pissed."

Tabitha worries about her ability to parent her children when she gets out. This has been a constant source of stress. The emotional turmoil she experienced during her pregnancy, birth, and postpartum period demonstrate clearly why the treatment and consideration of pregnant women behind bars needs to be closely scrutinized to determine how intention and outcome intersect. Her voice and her story beg us to question how the current system destabilizes or destroys families.

The social worker is recommending termination because I am here. I can't care for them like I want to from in here, so they are trying to terminate my parental rights.

As Tabitha says, "That's what they are out there for [to keep families together], and they are not doing it. They expect us to do certain things, but they're also shutting us down. It's like we're not worthy."

Finally, Tabitha expresses her concern for how the system affects all mothers. "It's not just me. It's other inmates too. I wish I could change the world around. This is no place for a pregnant mom to come."

Christy

My work as a doula with the birth attendants has been a tremendous honor. I have had the opportunity to support many women through their experiences of pregnancy, birth, and parenting while incarcerated and feel deeply connected to their struggles and triumphs. They have shown me what it means to be a true survivor. The stories I have heard and witnessed about how incarceration has affected their lives and their families have personalized and deepened my commitment to the struggle for human rights. Their experiences demonstrate clearly the inhumane and damaging effect of incarceration and suggest a need for alternatives that better meet the needs of people who are struggling with poverty and addiction. There are alternatives to incarceration for these mothers that would produce better outcomes for their health and improve the well-being of their families. If we care about mothers and children, we need to support those who are working towards these alternatives.

REFERENCES

L. A. Greenfeld and T. L. Snell. U.S. Department of Justice. *Women Offenders*, NCJ-175688. Washington, DC: 1999.

T. L. Snell. U.S. Department of Justice. *Women in Prison*, NCJ-145321. Washington, DC: 1994.

15

Pregnancy, Motherhood, and Loss in Prison

A Personal Story

Kebby Warner

My name is Kebby Warner. I am a twenty-five-year-old woman prisoner in Michigan. I have been incarcerated since October 17, 1997, for littering and publishing. Passing a $350 stolen check. My time has been one of struggle, heartache, pain, and desperation. Here is my story:

I spent my first month in prison being sick. Health Care told me my "illness" was a stomach flu and my other "symptoms" due to stress, but then they said I was pregnant. I calculated that the day I stepped through the razor wire and fence, I was ten days along.

I didn't know what to do. I was twenty years old, it was my first time being pregnant, and I was sitting in prison. I thought about abortion, something that I did not believe in for myself, though I am pro-choice. I thought of adoption, but I knew that if I carried my baby to term, I would not be able to let it go. The doctor handed me some pamphlets, sent me back to the cell, and gave me two hours to make the decision I dreaded. I walked back to my unit in a state of disbelief. This could not be happening.

I could not contact my husband that night, so I had to make the decision. After a night of crying, I decided to keep my child. I believed that I could count on her father, my husband, to take care of our child until I got out.

I am a type 1 diabetic and considered a "high-risk" pregnancy, so I was sent to a hospital in the "free world." I was grateful for this as I did not want to place the life of my baby in the hands of the Michigan Department of Corrections (MDOC).

By this time, I had made contact with my husband, who shared my excitement and who promised to be there for our child. He was the only person I had and the only one I thought I could count on.

Every time I went for a "medical" run, I had to get a humiliating strip-search when I left and returned to the prison. Prisoners are placed in belly chains and our hands are cuffed for the duration of the visit unless the doctor asks that they be removed. At about the sixth month of pregnancy, the strip-searches become difficult. By this time, my emotional state was up and down, and most of the time I left the "strip room" in tears from shame and humiliation.

At the first ultrasound, the technician looked at the monitor, got up, and ran out of the room, leaving me in a state of panic, thinking there was something wrong with my baby. She came back with the doctor and had a big grin on her face. The doctor looked at the monitor and informed me I was pregnant with twins. I felt pure joy when I looked at the image. I wanted so much to share this news, but the only person I had by my side was a prison guard. I couldn't talk to her.

Sometimes, I looked forward to the medical run-escape, even though I went in chains. Sometimes I got carsick, but because I was a prisoner, the guard couldn't stop by the side of the road. I was forced to be sick in the van. I couldn't feel the air-conditioning through the bulletproof partition, and they wouldn't let me open a window. The guards looked at me as if I was about to run at any moment, pregnant, with chains.

Inside the prison, I was placed in a "pregnancy unit." It surprised me that there were so many pregnant women in prison—sometimes as many as twenty—including some who came just before their due dates. I wondered about the cold-heartedness of judges who sent these women to prison when there are alternatives. Was there anyone to speak up for these women who were bringing life into the world?

A lot of us became close, and I was able to share my fears and worries with older women who had been through childbirth before. There was also a childbirth instructor. We had group therapy sessions in parenting, substance abuse, domestic violence, prenatal care, childbirth, and postpartum. The instructor also came to the hospital after delivery and checked on our progress and our plans for our babies. At times, she tried to talk me out of allowing my husband to take care of our babies, but I insisted.

At seventeen weeks, I received another ultrasound. Again, the technician ran from the room. I knew that something was wrong. Again she returned with the doctor, who looked at the monitor, looked at me, and stated that he was so sorry, but one of the twins' hearts had stopped beating. I was devastated. How could my baby die and why? I had so many unanswered questions. I spent the rest of my pregnancy in fear that I would lose the other twin.

Behind prison walls, women are not allowed to show emotion. Our anger, pain, and other feelings must be kept under tight control. To speak out or show our true feelings could lead to misconduct tickets from the guards. So except for tears, I kept all my emotions inside.

During this time, communication with my now ex-husband became almost nonexistent. He was in the world doing his thing. I tried to hold on to the hope that he would be there for our child, but it was not to be. When I was seven months pregnant, he disappeared, never to be heard from again.

Again the woman from Children's Services approached me, telling me my child would have to go into foster care. I just couldn't believe this and decided to contact my parents, from whom I'd been estranged for more than a year. They didn't know I was pregnant or in prison. After the first letter, they agreed to take my child until my release. We had our first visit when I was eight months pregnant.

These visits were full of the healing of old wounds, or what I thought was healing at the time. There were promises of change and unity in the family. My parents promised to keep my child until my release, with regular visits, photos, and letters.

On June 25, 1998, after seventy-two hours of hard labor, I gave birth to a healthy baby girl. She was perfect from head to toe. Looking at her, I forgot about the pain and only wanted to hold my baby.

No one was with me during labor, and guards stayed in my room most of the time, though I was not chained as I've heard others have been. Most of the nurses treated me as a human being instead of a prisoner.

But thirty minutes after giving birth, I was once again handcuffed and chained and wheeled to another floor. My daughter was allowed to stay in the room with me, instead of the nursery. That night I fell asleep with her in my arms, forgetting that I was a prisoner.

MDOC policy states that a woman can only spend twenty-four hours with her child before she is brought back to prison. I had to figure out a way to spend more time with her: I refused to eat.

I've seen women come back in a total state of shock and confusion after giving birth. One woman turned to pills, getting high by taking others' psychotropic medication to dull her pain. One night she OD'd and was rushed to the hospital, barely surviving. Later she was put in segregation, placed on suicide watch. At the time, I wondered how I would feel after I had to leave my baby. I used to lie on my bunk at night feeling her inside my body. I couldn't imagine the day I wouldn't feel her and couldn't talk to her anymore. When that day came, I was desperate.

Refusing to eat gave me a total of three days with my baby. Then they told me if I didn't eat, the baby would be placed in the nursery until I went back to prison. There was no use staying any longer.

I was given a chance to say good-bye to my baby before they put on chains and handcuffs. How do you say good-bye to your newborn child? These people could not really be telling me I had to leave her! I couldn't leave her. The guards began rushing me, telling me it was time to go. What did they mean? Time to go? Where were we going?

On that day, I made promises to my daughter that I would always keep her safe, that I would be home soon, and that I loved her with all my being, body and soul.

I told her that she would always be my Angel and my light. I named her Helen after my baby sister. Helen means "light." She is the light of my life. She is my reason for living. Even though she couldn't understand the words I was saying, I wanted to comfort her with my voice. I was comforted knowing that she heard me.

Then I heard the guard say, "Come on, Warner." I gave her to the nurse. With every click of the handcuffs and the sound of the chain being locked, my heart shattered. Before I was escorted out in a wheelchair, the nurse took Helen out of the room. My heart and soul went with her.

I was taken back to prison, tears streaming down my face. I was in shock and despair, hoping only to wake up from this nightmare. The guard said, "If you wanted to have children, you should have stayed out of prison." I can remember looking at her, full of hatred.

In my pain, anger, and desperation, I became defiant against the system, and with no other outlet, I began fighting with other women and receiving misconduct tickets. The guards labeled me a "management problem." My emotions tumbled out of control, and I couldn't think about consequences.

When my daughter was four months old, my father died. Fifteen days later, an attorney called, telling me that my mother had given my baby to the state, saying she would not raise a half-black baby by herself. In her selfishness and prejudice, she forgot about the innocence of her granddaughter.

After the first court hearing with a court-appointed attorney, I fought for two years to keep my child. I turned to other family members, but no one wanted to get involved.

Michigan law states that if a parent is incarcerated for two years, she is "neglectful" and parental rights can be terminated, as mine were in September 2002. I appealed the court's decision, but my court-appointed attorney said that if I did not stop the appeal, Helen would be placed with a family that would adopt her immediately and the file would be sealed. I stopped the appeal out of fear.

My daughter's foster family adopted her anyway, and it turned out that I was lucky to get a good family to raise her. They allowed me phone calls once a month. My daughter doesn't know who I am, but she talks to me.

MDOC has a policy whereby Sprint must receive a fifty-dollar deposit from all family and friends who receive a call from a prisoner. Without the deposit, we can't call that number. Three months ago, I wrote to the adoptive family explaining the Sprint system, but they have not responded. I fear that they no longer want me to contact her. Since the state has terminated my parental rights, the family has every right to stop our phone calls. With the new Sprint system, MDOC has stopped a lot of parents from speaking to their children.

I am starting an organization called the People Against Court Kidnapping (P.A.C.K.) to oppose legal kidnapping of children around the country. This organization will support incarcerated parents who struggle with the pain of never seeing their children again. Pregnant women behind bars have no one to turn to. And when mothers are forced to leave their newborns, they have no idea where the baby is going. The P.A.C.K. will support these parents.

At times, I am able to see pregnant women walking down the walkway inside the prison. The numbers go up and down, but there are always pregnant women here. How many mothers, as you read this, are leaving their newborns at hospitals and returning to prison? How many parents are fighting desperately inside America's courthouses for the right to keep their children? How many will never see their children again?

This is my voice, screaming out for help in fighting this unjust system. Where are their voices?

16

What the Parenting Program
at the Nebraska Correctional Center
for Women Has Meant to Me

Mary Alley, A. D., and C. S.

Mary Alley

In 1974, the Nebraska Correctional Center for Women (NCCW) housed about thirty-five women from Nebraska and from South Dakota, Wyoming, and Colorado, which did not have their own facilities for women.

At that time, children visiting their mothers came a long way for just a few hours. The warden, a visionary, developed a program that allowed children to stay overnight with their mothers.

The number of children who are wards of the state due to their mothers' incarceration has tripled over the past ten years. Some of these children get to see their mothers, first, for supervised visits, one-on-one, and then, over time, the visits can become unsupervised. If things go well, the mother can have overnight visits with her child and can get closer to putting her family back together. These mothers need only a job and approved housing before taking their children back after incarceration.

General visiting takes place in a crowded, noisy room where the child must share his or her mother's attention with a relative who may be angry over the circumstances or with a husband or boyfriend she is afraid of losing. The Parenting Program makes sure that the time is exclusively for mother and child. The mother may plan the day around activities such as baking or playing games and may give her child all the hugs and love she can manage. These visits are often the first time in a very long time that some mothers have looked at their children through sober eyes. A mother may realize during the visit just how her incarceration has hit the lives of the people she loves most and may find the motivation to succeed with her children at a time when she feels like a complete failure.

A child can see where her mother is living, that she is safe, that the environment is not what she may have seen on TV. For many of the children, visiting the Parenting Center creates some of their favorite childhood memories. Many have never seen their mothers sober before.

Some children find out that the Parenting Center is a safe environment for getting angry about being separated from their mothers. Many finally hear from their mothers that there is hope that things will get better.

Many of the children saw their mothers arrested and taken away, a terrifying experience. Staff treats the children gently and with respect. We see some children mellow with each visit.

At any given time, there are ten to fifteen pregnant women in our population. Some meet the criteria for living in the Nursery Unit, a secure area. The locked door opens up to bright colors and a warm, homelike atmosphere. Mothers sit and rock their babies, talk quietly, and give each other the support new mothers crave.

A. D.

When I came to NCCW, I had already been separated from my children for two years. I had been drowning in a selfish addiction and had been pretty successful in destroying almost all of my relationships, including those with my two children. To further complicate the situation, I was pregnant. So my first interaction with the program was actually being refused entry to the Nursery Program due to the length of my sentence.

This was by far the worst experience of my life, but it would also come to be one of the most valuable. When I was refused entry, I was forced to truly wake up. I came to realize that my actions had brought horrible, real, irrevocable consequences—and not just for myself but for everyone in my family. This was a vital revelation, and one that no other situation had brought to light for me.

When I began having day visits with all three of my children, this insight was further cemented in my mind. Having the opportunity to laugh, play, and snuggle with them was so important. Yes, I have created a lot of pain and mess, but look what I still had—this amazing family. Spending these days with them taught me what I never realized when I lived with them: They are beautiful miracles who can never be taken for granted.

Day visits aren't just about playing games, making snacks, and getting hugs either. They're also about changing diapers, wiping noses, and setting limits. The amazing thing is, though, that it's all beautiful, all of it. The fun, the mundane, the difficult.

My children benefit by spending time with their mom in a warm, casual environment. Their fears about where I am and what is happening to me are quieted. They get to experience for a short time what it's like to have a mommy. Best of all, the experience makes them hopeful.

I have also been able to have two of my children for overnight visits. I find it difficult to adequately describe how this has affected my personal relationships with each of them. When my six-year-old son came, it was the first time I had been alone with him since he was a year old. Getting to know him one-on-one was like falling in love. I found myself amazed by every new thing I learned about him. The more he was able to stay, the more I discovered.

Another incredible thing happened. I found that he was just as amazed by me. Through these visits, he and I have formed a very special bond. I can't imagine my life without this relationship now, but it was nonexistent before these visits.

I have also started having overnights with my youngest daughter, who is three and a half. Since she was born during my incarceration, this is the first time we have ever spent time alone together. We are building a relationship now and learning a lot about each other. These visits are the foundation for our future life together. Without the visits, we would essentially be strangers, which would make for a much rougher reunion when the time comes.

I have also been blessed to work in both the Parenting and Nursery areas, which has been a huge educational experience for me. Beyond all of the practical things I've learned, I've earned back some of my lost self-esteem by getting to help other mothers in the same situation.

The combined effect of these experiences is that I've been given a rare gift: the chance to use my time in prison to focus on and prepare for my future. Some people take for granted that this is what happens here, but usually it doesn't. If it weren't for this program, I think I would have left here much the same person I was when I came in—detached, distracted, lost, and broken. Being given the opportunity to focus on my children and work through my fears, guilt, and shame has made me much more than that. I am a more competent, committed, loving person. My children don't just have their old mom back. They have a much better mother and human being in their lives. This mother knows what she has been blessed with, thanks to this program and to the support, encouragement, and guidance of the people in it.

C. S.

Twenty years ago, if I had been asked my opinion about a mother in prison, I might have answered pretty self-righteously that she didn't deserve her children and should lose them. The program at the Nebraska Correctional Center for Women has softened my heart toward the women there, and any mother in prison. Each woman pays far more than her debt to society; she loses precious moments, and time with her children. She pays with the guilt and shame that society heaps upon her and that she heaps on herself.

In all these years, I have not stopped feeling the emotion of a child seeing his or her mother after months of separation, and the pain of leaving again, leaving her behind. I have grown in my capacity for compassion and forgiveness in my own life. I am grateful every day for my own children. I take very little in life for granted, because life can change in a heartbeat. I am constantly and continuously amazed at the love between a mother and child, the strength of it, and the need to cling to it.

17

The Storybook Project at Bedford Hills

Beth Falk, June Benson, Amorel Beyor, and Alte

Beth

Storybook projects inside prisons share basic features: inmates select books for their children, record themselves reading the books aloud, and include a personal message to their children. The tapes and books are mailed to the children, who can listen to their parent's voice and follow along as they read. The Storybook Project started in several corrections facilities in the early 1990s; now there are sites in more than twenty states.

All storybook projects focus on literacy as a vehicle for promoting healthy parent-child relationships. At the Bedford Hills Correctional Facility in Bedford Hills, New York, the project is known as Story Corner, and it is one of the facility's most popular parenting programs. Story Corner is a literacy program, a way to strengthen parent-child attachments and an important means of communication between mothers and their children. Many of the women's families live far from the facility. Visits with children may be rare, and phone conversations can be costly and hard to arrange. The Story Corner recordings may be one of the main ways children hear their mothers' voices, and they are the only way for many kids to have the experience of being read to by their mothers.

Several incarcerated women organize and run Story Corner. They are responsible for orienting new participants, helping women select books, and labeling and preparing the tapes for mailing. They also publicize the program, encouraging women to try it out. Peer outreach is particularly important to draw in non-English speakers and women who lack confidence in their reading skills. Community volunteers assist in several ways. They organize reading workshops and book-donation outreach and listen to recordings before they are mailed.

Below are the narratives of several women who have been participating regu-larly in Story Corner. June has been incarcerated for fifteen years and has recorded books for her children for nearly that long. Amorel started her sentence in 2006 and quickly became involved with the project. Alte has been at Bedford Hills for four years and reads both English- and Spanish-language books to her children. These women's circumstances, ethnic backgrounds, and sentence lengths vary, but several common themes emerge from their narratives. Story Corner is one of the few ways that incarcerated women can make active parenting choices, model pos-itive behaviors, and communicate messages of love, concern, and hope.

Many women who use Story Corner had not read to their children before being incarcerated. The joy of sharing a story or becoming engrossed in a book may be a new experience for them and may stimulate concrete parenting skills as well as a sense of focus and purpose in their relationships with their children. For many of the women, the act of recording transports them into a strong feeling of being present with their physically distant children. Recording sometimes brings up feelings of longing, guilt, and sadness as well, and the women speak about their desire to re-main positive for their children even when they feel great loss and regret themselves.

For the children, the tapes are often much more than a onetime listening expe-rience. Many of the children listen to the tapes multiple times and use them as a source of comfort and contact. Realizing the deep impact upon their children, the women in turn deepen their commitment to the Story Corner process.

Amorel

I have four kids: the oldest is twelve, then there are a ten-, eight-, and three-year-old. I've been here since September 6, 2006, and I started using Story Corner in October.

I think it's a wonderful program because I'm so far away and I can't see my kids that often. Collect calls are expensive. I don't get to call that much. When I send tapes, they get a chance to hear my voice. So I use the Story Corner, and it's great.

I don't think as a child I was ever read to; I don't remember it. But I think it's im-portant for my children, not just because I'm here. I've always been into books. When I read my kids books, it's like I'm actually at home interacting with them. I talk about the pictures, I ask them questions like, "What do you think of this, isn't that so cute?" just like I was there reading it to them. Before the book, I say, "How are you today? I love you, I miss you, I hope you like this book." I try to say I love them like a mil-lion times while I'm reading the book.

The tape reassures my kids that I'm okay. They were used to being with me every day, and now I just see them three times a year, so they need that reassurance, like mommy's okay, there's nothing wrong with me. It's especially important for my daughter Marie. She listens every night before she goes to bed, and she listens to the same tape a lot of times.

I think this is important for them. If I couldn't send them tapes no more, Marie would be kind of devastated, like why didn't you send them home? Through the tapes, I have a special bond with each one of them, because I read differently to each one. Say, if the little boy in the story plays baseball, then I'll say, "Edward, look you play baseball," because he was on a baseball team. So it really is like I'm interacting with my kids, but from a distance.

It has a different meaning to all of them, but they all love it. For Edward, he just likes that I'm there, because he lives with his father, but it shows that I care, I miss him, I love him. For Ann, the oldest one, it's like memories. The way her godmother explained, when she gets ready for bed at night, she's listening to the tapes. So I figure that's like my time with her. The little one, Lynn, she can't sit still that long, so she'll carry the book around with her. If it has her favorite princess on it, that's the bond. Like, "My mommy got me this book. This is part of my mom."

Usually when I talk to Marie on the phone, she'll cry. But the last time I talked to her, we were talking about the book, she was telling me about the one book I didn't read to her but sent to her. She was actually reading it and told me about it, and she didn't cry once on the phone, we had a perfect conversation. I felt really good about that because sometimes I don't even like to call her because I don't like getting her upset, but that was the most perfect phone call.

After I'm done recording, sometimes I feel really good, and sometimes I feel emotional, like I wish I was there with them. But I always feel good about sending it to them. The Story Corner helps me get through my time, because it reminds me that I have four wonderful children to go home to.

June

My youngest kids are three and five. Then I have a ten-year-old, a fifteen-year-old, and one who is twenty-five. I found out about Story Corner pretty soon after I got here. I was nervous at first. I don't know what I was nervous about exactly, maybe that I was reading into a recorder. Like you're in a room alone with a recorder, but once I sent that tape home with the books, and I got the reaction from my children, how happy they were, it was just great.

I see my children sometimes twice a month, sometimes more, depending upon my husband's schedule. I send out a tape once a month, and I've been doing it for fourteen years. I used to do it for my older daughter, who kind of aged out. But she reads all the time now, and I think she saved every tape.

I usually pick out what I think my kids will enjoy, and also by their ages. Like I know my two youngest like books with lots of pictures, lots of color, not big words, just fun. Sometimes they tell me what they want, a lot of times I just know. Over time I've become more creative with it. Sometimes I'll change the entire story, make it my own story, as long as it goes with the pictures. If it's a boring book, I'll make it fun by the way I read it. I incorporate their names into the story—like instead of using the person's name, I'll use one of the kids' names. They can't get enough of that!

I hear about the books every time I send one. I hear about them mostly on the visits. They tell me what they liked and didn't like and what they want to have. When I see them here, they really want me to read to them, and at home, they ask their dad to read to them too.

The experience when I read onto the tapes, it's like I'm there with them. I personalize it, for all of them. 'Cause I want to be there with them, and they want me there, so it's like we're just all sitting in this room. I do it for me also; it feels more intimate, if I can use that word. I can picture their enthusiasm while I'm reading. I can see their faces, I can see one of them jumping up, I can feel it.

I wasn't read to as a child, except in school. I didn't read to my kids before, because I had a different lifestyle. I was so busy just trying to live, I just didn't take the time. I talked to them a lot, but I never read them books, which seems amazing now.

I miss my children constantly, but I don't put that out on the tape, because I don't want to overwhelm them with what I'm feeling or how much I miss them. I tell them I love them and miss them, but I try to make it as upbeat as I can. When I finish taping, I feel great, because I know they are going to love it.

Story Corner has definitely had an impact on me as a mother. It's like it gives you definition as a mother. You don't really know the impact of reading to your child until you do it, and I never did it on the outside. It kind of makes the bond closer. You pick the books for the children, you read them, you realize how much the child loves being read to by mommy. It's not the same as anyone else. It kind of floors me how much they enjoy it.

Alte

I've been doing the Story Corner since 2003. I'm lucky because when I got here and I mentioned my kids, someone came and told me about it. I have four children, ages twenty-one, nineteen, fifteen, and my baby is fourteen. When my daughter first got a tape, she opened her mouth and was like, "Wow!" So I always say thank God for this, because it has helped me a lot about the kids, you know?

I send out a tape every month. I pick a book for each one still. Sometimes I do one book for the boys and one for my daughter, because she's the only girl. I send messages on the tapes each time, it's better for me that way. You know my English is not good, but I try to read something to them in English. Then when I talk to them, they'll say, "Mommy, your English is getting better, you're learning a lot." I read them the Spanish books too, now that we have them.

I also leave them a message that's funny. You might think it sounds crazy, but everybody likes it. Sometimes I try a little English, then I also speak Spanish to them. My English is funny to them, it doesn't sound that good, but they want me to speak it.

At home, I didn't read to my children. I did homework with them but not reading, because I had my four kids plus three more I was a foster parent for. But now, I make the tapes for the kids. The reading started here.

Story Corner is good because sometimes my daughter, she goes to school feeling down, you know, and she says when she hears my voice, especially when I say something funny, she tells me it's like she's next to me. Then she's laughing, and she forgets being sad. That's very helpful for me. My son goes to work in the morning and goes to school at night, so he has a big day. So sometimes in the morning, he'll listen to the tape before work. And in the tape I'll say, like, please put the dog out, take a shower, help clean the bathroom—you know, mommy things.

After I make a tape, I say something about God, and I'm laughing, I feel good. Sometimes I'm crying, because I think about when I had my daughter in my stomach and I don't believe it, until I saw her. I made a lot of goals, and then I think about mistakes, and I feel sad. When I talk to her on the tape, I think about it.

Talking about my kids, I get excited. My older son will graduate from college this year, and my other son will be starting in September. My older son loves to read, and when he comes to visit me, he'll bring two or three books. My daughter says she wants to be a doctor, I don't know which kind yet. But my baby, no, he doesn't like to read. Now he's only interested in basketball. I say "Poppy, if you don't read, you won't know about nothing. When you read, you know about what happened. Even read about basketball." I start to read a book on tape to him, and then I'll say, "Okay, Poppy, when I see you, I want to know what happened in the book." I think he's reading more now. So you know, I'm very serious about my goals for them.

Beth

I first heard about the Storybook Project on National Public Radio in the 1990s. I immediately knew that I wanted to be involved with this type of project locally, but I didn't take action for many years. I'm interested in parent-child attachment and in how family attachments affect one's life. Working on Story Corner with the women at Bedford Hills Correctional Facility and sharing the excitement of seeing the program grow connects us, despite the vast differences in our backgrounds and present lives. There is a lot that is unspoken, and much we don't know about each other, but the mutual respect and enjoyment of the work have been enriching and deeply satisfying.

18

A Trilogy of Journeys

Kathy Boudin

For my son on turning 18

I.

The day approaches
    when I begin
my yearly pilgrimage
    back in time,
the present no longer important,
only the exact hour and minutes on a clock.
They will bring me to that moment
    when you began
    the longest journey
    man ever makes,
out of the sea that
rocked you and bathed you,
out of the darkness and warmth
    that caressed you,
out of the space
that you stretched like the skin of a drum
    until it could no longer hold you
        and you journeyed through my tunnel
        with its twists and turns,
propelling yourself
on and on until
    your two feet danced into brightness
and you taught me

the meaning
          of miracles.

                    II.

Somewhere in the middle of the country
          you are driving a car,
sitting straight, seat belt tight across your well-exercised chest.
Looking into the horizon,
the hum of the engine dwarfed by the
                    laughter of your companions.
You are driving toward 18.
Two sets of parents
          on each side of the continent
await your arrival,
          anxiously,
And you leave them astounded
          by that drive,
always part of you,
to grow up as soon as possible.
You move toward the point
          That as parents we both celebrate and dread,
Foreshadowed by leavings that take place
          over and over again.
That leaving for kindergarten,
          that leaving for camp,
                    that leaving parents home on a Saturday night.
Until that time when you really leave,
          which is the point of it all,
And the sweet sadness.

                    III.

My atlas sits
          on a makeshift desk,
a drawing board
          between two lock-boxes.
It was a hard-fought-for item,
          always suspect in the prison environment
as if I could slide into its multicolored shapes
          and take a journey.

In front of me is the United States
        spread across two pages.
I search for Route 80,
        a thin red line
and imagine you,
        a dot moving along it,
You, an explorer now.
Davenport, Iowa; Cheyenne, Wyoming; then Utah; Nevada;
        until you reach
        the Sierras, looking down on the golden land.
Roads once traveled by your father and me.
As I struggle within myself to let you go,
        and it is only within,
for you *will* go,
I am lifted out of the limits
        of this jail cell,
and the road
        with you, my son,
who more than any map or dream
        extends my world.
My freedom may be limited,
But I am your passenger.

NOTES

This poem was previously published in *Doing Time: 25 Years of Prison Writing*, ed. Bell Gale Chevigny (New York: Arcade Publishing, 1999), 241–43. Grateful acknowledgment is made for permission to reprint.

PART THREE

Intimacy, Sexuality, and Gender Identity Inside

THIS SECTION COLLECTS POEMS and other forms of reflection on the possibilities for closeness among women inside, as individuals and as members of a community. The authors of the pieces here meditate on pleasure, danger, longing, and loss under the constraints of incarceration. Some of the poets, storytellers, and essayists write about the project of self-definition in gender and sexual identity. In almost all cases, authors are exploring terrain that is secret, discouraged, proscribed, and forbidden, to begin with, and that risks sanctions for those who enter.

Essays in this section are alternately ecstatic and despairing, as one might expect. Elizabeth Leslie's essay, "Who Said Women Can't Get Along?" is a powerful statement against sexist and misogynist assumptions that women can't support one another. Leslie begins, "Whoever said that women can't get along with each other—lied!" and she describes the loving support she found from other women in her drug rehabilitation program. In the end, Leslie asserts, "Women do need women," and she expresses gratitude to all the women who helped her on her journey to self-knowledge and self-confidence. Confronting the paradox of making a passionate human connection in an inhumane setting, Sheena King's piece, "Why? A Letter to My Lover," cries out, "Why did we have to meet and fall deeply, madly and ridiculously in love, in prison?"

In "Gender, Sexuality, and Family Kinship Networks," an excerpted section from her book *Chicana Lives and Criminal Justice*, Juanita Díaz-Cotto shows how incarcerated Chicana women creatively resist their families' and the prisons' oppressive gender-role mandates. She describes how incarcerated Chicanas challenge cultural

---

The Kiss. Photograph by Melissa Springer

and institutional rules and regulations, many rooted in compulsory hetereonormativity, as they build and nourish kinship networks to satisfy their "spiritual, social, and emotional needs." In "My Name is June Martinez," the transgendered Latina author offers insight into the unique hardships that incarcerated transgender women face, sometimes at the hands of prison administrators, sometimes via other incarcerated women. The dearth of support groups for transgender women makes it particularly difficult to meet the special health care, emotional, and safety concerns of imprisoned transgender women. Martinez calls for more resources and antidiscrimination measures so that transgender women can find support inside and upon release from prison. As the essays in this section reveal, self-love and loving and affectionate relationships between incarcerated women may be the ultimate act of resistance against the state's systematic attempts to dehumanize them.

Untitled

Celeste "Jazz" Carrington

Death
  And dying
Membership
  in the
Sisterhood
  of the
Living dead
  Loving madly
Living fiercely
  All we can
While we can
  Filling every moment
Knowing her / myself
  Now
No thought
  or gesture
Will gather
  Dust . . .

Analyzing Prison Sex

Reconciling Self-Expression with Safety

Brenda V. Smith

This article examines the complexity of prison sex and the challenges that it raises in the context of recently enacted U.S. legislation, specifically the Prison Rape Elimination Act (PREA). It first identifies a range of prisoner interests in enhanced sexual expression as part of an attempt to disentangle prisoners' rights in sexual expression from states' legitimate interests in regulating that expression. This article also directs policy makers and decision makers to mine international documents and human rights norms that both recognize the necessity of punishment and outline standards for the safety of individuals in custody, the protection of human dignity, and the acknowledgement of the right to sexual self-expression. Ultimately, many prisons do not have legitimate interests in prohibiting prisoners' sexual expression and should use their scarce resources to protect prisoners from nonconsensual and coercive sex by staff or other inmates.

THE PRISON RAPE ELIMINATION ACT OF 2003

In 2003, the U.S. Congress unanimously passed the Prison Rape Elimination Act. PREA establishes "zero tolerance" for rape in custodial settings, requires data collection on the incidence of rape in each state, and establishes a National Prison Rape Elimination Commission. The commission is required to issue a report on the causes and consequences of prison rape and to develop national standards for the prevention, detection, and punishment of prison rape. PREA creates a system of incentives and disincentives for states, correctional agencies, and correctional accrediting organizations that fail to comply with its provisions. Correctional agencies must, upon request by the Bureau of Justice Statistics (BJS), report the number of instances of sexual violence in their facilities. The three states with the highest incidence and the two states with the lowest incidence of prison rape must appear before the Review Panel on Prison Rape to explain their rankings. States and accrediting organizations stand to lose 5 percent of federal funds for criminal justice activities if they fail to implement or develop national standards. As an incentive to comply with its provisions, PREA provides grant assistance to states to implement practices that reduce, prevent, or eliminate prison rape. PREA does not change the traditional definition of rape. It does, however, recognize that sexual assault can be accomplished not only by actual force but also through fear and intimidation. In addition, PREA gives BJS the authority to create another definition of rape for the purposes of conducting its statistical analysis and reviewing the prevalence of prison rape. This distinction is important because BJS has chosen to collect data on a broader range of sexual conduct—nonconsensual acts, abusive sexual contact, staff sexual misconduct, and staff sexual harassment—than is covered by legal definitions of rape. BJS data collection includes inmate-on-inmate conduct as well as staff-on-inmate conduct. The data will come from a variety of sources, such as records, reviews of correctional agencies, victim self-reports while in custody, and surveys of former and soon-to-be released inmates. Yet any discussion of rape necessarily includes a discussion of consent. Recognizing the complexity of sexual behavior in correctional settings, the proposed BJS National Inmate Survey also asks about consensual sex. BJS data collection has prompted discussions among stakeholders about the nature of consensual sexual interactions in prisons between inmates and between staff and inmates. Although correctional officials, advocates, and prisoners are clear about the need to end prison rape, some people have other, more complex agendas. Correctional authorities are interested in minimizing the number of sexual interactions between inmates that they define as rape so that they can lower their numbers for the BJS data collection and limit their potential legal liability for prison rape.

Human rights organizations are concerned that correctional authorities will respond to PREA by strictly enforcing existing prison policies that prohibit all sex between inmates and in some instances, bar all sexual expression, including masturbation.

This retrenchment could subject prisoners who engage in consensual sex to disciplinary measures or criminal prosecution. Further, human rights activists are concerned that the acknowledgment of consensual sex in correctional settings will allow prison authorities to cast rapes as consensual, thereby reducing the number of rapes reported to BJS and the attention paid to investigating and disciplining perpetrators.

Prisoners are rightfully concerned that although this heightened scrutiny may result in fewer assaults, it gives correctional authorities a potent tool to sanction inmates selectively for any sexual expression. Currently, prisoners engage in sexual activity with other prisoners and with staff. Although sexual relations with staff pose obvious risks, sex between offenders and their nonstaff partners poses fewer risks and potentially more benefits. Prisoners are concerned that agencies, in their desire to comply with PREA, will allow even fewer spaces for sexual expression. They are also concerned that any act of self-expression will be labeled an infraction and result in punishment.

INMATES' INTERESTS IN SEXUAL EXPRESSION

Most advocates and correctional authorities agree that sex between staff and inmates can never, as a legal matter, be consensual. Staff members' sexual interactions with inmates can jeopardize prison safety and security. Both domestic law and international standards for prison practice recognize that an inherent power imbalance exists between staff and inmates. Correctional staff control every aspect of the prison experience. Moreover, there are many reported incidents of staff relationships with inmates that have resulted in escapes, death, and other outcomes that compromise the safety of other staff and inmates. Finally, as a policy matter, allowing staff and inmates to have consensual relationships puts the legitimacy of the state's care and custody of inmates in question. From the prisoner's perspective, however, sexual expression in prison yields a different result. Prisoners have an interest in sexual expression separate from that of the state.

Sex for Pleasure

Despite society's sense of the desirability or deservedness of prisoner sex, prisoners have an interest in sex for pleasure. Prisoners engage in a variety of sexual behaviors, including masturbation and sex with other prisoners, visitors, and staff. Although these behaviors are prohibited by most state policies, arguably only sex with staff has the potential to disrupt prison safety and security. The other three—masturbation, sex between prisoners, and sex with visitors—are not clearly a threat to safety and security, particularly if properly managed. In enforcing the prohibitions against all sex, correctional authorities miss opportunities to educate inmates about violence in relationships and to encourage safe sex and healthy relationships that could offer support upon return to the community.

Sex for Trade

In prison, sex is valued because it is highly desired and forbidden. Therefore, prisoners use sex as a commodity to gain access to items they would not have access to otherwise. They engage in sexual practices in exchange for common items like cigarettes, candy, chips, or a phone call. This system of bartering has arisen because inmates frequently lack legitimate methods of gaining access to those items or decreasing their desire for them. In other iterations of the exchange, prisoners who have desired items are vulnerable to sexual exploitation and intimidation by those who want their goods. The prison's interest in safety and security suggests that sex for trade should be prohibited. The potential for violence is great because staff and inmates often do not deliver what they agreed to exchange. In these circumstances, sex becomes less the prisoner's choice than a commodity that is necessary for obtaining goods.

Sex for Freedom

For many prisoners, sexual expression is a corollary of freedom. Whether inmates are imprisoned for short or long sentences, sexual expression, although limited, is one of the few acts that they control. Making the choice to have sex when it is prohibited is an expression of freedom. The state should not regulate expressions of sexual freedom that do not impede safety or security, as is clearly the case in staff-inmate sexual interactions.

Sex for Transgression

In the world outside of prison, sexual expression can be a source of freedom. Often freedom of expression is closely associated with transgression—breaking rules, defying the normative structures imposed by society, the state, and other institutions. Sexuality and gender are society-imposed normative structures. Prisoners use sex to transgress these normative structures. Prison sex is also transgressive because it is against prison policies and rules. Sex becomes a prisoner's tool to thwart, control, embarrass, and harm those who control them within the confines of prison. Having sex with staff members, who are symbols of power, is the ultimate way to transgress because the prisoner has the potential to affect the state's and the prison's system of control.

Sex for Procreation

Procreation is another aspect of sexual expression that survives imprisonment. Vestiges of early reformer and eugenic sentiments still exist, holding that criminals should not bear children for a variety of reasons. Yet both male and female prisoners often want to conceive, want aid in conceiving, and want to bear and raise children. Given the construct of U.S. prisons, where prisoners have very limited contact with their partners and existing children or lose custody of their children as a result of their imprisonment, conceiving or fathering children becomes the primary mode of this form of sexual expression. A recent case, *Gerber v. Hickman*, illustrates this point. William Gerber, who was serving life without parole, sought permission from the California Department of Corrections to provide, at his own expense, a sperm sample to impregnate his wife. A deeply divided en banc Ninth Circuit, over vigorous dissent, held that the right to procreate was inconsistent with imprisonment and that Gerber had no interest in inseminating his wife because he would never be able to leave prison to assist in raising the child. Given that he was not allowed conjugal visits, his only remaining interest, considering his limited opportunities, was in providing the means for his wife to conceive a child. This act was also one of the few remaining ways for him to express his sexuality. Gerber's solution—which did not involve physical contact, only collection of his sperm—was an appropriate and nonintrusive way to exercise his constitutional right to procreate while maintaining the prison's interest in security.

Sex for Safety

Concern for physical safety is a key motivator for sex between inmates and between inmates and correctional staff. Social scientists have identified the concept of protective pairing, in which inmates have sex or become involved with someone to protect themselves from other inmates or staff. Both legal and other narratives are replete with stories of prisoners having sex with other prisoners or with correctional staff to secure their safety. Notwithstanding the passage of state laws, prisoners still receive little protection from forced and coerced sex. Although the full scope of sexual violence in prison is unknown, reports from correctional officials should cause concern.

A recent study by BJS found that inmate perpetrators of sexual abuse are more likely to be sanctioned and prosecuted than staff perpetrators and that even when staff are prosecuted, the sanctions they receive are minimal. Given the unlikelihood of receiving protection from either the corrections agency or the state through investigation, discipline, or prosecution, inmates' decisions to have sex with staff and other inmates in an effort to secure their safety is a reasonable response. Regulating sex for safety is an appropriate exercise of state authority because the state is obligated to protect inmates from harm.

Sex for Love

Often prisoners engage in sex for love or desire. Even in this setting, where individuals are legally stripped of their autonomy and dignity and face violence from other prisoners and staff, prisoners manage to establish meaningful and loving relationships. Accounts of prison officials at all levels indicate that they are aware that sexual relationships between inmates occur and are part of the fabric of the correctional experience for both staff and inmates. Still, the role of the state in limiting loving sexual relationships between inmates is unclear. Correctional staff members' accounts indicate that they have already developed some tools to address these relationships, identifying, intervening, and disciplining when appropriate. A clear written policy or procedure from prison officials that recognizes the existence of intimate relationships between inmates would provide the opportunity not only for inmates to express those relationships but also for corrections officials to address them explicitly in a manner congruent with their correctional mission of safety and security.

IMPLICATIONS FOR STATE
REGULATION OF PRISON SEX

Taking as a given that sexual expression is a fundamental right, should this fundamental right survive imprisonment? Unfortunately, the legal response is not promising. So far, court decisions set parameters only for sexual expression that raises questions of sterilization and abortion: the state cannot sterilize an inmate, and in deciding whether to allow prisoners to obtain abortions, the holding state must follow the same law that governs its general populace. The terrain in between remains uncharted but seems terribly forbidding.

Certain penological interests, however, would be served by enhanced prisoner self-expression. First, the Prison Rape Elimination Act requires correctional agencies to report all incidents of prison rape. Appropriately identifying acts that are consensual rather than coerced would permit corrections officials to provide more accurate information to BJS and to meet the act's data collection requirements. This step would enhance national, state, and local interests in assessing prevalence and risk and in ineffectively deploying scarce investigative, medical, and administrative resources to address forced or coerced sex in prisons.

Second, policies that recognize and allow greater prisoner expression would give correctional officials a greater range of categories in which to situate sexual behavior, which would prompt improvements over current policies that simply provide a blanket prohibition against sex. Currently, correctional staff ignore or selectively enforce prison policies that prohibit sexual conduct, thereby fostering a culture of disrespect by both staff and inmates and calling into question the necessity for following other rules. This policy change would enhance the credibility of correction agencies with both staff and inmates.

Third, sex in prison, whether consensual or nonconsensual, poses serious health risks to the community. For example, recent studies estimate that the rate of infection for hepatitis and HIV is three times greater among the prison population than in the general population, and it is even higher among female inmates. Acknowledging that a broad range of sex occurs in correctional settings for a variety of reasons would enable prison officials to take appropriate health measures, such as condom distribution, HIV/AIDS education programs, clinical trials, and specific interventions that target risk behavior in prison settings. Such measures would protect the health of staff, inmates, and the communities to which prisoners return after their incarceration.

The fourth penological interest in recognizing and encouraging a broader range of sexual expression is to ease prisoners' reentry into the community. Strengthening and preserving family bonds are the goals for most conjugal and family visiting programs. These programs enhance family support for inmates during their imprisonment and sustain important connections that they can return to once their sentence is complete. Inmates who have family support are less likely to become repeat offenders and return to prison. Many correctional agencies also use family and conjugal visits as an inmate-management tool. By explicitly regulating visitation, prison officials can control and implement their policy strategically to further correctional goals of safety, security, and rehabilitation.

Fifth, recognizing and granting inmates a degree of sexual expression may enhance inmate safety by decreasing prison rape. By recognizing and regulating such conduct, states can better prevent incidences of violence and stem the spread of diseases associated with prison rape, and they can help prisoners learn healthy and responsible sexual behavior before returning to their communities. These interventions have already been used in situations involving illegal sex (e.g., prostitution and prohibited sex) in other institutional settings (e.g., nursing homes, homes for the mentally retarded, and psychiatric settings). Finally, permitting a greater degree of sexual expression recognizes the inherent dignity and autonomy of human beings, which also survive imprisonment.

HUMAN RIGHTS NORMS AND PRISON SEX

Increasingly, U.S. courts have turned to international human rights law to enrich the nation's impoverished constitutional rights jurisprudence. Both preventing sexual abuse and permitting greater sexual self-expression are congruent with international human rights instruments. Several international instruments provide norms for the treatment of prisoners. Article 60(1) of the Standard Minimum Rules for the Treatment of Prisoners provides that the "regime of the institution should seek to minimize any differences between prison life and life at liberty which tend to lessen the responsibility of the prisoners or the respect due to their dignity as human beings." Another source, Article 10 of the International Covenant on Civil and Political Rights (ICCPR), which the United States has ratified, provides that "all persons deprived of their liberties shall be treated with humanity and with respect for the inherent dignity of the human person." Finally, in the case of *Prosecutor v. Kunarac, et al.,* the Appeals Chamber of the International Criminal Tribunal for the former Yugoslavia held that the act of rape, by definition, implies severe pain or suffering and constitutes torture when it is used to intimidate and coerce the victims. Under this definition, many instances of prison rape are a violation of the United Nations Convention against Torture (CAT), to which the United States is a party.

In addition to signing on to these international instruments, the United States has ratified and is bound by regional human rights instruments as a member of the Organization of American States, including the American Declaration of the Rights and Duties of Man and the American Convention on Human Rights. These instruments require the humane treatment of prisoners and mandate that "punishments consisting of deprivation of liberty shall have as an essential aim the reform and social readaptation of the prisoners."

Unfortunately, the United States has a history of exceptionalism or opting out of human rights obligations. It has limited the application of the ICCPR, the CAT, and regional instruments like the Organization of American States declaration and convention to its obligations under the Fifth, Eighth, and Fourteenth Amendments of the U.S. Constitution. These exceptions limit the formal structures for holding the United States accountable for compliance with international human rights norms, but the norms are still powerful and persuasive guides to practice in other countries. The challenge is to use these norms to influence U.S. policies and practices.

Notwithstanding its exceptionalism and antipathy toward international law, the United States, like any other country, is influenced by the practices of other countries. In the area of granting greater sexual expression to prisoners, however, the country lags behind.

Although the Standard Minimum Rules for the Treatment of Prisoners are silent about sexual relations, Rule 60(1), the principle of normalcy, "implies that sexual contact between prisoners and their partners should be allowed if [it] is possible under relatively normal conditions."

Many other countries permit sexual expression in institutional settings, define these visits under the rubric of either intimate or conjugal visits, and permit prisoners to have intimate and other contact with spouses, partners, and family. For example, Brazil has implemented a "communal visit," which allows prisoners to visit with family and friends without physical restrictions, and an "intimate visit," which allows prisoners to receive visits from their partners or spouses in individual prison cells. In the Czech Republic, the director of the prison may allow married couples to visit in rooms specifically designated for intimate contact. The Czech policy also allows prisoners to receive visits from four close relatives at a time. In Spain, inmates who cannot leave the institution may receive conjugal/intimate visits once a month for one to three hours. Finally, Denmark has implemented a "prison leave" system for prisoners with sentences greater than five months. The leave can last from one day to an entire weekend. Denmark "see[s] leave as a helpful tool in maintaining a stable atmosphere in the prisons and furthermore by keeping contact with relatives outside it is believed that fewer prisoners try to escape." These leaves and visits enhance prisoner sexual expression by recognizing that sexual identity and expression are a core element of personhood. U.S. corrections agencies would enhance the safety of the nation's prisons and inmates by doing the same.

CONCLUSION

The desire for sexual intimacy and sexual expression is powerful and survives imprisonment. Individuals in custody, despite society's view, maintain their humanity and personhood. As Judge Richard A. Posner has written, "We must not exaggerate the distance between 'us,' the lawful ones, the respectable ones, and the prison and jail population; for such exaggeration will make it too easy for us to deny that population the rudiments of humane consideration." There is great benefit to acknowledging that inmates do not lose their sexuality once they enter prison and to seeing the management of these interactions as part of the work of corrections agencies. Moreover, appropriate intervention in these interactions can enhance the safety of inmates and staff, help agencies realize their correctional goals of providing safe and secure correctional environments, and encourage the rehabilitation of inmates. This approach preserves scarce correctional resources for serious incidents of sexual violence that occur in institutional settings, and it enforces the dignity of prisoners. Although much work remains to outline a workable and humane approach to enhancing opportunities for inmate sexual expression, this article serves as an initial step in that direction.

Editors' Note: The complete version of this article, *Rethinking Prison Sex: Self-Expression and Safety,* was published in the *Columbia Journal of Gender and Law* 15, at 185 (2006).

21

Who Said Women Can't Get Along?

Elizabeth Leslie

Whoever said that women can't get along with each other—lied! I, too, believed that poisonous propaganda. People misinformed about women misinformed me for years. I read stories of the evil-wicked stepmother, jezebels, man stealing, creeping and cheating, cat fights, etc. I was definitely scared of women!

In June 2005, I was blessed by being sent to a drug rehabilitation program as an alternative to incarceration, Project Greenhope Services for Women. Project Greenhope houses fifty-three women in multifaceted components (alternative to incarceration, outpatient, intensive outpatient, relapse prevention, and parolees). Fifty-three women! Fifty-three personalities! I was scared to death and definitely not thrilled. Just the thought of all those WOMEN!!!

I was elated to be out of jail, to have a chance to deal with my drug addiction, to visit my family on the weekend, and to serve my time in a safe environment. The only dilemma was being in an all-women facility. I really dreaded the prospect of living with fifty-three women. The worst punishment for me was being with women.

I kept thinking, I can't get along with women! All I could focus on was, these women are my enemies. They are jealous of me. They want something from me. They look better than me. They might find out who I am, and they will surely want to take my throne of Queen Bee. I was brainwashed. I didn't have a clue that these women would be the ones to help me in my recovery.

In my active addiction, I had to compete with women for johns/tricks. Growing up, I had to compete with other girls for boyfriends. Girls bullied me in my school. Everyone competed to be the smartest, the prettiest. I carried all these resentments about women with me to Greenhope.

Also, I came to Greenhope with anger, resentment, abandonment issues, molestation, domestic violence, verbal abuse, physical abuse, and any other type of abuse you can imagine, a lot of it inflicted by women. You know I wasn't enthused about being in an all-women program.

After a few weeks in the program, I began developing relationships with the women. I didn't put much effort into it at first because I had tunnel vision. I had already decided that I was only going to deal with these women on a surface level, just to get through the program.

But there was no way to get around these women! I tried to wear my back-off-of-me mask to push them away from me, but to no avail. I used my representative to portray me as a distant, isolated, noncaring, coldhearted, rude, and hateful woman. But I had to be in groups with them, eat with them, sleep with them, shower with them, and the scary part was, I had to share all my innermost fears with them. I was stuck!

Finally, I started to sincerely interact with the women. I gradually started to put my guard down and take off the deceptive mask. One day while sitting in a group, I heard my own story! The women shared the same pain, anger, loneliness, fear, and resentment that I felt. I was astounded. One woman talked about being raped and molested at an early age by a family member, being a victim of domestic violence, living in degradation, feeling inadequate and ashamed, and she cried like a baby while she let out her suppressed pain. It was then that it dawned on me that women need women in order to heal. It was then that I acknowledged that the other women and I were more alike than different. The more I accepted and embraced the women, the more comfortable I became.

We cried together in groups, we offered each other support, we gave each other constructive criticism, we told war stories and were able to laugh at our insaneness during active addiction. We became our sister's keeper.

I was very fortunate to meet a few phenomenal women while in Greenhope who are still a part of my network and support group and remain my confidants. We were the women who endured the good, the bad, and the ugly. We were the women who took risks and got gut-level in groups. We became willing to change our lives. We all wanted to be free from active addiction, to stop recidivism, to reunite with our families, and to become productive members of society. We also wanted to claim our crowns as the Queens we were born to be.

Pamela, Beverly, Monica, Ida, and Irene are five women I bonded with while at Greenhope. What made our pact so genuine is the fact that we were not afraid to give each other constructive criticism within the context of unconditional love.

Pamela and Beverly worked with me on my negative disposition, informing me when my attitude was outrageous. They couldn't understand how I could be the most loving/caring person one minute and then transform into a verbally abusive monster. I was in total denial, ignoring how mean I got when I couldn't get high or when I finally realized the mess I had made of my life.

Pamela and Beverly showed me how I was hurting my sisters. They helped me to embrace my loving, caring, and giving assets. Honestly, I was resistant at first. I would get angry and curse them out, throw tantrums, and become closed-minded, but all my drama didn't stop them from helping me. That's unconditional love!

Monica was the oldest of us, and she had acquired wisdom, power, and spirituality over the years. Monica had been in and out of programs and jails and was sick and tired of being tired and was determined to succeed at Greenhope. When I met Monica, I wanted what she had!

I was blessed to have Monica as my roommate. Monica loves music just like I do, and when we went to our room, she would play positive music. She had a large collection of contemporary gospel. Her favorite was Donnie McClurkin's, "We Fall Down," which soon became my favorite. I would be on the top bunk crying like a baby, snotty-nosed crying. I cried because I was in pain, I cried because I felt every word of that song. I cried because the lyrics of that song offered me hope, solace, and empowerment. I thought God was talking to me through Donnie McClurkin, telling me that even though I fell down, I could get back up again. That song was a part of my healing.

Monica was part of my healing, too. She played a major role in helping me restore my spirit. She gave me hope, especially after I heard her experience and got to know her strength and spirit.

Ida was very outspoken and controlling, a people pleaser, and self-centered. As a matter of fact, Ida's character defects were just like mine. We didn't like each other very much, but we got along for program purposes, at first. We are both great cooks from South Carolina and love making people happy with our delicious food. Ida came to Greenhope first and established her slot as the best cook, but then I came with my good cooking self. That was our first hard encounter, not really about food but about control, and neither of us was going to bend.

Ida wore her mask longer than I did. She was a positive sister, but she had an image to deal with. She played it safe, afraid to let the women know how vulnerable she was. I didn't compromise and was very open about who I was and took full advantage of the chance to change. Ida wanted to take off her mask but she was afraid to. She wanted to change, but didn't know how. I was perturbed with Ida because I knew she was strong, positive, giving, dedicated, and loving. She was a diamond in the rough but acted like a piece of broken glass. I knew she was fronting because I had fronted for so many years.

We finally aired our differences, and now we are very close despite our control issues. Ida taught me that friends don't have to agree all the time. We learned that we don't always have to be the "Queen Bee." We learned that we could tell each other about our own accomplishments and be proud of each other.

Irene came to Greenhope when I was in my transitional stage. She was such a cry baby, in so much pain from her abusive childhood, and she came in the door talking about her pain. She was ready to get help. She had courage! She was ready to heal, and by any means necessary.

Irene paid attention when the counselors said, "Hang with the winners." She was watching me because, by now, I was a role model in the facility. She wasn't envious; she just wanted to know how she could get where I was. She came up to me one day and said, "I want what you have. Can you show me or help me get there?" I was truly shocked because I still was suffering from low self-esteem, and I didn't think I had anything worthy to give anyone, even though I was taking a leadership role.

I was the house coordinator, and running the house immaculately was my goal. I became an advisory council member of Women of Substance, a public education project of JusticeWorks, a grassroots organization in Brooklyn, where I talked about the impact of incarceration on women and children. I attended church at least two times a week and brought so many women with me to church that the bishop named me the "missionary." By this time, I was creating group topics to help women work through their issues, and I was facilitating groups. I was writing and reciting motivational poetry for the women. Staff loved me and often asked my advice. I was active in Narcotics Anonymous. I was growing up to be a woman of substance, like Monica.

Because I knew Irene was watching me, and I knew she wanted what I had, I stayed on top of my behavior and my thinking. I had to practice what I preached. I didn't want to be a hypocrite, and I was dedicated to helping her. This meant learning to share. I learned that I couldn't keep it unless I gave it away. Now, when I reminisce about when I came to Greenhope, I was Irene and Irene was me.

There was always something to learn from the women in Greenhope, but the six of us taught each other how to have a loving healthy relationship with a woman. We call each other on a regular basis. We empower each other. We encourage each other. We are support for each other. We motivate each other. We share our day-to-day experiences. We confide in each other. We trust each other. We help each other stay clean (also serene). We care about each other's well being. We love each other unconditionally. We teach each other. And most importantly, we are our sister's keeper.

After all this time, now I know: women do need women. It takes a woman to teach a woman how to be a woman. A man will tell a woman what he thinks she wants to hear, but a woman will tell a woman what she needs to hear. The life lessons I learned by creating relationships with women helped me to become the phenomenal woman I was born to be. I can never repay these women for the love they gave to me. I can give the love to another sister. There are so many diamonds in the rough that just need to be polished. Who said women can't get along?

22

Sorry

Tina Reynolds

imprisoned in this corner
this darkness that felt so comfortable
this place of *sorry*
voices loud
voices soft
crying
yelling
giving
talking
whispering
you are sorry
girl you are so sorry
people told me I was *sorry*
I almost believed them
but that meant I didn't deserve those hugs
those kisses
didn't deserve to hear
I love you Mommy

imprisoned within this image of feeling *sorry*
this relationship so thick with time
no empathy
no concern
no good morning

playing this game of tug of war
and being on both ends
dragging myself closer to the mud hole

gates slamming
gates within gates
squeezing myself between them
no escape
can't grease myself to get between these bars

there's another gate after this one
my tears drop to the floor
on my hands and knees
thinking about kicking and screaming
but worried about who's watching
I'll have to say *I'm sorry* for that too

another identifier other than
badmomprisonercrackhead and
what's my name
trying to remember cus they call me
95G1525
95G1525

shackled and handcuffed so much
I believed I was *sorry*
believed I was an isolated incident
sittin in the bullpen next to Sheila
stepping over Pam,Alberta,Denise
to get a bologna sandwich
lining up to squat
waiting 24 hours for a decision to be made
one more that I wouldn't be making for myself

we stopped making decisions for ourselves a long time ago
we all took different paths to end up in this valley
feasting on the addict attitude

I can't possibly cut that with a spin on the truth
I was not an isolated incident
I am not an isolated incident

I was *sorry*
at that moment believing I was
undeserving
unwanted

used up
and nothing to nobody
even I didn't want me

girl I knew I needed your mercy
even if I didn't believe a word I was saying at the time

I found a box and each day I locked away words like
courageous
loving
capable
deserving
intelligent
compassionate
sane
beautiful
locked these words away from myself
until they meant something
hoped and prayed one day
these words would hold water
saturating the dry parched sponge that was me

23

The Chase

Holli Hampton

I love the lady living 3 cells down.
But she doesn't know it.

I watch her all day at work.
But she doesn't know it.

I wait for a shower so I can see her body.

I fall in line so I can devour her scent.
But she doesn't know it.

I touch myself, wishing it were her.
But she doesn't know it.

I hear her cry every night until the wee hours.
But she doesn't know it.

I love the lady living 3 cells down.
And she's gonna know it.

24

Why?

A Letter to My Lover

Sheena M. King

I've had so many lovers before you, both male and female, so why did *you* touch me in such a deeply profound way? Why did you cross my path at that crucial moment when I was in therapy trying to heal from the past and learn for the future? Why did we have to meet and fall deeply, madly, and ridiculously in love, in prison? Why did it have to happen here? When we could no longer deny what we felt. When we had shared our minds, hearts, hopes, dreams, and desires and decided we were best friends, why did we enhance it by exploring each other's bodies? Merging our souls? Sealing our fates? Why couldn't we deny mutual attraction?

Why did we have to make love in closets, bathroom stalls, in secret rooms, in showers and over toilets, with quick touches in corners? If we lay in my cell or yours, we needed someone to watch for us while we quickly but passionately quenched each other's fire. No pillow talk, no extensive cuddles or falling asleep in each other's arms for a night, to awaken to your beauty by sunlight. Why? Why was our relationship so stifled? Why did we have a visit together, only to be forbidden to talk to each other, like we were strangers, because of "Visiting Room Policy"? Why did we pretend our relationship didn't exist so we could live together—not in the same room, just in the same building? Why couldn't I hold your hand and smell your face when we were walking around the yard or the dining room? Why were unhappy, lonely people so jealous of our obvious love and adoration of each other? Why did the staff watch our every move, as if we were going to strip naked and taste our love in the middle of the floor? Why were they so against our being together when our marriage was so nurturing, positive, loving, and progressive? Why did our fellow convicts and inmates think it necessary to tell, like children, whenever we could sneak a moment to touch, kiss, explore, or make love? Why? How was our private life a public nuisance when we kept our personal life to ourselves? Why was our love and joy disrespected though we weren't disrespectful? Why are prison officials homophobic when so many of their staff are loving the same sex?

Why did we complement each other in our external beauty and also in our inner beauty? Why are we so similar in every aspect? Why did you complete me and unselfishly give me the best three years of my life? Why did I have to be sentenced to Life and you leave me here to yearn and burn for you while you yearn and burn for me? Why do I walk through this institution with feigned happiness as if I'm not an empty shell, attempting to continue in wholeness while we live spiritually together but physically apart? Why do people say your name knowing the sound of it drives a knife through my heart and through my bones to the marrow?

Why did we jump off the cliff and gladly fall into the abyss of love when we would have to separate? Why doesn't the pain stop? Why, Charlotte? Why?

25

Gender, Sexuality, and Family Kinship Networks

Juanita Díaz-Cotto

Chicana pintas struggled with demands placed on them simultaneously by their families, their barrios, and the state.[1] Gender roles, sexuality and sexual identification were arenas within which pintas challenged such expectations. As such, pintas took advantage of the institutional setting to experiment with many different types of relationships with other women, some of which were sexual in nature. They also had both voluntary and involuntary sexual contact with female, but most often, male staff.[2]

This essay asks questions such as: How did pintas incarcerated at Sybil Brand Institute for Women (SBI), Los Angeles's women's jail, seek to exert their independence from oppressive gender role expectations placed on them by jail administrators and staff? What types of sexual and nonsexual relationships and networks did pintas form while incarcerated? What were their motivations for participating in such relationships? How did penal staff react to same-sex relationships between women?

SEXUAL IDENTIFICATION

Sexual identification for most pintas interviewed varied throughout the years. It hinged upon the pressures they received from their families and peers to be heterosexual, whether or not they were incarcerated, and their personal preferences at any one time. While almost all the pintas interviewed had at least one lesbian encounter or relationship in their lives and a number of them identified themselves as lesbians when they were teenagers, not all of them did so at the time of the interview.[3] Some who knew they were lesbians from an early age had married men and had children at some point in their lives to please their families. A few lived only as lesbians or heterosexuals whether they were in or out of institutions. Others became involved in same-sex relationships while they were incarcerated, only to return to heterosexual lives upon release from the institution. Still others identified themselves as bisexual throughout their lives or at the time of the interview. Graciela illustrates how sexual identification could be fluid.

> *Graciela:* [I was gay] since I was 13. I got married when I was 17 and I separated three years after that, in '81, and I went back to women. And then I've been in and out of prison since '84 and I just messed around with women. And then I . . . decided I wanted to have a baby. So then I got pregnant with my daughter. I had her in '91 and I haven't been with nobody. . . . Just this past few months I've had a relationship with a man. [I'm now] bisexual.

Pintas, like other incarcerated women, frequently explored their sexuality for the first time while incarcerated.

> *Rosa:* A lot of times the women would come in straight and end up being homosexual when they got there. And then left straight again. . . . It happened within all the races.

> *Deborah:* And they come out into the streets and . . . they're with their . . . old man and their kids again, and they act like they're not like that at all. . . . It's like the person that does religion in the jail and then when they get out they're no longer religious.

> *Mercedes:* I had an encounter with a . . . woman . . . at Sybil Brand. Something that I said I was never going to do. . . . She was a Chicana. . . . I had this homosexual experience and, you know what? I had the greatest time of my life! I lived it for every moment knowing that this was not my life. Knowing that this was not what I wanted. . . . We did intimate things. And it might sound crazy but the intimate thing there was . . . to feel close, . . . to have your socks washed, to . . . get your hair brushed. . . . Of course we had sex!

Most of these jail affairs were not long lasting.

> *Victoria:* A lot of . . . like . . . "fly by night" sort of things. You know, women they . . . meet each other, they hook up, and . . . then they're like with someone else. . . . And . . . it's kind of like with a soapish opera sort of . . . ring to it. . . . A lot of drama. . . . And I think maybe some people like feed off of that.

Pintas gave various reasons why prisoners who did not generally identify as lesbians became involved with other women while incarcerated.

> *Deborah:* I just think that they do that just to fit in. It's a protection thing. . . . It's kind of like a back-up thing, you know. . . . Maybe they can't go without sex. . . . (laugh)

Though prisoners did have interracial and interethnic relationships with other prisoners, the tendency at SBI was to stick to "your own kind." When involved in interracial relationships, Chicanas tended to prefer white over African-American prisoners. In fact, relationships with African-American prisoners were discouraged by other Chicanas.

> *Graciela:* You were looked down on. They just didn't like the idea of you going with a Black person.... They'd call 'em names. Call 'em *mayateras.* ... Or they would use the word "nigger lover." You were just a disgrace.

> *Cristina:* They would walk up and tell you, "You don't hang around with them. You hang with your own kind. If it goes further than this then, yes, I will kick your ass."

While interracial relationships were still frowned upon, by the mid-1990s pintas agreed that the attitudes toward such relationships had changed somewhat.[4]

> *Graciela:* Back then it was very seldom seen. Now ... you see it more.

Regardless of how women defined themselves sexually, the overwhelming number broke institutional rules to have such relationships.

Guards' reactions to same-sex relationships between prisoners varied. Some guards tolerated such relationships and a few even went out of their way to support them. They housed lovers together and ignored outright signs of affection between them. Some, while not approving of such relationships, gave prisoners verbal warnings.

> *Victoria:* And . . . there was this one officer [a Chicana] and . . . she hooked it up for us to be in the same dorm. And . . . she just said, "You know what? You guys could stay together but, yeah, I better not see not one hickey on your neck . . . or else . . . I'll send you straight to Lockup and I'll separate you two. . . . " Eventually . . . we both had hickeys on our neck. She'd seen one time and she didn't do nothing about it.

While some prisoners could claim that they got hickeys during sexual encounters with male staff, they did not generally make reference to such incidents. On the one hand, sexual contact between prisoners and staff was also prohibited. On the other hand, the staff in question could always deny it. Rita declared, "Yeah, . . . but they have to catch you in the act and it's your word against theirs."

Most guards frowned on same-sex relationships and enforced institutional regulations that penalized prisoners for having "personal contact," or "homosecting," with other prisoners. Personal contact included sitting in each other's beds, combing each other's hair, "standing too close," hugging, kissing, having hickeys, and making love.

Administrative policies frequently included asking new prisoners if they were "homosexual" and if so, if they were "femme" or "butch." Regardless of how prisoners identified themselves, those deemed to be masculine in appearance and demeanor were automatically labeled "obvious homosexuals." They were also referred to as "butches," "dykes," "daddies," "little boys," and "stud broads."[5] While prisoners also used such labels to refer to other prisoners, they did not generally tend to do so in a pejorative manner.

At times guards sought to discourage prisoners from engaging in same-sex relationships by repeatedly charging at least one of the partners with rule violations. Likewise, they went out of their way to penalize the butches, who were labeled a priori as "troublemakers" because of their demeanor and appearance. Pintas also argued that guards set butches up for further punishment by sexually harassing the butches' lovers in front of them.

> *Carmen:* They would . . . pat 'em down, touch 'em in front of you. And . . . what I experienced is . . . they would like try to play on 'em and . . . flirt with them in front of you and tease you about it. . . . Well, we'd get pissed off and we would cuss back and tell 'em things and then we'd get in trouble.

The butches responded in anger not only because they wanted to protect the femmes but also to show guards and other butches that they were willing to stand up for themselves.

> *Carmen:* When you're in that kind of . . . environment, life, it's like you have this pride. . . . You will tell back a CO and you will speak up because it's like you got a lot of other little boys listening to you and watching you. So you . . . gotta carry that image. . . . 'Cause it's like every little boy's trying to be better than the next little boy. So it's like you gonna say something. You gonna do something. . . . If not, . . . you ain't gonna look good in the system.

Prisoners were also routinely ridiculed, threatened, and punished by guards for such relationships.

> *Carmen:* Oh, well, . . . they would say, "Oh, you think you're slick, huh? We caught you!" . . . Some of them would make fun of it. . . . Some would say, "You're going to the Hole." Some of them would say, "I . . . hope you thought it was good because you gonna pay a big price for it."

Verbal reprimands and ridicule were accompanied by write-ups, which were placed in prisoners' institutional files. Once a certain number of write-ups accumulated, a prisoner could lose her "good time" and/or be sent to Lockup for a period of time.

> *Victoria:* They'll get locked up for "PC," . . . "personal contact." . . . They'd get sent to Lockup. . . . And . . . they try to separate them like for the rest of their stay.

Write-ups, always included in prisoners' files, were accessible to staff and parole board members. On occasion prisoners' families were also informed when their relatives were sent to segregation for "homosecting."

In spite of the many regulations, prisoners found ways to both continue having sexual encounters with one another and reduce their chances of being caught by guards. Regulars would request assignment to those living spaces in the dorms that were the furthest away from the Cop Shop.

> *Mercedes:* There's certain areas in the dorm where . . . all the regulars would have, and that was always the back of the dorm. . . . We never had to fight for that area. . . . Since we're regulars we pretty much requested it.

During those times when at least some pintas were housed in individual cells, it was easier for them to maintain sexual relationships. For those whose roommate was also their lover, it was an almost perfect arrangement. Those pintas who had sex in the dorms took the chance that other prisoners would snitch on them.

> *Victoria:* A lot . . . of women didn't like it and a couple of times we'd gotten complaints 'cause we were having sex there and . . . doing whatever we wanted to do. . . . Like . . . somebody wrote a written complaint . . . and they had said that we were doing "lewd and vulgar acts" and that we were a bunch of "lesbian pigs" and . . . "dykes." . . . You know, just really bashing us.

Such snitching, however, was not that common, as most prisoners were either involved in same-sex affairs themselves, feared retaliation, or decided it was none of their concern. Pintas housed in dorms sought to have some privacy as well as protect themselves from snitches by covering their beds with sheets while having sex. Pintas had a number of other places in which to have sexual encounters.

> *Carmen:* We would have sex in the room if people would pin [lookout]. . . . It could be always anywhere, the showers . . . in the kitchen, in different . . . isolated areas . . . in the Library. . . . A lot of times the art room and sewing room.

> *Rita:* Well, in the Kitchen . . . you can't have sex but you can mess around. . . . They catch women in bed together in the dorms, . . . in showers. Or they see hickeys all over and they know you've been there for a long time. They . . . know you have had sexual contact with another female.

Even when lovers were separated in different housing units by guards, pintas found ways to visit one another.

> *Victoria:* It used to be different-color dresses but over the years that changed and then it was just a different-color wristband. So they'd have like a red wristband and then a yellow wristband, green, purple. Anyway, so, I would . . . just trade the different-color wristbands. . . . with someone else. You know, give 'em 5 dollars. . . . You know, trade with someone else . . . that's in that dorm.

Such roaming was possible because of overcrowding and guards' lack of interest in getting to know prisoners. Even then, repeat offenders who became known to guards had to be particularly careful.

Showering together was another activity that required much coordination between lovers and their "pointers," generally friends who covered or pinned for them.

Pointers were also necessary when prisoners were engaging in sex in the dorm or even just sleeping together.

> *Rosa:* Usually there would be people that would be pointers, you know, friends. And you'd put a blanket across . . . the bed area. And some people don't care. They don't even do that. And if the officer was coming, they'd let you know. . . . "Stop!"

Spending the night together required more coordination and the cooperation of additional prisoners.

> *Victoria:* Well . . . we would trade like beds with someone . . . else. And . . . just that night for . . . roll call or wristband check, we'd . . . sit down, you know, they'd get us on our . . . rightful bed. And then at night when the lights were out we'd just trade. You know, the girl knew, "Hey, I'm sleeping here. Go to my bed." And then she would go and then me and her were able to sleep together. We would even push our bunks together so we would . . . almost like imagine that we were in our own house sleeping in . . . our full size bed.

Some prisoners caught homosecting were fortunate enough to avoid being sent to Lockup.

> *Victoria:* What had happened was that we . . . got a . . . verbal warning. . . . You know, the lights are out so we were able to finagle. Half . . . of the dorm is gay, supposedly when they're in jail. . . . And . . . we were able to say, "You know, that wasn't us officer. . . . That must have been . . . Joan Doe who sleeps right next to us. Oh, she has all kinds of girls in her bed." "Well, what's her name?" "We don't know," you know, sort of thing, so.

> *Mercedes:* Yeah, we got caught sleeping together. We got pulled out to the door like 3 A.M. . . . They kept us there forever . . . standing in the hallway. . . . freezing to death in a little . . . nightgown. . . . They call them gunnysack nightgowns. . . . I don't recall them doing anything about it just scolding us and telling us we couldn't do that, no homosexual . . . activities. . . . They were basically women guards. They were Black and Chicanas.

When one of the partners in a couple was sent to Lockup it became harder to maintain the relationship.

> *Victoria:* So she got caught stealing sugar . . . into the dorm . . . and . . . they took her to Lockup. . . . But I would write to her every single day little notes. And one of the girls that used to go down and clean the bottom floor, she'd like would throw it in there and she'd get my notes. . . . Sometimes she couldn't get to 'em or sometimes the sheriff picked it up . . . and wondered, "Where's this from?" sort of thing. . . . That's how we kept in contact, writing letters to one another.

Even the most stable relationships, however, were affected by the release from SBI of one of the partners. At times, pintas resumed their relationship once both were released from jail.

Victoria: And she went home. It was the saddest day of my life. We had seen each other for a couple of months. . . . When I met her I was like, " . . . This is gonna be a one night stand. That's cool with me." . . . And it just turned out to just be more. . . . We haven't left each other yet.

LESBIANISM AS INSTITUTIONALIZATION?

Some prisoners, like Lucy, believed that over a period of time heterosexual prisoners could evolve into lesbians as a way of adapting to institutional life. She felt that this was easier than getting clean and sober and coping with life on the outside. While Lucy saw becoming a lesbian as a natural extension of institutional life, she did not see it as something "natural" for herself.

> For most people, I believe, . . . especially if they'd been institutionalized, it's . . . a form of adaptation, like evolving. Like how they say that fish evolved and so began to walk on the earth from the water into there. I believe actually that for some people that were doing time, that eventually, that they may evolve into being . . . a lesbian. . . .
>   It's a lot more acceptable to change that route than actually change every other part of your life to make it outside in the society.

Despite her reservations Lucy found herself becoming more and more attracted to such relationships with each subsequent incarceration.

> Where in the beginning it was, "I like you," because it was out of necessity, . . . after, when . . . I was making money from having my own store and . . . selling cigarettes, . . . it was more of a game. . . . I got scared because I'd seen that I was getting real comfortable and I was never comfortable in jail. . . . Not until this last time when I was there . . . in '93. . . . You know, where I could see that . . . I was that much closer to even going that route. You know, of . . . being with another woman. . . . Not just the lifestyle of being, . . . I would have to say bisexual, but the whole jail environment itself, . . . women, the dope running in there, . . . the scenes. . . . I think I was going for . . . the whole . . . enchilada. . . . Where I had finally found that I fit in. . . . Actually seeing where it could be comfortable, that's what scared me . . . because I always never got loaded, never played in there, was always saying, "Know what? There's a life out there for me. I'm going to be something." And then all of a sudden the life out there was more scary for me. . . . And I was starting to lose . . . what . . . was real to me, you know.

Unlike Lucy, the other pintas interviewed saw their sexuality while incarcerated more as a choice than an imposition and did not tend to consider either lesbianism or having lesbian relationships on the inside as a sign of institutionalization.

LITTLE BOYS AND FEMMES

While the sexual identification (i.e., lesbian, heterosexual, bisexual) and gender roles some pintas assumed depended on whether they were in or out of jail, they expressed their sexuality within the confines of traditional male/female gender roles (i.e., butch, femme). This was so even when individual prisoners sometimes changed those roles in midstream. Such as when they were heterosexual and femme when arriving at the jail but "turned" lesbian and butch once in the institution or when a butch "dropped her belt" and adopted a feminine role.

For other pintas their sexual identification did not change when institutionalized. However, the way they felt about it did. For Carmen, who was state-raised and butch-identified throughout her life, SBI became a safe haven in which to express her sexuality because same-sex relationships were the norm.

> *Carmen:* Well, in jail . . . it was easy. . . . I was so used to doing time, for me it was like home. . . . It was comfortable. I felt safe. I felt like I was accepted . . . being a homosexual. . . . You know, everybody around me was gay. It was like a little world of gayness. . . . And . . . it was easy to compete against people in there . . . compared to out here, you know, it was so hard. It was so much bigger and more expanded, and there wasn't so many people that I knew that were gay. All of them I knew that were gay were in . . . jail or far away.

Butches cut their hair short and dressed like working-class men of their own ethnic groups. Carmen, who described herself as a "lesbian," a "homosexual," and a "little boy," described what that meant in her case.

> I was masculine . . . all the time . . . through all my homosexuality. . . . I dressed like a little boy. You know, I tried to have short hair and dress like . . . a cholo would dress. The Khakis or sweatshirts and slingshots, . . . maybe T-shirts. . . . That's the way I was in the system.

For some, embracing the role of butch meant finally giving into an outward physical appearance that reflected how they felt about themselves. In this sense, going to jail was a liberating experience for some Chicana lesbians, not only because they met women with whom they identified, but also because their appearance and "aggressive" (mannish) demeanor, criticized and ridiculed on the outside, was highly valued and respected on the inside.

> *Graciela:* When I was 13, okay, and I was . . . with women, it was always like kept in the closet. When I got taken to jail and I seen this is what I was. I seen gay girls that were aggressive, how they dressed like boys and they looked like boys. . . . I've always been aggressive. . . . That was just the way I was and . . . even when I was younger I used to dress like a boy. . . . I didn't like wearing girls' clothes. . . . So I decided I was gonna cut my hair off. And I did. And . . . that's when I decided to come out of the closet. My behavior didn't change, just my appearance.

As discussed earlier, butches were granted special treatment by women labeled femmes, much as men are given deference by some women. Although self-identified lesbians who were butches also benefited from such privileges, they ridiculed and resented prisoners who were just playing the role of "little boys" while incarcerated.

Asked why the femmes would cater to the butches, Rosa replied.

Rosa: Because . . . for one thing, there's no men around. And I don't think that you can take sex completely out of a person. And they're gonna find a substitute whether they're straight or not. . . . And a lot of those daddies, they acted like men.

Carmen: They would do anything for us. I mean, . . . even to the . . . fact that . . . if we might have had another old lady in another yard, they would still put up with it 'cause . . . there wasn't very many little boys.

Some butches, however, argued that they provided femmes protection and sex.

Carmen: Well, we took care of them. We protected them. . . . It's like nobody would bother them. You know, they had their needs met. It involved sex, yeah.

Asked what the daddies had to offer femmes in jail, however, Rosa responded, "They didn't offer anything." For Rosa, who was a self-identified femme, the daddies did not even offer protection. This was so because she and her butch lover were involved in an abusive relationship.

Most of the time we had such a violent relationship that we were fighting each other. So I don't know who we were gonna protect each other from.

THE "DADDY TANK"

Deemed by administrators as "mentally ill" and considered to be a bad influence on other prisoners, during the late 1960s, the harassment of butches at SBI led to the confinement of lesbians in Cellblock 4200, a maximum-security cellblock also known as the "Daddy Tank." The policy was supported by a California state law at the time that required the separation or "exclusion" of identified lesbians from other prisoners.[6]

The Daddy Tank was a separate housing area for "obvious homosexuals."[7] There they remained locked down (two to three prisoners in a small cell) unless they had work assignments, went to meals, had visitors, or were let out for brief periods of recreation on Saturdays. Such restrictive housing also meant that prisoners labeled homosexual were excluded from participating in the few programs available to other prisoners.[8] Lesbians also felt guards were more likely to harass them than nonlesbians and place them in solitary confinement.

Luisa: They had a Daddy's Tank. Nothing . . . but *lesbiana* women used to be there. But it was for the ones that were. . . . the aggressive, the butch.

Rosa: It was a cellblock and it was called 4200 and the women worked in the laundry at night.

Carmen: The Daddy Tank . . . it sucks because it was like they kept us separated. We couldn't get to any of the . . . femmes . . . You could get out of the unit to go to . . . where they put you to work. And then, it was a lot of craziness going on in the jobs to where the . . . sheriffs were coming down on you even harder. And you found most of the . . . little boys in discipline. Either in the Daddy Tank or in discipline.

Prisoners interviewed by Kathryn Watterson at SBI also said that women held in the Daddy Tank were often mistreated by guards.[9]

In spite of being segregated, the daddies were still popular with prisoners in General Population.

Rosa: They dressed in blue. And I always looked at it as being an "elite" thing, right, because whenever they walked in, the rest of the women would sort of sit up and take notice. 'Cause it was like . . . men coming in. . . . It's so hard to put into words. It was like looking at men!

Rosa: They had to wear dresses. At that time there was no pants.[10] And, oh, God, they hated it. You could see they hated it. But they had their hair cut . . . and they walked very boyish and the did the best they could to look boyish, in dresses!

The only time Daddy Tank prisoners were allowed to mix with the General Population was during the weekly Saturday recreation period and in the dining room. While the interaction between the daddies and General Population was strictly monitored, prisoners managed to communicate with one another.

Rosa: The only time that they would mix with the other women would be on Saturday. They had a . . . day that you would go out into the yard. Everybody would be able to go out there for about an hour. . . . And also in the dining room, you know, you looked, you winked, you talked, you'd throw kites. . . . You really can't keep them apart.

Sometimes lovers arranged to have visitors from the outside come at the same time so that they too could visit with one another.

At the end of 1976, SBI moved prisoners housed in the Daddy Tank to a dormitory where lesbians were granted more freedom of movement and the ability to participate in some programs.[11] However, prisoners identified as homosexuals remained housed separately from the rest of the jail population.[12] The dorm, nonetheless, was opened to include both butch and femme lesbians.

Rosa: There was some kind of thing going on in Sybil Brand where classification was changing. And they were gonna put every homosexual away from General Population. See before that there used to be a tank for homosexuals that were very dominant, stud girls. . . . Those girls got put into 4200. The other women were left out in that General Population. And all of a sudden this drive came through because of this classification officer, sergeant, that decided that she was gonna put away all the homosexuals in a tank to themselves. And because I came in with my girlfriend, I was classified with them. . . . Everybody went to homosexual tank whether you were femme or a daddy.

The reclassification, however, backfired on administrators.

> *Luisa:* And then they just mixed them all together. A lot of hanky-panky going on. It was more like a casino. (laughs) Everybody be making out or having sex. A lot of the women they jump from one bed to another, you know. I was too scared . . . to get caught. (laughs)

> *Rosa:* A lot of women were trying to get in there, . . . especially if they had a girlfriend . . . in there. . . . I guess they thought it was gonna be fun.

During the 1980s, SBI administrators ended the policy of segregated housing for lesbians. On the one hand, prisoners organized against it. On the other hand, prisoners' demands for an end to segregated housing was complemented by those of prisoners' rights activists on the outside, particularly women's groups and attorneys. These advocates picketed and demonstrated outside of SBI demanding an end to discriminatory policies and a change in the overall conditions at the jail. Advocates also brought attention to the plight of prisoners at SBI in the media.[13] Ultimately, the segregation of lesbians was terminated because, as prisoners alleged in *Inmates of Sybil Brand Institute*, a class action lawsuit, it was a violation of prisoners' civil rights.[14]

> *Carmen:* Well, they put a committee together . . . to take the Daddy Tank out. . . . I think that had a lot to do with it though . . . They did it from both sides . . . of the jail houses. . . . They did do away with the Daddy Tank I think about 10 years ago or 15. I think they probably got rid of it 'cause it's against the law to keep people segregated like that.

PSEUDO-FAMILY/KINSHIP NETWORKS

Pintas also supported one another in SBI by forming pseudo-family/kinship networks, what prisoners referred to as "play families." That is, networks in which prisoners adopted or were assigned the roles of male and female members of a family such as "father," "brother," "mother," "daughter," etc.[15]

> *Estela:* Like the Mexicans[16] . . . like the stud broads . . . say, "Oh, that's my brother. . . ." And like the femmes say, "That's my sister." . . . And . . . if somebody was . . . real older, they'd say, "Oh, that's my kid." And they would call that person, "Mom."

Prisoners who participated in pseudo-families could identify as lesbian, bisexual, or heterosexual. While the heads of a family could be a lesbian couple, this was not always the case.

The primary purpose of pseudo-families was to help prisoners survive incarceration by providing emotional support and reducing prisoners' fears and sense of isolation. Such networks also helped familiarize prisoners with institutional rules and regulations as well as prisoner codes, thus socializing Chicanas into institutional life. They provided continuity and stability in an environment where the prisoner body was constantly changing and where rules and regulations were enforced arbitrarily by staff members. Most importantly, they provided prisoners protection from their peers.

> *Deborah:* Well, I just think that it . . . was . . . just a group thing. I mean, we stuck together. . . . It would keep probably other people, like the Blacks or the whites, to be aware of, you know, "It's not just one person. This is a group that you're messing with. Even if you see this person outside of this group, you're not to mess with that person 'cause they do get along with this whole crowd over here."

Roles were assigned according to how close prisoners felt to one another. Thus, pintas were careful when assigning such labels. The closeness also carried with it gender role expectations as prisoners were labeled butch or femme. "Male" relatives were expected to protect those they took under their wing. Female relatives were expected to be emotionally supportive.

Graciela and Victoria claimed that Latinas seemed to engage in pseudo-families more frequently than other racial/ethnic groups. Some pintas, like Rita, went further by stating that bilingual Chicanas were more likely to participate in pseudo-families than nonbilingual Chicanas and Latin American immigrants.

While most pintas interviewed said they had not formed part of pseudo-families, they gave examples of times when other pintas either referred to them as "Moms" or assigned them male roles, or when they themselves called other pintas "Mom."

> *Deborah:* I've had people say, "This is my cousin" but I'm not. You know, "This is my sister" . . . but I'm not related to them. . . . '91 I had a youngster call me Mom. . . . I never did it.

Sometimes groups of prisoners developed closeness with one another because they had done time together. In such cases, they related like an extended family network.

> *Graciela:* Someone can be from a different town, that I met in there. 'Cause to me it's like we have a family reunion. Every year I've seen the same people. . . . We're used to being in the system with each other, not out here.

Some social scientists have argued that competition among different pseudo-families kept prisoners from forming coalitions to demand prison reform.[17] Pintas interviewed for this book as well as other Latinas, maintain that other factors kept prisoners from forming coalitions.[18] These included fear of guard retaliation, lack of adequate outside sources of support, the length of a prisoner's sentence, and interracial/interethnic hostilities among prisoners. Despite such obstacles to organizing, pintas agreed that if family heads asked family members to join them in reform-oriented activities, they would do so because they would obey their "parents'" wishes.

> *Graciela:* Like if the "mother" or the "father," if they ask the "daughter" or the "kid" what . . . you want them to do, they're gonna do it.[19]

At their best, pseudo-families reproduced the comfort, companionship, love, and acceptance some pintas had received from loved ones on the outside. The emotional and psychological support pintas received from such kinship networks was particularly important because, while all prisoners were scarred by their experiences within penal institutions, not all survived incarceration. Some died in jail as a result of diseases, staff negligence, or suicide.

Others pintas, like Victoria, felt pseudo-families fulfilled only superficial roles giving members, "a false sense of security and a . . . false sense of family." Likewise, sometimes family members reinforced and supported the negative behavior of their members. Such was the case when the members dealt drugs within the institution and victimized other prisoners. Rita went further by stating that members of pseudo-families tended to exploit other family members.

> *Rita:* And I'd also seen people that used other people because they know . . . they got visits every day, and they gonna latch on to them. And they're gonna say, "Oh, yeah, just call me 'Mom'" . . . And if you're dumb and stupid in there, you're gonna . . . give these other people money.

In summary, being forced to live in a women's institution gave pintas the opportunity to experiment with diverse types of gender role and sexual identification as well as relationships with other women. While some chose to sexualize those relationships, others did not. Nowhere was the mixture of roles and sexual identities more apparent than in the pseudo-family/kinship networks women created to satisfy a host of spiritual, social, and emotional needs.

It is clear that the various types of gender and sexual roles pintas adopted in jail significantly challenged not only society's heterosexual role expectations for women and Chicanas but also institutional rules and regulations. This was true even when pintas adopted a butch role and imitated male behavior or when femmes catered to the butches. The behavior of butches posed a particular threat to male guards who felt their masculinity challenged by prisoners who had the ability to attract other women's attention.

Those pintas who opted to barter sexual favors with staff for desired goods also broke with institutional rules and regulations even when they did not necessarily break free of traditional gender roles nor oppressive relationships.

NOTES

From *Chicana Lives and Criminal Justice: Voices from el Barrio,* by Juanita Díaz-Cotto, copyright © 2006. By permission of the author and the University of Texas Press.

1. Within Chicana/o communities, the term *pintas* is used to refer to both current and former female prisoners. This essay is based on ten of the twenty-nine interviews conducted by the author between 1995 and 2001 with Chicana ex-prisoners who had been incarcerated at Sybil Brand Institute for Women, Los Angeles's women's jail, between November 1963 and 1997 when it closed.

2. Joyce Ann Brown, *Joyce Ann Brown* (Chicago: Noble Press, 1990); Juanita Díaz-Cotto, *Gender, Ethnicity, and the State: Latina and Latino Prison Politics* (Albany, NY: State University of New York Press, 1996); Rose Giallombardo, *Society of Women: A Study of a Women's Prison* (New York: John Wiley and Sons, 1966); Human Rights Watch, Women's Rights Project, *All Too Familiar: Sexual Abuse of Women in U.S. State Prisons*, December 1996; Barbara Owen, *In the Mix: Struggle and Survival in a Women's Prison* (Albany, New York: State University of New York Press, 1998); David Ward and Gene Kassebaum, *Women's Prisons* (Chicago: Aldine-Atherton, 1965); and Kathryn Watterson, *Women in Prison*, rev. ed. (Boston: Northeastern University Press, 1996).

3. At the time of the interviews, ten of the nineteen pintas for whom information was available identified as lesbians, seven as heterosexual, and two as bisexual. For more on Latina lesbians, see Gloria Anzaldúa, *Borderlands / La Frontera* (San Francisco: Spinsters / Aunt Lute Books, 1987); Cherríe Moraga, *Loving in the War Years, lo que nunca pasó por sus labios* (Boston: South End Press, 1983); Cherríe Moraga and Gloria Anzaldúa, eds., *This Bridge Called My Back: Writings by Radical Women of Color* (Lantham, NY: Kitchen Table Press, 1983); Juanita Ramos, ed., *Compañeras: Latina Lesbians / Lesbianas latinoamericanas*, 3rd. ed. (New York: Latina Lesbian History Project, 2004); Mariana Romo-Carmona, ed., *Conversaciones: Relatos por madres y padres de hijas lesbianas e hijos gays* (San Francisco: Cleis Press, 2001); *Sinister Wisdom 74: Latina Lesbians*, 2008; and Carla Trujillo, ed., *Chicana Lesbians: The Girls Our Mothers Warned Us About* (Berkeley, CA: Third Woman Press, 1991).

4. White male guards also frowned upon interracial relationships, particularly between African-American and white prisoners.

5. Juanita Díaz-Cotto, "Lesbian Prisoners," in *Encyclopedia of Lesbian Histories and Culture*. ed. Bonnie Zimmerman (New York: Garland Publishing, 2000).

6. "Law Requires Segregating Lesbians," *NewsWest*, October 15, 1976.

7. Lois Johansen, July 14, 1996 (interview with author); and *Los Angeles Times*, April 10, 1973, July 13, 1986.

8. Kathryn Watterson, *Women in Prison*, rev. ed. (Boston: Northeastern University Press, 1996).

9. Ibid.

10. The daddies were subsequently allowed to wear overalls depending on their work assignment. Lois Johansen, July 14, 1996 (interview with author).

11. "Lesbian Inmates Gain Freedoms," *NewsWest*, December 23, 1976–January 6, 1977.

12. Ibid.

13. *Los Angeles Times*, June 19, 1972; and "Lesbian Inmates Gain Freedoms."

14. *Inmates of Sybil Brand Institute for Women, et al. v. The County of Los Angeles, et al.* App., 181 Cal.Rptr. 599. (1982); and 2d Civil. No. 61642 (1982).

15. Brown, *Joyce Ann Brown*; Díaz-Cotto, *Gender, Ethnicity, and the State*; Giallombardo, *Society of Women*; Owen, *In the Mix*; Ward and Kassebaum, *Women's Prison*; and Watterson, *Women in Prison*.

16. Meaning Chicanas and other women of Latin American descent.

17. Giallombardo, *Society of Women*.

18. Díaz-Cotto, *Gender, Ethnicity, and the State*.

19. Díaz-Cotto (1996) found that in some cases heads of households were leading organizers of prisoner coalitions. There were also times when pseudo-families were behind the creation of formal prisoner groups and were the most active prisoners in these groups.

26

Getting Free

Amy Stout

I come here about six months ago, and I'll be here a while longer. Longer than that if I trip up. But so far I've gone along with the program, so I think I'll be out on time. Ever since I come in, I've had such a hole in my heart you wouldn't believe. Something just eats away at me. It's there when I wake up and there when I go to bed. I'd sleep it away if I could, but I'm nervous during the day and so I can't sleep. I just try to get through every minute even when the minute feels as solid as a brick inside of me.

Ralph comes to visit me every month. I don't know why he comes half the time, to tell you the truth. I tell him he doesn't have to come just because I'm his mother. Most of the time he just sits and stares at me, not saying anything. I don't know what in the world to ask him, so I ask him the same thing every month. How's work? How's the kid? How's anything? He gives me his answers in one word or less, and then we're back to staring at each other again. Sometime I sneak a look at the other inmates to see what they're doing with their loved ones, and I see them talking away like I think Ralph and I should be. But we never did have much to say to one another. Not since he grew up anyway. He was very sweet when he was small. He really was. He's laughing in almost every picture I have of him. I don't know how he got so shifty as an adult.

Seeing as Ralph is the only company I get that I don't seek out—because I am stuck with three other people in one room—I do get a little lonely. Actually, I get very lonely. I'm not much of a reader, though Lord knows I have tried to read in this place. I went straight to the library when I arrived, all ready to check out books, but I just couldn't find one that would hold my attention very long. The noise in here is constant and unnerving. Doors slam, people shout at one another, the prison machines turn and turn endlessly.

Then I got the idea to put an ad in the paper for a pen pal. I wanted something a little romantic, too. The kind of letter I'd really look forward to reading, you know? It would be much better than a book because, of course, it would be real. The hard part was writing the ad, because I wanted to attract just the right sort of person. I didn't want someone who wrote to a lot of inmates because then I wouldn't be special. And I didn't want some old lady who was just doing it to be charitable and would ramble on about her flower garden page after page. I wanted someone I could really talk to, someone who could remind me of what life was like on the outside. I crawled out of bed where I was lying, holding my gut because of that hole inside of me, and worked on an advertisement for myself. "Middle-aged woman seeks romantic friendship with person not currently incarcerated. All races welcome."

I liked that part about the races. It would show them right up front that I was open-minded. There's a lot of racism in prison, and people always seem to know that, but I'm different. I always taught Ralph different, too. All races really were welcome. I didn't care if someone from China wrote me back, just so long as she spoke English. So I sealed up my ad and mailed it off to the newspaper.

When Ralph came to visit, I told him about the pen pal idea. I hoped he'd be pleased. But he just said,

"What kind of lunatic would want to write to someone in prison?"

I reminded him that he never did like writing letters, even thank-you notes, and that a lot of women like to write letters to one another.

"Yeah, well what kind of friendship are you looking for?"

He looked at me with those rat eyes of his father's. He never liked me going with women, probably because I didn't start until he was old enough to have an opinion about it. I told him I was just looking for something nice, maybe a little romantic, but harmless. I tried to explain that I was all alone in here, that I was starved for a little human understanding. I didn't get through to him, as usual, and he just rolled his eyes.

It took forever to get a response. The letter came from Michigan, which I've never been to. It was neatly written on paper that had little flowers etched on it around the edges. That was very nice, I thought. I set it carefully aside waiting for the other letters to come so that I could select the one that I liked the most. I waited a month, expecting letters every day. But I only got the one response. Can you believe it? I thought surely I'd get more, but I only got one.

Dear Dawn,

I liked your name, so I chose you to write to. Your ad was too short to say much. How old are you? Why are you in prison? What kinds of things do you think are romantic? I am 23. I just finished college last year, but I couldn't find a job so I am cleaning houses. Did you go to college? If so, where? I studied sociology. It's pretty useless but I studied hard all the same.

Romantic for me is watching a good movie. Do you get movies in prison? I also like walking along the water. Where are you from? Do they have beaches there?

O.K. I've asked you enough questions for now. Please write back soon. Yours is the only ad I answered, but if you don't write back I'll probably try another. Why do you want a pen-pal? Is it hard to find people to talk to in prison?

Sincerely, Wanda

That was her letter. Just full of questions. Still, it gave me somewhere to begin. This was a brand-new friendship with nothing screwed up about it. Why did she want a pen pal? I wondered. Well, I would ask her. I worked on my letter for days. I told her that I'd been in for six months and that Ralph came to visit me every month. I told her I'd cleaned houses for a job once, too, but I didn't go to college. In fact, I wasn't quite sure I knew what sociology was. I didn't tell her why I was in here; I just skipped that question.

I told her the important stuff—that I was 5'7" of medium build with blond hair and blue eyes. I told her I liked movies, but that the most romantic thing for me was making dinner for someone special. I asked her what she looked like, and could she send a picture? I ran out of things to say pretty quick, unfortunately, so I kept working on the letter. One day I wrote a lot. I wrote about how lonely it was in here, how I missed the sunshine and the sky, and doing what I wanted, and cooking for myself. I told her I missed having someone next to me, waking up next to someone and having someone to kiss in the mornings. I mailed the letter before I was too chicken to follow through.

Wanda wrote back right away, full of stories. She didn't send a picture, but she said she was small and dark-haired with glasses. Glasses! I hadn't expected that. She told me about the bar scene where she lived in Michigan, about some of the characters that hung out there. Her letter was the closest thing to love I'd felt in a long, long time, and I began working on a new one right away. I told her about where I was from, my brothers and my grandmother who'd grown every kind of vegetable imaginable. I told her about Ralph's dad, how he was no good, but how I'd loved him anyway for a while. And I told her how I wanted to get out of this place and get a job, and this time I would just enjoy living and not ask too much, not get into trouble.

We wrote back and forth for months. I worked so hard on those letters! I even went to the library to get information for Wanda. I wanted to tell her about my hometown, so I looked it up in a book about industry and found out that soybeans and hogs were the main sellers. I knew she'd like this because she went to college. I filled my letters with information about me, everything I'd ever thought about saying to someone but never had anyone to say it to. Wanda's letters worked on me like the tide, pulling out emotions I never thought I'd share.

After a while, Wanda asked if she could visit me here. I didn't know what to say. I was excited and scared at the same time. What would she think of me? She was near Ralph's age! I'd seem so old to her. And I didn't look so good having been in here for a while. I was pale and the food wasn't good. I'd lost weight and the skin was hanging on me a little. But the thought of seeing her, so young and healthy, and after all we'd shared! I asked Ralph on his next visit what he thought.

"Your pen pal? Who the hell is she?"

Just a girl, I told him, about his age, who wants to come all the way from Michigan to see me.

"Michigan? Who would drive three states to see someone they never met in prison?"

I tried to tell him that we'd been writing letters, that we'd gotten to know each other real well.

"You'd like her," I pleaded, knowing full well that wasn't true.

"Why're you asking me?" he asked, bored.

I told him I wanted his opinion, to know what he thought.

"Yeah, I don't care if your girlfriend comes. Is that what she is, your girlfriend?"

"No, not really, just a friend," I told him.

So I'd tell her to come—I was so excited. I didn't care what Ralph thought anyway. He only visited out of habit anymore. After he left, I began a letter immediately inviting her to visit.

Wanda's response came quickly. She'd drive to see me in a month and stay somewhere nearby. The days went by so slowly. I couldn't wait for Wanda's arrival. People must have noticed a difference in me. I started caring more about my appearance, combing my hair and washing my face in the mornings. I even tried to eat a little more of the food, mostly soggy soy products and limp vegetables, to fill out before she arrived.

Finally, the day came. I·hated that I was in prison clothes, which were so humiliating. I tried to look my best that day. Out in the visitors' waiting room, I sat patiently waiting for someone small and dark, with glasses. Just after visiting hours began, she came through the door. She was just as she'd said; I recognized her right away.

"Wanda!" I said. "Over here!"

And I waved my arm frantically, getting her attention. She smiled and took the chair across from me.

"Dawn. It's you. Wow!"

She reached out her hand and took mine.

"It's nice to meet you."

I just looked at her, mute, marveling at our meeting and wondering what to say.

"I got your letter," I said.

"Yeah, I got yours," she replied.

And we both sat in silence, not knowing where to begin.

. . .

That was three years ago, and Wanda still came to visit me whenever she could. We wrote letters even when we'd run out of things to say. It's a strange feeling, being so close to someone you've barely touched and never even kissed. She gave me a piece of the outside every time she visited or wrote me a letter.

We talked about getting together when I got out. Wanda wanted me to come to Michigan to stay with her. But what about Ralph? I wondered. The idea of actually building a relationship on what we had scared the devil out of me. We were so close, don't get me wrong. In some ways, Wanda knew me better than anyone did. But she didn't know the life I'd had. The real life—the stuff you have to contend with day to day—not just what makes sense in a letter.

Still, I thought I'd go to Michigan with her. I couldn't stand the idea of saying no after all this time, to her sweet openness. Moving away would give me the chance to start a new life. I knew her friends must think she was crazy for inviting me to live with her. I wanted to prove her right for believing in me. I wanted to show her she'd done the right thing by writing to me. Wanda said she'd be waiting at the gate when I got out. Ralph said he wasn't coming if Wanda was going to be there.

"What's the point if you're just going to run off with your girlfriend?" he asked.

I tried not to care and just thought about Wanda in her glasses ready to take me home to a place I'd never been.

She was there at 11:00 A.M., all right, standing in front of a midnight blue Chevy across from the prison gates. I couldn't believe it was really happening. Wanda looked like she'd just stepped out of the sea, unencumbered by any of the heaviness that had been dogging me those long years on the inside. It was like I'd known her forever and this was any ordinary day. I stopped two feet from her and just stared, dropping my bag on the ground.

"I got your letter," I said. I thought I would cry, but before I had a chance, she took my hand and pulled me close to her, giving me the most long-awaited kiss the world has ever known.

27

My Name Is June Martinez

Prison Environment for Transgendered Persons
A Report Delivered at Sociologists for Women in Society
and Transgender 102 Meeting, Philadelphia, August 2005

My name is June Martinez, and I'm a transgendered Latina. I was asked to speak today, but unfortunately I am unable to be here, so I've asked my friend and case-worker Sabina Neem to distribute this report.

I would like to inform all of you here today about life behind bars for trans women. I know that many speculate about how easy it must be for trans women because they believe that being surrounded by men all day long is a pleasure. Trust me, it's not, and for those people who think that trans women have support systems in prison, they are wrong.

I am a third-generation transgendered woman. I have an aunt and great aunt on my mother's side who are transgenders, and I learned a great deal from them. I am well accepted in my family, and all my brothers and sisters treat me as a female. But not all trans women have been as fortunate as I have. Many come from broken homes and are outcast from their families, and they grow up in the streets where they learn nothing but a life of drugs and prostitution and other crimes. They are constantly being discriminated against so they become used to harsh treatments.

When they are incarcerated and they can't get away from this treatment, they get involved in many types of sexual acts to find protection, financial support, food and other items, and, in various cases, drugs. They figure that if no one cared about them in the outside world, why should anyone care for them in here? I can relate to that, because I've had my share of rejection from loved ones since I've been incarcerated.

Many of us try to find spiritual solace or guidance by going to church. But even if we are on our best behavior, there is always someone putting negativity into other inmates' minds and into the minds of the chaplains. Many trans women are told to either sit in the front row of the church or leave. Many inmates see this type of treatment from staff members and think that it's okay to treat trans women in such a degrading manner.

Then, you hear the preachers talking about how all gay men go to hell and that homosexuality is a sin. You have other religious leaders in here telling their followers other negative things about gay men in general.

I don't feel that we in the transgender community are any better than any other gay community, but we are different and have many special needs. For example, we need female hormones, and we need to be in constant social settings with women. In prison, it's hard to obtain female hormones, and many of the female staff members in these prisons don't care about the special needs of the trans communities and would rather stay away.

I have never seen or heard of any support groups for gay men and trans women in prisons. When a problem occurs for people in either of these groups, they are sent to see a shrink. When we as trans women try to reach out for help, there is no one to understand us. They think we are all sick and that we all have either HIV or AIDS. Many of us are lonely, and some see sexual activities as a way of being part of something in prison. Eventually some of these people do get sick.

I strongly believe that if outside gay groups got involved with the Department of Corrections, much of the discrimination beyond these prison walls would be eliminated and the staff members could learn more about the lives of gay men and trans women.

We all know that there are many gay men and women staff members, but they are all in the closet and would rather keep it that way. They are not helping the gay communities in prison or helping to make others see things in a different manner. Instead, they make things harder on the inmates. They get away with so much, and it's just getting worse because there is a whole new generation of young inmates coming through these prisons every day and they are just so uneducated and very ignorant. These young men need to fit in with the inmates and they'll do just about anything to be accepted, so they play the hate game and at times it gets out of hand.

Many of the medical staff members don't have the knowledge to deal with the needs of trans women. We know that trans women are very emotional beings, and they cannot help how certain situations affect them. We know that trans women have many of the same emotional experiences as women, but the staff is not willing to accept this and they treat trans women very poorly. Humiliation is their priority, and I have seen many trans women break down in tears due to how they are treated by certain staff members. Many staff members have told me that they have never seen drag queens in person and they don't have people like that in their communities. Many have said that there are no gay men in their neighborhoods and that if there were, they would have done something about it. Now we all know that there are gay men in every community.

Today, I talk to all gay men, transgendered, down-low brothers, Latino men, and heterosexuals about HIV/AIDS, and I feel good about what I do. I know I have touched many nerves, and I don't care. If I can prevent someone from getting sick, I will do my best. I have also set many standards for the gay and trans world in this prison to let everyone know that we will not stand for discrimination anymore.

I hope and pray that in some way people from the outside world can get involved with the gay and trans world behind these walls and help these prisoners overcome their fears and make better persons of themselves.

We are not many in prisons, but we are human beings, and we need your help and would like to see one day the equality of all inmates. I know that race has a great deal to do with discrimination in prison, not just for heterosexual inmates but more so for the gay men and trans women. There are laws against discrimination in prisons, but what can we do when the very ones who put up these signs about the laws are the ones practicing hate crimes and discriminating against gay men and trans women?

With more education about our communities to all institutions, a great deal would be accomplished and the trans women in prisons could do better in programs and would focus on someday going home. Many are afraid of going out into the world because many do not have employment waiting for them and don't have family support or friends to help them with the transition from here to the outside world.

In 2004, when I was home on prerelease, I had the help of two wonderful young ladies who gave me a chance and provided me with employment as a health education specialist at The GALAEI [Gay and Lesbian AIDS Latino Education Initiative] Project and the TIP [Trans-health Information Project]/Prevention Point Phila[delphia]. I found so much peace within myself and the courage to stand up for what I believe, and that is helping others. I've met so many people from all walks of life at various conferences and meetings with the trans world, and I must say that we are people with a lot of pride.

We must help all trans women behind these walls, but we must also bring awareness to our younger sisters and help them stay in school and get proper education, help them find employment and be respected as human beings.

The goal here today is for all of you who can make a difference in these prisons to do something about it and help trans women find resources and employment, so that when they do go home, they will not have to return to the life they left behind.

I wish that I could have been here today in person, as I would have liked to meet and talk with all of you.

I have not included statistics in this report about transgender discrimination, because I am of the opinion that no serious study of these problems has been recorded or documented. My purpose here is to enlighten the reader by providing a couple of firsthand accounts of the discrimination against transgendered inmates.

28

King County (WA) Gender Identity Regulations

Department of Adult and Juvenile Detention

Adult Divisions
General Policy Manual
Chapter 6: Inmate Classification and Discipline

6.03.007 Transgender Inmates
Policy Draft updated 08/01/06SR
Excerpts

Purpose

To establish protocols on providing the appropriate treatment of transgender, transsexual, intersex, and gender variant persons who are incarcerated and housed within King County's Department of Adult and Juvenile Detention [DAJD].

Policy

Having guidelines for proper treatment of transgender, transsexual, intersex, and gender variant inmates by all jail staff (custodial, administrative, healthcare, and all other support and program access staff) and volunteers ensures not only that the inmate is treated with dignity, but that staff have the information and support they need to be more effective.

A. General Guidelines
   1. All DAJD forms, formal interaction, addresses, and valid law enforcement discussions shall include the arrestee's birth and/or legal name or the name the inmate has been booked under.
   2. Staff should address inmates by last name and refrain from using forms of address such as Mr. or Mrs.

3. If staff are uncertain about names or pronouns, they should respectfully ask the inmate.

4. Inmates shall not be punished for respectfully clarifying name and pronoun usage by staff.

5. Unless such questions are part of a formal investigation or other situations that affect the safe and secure operation of the facility, staff shall not ask personal questions related to sexual identity, gender identity, or gender expression.

6. Transgender, transsexual, gender variant, and intersex inmates shall have access to all necessary medical and mental health care.

7. Transgender, transsexual, gender variant, and intersex inmates will be provided with a commissary form that conforms to their housing assignment and security level.

   a. As long as it does not disrupt the safe and secure functioning of the facility, transgender, transsexual, gender variant, and intersex inmates shall be permitted to wear the same items as anyone else of their adopted gender (i.e. transwomen will be provided with bras and personal supplies given to other females).

   b. For male-identified inmates who have not or are not having chest surgery, DAJD will, upon request, issue shirts that are large enough to fit loosely over the chest area to help the inmate maintain a gender-congruent appearance.

   c. Menstrual hygiene supplies are available on an as-needed basis.

   d. Shaving supplies are available through the facilities commissary.

   e. After reviewing an inmate's medical history, and if approved, JHS [Jail Health Services] shall provide transsexual inmates with necessary continuing care items such as stents and post-operative supplies.

C. Behavior Toward Transsexual/Transgender/Intersex/Gender Variant Inmates

   1. Following Department policy *1.03.020 Anti-Harassment,* the following activities constitute harassment of inmates and must not be engaged in by DAJD staff or other inmates.

      a. Talking within hearing/sightline of a transgender, transsexual, intersex, or gender variant inmate about their own gender identity or gender identity in general in a derogatory or hurtful manner.

      b. Talking about or ridiculing transgender, transsexual, intersex, and gender variant inmates specifically, or these populations in general, to the larger inmate population. This could have the effect of sanctioning and bringing already existing prejudicial feelings to the surface in other inmates, which could make things unsafe for transgender, transsexual, intersex, and gender variant inmates.

      c. Asking an inmate personal questions about what their genitals look like, why they want to undergo gender reassignment, or anything else related to their gender identity or its presentation.

d. There may be necessary exemptions which include, but are not limited to:

    1. Jail Health Staff personnel, when performing their duties relating to the sexual and gender identities of inmates.

    2. Departmental investigations or other formal inquiries.

    3. As part of the Classification process.

Mother

Mayra Collado

Mother, you weren't always the best parent
Sometimes we didn't flow at the same current
I know I haven't been the best daughter
Now I have one of my own,
and I couldn't even fight for her
What I want to be for you
Is what I want my daughter to be for me
But I am the one lost between you two
This day I never thought would come for me to see
This here I see is my fate, my destiny
I made my own bed, and lie in it
I dragged her down,
Now she'll find a place in someone else's life to fit
Will I ever find myself one day
Will I ever see her again some day
Will you both forgive me in some way
I'll try to make you happy momma
I'll try to find you Patricia
Please God this time in my life let them stay,
and I promise to never stray

Daddy Black Man

Cassandra Adams

I had a dream that one day daddy would love me like I thought he
   should
         No lying words from his mouth at a
Constant rate
My tears falling for an act I hadn't committed
BLACK MAN!
I didn't ask to be born
Love me if you wanted!
Your shoulders another woman's child sat upon
         Me? I sat upon my mother's lap
She nurtured . . . loved . . . tried
         Failed and tried again
Never giving up even when she was fed up. With my nasty atti-
   tude and
Smart mouth
         Places she could have sent me but didn't
Frustrations. You! Left behind couldn't be taken out on me
         Because although you didn't want me—I am You!
The black girl you left
Always wondering if I'd find love.
         The woman I am . . . caramel burnt skin
Big doe eyes, cheeks. They belong to you.
Every admirer I've had was looking at the reflection of a girl her
   daddy didn't want.

Mistakes made—we all make them
Some last longer—hurt longer
Eyes laced with hope something better would come
A mindset to do better than the last generation
        Study, work and do well!
Dreams of men-love-babies and GOD that would always protect
        Completion.

31

Watershed

Kinnari Jivani

she disn't even know
i existed
until after
she drenched in raving red shred
until after
red dried to entrust patched skin and semi-stiff hair

news came to her as collision
unveiled secret love sketched back to valentine's time
the moment she wanted to cherish
came when she wished herself dead
walking sandy steps on sticky lane
downhill fate

our soul shivered as
butcher-faced hacked the union
then badge-chest stole dead me
installed in ice box
to trace DNA strands

they called her "coward"

she watered long nights grieving
for raving red shred and

a piece of herself immersed in water
immersed no more

can ocean be ocean
after someone snatch it empty?

tree's story is seed's
seed's story is tree's
it cannot be departed
so how can mine from hers?

PART FOUR

Creating and Maintaining Intellectual, Spiritual, and Creative Life Inside

AS MICHELLE FINE AND HER TEAM of participatory-action researchers at Bedford Hills prison point out in "Changing Minds," an essay about a unique coalition of insiders and outsiders resisting the termination of educational programs at that prison, more than three hundred college programs in prisons nationwide were shut down in the mid-1990s.

The same politicians who ended welfare and systematically reduced funding for public education at all levels also cut programs for prisoners around the country, despite what we know about the good outcomes associated with the education of incarcerated and free persons. Life inside got much bleaker, and prospects for life after prison were materially damaged.

Since the mid-1990s, volunteers from educational institutions, religious organizations, and other entities have streamed into jails and prisons, determined to recognize, honor, and nurture the minds and human spirits of incarcerated persons. To varying degrees, jails and prisons have been receptive. This section presents essays describing some of these efforts as well as the creative writing of a number of incarcerated and formerly incarcerated women.

Ann Fowell Stanford describes the work of women in a writing program at Cook County Jail in Chicago. She analyzes the language and the politics of the incarcerated poets she teaches there as if their poetry were as beautiful and illuminating as Audre Lorde's or Grace Paley's, which Stanford clearly believes it is. Lynne Haney and András Tapolcai write a fascinating comparison of the subject matter and perceptions of their incarcerated writing students in California and Hungary. Haney

HIV Isolation Unit. Photograph by Melissa Springer

and Tapolcai come to surprising conclusions about the cultural differences —the relation between guilt and redemption—in these women's worldviews. Tanya Erzen explores meanings of "citizenship" with her incarcerated students, and Megan Sweeney catalogues the reading habits of the incarcerated women she teaches and the roles of novel reading in their lives. All these essays record and report on the one infinitely complex place that incarcerated women can explore, map out, and expand, infinitely: their minds. Sister Suzanne Jabro and Kelly Kester-Smith provide a rich example of the many ways that spirituality can become the golden anchor and sustenance for women stranded inside.

Interspersed between these descriptions of exemplary intellectual, artistic, and spiritual programs are several poems by incarcerated women that demonstrate the close relationship between expression and existence.

Lit by Each Other's Light

Women's Writing at Cook County Jail

Anne Fowell Stanford

What poetry is made of is so old, so familiar, that it's easy to forget that it's not just the words, but polyrhythmic sounds, speech in its first endeavor (every poem breaks a silence that had to be overcome), prismatic meanings lit by each others' light, stained by each others' shadows.

ADRIENNE RICH

Jail is, among many other things, a liminal space, a place of crisis, where the life narratives of those who have been incarcerated unravel. For most of those detained in a county jail, it is a place between arrest and conviction, a place of waiting, a twilight zone where rules arbitrarily shift, cell mates come and go, anger is dulled by drugs, and tier assignments change for no apparent reason. Cook County Jail ("County"), where I spent over seven years writing with women (and the last two years training adult students to do the same), is a place of radical dislocation, in which the writing that emerges often becomes both grounding and liberating. Words come together to reweave broken narratives, break through silence, and create new worlds, new visions. Within the dehumanizing social practices of the jail, writing becomes an act of resistance, sometimes obvious, sometimes masked. Some of the women write against the official discourse of the jail, some write with it, some do both at the same time. This writing is dangerous because it proclaims a making and remaking of selves despite state attempts to confine, fix, and stabilize identities as "inmates" (compliant/unruly). It is also dangerous because it proclaims a "we" within the confines of the razor wire and disrupts the individualistic discourse and practice on which any system of oppression depends. It is brave writing, scripted from the front lines of a battle for psychic, spiritual, and even physical survival. It is raw and immediate writing. It is an exercise of power in a place that attempts to deny power to those who are imprisoned there. This work repays careful attention.

Chicago's Cook County Jail detains between 1,100 and 1,200 women on any given day, most of whom are there for nonviolent offenses. Some of the women will be released; some will be sent to state prisons. Each of them has become a statistic in the shameful record of the United States' escalating political and economic reliance on a prison-industrial complex whose annual costs have skyrocketed into the billions, in many states rivaling educational funding. This explains in part how it has been possible for the number of prisoners in the United States to increase over the last two decades from 500,000 to more than 2 million.[1] At the end of 2002, 6.7 million people in the United States were on probation, in prison or in jail, or on parole—1 in every 32 adults. Norval Morris points out that whereas 491 of every 100,000 white males were incarcerated in 1999, an astounding 3,253 of every 100,000 black men were incarcerated that year.[2] Whereas 5 of every 1,000 white women will be imprisoned during their lifetimes, 36 of every 1,000 black women and 15 of every 1,000 Latina women will be subject to incarceration during theirs. Although only 26 percent of Cook County's residents identified themselves as African American in January 2000, 72 percent of the women in Cook County Jail identified themselves as African American, a statistic that is readily apparent when the women at County are gathered.[3] (This finding brings to mind an incident during a visit by a South African guest to the juvenile prison in Joliet—"Little Joliet." During the tour, he innocently asked his host to show him where they kept the white children.)[4]

Cook County Jail, the largest single-site county predetention facility in the United States, sits on ninety-six acres in Chicago's densely populated West Side. In the past ten years, detention rates for women in Cook County have increased 89 percent. Most of the women have been through the system many times, and most women who go on to become incarcerated in Illinois state prisons have been arrested in Cook County.[5] At County, the women are waiting—some of them for weeks, some for years—for sentencing, reprieve, another life, their children, husbands, partners, jobs. They are given blue uniforms and assigned identification numbers, tiers, and cell mates. The passivity coded into the official discourse ("feeding time," "being medicated") matches the rules, which emphasize absolute obedience, quiet (despite the overwhelming and nearly ceaseless noise of televisions, shouting, and door slamming), and military deference to guards ("officers"). Breakfast is served on individual tiers at 3:00 or 4:00 A.M. (after which the women are sent back to bed in their cells), lunch at 10:00 or 11:00 A.M., and dinner anywhere between 4:00 and 6:00 P.M. Families and friends are usually frisked, and a sign points out that they are about to enter the "visitors' cage," in which they are not permitted food or drink. Not only are the women penned in, but their visitors are also relegated to their own dehumanizing spaces.

LIVES FOGGED WITH SWEAT

I started offering writing workshops shortly after a small group of volunteers and a supportive superintendent established a library in one of the conference rooms of the women's division at County. At first, I ran one-and-one-half to two-hour workshops with a different tier each week to allow more women the opportunity to write. It became clear, however, that the few hours, fun though they were, were ultimately frustrating for the women and me. The lack of continuity precluded the opportunity for the women to develop as writers and as a community. I was concerned that I was offering only palliative moments and, in so doing, actually supporting and making the very system of which I am so critical look good. My acute awareness of privilege as a white middle-class academic, free to come and go in this enclosed space, added to my unease and growing sense of collusion (this issue alone warrants a separate essay). Instead of offering the one-time sessions, I switched formats and began holding workshops that lasted four to six weeks per tier. Although this change obviously did not resolve the issue of racial and class privilege or collusion with the system, it did offer participants some continuity and the opportunity to create a body of work. Even so, the jail workshops are different from those in prison that, when funding or volunteers are available, may continue with the same participants for months or even years. Jail settings are chaotic and changeable, and the writing that emerges in this setting is immediate and sometimes quite raw, not unlike poetry penned quickly on the front lines of war zones. I think of Martin Espada's comments about "poets of the kitchen":

> Their lives are fogged with sweat, loud with the noise of their labor. To be heard over the crashing of pots, these poets may shout, in a language understood by the other workers in the kitchen, to remind them of their humanity even in the midst of flames. As always with kitchen work, many of the poets are dark-skinned or female; there may be no English, or a new English. The kitchen, for these poets, may literally be a city jail, a welfare office, a housing project. . . . This poetry has the capacity to create solidarity among those in the kitchen and empathy among those outside the kitchen. . . . Perhaps the vocabulary is more urgent than usual, but then again the house is on fire.[6]

The poetry is work that, as Espada says, "has capacity" and is unfinished in the best sense of the word. It is also liminal work. The women themselves are in transition, often not sure what the next step will be in their lives: prison, treatment center, or release. If the workshops had lasted much longer than six weeks, we would have an entirely different group. Each workshop usually has between seven and fifteen women. Because of the transitory nature of jail life, a number of the women who begin the workshops leave for home or "shipment" to prison during those weeks; but others often wish to join, so the group constituency changes somewhat. Within the groups of women, a core usually takes shape, however, and from that core frequently come leadership and strong writing.

At the end of each four- to six-week session, the writers receive an anthology of the group's work and a certificate of completion. They occasionally take these items to court as evidence of having done productive time in detention. And indeed, within those few weeks, a great deal happens. Although some of the women have been writers long before coming to jail, many have never tried it; and whereas some are eager to try, others are frankly scared of the idea. They may first attend simply out of boredom, because a friend comes, or perhaps because they have heard they will get a certificate and see their work typed up.[7]

WRITING AND SUBVERSION

We start slowly with warm-up exercises; usually we will write a poem based on our name. We read other poets (Nikki Giovanni, Maya Angelou, Mary Oliver, Gwendolyn Brooks, Jimmy Santiago Baca, Kathy Boudin, Sandra Cisneros, for example), using their work to inspire our own. Everyone in the workshop writes, including visitors. Sometimes the women come up with their own exercises. They offer praise and encouragement to each other. If someone is simply too overcome with emotion or shyness to read her work, another writer may step in or the group may make suggestions. If some of the women talk while a writer reads her work aloud, she may (and usually will) ask for "Respect, please, ladies!" We try to make respect, imagination, and fun the coins of the realm.

Over the years of reading and typing hundreds of poems, I have thought a lot about what the women's writing represents. The process of typing their work has given me the opportunity to think about what and how the women write. Trying to make sense of these poems as a whole has been a fascinating and necessarily failure-ridden process. The voices are multiple, and they resist categorization. For years, I did not write about the work or the poetry because I wanted to avoid as much as possible influencing the kinds of assignments and exercises I gave the women. Indeed, I privilege certain kinds of writing—appreciating pieces in which the women feel they can critique the system and articulate a broader social and political context for their experience than the individualistic one bandied about in most social institutions. I like seeing complex poems with multiple meanings and strong imagery. This emphasis fits with who I am and what I seek to bring to the workshops. But because I also believe that simply picking up pen and paper and writing behind bars is a subversive act, I celebrate all of the writing that emerges, with few exceptions (the exceptions being pieces that are hurtful or insulting to a person or group of persons).

Choosing the poems to discuss in this piece, however, has brought up the thorny issue of my own biases. Readers will see that I have culled poems that illustrate several points I wish to make about the writing emerging from Cook County. Space permitting, I could have chosen additional poems and made other points. What has fascinated me is how much of the work resists the state's attempt to erase the identities of inmates and discourage individualistic discourse—a form of suppression on which society depends to continue its exploitation and oppression of poor and marginalized people—and how passionately the work seeks to expand the tightly enclosed spaces of possibility mapped for poor and marginalized women.

This poetry has the potential to wake readers up from the numbing effects of statistics and to clear a discursive space in which new alliances, new solidarities, and new actions are possible.

I have wanted to call the women's writing resistance literature, but it is not strictly so. Barbara Harlow defines such literature as that which "calls attention to itself, and to literature in general, as a political and politicized activity" and that "sees itself furthermore as immediately and directly involved in a struggle against ascendant or dominant forms of ideological and cultural production."[8] Although such politicized self-consciousness is usually not present in the writing coming out of Cook County Jail, the work does challenge "dominant forms of ideological and cultural production" by its very existence. And yet as the writers resist power and dominance, they often weave official discourses into their language as well. Religious or romantic poetry, poems that sound mawkish or appear to be regurgitations of the latest soap opera or the most recent sermon, have within them the seeds of subversion simply because of their social setting and context (the jail) and the life worlds out of which they arise. In addition, careful reading reveals fascinating kinds of resistances, even when masked in religious language. For example, in a poem about freedom, one woman writes, "I'm trying to be free and I'm trying with all of my might," but then offers a predestinarian explanation: "Only God can decide my fate, / only he knows when I can walk out these gates / And when the time comes to walk into a gate. / A gate that I love, that will be the Pearly Gate in Heaven above." Jail becomes the antithesis of heaven, thus figured as hell, the "other" gate out of which the writer will be escorted by God and, by analogy, by the superintendent (or perhaps more broadly, the poem casts County jail as the devil himself.)

I also think that much of the poetry created in jails and prisons shares elements with the literature of testimony and witness. The women both produce the powerful literature of testimony as they write and engage in an act of witnessing when they read and listen to each other's work. Every time they pick up paper and pen—whether in or out of the workshop—the writers potentially engage in acts of resistance, witness, and testimony. Their work insists on giving faces, names, details, and heart to dry statistics. Moreover, the process of writing in a context of silence and invisibility (to the outside world, to the guards, and at times to each other and to themselves) constitutes a political and subversive act.

The writings I focus on in this chapter are subversive in several general ways. First, in writing at all, each author insists that her voice counts, that she has something important to say, that she is potentially an agent in the world. Second, often writers begin to see themselves as a "we" and thus subvert the individualistic rhetoric that permeates the discourse of rehabilitation and punishment. As part of the workshop's "we," they also function as witnesses to each other's experiences, as rendered in the poems. Third, some of the writers reflect on and critique the oppressive system(s) in which they find and have found themselves. But even when such a critique is not deliberate, the poems frequently serve to disrupt dominant modes of thinking about incarceration and prisoners. Finally, the writing becomes a means of constructing (and often rediscovering) the self as a contributing member of society.

CONSTRUCTIONS AND RECONSTRUCTIONS OF THE SELF

We sit around the table in our small one-room library, surrounded by book-laden shelves, and I insert a tape into the recorder. We listen to Nikki Giovanni reading her poem "Ego Tripping," accompanied by syncopated hand percussion while the women follow along with the written text.[9] Soon many of us are snapping fingers as we get into the so-alive rhythms of the poem. The speaker's claims are outrageous and fun ("I am so hip even my errors are correct / . . . . I am so perfect so divine so ethereal so surreal / I cannot be comprehended / except by my permission"). She creates multiple, unfixed identities for herself. After listening to the poem, we talk about the kinds of constructions the outside world gives to women in general and particularly to women of color. We look at how the speaker of this poem confounds and recasts those constructions. Each writer in the workshop chooses a word or a line from the poem and uses it as the beginning of her own "ego-tripping" poem. The resulting versions of the self—those based on desire and/or reality—demand that the speakers be seen beyond their ID numbers and uniforms.

One writer declares that she is a queen who "was reared and nurtured by / the village of our ancestors through their words and wisdom. I take that st and. / My body is a sponge to absorb their pain, sorrow, and their misery." Sounding almost biblical in tone, the speaker goes on to imagine herself leading children toward justice and equality within an Afrocentric worldview. She embodies the ancestors' pain and uses it to create herself as a leader. Another participant constructs a remarkable creation myth in which the speaker is told by her "Father" that she was born of a Virgin ("my Big Brother laughed"). Her Father speaks directly to her, explaining that she must enter the human world, that she is "going to be colored,"

> . . . that means a black Nubian Queen; you have to be just like them. You can't work any miracles too soon [or] they'll have you on Oprah or Springer too. You will have to be homeless, hungry, you will have to deal with the horror of their hatred and sorrow, pain and abuse.

Later the speaker pointedly tells readers, "But remember, most of all, I'm in a blue uniform, number for my name. I have a cell for a house. / But most important, I'm just like you." Turning her incarceration around, this writer recasts it as divinely ordained, not as punishment but as a way to redeem the world. She constructs a self who is not an inmate but is Jesus's sister. Moving from incarceration to incarnation, she is like Jesus, "just like" her readers, the "you" of the poem, and thus she both reaches out to readers with grace and implicates and draws in readers who might wish to distance themselves from an incarcerated speaker such as herself.

After reading Judee Norton's poem, "Arrival,"[10] Deborah McKinzie writes about her arrival at Cook County Jail in a slightly humorous vein:

> Oh no: me
> in blue D.O.C. you
> too. This can't be true
> Heaven is not like this. None of us are supposed to be here
> Where's the tub? May I
> use the washing machine? Where's
> my
> key
> to my room?
> When
> do
> I
> get to touch my children?

The wry humor in the speaker's search for a key and request for permission to use the washing machine is undercut by line breaks that emphasize the fragmentation on arrival and the assault on her sense of self. The final harrowing lines remind readers not only of the pain to the mother but of the violence done to children when they are separated from their mothers. (Indeed, 82 percent of the women at Cook County Jail surveyed by the Chicago Coalition for the Homeless in 2001 were mothers.)[11]

SOLIDARITY AND COMMUNITY

Although poems asserting the self or multiple selves become utterances of resistance, writing that affirms a "we" in jail is itself radical work. Although the women are encouraged to get along with each other, a great deal of the public rhetoric emphasizes individualism, the redemption of individual lives, and the return to one's "own" family (read, husband and children). The women's solidarity with each other can become a threat to an efficiently run jail and to a system of incarceration that relies—in part—on the myth of individualism and rehabilitation to maintain itself in society. When the women begin to see themselves as part of something larger than their individual life stories (many times narrated in terms of sin and salvation), they become dangerous because together they can more strongly critique the system in which they find themselves. As Indres Naidoo points out about political detainees on Robben Island in South Africa, the use of "we" was forbidden there.[12] Although the women in Cook County Jail are not political detainees in the strict sense (one could argue that their detentions are indeed political), the notion of collectivity is antithetical to the overall system of incarceration, which relies on detainees' dependence on authority (or the spectacle of authority) to maintain control. Thus, within this context of the jail, where community is discouraged and punished, the work becomes especially courageous and innovative. As we read work such as Pat Mora's "Let Us Hold Hands" ("In this time that fears faith, let us hold hands / In this time that fears the unwashed, let us hold hands") or Maya Angelou's "And Still I Rise" ("You may write me down in history / With your bitter twisted lies / You may trod me in the very dirt / But still, like dust, I'll rise") or Marge Piercy's "Poem for Strong Women" ("A strong woman is a woman weeping"), frequently the participants will begin writing about themselves as members of a group of other struggling women.[13]

One writer, in "The Only One," uses repetition to affirm the power of witness and testimony in healing from trauma:

> When I got high for the first time I thought I was the only one.
> When I had a sick daughter I thought I was the only one.
> When I got raped when I was little I thought I was the only one.
> When I had no parents in my life always in jail or abusing drugs
> I thought I was the only one.
> But God let me hear the testimonies of other women in this
> jail to
> let me know
> that I am not alone.

The point is not simply that she learns that she is not alone but that she learns this fact from other detainees. The list of abuses and trauma that are detailed in this poem is daunting, but the speaker acknowledges a particular grace in knowing other women in this situation who can help her make sense of her own story.

CRITIQUE

In writing about her "worst day in jail," one poet describes the day that she woke up to the facts that "this business of incarceration is a billion dollar industry" and that "my sisters had nothing to do but what they were doing [gossiping and fighting on the tier], not realizing that in a sense our lives are at stake, held hostage by the courts and by our ignorance." Understanding at once the role of economics, ignorance, and corruption in creating and maintaining the prison-industrial complex, the speaker inverts the terms of crime with her use of the word *hostage*, thus recasting the state as terrorist and criminal.

Another woman's poem, "Alternatives to Jail," takes on the growth of the prison-industrial complex: "They say there is a growing need for jails. / . . . They say crime has gone up. Why?" First interrupting the official discourse with a simple question, the speaker asserts, "This world is so full of lies and deceit, / From every corner on every street," and points out, with quite a bit of restraint, that those in authority do not always make "proper choices." Using a nice figure for powerlessness—one that recalls Gwendolyn Brooks's early poetry—she asks, "So should we jail all the little feet!" Understanding that the "little feet" are the ones who get sentenced and labeled, she argues, "Not everyone [in jail] deserves to be labeled BAD" and calls for structural adjustment to the whole system. She says, however, that if one were really to take the idea of prison reform (and real justice) seriously, those people would be looked at as weak ("in need of help too"). Thus, the speaker sends up notions of jail/prison as a place of rehabilitation and links any attempt at meaningful structural change to behavior that would be quickly repressed and criminalized by the system. The speaker despairs that "More jails is all that / It seems I see."

Peggy Thomas describes jail as a place in which people shut down internally as the system encourages them to become passive, "programmed to receive," and points out that (to borrow from the Eagles), "you can check out anytime you like, but you can never leave." Several poems take the jail guards and officers as their subject, at times critiquing the majority by singling out one of the few who displays exemplary behavior or, as in the following case, comparing the incarcerated women to the guards: "I view you as though in my own likeness. / A woman. / . . . The difference is that after eight hours, / you can leave. . . . Without your navy blues / and your silver Smith & Wesson, / you'd probably be here / also learning some type of lesson."[14] Paring down the difference to uniform and gun, Thomas makes the trenchant (and unwelcome) observation that officers and incarcerated women have parallel life histories and backgrounds.

CONTRIBUTIVE WRITING

The women in my workshops write many poems for their children, grandparents, parents, lovers, spouses, and friends. Many of these are expressions of sorrow and love, but many, especially their poems to their children, speak in a contributive voice—the voice that asserts its place in civic discourse. Not long ago, a colleague and I were invited to present a workshop at the Cook County Juvenile Temporary Detention Center (formerly the Audy Home). The night before the workshop, I was at Cook County Jail and asked the women if they had anything to say to the girls in the Audy. They were so energized by this proposition that they wrote poems to the girls. In these poems, the "we" of the workshop reached out to the girls in detention at the Audy, building a bridge of solidarity between (or rather, over) the two institutions. The poetic voice was one of counsel, warning, sympathy, and encouragement. This voice asserted and demanded a hearing, declaring its role in shaping the future of society.

One poem, entitled "To all my little soul sisters, a few things to consider," argues that "sitting here ain't no joke / I mean here in this place / You're just a number, not a face." The speaker warns about the revolving door of incarceration: "It seems some have made a career out of going back and forth to jail, / but each time the judge is harder; / he raises the bail." Finally the speaker exhorts the girls, "You have your whole life to be a person of your own, / don't sell short your career goals, your destinies, not soon. / Your freedom for long doesn't have to be blown. / Believe me, you ladies, jail is hell." Adopting an individualistic discourse—"be a person of your own"—the speaker nonetheless critiques the system, noting that bail, not crime, is the issue for the swelling ranks in Cook County Jail. The speaker understands all too well the injustice of a system in which bail is arbitrarily used to detain some and not others and in which having money is a predictor of whether a person will serve time in jail or not. Another writer claims that she and the other poets are "here to help you try to keep you away from / this Horrible institution that we're in today / and we're telling you sincerely that / CRIME DOESN'T PAY." Again, mixing discourses, the speaker mimes the official slogan while asserting the horrors of the institution.

Several of the poems adopt a tone of firm compassion. The writers strived to paint a realistic portrait of jail life. Many of them challenged the young women to use their experience in jail as a deterrent to coming back. For example, in the following poem, Irene Sanchez first says that she is not going to preach to anyone because she's been in County twelve times, but "I'm just gonna let you know how it is. / You all make your own choices and if you think you're a bad ass, / you'll end up here." The poem is long, detailing life in a six- by-nine-foot cell shared with one, sometimes two, other people, breakfast at 2:30 A.M. and another 7:30 A.M. wake-up call, "You do what you're told; never what you want. / . . . Cold food all day long. . . . Showers are mandatory; / you better get in there first thing in the morning / or you'll be taking a cold one." She describes the arguments; the "hole" where women are sent if they are caught fighting; the struggle to make phone calls, to watch television, to have time alone; the struggle to keep sanity. Sanchez ends the poem with a "personal invitation":

> come right in and bring a friend,
> you won't be together for a very long time;
> you'll both be sent to different tiers.
> It's a long, lonely road:
> drive it if you want to.[15]

The next day, when we took in typed copies of the poems, the girls in the Audy workshop read them aloud and were galvanized by the idea that the women at County had written to them. They, in turn, wrote poems back to the women, offering them their own encouragement and thanks, as well as their descriptions of life in the Audy. They also reached across institutions with their expressions of solidarity. One young woman, L. B., wrote, "To my big sistas in the County, / I want to thank you for your poetry. / I don't feel so alone. I can share my pain. / When I shed tears it won't be the same. / I will pray for you all in hopes and dreams. / that you get out soon and start a new scene." Another anonymous writer sent her sympathy: "It's bad you have to be there under bogus circumstance / but that how it is. / Deal with matters at hand," she sagely advises her older counterparts. The girls, in many cases, took on an adult voice; in others, they sounded like frightened girls ("Who can I trust?") or angry ("Water hard hit / Mad angry feelings sad / Wet drops falling down"). This brief written exchange showed me that many of the older women would be good mentors for the younger women and that intergenerational community writing projects for released women and girls would make a great deal of sense.

In August 2000, a professor from my university's English department asked me if he could bring his freshman seminar into the jail to meet some of the writers whose work had been published in that summer's issue of *Real Conditions*. I arranged for the group of thirty students to come in and listen to the women read their poetry. They also heard the women discuss their choices of line breaks, imagery, and language and talk about the relationship between their poems and their life worlds. In addition, when the Cook County writers led small groups of students in writing their own poems, the energy in the room was electric. Here were jailed women leading college students in a poetry exercise, helping them produce poetry of their own, much as they had learned to produce it while in (or perhaps before) jail. The experience reminded me of a few lines from Marge Piercy's poem "To Be of Use": "The pitcher cries for water to carry / and a person for work that is real."[16] After the students left, the women and I talked about the experience. Not surprisingly, they loved reading and discussing their work, but they had been deeply moved by helping the university students write their own poems. They had done good intellectual work, and they wanted more of it. Instead, of course, they had to return to their cells.

Behind those locked doors at County reside much talent, resilience, and courage. These women are in the main survivors of a system that is unjust and out of control. To be fair, some individuals within Cook County Jail—officers, superintendents, workers—care a great deal about the women and struggle against insurmountable odds. They are not the ones against whom I (or the writers of the poems) direct the critiques. An alarming symbiosis is at stake: at the same time that local economies are collapsing, we are building larger and more expensive prisons that provide livelihoods to those locales; but to function, these institutions need prisoners to fill them. For politicians to get elected and stay in office, they must make their constituencies feel safe. Prisons and anticrime rhetoric are part of the myth of safety that tilts the ballot boxes. And so on and so on. Meanwhile, the women who are behind bars, separated from their children—most of whom are imprisoned for nonviolent offenses and most of whom have survived domestic violence and/or been sexually abused, have little education, and are poor—continue to survive in conditions that would break most of us on the outside in a fraction of the time they have endured them.

I end this chapter with one writer's words as she imagines leaving jail, understanding the odds she is up against in trying to stay out. She writes with spirit and rocks her way through the poem, ending with a call for what she and so many women, locked away, deserve: a future.

> Bustin'
> Bustin' out these walls
> is like a soldier throwin'
> grenades at his foes.
> Watch your block—avert the
> glock. Enlight my life with happiness.
> Select my career, find who I am,
> live righteously, dammit,
> don't throw me negativity—Swing
> my way wit the good life.

NOTES

"Lit by Each Other's Light" originally appeared as "More than Just Words: Women's Poetry and Resistance at Cook County Jail" in *Feminist Studies* 30, no. 2 (Summer 2004): 277–301. By permission of the author and *Feminist Studies*, Inc.

1. Bureau of Justice Statistics; http://22.ojp.usdoj.gov/bjs/correct.htm.

2. Norval Morris, "Mass Incarceration: Perspectives on U.S. Imprisonment," *University of Chicago Law School Roundtable* 7 (2000): 91.

3. Samir Goswami, "Unlocking Options for Women: A Survey of Women in Cook County Jail" (Chicago: Chicago Coalition for the Homeless, April 2002), 4.

4. Thanks to Ora Schub and Cheryl Graves of the Community Justice for Youth Institute for this account.

5. Goswami, "Unlocking Options for Women," 5.

6. Martin Espada, "Zapata's Disciple and Perfect Brie," in his *Zapata's Disciple* (Cambridge, MA: South End Press, 1998), 10, 11.

7. The writers consistently ask me to edit their work. I have tried to keep each poem as true to the original as possible, changing spelling and, occasionally, number and tense. Most of the line breaks are the poet's own. After I typed each poem, I asked each woman to inspect it before it became public. Unless the writer's work has been published, I have omitted her name, referring to her as a "writer" or a "poet." In quoting works that have been published, I have used the poets' names and cited them in the notes. All the published poems appeared in *Real Conditions,* a journal of the Community Writing Project,

affiliated with the University of Illinois at Chicago. The editor, Hal Adams, generously allowed me to edit two issues dedicated to the poetry of women from Division 4, Cook County Jail.

8. Barbara Harlow, *Resistance Literature* (New York: Methuen, 1987), 28–29.

9. Nikki Giovanni, "Ego Tripping," Truth Is on Its Way, Black History Series Col-CD 6506, Collectables Records, 1993.

10. Judee Norton, "Arrival," in *Doing Time: 25 Years of Prison Writing (A PEN American Center Prize Anthology)*, ed. Bell Gale Chevigny (New York: Arcade, 1999), 25.

11. Goswami, "Unlocking Options for Women," 5.

12. Indres Naidoo, as told to Albie Sachs, in Sachs, *Robben Island: Ten Years as a Political Prisoner in South Africa's Most Notorious Penitentiary* (New York: Vintage, 1983), 241.

13. Pat Mora, "Let Us Hold Hands," in *Agua Santa: Holy Water* (Boston: Beacon Press, 1995), 116–17; Maya Angelou, "And Still I Rise," in *Poems* (New York: Random House, 1994), 154; Marge Piercy, "For Strong Women," in *The Moon Is Always Female* (New York: Knopf, 1982), 56–57.

14. Peggy Thomas, "Miss Rosie," *Real Conditions* 1 (August 2000): 14.

15. Irene Sanchez, "To the Girls at the Audy," *Real Conditions* 2 (July 2001): 17.

16. Marge Piercy, "To Be of Use," in *To Be of Use* (New York: Doubleday, 1973).

33

Tuesday SOUL

Kinnari Jivani

Becoming a writer
was not my childhood dream.
But inside the closed fence
                with the closed door
writing became my on and off companion
writing journal was something that
I learned to do
                to ease my pain
                        my anger
                to survive
                to jot down the scrambled thoughts
                to drop all the masks
                        of merry-go-round myths
                        in search of my true self.

Joining SOUL
has added new spices
in my recipe for writing.
Like breeze in the air
that helps the kite fly smoothly
it provided boost for
my creative ink
to run the quality mile
to grow hummingbird wings.

Being a sister of SOUL
is a growing experience
for me and my pen;
we learn
      to listen
            to the ocean waves in the desert
      to read
            with the writers glasses
      to observe
      the details from a spider's eye
      to water
            the writing plant that grows in the mind
      to write lighter
            like fluffy snow flakes ride the air
      to write stronger
            like banyan tree trunk stand
      to write
            to be heard

34

"I *lived* that book!"

Reading behind Bars

Megan Sweeney

Freedom for me was an evolution, not a revolution.
SOLO, INCARCERATED IN A MIDWESTERN WOMEN'S PRISON

"They lull us to sleep with romance! I'm telling you, four shelves of romance! Danielle Steel has a whole big huge section!" So says Solo, a fifty-six-year-old African American woman, in discussing the library at the midwestern prison where she is currently incarcerated. According to Solo, the prison library includes "books mainly to entertain"—no political magazines or books that will "incite us to become conscious of the fact that you may be infringing on my rights"—and it caters to prisoners' "fantasy" of "being a[n] entrepreneur or falling in love." Rather than offering numerous books about starting your own business, the prison library should provide more "realistic" books about "how to get out and stay out," Solo argues. "I'm one of the ones who they didn't expect to come back. But I had other issues. So we need to have books dealing with those issues. 'Cause you pack all these people into these compounds and you don't have the staff nor the time nor the resources, including money, to really deal with *why are you an inmate?*" Solo then sharply criticizes current reductions in educational opportunities for incarcerated women:

> If you have a drug offense, you can't get a Pell grant . . . You leave me no choice but to start drugs again and hope I don't get caught. 'Cause you won't let me go to school! It's crazy! . . . And in ten years, they're gonna regret these decisions. . . . You cannot beat the sin out. You have to nurture the sin out. . . . You just want to beat me, beat me, beat me, punish me, punish me, punish me. And then expect me to come out of prison reformed! . . . At some point I'm just gonna become what you expect me to. I'm gonna become that monster.

As Solo indicates, the draconian political climate in the United States has con-tributed to an evisceration of prison libraries and a substantial reduction in the ed-ucational and rehabilitative programs in prisons. This trend bespeaks an increas-ing dehumanization of incarcerated men and women that makes it difficult to regard them as readers, let alone as human beings capable of deep thought, growth, and transformation.

Despite these bleak prospects for reading behind bars, I have discovered that some incarcerated women engage in highly resourceful reading practices with the limited materials available to them. As part of a larger study about cultures of read-ing in women's prisons, I have been conducting interviews and book discussions in a midwestern women's prison. Each reader who volunteers for my study partic-ipates in one life-narrative interview, two interviews about her reading practices, and six group discussions of books. The following pages provide snapshots of the varied and vital ways in which these women use reading as a means to re-story their lives: to learn about themselves, mediate their histories of pain and violence, gain knowledge and inspiration from other women, and narrate—and sometimes redirect—their own journeys.

"THE UNDERGROUND BOOK RAILROAD": "KEEPIN' IT REAL" WITH URBAN FICTION

Perhaps the most popular genre in the women's prison is African American urban fiction, written by authors such as Vickie Stringer, Zane, Teri Woods, and Noire. Bearing titles such as *Sex Chronicles, G-Spot, Thug-A-Licious,* and *Thong on Fire,* African American urban books have become a booming industry since 2001, and young black women constitute their primary readers. Darlene, a thirty-five-year-old African American woman who is an avid fan of the genre, explains that the books typically feature "a pimp or killer or drug dealer" or "just a[n] everyday life situa-tion: prison, baby mama drama, having a guy being a player." The books often start with the protagonist's childhood, "how they used to see their mother get beat up, or how they went to different groups and foster homes and prison," and they often involve courtroom scenes and characters' efforts to flee the police. According to Dar-lene, urban books are "so real you can actually feel what they're goin' through or been through. . . . I can find bits and pieces of me or somebody that's close to me in the urban books."

Although the prison librarian receives multiple requests for urban books each week, she excludes them from the library due to their emphasis on crime, drugs, and violence. The chief librarian for the state's penal system describes the genre as "street life–type novels that are just horrendous." While conceding that the books typically feature a female protagonist who "has gone to prison or is trying to change her life," the librarian asserts that "all the events leading up to that are gory and sensational. Then the author has the nerve to put study questions, like what did you learn from this? Come on!" Vickie Stringer, a formerly incarcerated woman and founder of a major urban-book–publishing firm, spoke at the prison and tried to donate her books, but the prison refused to accept them.

Nevertheless, some incarcerated women are permitted to purchase urban fiction from outside book vendors, such as Black Expressions, and these women often circulate their books through what one woman calls the "Underground Book Railroad." For instance, Brenda—a thirty-nine-year-old African American woman—has amassed more than ninety urban books and has established her own system for lending them, including a three-day limit for borrowing. Darlene describes the underground book traffic in these terms: "You'll have about three hundred people in this compound waiting to read a book. So it's like a list that the [book owner] keeps on who got the book [and] how much time they got to read it and get it to the next person." Darlene also notes that during her month-long stay in the segregation unit, sympathetic correctional officers brought her more than forty urban books, and she says of those books, "They were my best friends."

Some prisoners agree with the library's prohibition of urban fiction. Denise, a forty-six-year-old African American woman, recognizes that fans of the urban genre find it "amazing that somebody has put their lives in a book," yet she considers the books "garbage" because they glamorize an urban-gangster lifestyle. "It's what these girls have lived all their lives," she argues. "It's what brought them to the penitentiary, and it gives them a hype that this is what they should [a]spire to be." In Denise's view, urban books are "tragedies" in which "a lot of people die," yet women see only that the characters "live flashy"; they fail to recognize that only "one out of a hundred people" manages to live such a life.

Incarcerated fans of urban fiction articulate a range of reasons why they like the genre, but all emphasize that they can relate the events and issues depicted in the books to their own experiences. Darlene particularly enjoys books by Zane, which focus on "relationships and women having sexual problems. . . . It's always somethin' deep involved in it that you can relate to, whether you were raped, or a woman's sensuality and [need] to be affectionate." Countering critics' objections that Zane's books are too "explicit as far as sex or violence," Darlene echoes several women in noting that the prison library's extensive collection of romance novels and crime novels—which focus on white people—include just as much sex, crime, and violence. Zane's books are "real healthy," Darlene insists. "They help you get strong" and teach you "to speak your mind, or even open your mind."

In addition to learning from characters' struggles, Darlene values urban books because "they inspire a lot of us to write our own books, and tell our own stories." In her view, urban books "keep it real," not only by reflecting women's experiences but also by reflecting their language style. Although editors "wanted to change

[Zane's] words around," she explains, Zane "didn't change nothin' . . . and now she's like a *major* writer." Darlene also appreciates the fact that authors of urban books invite readers to correspond with them and engage in dialogue about reading and writing: "Some of the authors even ask you do you have a story to tell, or how could you relate to this book," and "they even say you could write me a letter here and I will respond." In writing her own book, Darlene uses urban books as a guide. "I'll say, well damn, this thing in her book was just the bomb!" she explains. "So I'll go back and read it like three or four times, but I want mine to be ten times better than hers, the high point of the book. So people can remember and so they can talk about it."

Prison restrictions prevented us from reading current urban fiction for our group discussions, but we did discuss a book that many consider the progenitor of the urban genre: Sister Souljah's 1999 best-selling novel, *The Coldest Winter Ever*. Sister Souljah's book—which several women were waiting to read once their names came up on the waiting list—features Winter Santiaga, a selfish young woman whose father is a wealthy drug kingpin. When her father gets arrested, Winter's own ruthless acts land her in prison. Although some readers in the group objected to the novel's thinly portrayed characters, others championed *The Coldest Winter Ever* for telling it like it is. Jacqueline, a forty-one-year-old African American woman, passionately argued, "This how it goes down! This is the life! This is it! So, I think she did a wonderful job enlightening the public about this world." Referencing the novel's implicit call for women to develop a sense of self-worth not based on wealth or physical beauty, Jacqueline added, "This book made me want to talk to [my daughters] more and it made me want to be a better example for my girls."

Other women found Sister Souljah's novel an important catalyst for self-reflection. Vanessa, a thirty-three-year-old white woman, commented on the fact that Winter sells crack to her own mother in the book: "I sold drugs to my old man's mom! I'm no better than this woman in this book! It makes me sick to think that I did that!" Vanessa then shared, "I'm getting ready to leave in thirteen days, and I'm scared shitless because I don't want to be a Winter. . . . I have to start all over and I'm scared, because all I know was to sell drugs, trick, rob, steal, be a mule. . . . This book was so real for me because somewhere in this book that was me." Denise experienced a similar shock of self-recognition in reading *The Coldest Winter Ever*, despite her general dismissal of urban fiction. "This book was really good for me," she admitted. "I saw the way I raised my children in each one of those characters. I saw Winter in me. I saw Winter in my daughter. Little pieces [of the novel] would jump out at me and would like stab me. Like, oh God, this is what I done did to my child."

My interview with Lakesha, a twenty-seven-year-old African American woman, serves as a crucial reminder of the important role that urban fiction plays in some incarcerated women's lives. As Lakesha was discussing her favorite urban-fiction authors, she became increasingly anxious about mentioning books that she suspects are not sanctioned by the prison, even though she has found them in the prison library or received them through the mail. "I don't want to go to the hole over no book," she said. "Don't you think that's like an oppressive state? I'm reading a book. It's not telling me how to go out there and kill people, harm people or nothing. Why don't you want me to read it? . . . Why you trying to take another black author off the shelf? . . . But I can watch *Prison Break* and I'm sitting in prison! So what's really your story?" After articulating her concerns that my study would lead the prison to impose greater restrictions on women's reading, Lakesha decided to withdraw from the study. "I want my books," she explained, "and I want other inmates to get the opportunity to read stuff, too." Lakesha's final comment was, "Maybe you should write another book called *Fear of Books*."

"THE TURN OF THE CARD": READING JOHN GRISHAM

Although the prison restricts women's access to African American urban fiction—due to its emphasis on crime—crime novels written by and about white people occupy several shelves in the prison library. Incarcerated women who enjoy reading these crime and legal thrillers often cite John Grisham's books as their favorites. Mildred, a forty-two-year-old African American woman, reads "four hours a day, every single day," and her reading consists almost entirely of Grisham's dramas.

Mildred attributes her fascination with John Grisham's books to the fact that she has "always wanted to be a lawyer or a judge." During the two years before her current incarceration, Mildred spent every day observing the activity in a particular judge's criminal court because she wanted "to get a better understanding about . . . what's involved with certain crimes" and wanted to see if she could "find [my]self in the defendants." Mildred would spend "every day" in the prison law library if she were "educated enough to understand," but she finds legal reading too difficult. She therefore reads John Grisham's books as a sort of ersatz legal training. "If I have to write a letter to a judge," she explains, "I use that reading knowledge that I learned in those books to prepare a letter that's more presentable for somebody as important as a judge." Reading John Grisham's novels also helps Mildred "get a better understanding of the prosecutor, the judge, and the defense attorney." She considers such knowledge important because her son is involved in crime. "If he gets in trouble, I want to go in the courtroom and know how to talk to the judge and the prosecutor . . . I don't want to see my child in prison." In addition to these practical applications, Mildred enjoys Grisham's focus on white-collar crime because it highlights "that white and black people think alike, as far as trying to get money" or "a little extra something in life." In her experience, the judge and the prosecutor are "usually white men," so Grisham's novels enact a "turn of the card" in depicting legal authorities "finally seeing their own kind."

"SHE WAS TELLING MY LIFE!": NARRATIVES
OF VICTIMIZATION AND SURVIVAL

Narratives that foreground characters' experiences of victimization help many incarcerated women to reckon with the roles that violence, particularly sexualized violence, has played in their own lives. Upon the recommendation of some study participants, we focused one of our group discussions on T. D. Jakes's 2004 novel *Woman, Thou Art Loosed!*, which tells the story of an African American woman who struggles with poverty and addiction and eventually goes to prison for killing her sexually abusive stepfather.

In our conversation about Jakes's book, the women discussed their intense sense of identification with the protagonist, as well as the lack of available resources for helping them come to terms with their own experiences. Wendy, a twenty-eight-year-old African American woman, explained, "I was totally, you know, feeling where this woman's at. . . . That could have been me." Discussing the protagonist's depression and need for treatment, Wendy then reflected, "Here in the system, they'll give meds but you're on a waiting list for a counselor! You know, I don't want to be high . . . I just want to talk with someone." Although the prison is called the "Department of *Rehabilitation*" and the "Department of *Corrections*," Wendy observed, "they'd rather just shut you up. . . . They don't want to get to the root of the problem and deal with it."

Jacqueline likewise expressed extreme frustration with the lack of counseling resources available to her in prison, and she described Jakes's novel as a substitute form of therapy: "I related so much to this girl. I never cried so much since I've been locked up because I was having flashbacks. . . . 'Til this day [my mother] thinks that I made a move on her man, and I was a little girl. . . . Reading this woman's story, [I realized] that's why I started using drugs. And it escalated to crack cocaine, you know, trying to work from the pain." After talking at length about her experiences, Jacqueline noted, "I'm usually afraid that somebody will spread my business, but I just needed to talk." I later discovered that Jacqueline actually skipped two meetings with her psychiatrist—which conflicted with our book discussions—because she found the book discussions more useful.

Marlena, a twenty-four-year-old white woman, illustrates how women sometimes use even the most unlikely genres in therapeutic ways. She says that V. C. Andrews's fictional book series, which depicts incestuous relationships, child abuse, and other taboo forms of sexuality within families, has helped her come to terms with her "traumatic" experiences. At age seven, Marlena discovered that she is the daughter of her mother and her maternal grandfather, and at age twelve, she was raped and gave birth to her first child. Highlighting Andrews's portraits of parents who "psychologically screw up these kids into their twisted morbid game," Marlena explained, "My biological family was like that. They were sick-minded, and I don't believe I am, but I want to understand them. So I read books that are kind of like what they were doing." Reading Andrews's books "brings me peace" and "answer[s] my internal questions," Marlena says, such as "how incest affected me . . . Now I can accept it and move on. . . . It's not my fault that they did that. I'm just a product of it. I know I'm a good person inside that's just made some bad choices."

Among narratives of victimization and survival, Iyanla Vanzant's *Yesterday, I Cried: Celebrating the Lessons of Living and Loving* emerged as a favorite of many imprisoned readers. In this 1998 best seller, Vanzant discusses her experiences with abuse, abandonment, and self-doubt, and she offers lessons about using hardships as occasions for growth and healing. Solo, whose reflections open this essay, started our group discussion about Vanzant's book:

> I first experienced this book when I was in County [jail]. And I was in a very dark place at that time. I didn't want to come back to prison. I felt like such a loser. . . . I wouldn't eat. I didn't shower. I just stayed in my room under this heavy, wool, grey blanket. And it got to the point that the girls would knock on the door and just say, "Do you want your tray?" No one cared enough to say, "[Solo], come out." . . .
>
> [But] one girl came by with a book, and it was this book . . . and she said, "You may as well read it." . . . Well, I got up, and I did read. And as I was reading it, I was doing just what it says on [page] 222 at the bottom: "The earth sheds each year. The trees and flowers let go of their identity. As the old identity dies, a new identity is born. . . . The heart and the spirit also shed. They shed the emotions and experiences that we no longer need. They shed the things that stunt our growth. . . . It feels as if we are dying. We are; just like the flowers and trees we are dying to an old identity. This shedding or death is not the end of us. It is the beginning."
>
> And that's the [Solo] that you see today. From that girl having that much compassion for me, I got up, I came out, I showered. I let somebody braid my hair . . . and the women sort of gathered around me, and I fed from their energy. I played cards that day, I ate that day, and I smiled that day. And I had hope. Had I not read this book, I don't know what would have happened to me because I was so close to that brink, there's no telling . . . All it took was one kind gesture, and that was this book.

Mildred, the avid John Grisham fan, found Vanzant's memoir equally powerful because it helped her to articulate her own experiences. "Her story told my story. . . . I couldn't word my life that way if I wanted to word my life that way. I couldn't word it that way 'cause I didn't know how to put the words together. I would have stumbled on the words trying to put my life on paper or explain it to somebody. But I had to copy some of these pages down because this was my life she was talking about! I mean, . . . my abuse wasn't as graphic as hers was . . . But this was my life story!"

Mildred later elaborated, "I wrote a letter! . . . some of the passages in the book I used in my letter! Like the passage of 'Who I am is not who I used to be. But who I am is all of who I used to be.' I love that!" Again underscoring her profound sense of identification with Vanzant's narrative, Mildred then said,

In a period in her life [Vanzant] was trying to kill herself, I mean, taking all the pills, and then when she went to the psychiatric hospital. That part right there, you know, I've experienced all of it. Several times. And seeing that after she did all that, she started writin' books! . . . She grew! Even after she tried to kill herself! I've experienced all of that except writing the book. I knew where she was coming from. She didn't feel loved . . . She didn't know about herself. And she was hurtin'. And her pain and her hurt was my story *all day long!* . . . All the books we have read, it shows how to put your pain and your hurt on paper when I never knew how to do that.

For Mildred and so many of the incarcerated women, reading about others' pain, hurt, and survival serves as a vehicle for encountering themselves, realizing the healing potential of translating experience into words, and re-envisioning the path that has led up to—and will lead beyond—the prison door.

· · ·

Through their creative uses of the limited reading materials available to them, the women featured in this essay challenge prevailing conceptions of prisoners as static, one-dimensional, unintellectual, and incapable of change. Powerfully demonstrating how reading can serve as a vehicle for critical insight and transformation, these women engage in reading practices that involve sustained and often painful efforts to reckon with, and to rescript, their life narratives. In the words of Solo, from her poem "Freedom," the incarcerated readers model the vital, evolutionary work of claiming their freedom in the midst of restraint, of learning to stand up "a woman who knew her name, knew her purpose, knew her past was that and nothing more than that, knew her life was meaningful, worthy of saving from both prison and abuse."

SOURCES

Kay Schaffer and Sidonie Smith. *Human Rights and Narrated Lives: The Ethics of Recognition.* New York: Palgrave MacMillan, 2004.

Robert Worth. "A Model Prison." *Atlantic Monthly,* November 1995, 38–44.

Barbara Zahm, director. "The Last Graduation." New York,: Deep Dish Television, 1997.

35

Changing Minds

A Participatory Action Research Project on College in Prison

Michelle Fine (The Graduate Center, CUNY), María Elena
Torre (Lang College), Kathy Boudin (Teachers College, Columbia
University), Iris Bowen (Bayview Correctional Facility), Judith
Clark (Bedford Hills Correctional Facility), Donna Hylton
(Bedford Hills Correctional Facility), Migdalia Martinez (Gay
Men's Health Crisis), Cheryl "Missy" Wilkins (Lehman College),
Melissa Rivera (El Centro, Hunter College), Rosemarie A. Roberts
(Connecticut College), Pamela Smart (Bedford Hills Correctional
Facility), and Debora Upegui (The Graduate Center, CUNY)

In 1995, President Bill Clinton signed the Violent Crime Control and Law Enforcement Act, which effectively stopped the flow of all federal dollars (in the form of Pell Grants) enabling women and men in prison to attend college. As a result, at a New York State maximum facility for women, a vibrant fifteen-year-old college program closed, as did more than 340 other programs nationwide. The air in the prison thickened with a heavy sense of disappointment and despair on the faces and in the bodies of women who had been participating in the college, precollege, GED (high-school equivalency), ESL (English as a Second Language), and ABE (Adult Basic Education) courses. Some corrections officers who believed that college was foundational to "peace" in the prison expressed concern.

Within months, a group of prisoners organized with administration, community volunteers, and local universities to resurrect college. The College Bound program has been in place in the prison for almost ten years, supported entirely by a private, voluntary consortium of colleges and universities. Women can earn a bachelor's degree in sociology, taking classes offered by faculty from a consortium of eight to ten local colleges and universities. At the time of our writing, more than 130 women—constituting close to one-third of the prison population, excluding those in "reception"—were enrolled, with others in GED and precollege courses.

The physical space of the Learning Center, the hub of the college, is equipped with nonnetworked computers (no Internet), books, magazines, and newspapers, all of which are donated by colleges and universities in the consortium. Here, according to the women in the education programs, "If I need help I can find it—even if that means someone to kick me in the ass to get back to work and finish my papers."

College fills every corner of the prison. In the "yard" are study groups on Michel Foucault, qualitative research, Alice Walker. One woman told us that after dusk, on her cell block, she could hear the staccato ticking of typewriter keys late into the night; or a "young inmate may knock softly on [my] wall, at midnight, asking how to spell or punctuate."

Eighty percent of the women at this prison carry scars of childhood or adult sexual abuse. Most have biographies of miseducation, tough family and community backgrounds, long lists of social and personal betrayals. College—even in prison—is an opportunity to learn to trust, ask for help, revise the past, give to others, and reimagine the future. For some, this is the first time such an opportunity has been available, at a place where they are out from under the thumbs of family or partner threats, violence, and/or endless responsibilities.

In 1995, some of the "older" prisoners who knew we could no longer take the college program for granted asked Michelle to conduct an evaluation of the impact of college. To us, conducting a participatory action research (PAR) design behind bars appeared to be nearly impossible—yet essential. We consulted with the superintendent, who agreed with the design, after the New York State Department of Correctional Services provided official approval. Rosemarie A. Roberts and Melissa Rivera, then graduate students, taught an undergraduate course in the prison on research methods in which a broad cross-section of fifteen students crafted questions of personal meaning about the impact of college in prison. With creativity and varied subjectivities, they generated questions that touched down at the intersection of autobiography and the umbrella question of the project.

Their ideas for questions took varied forms: What is the impact of college on your religious beliefs? How does college change the lives of women who have been abused by parents and/or men for most of their lives? What's the impact of college on mothers? On children? On lesbians? How does college affect young women from "bad" high schools? What do the officers think of the college program?

For each question that a student generated, she conducted five interviews with other women prisoners of her choosing (which she documented via typed or handwritten notes; not a tape recorder). At the end of what many considered a rigorous course and others considered an exhilarating semester, we collectively gathered seventy-five interviews. Seven of the fifteen women opted to join the College in Prison research collective.

The research team—Kathy Boudin, Iris Bowen, Judith Clark, Aisha Elliot, Michelle Fine, Donna Hylton, Migdalia Martinez, "Missy" Wilkins, Melissa Rivera, Rosemarie A. Roberts, Pam Smart, María Elena Torre, and Debora Upegui—met every two to four weeks for four years. Half of us were prisoners, and half of us were free to return to our homes. All of us shared a desire to resurrect college within prison walls. We hailed from New York, Jamaica, Maine, Puerto Rico, and Colombia. We were convicted and not; immigrant and native; lesbian, straight, bi, and all of the above; victims of violence and women accused of murder. Some of us lived on the "honors" floor, some were "trackers" (under constant surveillance), and some of us could go home. All of us spoke English, and a number spoke Spanish too. We had varying levels of interest in politics, activist research, nail polish, hair and clothes, the approval of the warden, and the long struggle for justice. Encumbered by limitations on privacy, freedom, contact, and time, we carved a small delicate space of trust and work. We spent our morning sessions between 9 and 11 laughing, discussing, disagreeing, gossiping and writing, negotiating about what matters we should study, speak about, or hold quietly among ourselves.

We engaged in discussions that Paulo Freire would call "dialogue," which "always submits . . . : causality to analysis; what is true today may not be so tomorrow." Freire sought to create educational spaces—in our case, we were both a community of learners (college) and a community of researchers (PAR collective)—in which "facts" were submitted to analysis, "causes" reconsidered and, indeed "responsibility" reconceived in critical biographical, political, and historical contexts. The task was not merely to educate us all about "what is," but to provoke critical analysis of "what has been" and as Maxine Greene would invite us to do, to release our imaginations for "what could be." We created what bell hooks would call a "space of radical openness . . . a margin—a profound edge," a risky place that is also a community.

We were such a community. The most obvious divide was between freedom and imprisonment, but the other tattoos and scars on our souls wove through our work, worries, writings, and our many communities. Despite our shared commitments, the structures and waterfalls of white supremacy and global capital had washed over our biographies and marked us quite differently.

Usually our differences enriched us. Sometimes they distinguished us. At moments, they separated us. We understood ourselves to carry knowledge and consciousness that were, at once, determined by where we came from and shaped by who we had chosen to be. We had hard conversations about "choice." Those of us from The Graduate Center were much more likely to offer structural explanations of crime and mass incarceration, whereas the women in the prison were stitching together a language of personal agency, social responsibility, and individual choice(s) within structural inequities. This difference was not a simple dance between progressive and conservative ideologies. Our conversations and differences had everything to do with experiencing privilege, surviving institutionalization, and waking up (or not) to the images of bodies or screams from the past.

We worked together for four years and elaborated a complex multimethod design that included archival research into years of college records and documents;

nine focus groups with current students and dropouts; twenty interviews with women on the outside; interviews with a number of corrections officers who were considered sympathetic and others who were hostile to college in prison; surveys by faculty and university administrators; and a focus group with adolescent children of prisoners. To the extent possible, researchers from The Graduate Center and "inside" researchers worked together to facilitate all of these methods. At the same time, we asked the New York State Department of Corrections to undertake an extensive, quantitative longitudinal analysis of thirty-six-month recidivism rates for thousands of women released from prison, stratified by those who participated in college and those who didn't.

We refer you to the website www.changingminds.ws for the full reporting of our methods and findings. In brief, the material we gathered strongly confirmed the impact of college in prison on women, their children, "peace" in the prison, postrelease outcomes, the level of leadership that women provided in communities after their release, and the tax benefits for society of not having to subsidize those who return to incarceration (at $30,000 per year).

The New York State Department of Corrections conducted a longitudinal study of 274 women prisoners who were enrolled in college prior to release and compared them to 2,031 women who were not enrolled in college prior to release (trying to control for crime and level of education when they entered prison). In this analysis, conducted over a thirty-six-month period, recidivism rates dropped from 29.9 percent (without college) to 7.7 percent (with college). Further, in our focus groups and surveys, women, children, faculty, and a number of correctional officers spoke of the transformative changes that occurred in the college culture and the women. Women in prison who have, for the most part, spent the better (or worst) part of their lives under the thumbs of poverty, racism, and men, could, in college, "hear my own voice" or "see my own signature" or "make my own decisions." The women, and their children, viewed themselves anew as agents who had made certain choices and could make other choices to repair the wounds left behind. College students exhibited strong leadership within the prison, and after they were released, they launched projects on topics such as HIV/AIDS, education, foster care, alternatives to incarceration, mothering from prison, and programs for teens. With knowledge, academic experience, and newfound skills, they were designing personal and social futures not overdetermined by the past.

The intimate relationships that knit us together as a research collective brought a fever to the work. We were, of course, always under scrutiny. And we knew that the futures of the program and our collaboration were always in jeopardy. In research meetings, we often jogged between hope/possibility and despair/fear, but our collective unconscious wouldn't allow us to settle on the latter terms for too long. Sometimes in a research meeting, or the graduate seminar, we would pause as a research member detailed the difficulty of registering new students eager to start the program with one or two courses and expressed her fear that the program might close before these students graduate; or as someone in the Learning Center wept because a visit with her parents, who had traveled from Nevada to see her, was canceled because prison personnel couldn't find the paperwork; or as we listened to details of a botched kidney transplant; or as we held each other because a mother, a student in the college, serving twenty years to life had just learned that her son was selling drugs and she couldn't stop him; or as we discovered that another student was sent to Solitary Housing Unit because she tried to cut herself. Other times we deliberately stayed clear of such conversations, keeping "on task" as a way to exert control where little was available. The context and physical environment of our research was harsh, noisy, and without privacy, by design.

At our rectangular, cramped, uneven wooden table in the Learning Center, we huddled around snacks and our writings. Many long conversations took place there, as other women—students in the college program—completed research papers, studied for the GED, tutored "new women," cared for dogs they were training to become seeing-eye dogs. Each of us in the research collective brought in the writing we had done on our distinct sections and concerns.

Later in our research process, in March 2000, when we had completed the research, we tried to figure out how to write our text. Should we write with one voice or display our multiple voices? Should we fill our report with the questions and contradictions of participatory work, or should we aim for a coherent and authoritative tone? Should we stuff our analysis with feminist complexity or aim for social-science parsimony? How should we designate authorship—in alphabetical order? in separate lists of prisoner researchers and Graduate Center researchers? with Michelle's name first to confer "legitimacy"? with some of the high-profile prisoners' names later in the list because of concerns about perceptions?

Our primary goal was to write convincingly about the data we had collected; to show the New York State legislature that it made political, economic, and social sense to restore funds for college-in-prison programs. But we also wanted to produce materials of use on college campuses, in other prisons, to prison advocacy groups, to families of persons in prison, and others. So we decided to craft multiple products. Our primary document would be a single-voiced, multimethod, rigorous, and professionally designed report, available widely as a website (www.changingminds.ws), with quotes and endorsements from people on the political left and right. The prisoners wanted Michelle Fine to be the first name, and "Missy" insisted on using that name. This report was distributed to every governor in the United States and all the New York State senators and members of the Assembly. We would, as well, construct additional essays on feminist methodology in which our contradictions would be interrogated,[1] and we produced one thousand organizing brochures in English and Spanish that carried a strong voice of advocacy and demands for justice and action. These brochures were distributed to a series of community-based organizations, national advocacy groups, and colleges and universities. We created (and have sustained for four years) a website where activists, organizers, students, faculty, criminal justice administrators, and prisoners and their families can download a full copy of the report, loaded with photos, letters, charts, graphs, cost-benefit analyses, and the rich words of the women. To date, the website has had more than five thousand hits. The California State Department of Corrections has ordered fifty copies of the report; feminist and critical education faculty have assigned the report in class; a father whose daughter committed suicide in prison has decided to sponsor a college-in-prison project, and he too ordered enough copies for a number of administrators in his home state.

As we struggled with the section defining the "we" of the research collective, Michelle naively offered, "What if we write something like, 'We are all women concerned with violence against women; some of us have experienced [it], most of us have witnessed [it,] and all are outraged.'" To which someone said, "Michelle, please don't romanticize us. Your writing is eloquent, but you seem to have left out the part that some of us are here for murder." Another woman extended the point: "And some of us [are here] for [the] murder of our children." The argument was becoming clear: "When we're not here in the college, and we're alone in our cells, we have to think about the people affected by our crimes. We take responsibility, and we need you to represent that as well as our common concerns as women, as feminists, as political people . . . "

In prison, as in any institution under external surveillance, insiders know details of daily life, understand the laserlike penetration of external scrutiny, and are more likely to refuse to romanticize the events within. Indeed, in our collaborations, the women who were prisoners and researchers were the ones who recognized that our design needed to include dissenting voices, narratives of critique, and perspectives from dropouts; prisoners and former prisoners insisted that we talk about responsibility, choices, and remorse.

As powerful as PAR has been behind bars, we offer cautions. The women in prison were always more vulnerable than the outsiders. Cells could be searched, and private papers could be confiscated. And the critical consciousness that accompanies participatory research comes with anger, outrage, and a recognition of injustice that boils in prison and beyond. PAR speaks to an outside world, but often the women inside see few changes.

At one state legislative hearing, two of us (Michelle and Maria) presented the findings and concluded, "College in prison is morally important to individuals, families, and communities; financially wise for the state; and it builds civic engagement and leadership in urban communities. In fact, college in prison even saves taxpayers money. A conservative Republican, as well as your more progressive colleagues, should support these programs . . . unless, of course, the point is simply to lock up Black and Brown bodies at the Canadian border." One of the more progressive state legislators responded, "Doctor, I'm afraid that is the point. You know that in New York, downstate's crime is upstate's industry." In other words, the social fabric of New York State is divided, with a relatively white and rural "upstate" and substantial poverty and communities of color "downstate" in New York City (with pockets of urban poverty distributed throughout the state).

Prisons and their justifications have infected our national consciousness, our national economy, and the global economy. In modest response, in the midst of a global struggle against the mass incarceration of people of color, and women in particular, this participatory action research project on college in prison sparks an electric current through which critique and possibility travel. PAR projects are born in dissent, strengthened by difference, organized through a bumpy democracy, and motivated by desire for contestation and justice.

UPDATE

More than ten years have passed since Clinton pulled the funds out of college in prison. In fact, the Bedford Hills college program just celebrated a decade anniversary.[2]

Recently, a new PAR collective formed to take up another piece of research on mass incarceration: a study of men and women who have been released after serving long sentences (longer than eight years) or violent crimes. With a strong advisory board of men and women who meet these criteria, we are analyzing state reincarceration rates and conducting fifty life interviews with women and men who fit these criteria. With an analytic eye on the nature of the original crime and gender, we are studying reincarceration rates, parole denials, and the consequences of mass incarceration on families and children. Thus far we have learned that these men and women—especially the women—have remarkably low rates of reincarceration (see chapter 57, by Kathy Boudin, in this volume).

This new project seeks to re-present women and men who have been charged with violent crimes, enabling them to tell their stories of crime, responsibility, prison, and release. Equally important, with this work we hope to pry open all the ways in which gender, race, and class move through the system, landing unjustly on women's backs—to investigate why so many women plead guilty while male codefendants refuse to plead and go to trial, receiving often lighter sentences; why women "hide the gun" after men pull the trigger and they both get long sentences; why men know enough to turn state's evidence and rat on others so that they can receive reduced sentences, whereas women know little and are sent off to prison; why men who go to prison have women to raise their children and visit them, whereas women who go to prison often lose their kids to foster care, with few visits and terminated parental rights—a lifetime sentence.

Our work, past and future, seeks to pierce the national anesthesia and to offer critical gender, race, and class analyses of the devastating politics of mass incarceration.

NOTES

1. Michelle Fine, Maria Elena Torre, Kathy Boudin, Iris Bowen, Judith Clark, Donna Hylton, Migdalia Martinez, Missy, Rosemarie A. Roberts, Pamela Smart, and Debora Upegui, "Participatory Action Research: From within and beyond Prison Bars," in *Qualitative Research in Psychology: Expanding Perspectives in Methodology and Design,* ed. Paul M. Camic, Jean E. Rhodes, and Lucy Yardley (Washington, DC: American Psychological Association, 2003).

2. The update was written by a subgroup of us who are no longer in prison.

36

Imagining the Self and Other

Women Narrate Prison Life across Cultures

Lynne Haney and András Tapolcai

On an afternoon in the summer of 2002, a dozen inmates gathered in a California prison for incarcerated mothers for the first meeting of our creative writing class. We began with a writing exercise that had worked well in similar settings: We asked the women to list ten feelings, which we then wrote on the blackboard. "Sorrow," Maria called out. "Grief, fear, and depression," Chanel added. "You've got to put anxiety and frustration at the top," Melissa demanded. "No way," Claire interjected. "Guilt and regret should be up there." The list concluded with "disappointment" and "loneliness." Looking at the list, we were struck by the fact that all the suggestions were negative feelings. Before we could comment, Maria jumped in to explain their choices: "This place is all about depression and guilt . . . What kind of positive feelings do you want from us?"

Three years later, on another summer day, we were in Hungary's only maximum-security prison for women doing the same writing exercise. "Love and passion," Timea suggested. "Happiness and sadness," Maria said. "Anger?" Kinga asked. Others threw in "calmness," "ignorance," and "distrust." Zsuzsa concluded the list with "exhaustion," prompting everyone to talk about how tired they were after their eight-hour workday in the prison's factory. Then Timea, who had been intently looking at the list, began to brainstorm about which emotion had the most literary potential—maybe passion, because it conjured up so many raw feelings. Or perhaps anger. A conversation then ensued about how to relay emotions in writing through innuendo and insinuation. Soon, the women started writing for the day and silence fell over the room.

In the past decade, as female incarceration rates have increased across the globe, feminist scholars and activists have done extraordinary work studying how mass imprisonment affects women. Their work has revealed how women's lives are transformed by imprisonment: their employment options, familial relationships, and survival strategies all bear the imprint of incarceration. Over the past few years, as we have taught creative writing in women's prisons, we have begun to see another level at which prison cultures operate: they have a profound influence on inmates' imaginations, shaping how female inmates envision their past and future. They provide narratives through which inmates filter their experiences, hopes, and dreams. And they structure the frames available for inmates to interpret who they are and who they might want to become.

This paper describes the effects of incarceration in two very different penal contexts: a community-based prison for women in California and a maximum-security facility for women in Hungary. Based on years of conducting creative writing classes in these prisons, we trace the imprint the environments left on inmates' imaginations. On the one hand, we describe how the institutional scripts available to the U.S. inmates centered on the individual—usually through narratives of addiction and pathology. Their stories focused on the emergence of new selves freed from old pathologies and ways of being. This focus then led the women to rely exclusively on the "I" in their writing and to represent their experiences in purely personal terms. On the other hand, we show how the Hungarian inmates rejected references to the self. Instead, their scripts emphasized the social and relational, which then gave rise to an imagining of alternative relationships and experiences that bypassed the individual. This focus led the women to insist on writing in third person and to create characters that, while based on their own lives, were not personal replicas of them. In addition to describing these differences, we discuss the possibilities and limitations of both imaginary modes and their links to the larger penal cultures in which the women lived.

WRITING THE "SELF" IN U.S. PRISONS

In the mid-1990s, California began an experiment in its prison system: after pressure from feminist lawyers and activists, it established four facilities in which female inmates could reside with their children. These facilities, part of the Community Prisoner Mothers Program (CPMP), prompted optimism. Designed as alternatives to traditional corrections, they promised to end the cycling of prisoners' children through the foster care system by allowing women to raise their children while incarcerated. They also promised to "empower" female inmates by helping them understand and resolve their problems.

By 2002, when we began our work in one of the first CPMP facilities, a consensus had formed around what these promises implied for the program, Visions. Alternative orientation had come to imply therapeutic intervention, whereas empowerment meant therapeutic recovery. In fact, in all of its glossy promotional

material, Visions represented itself as a "therapeutic community," replete with clin-
ically trained counselors and addiction specialists. In concrete terms, this orientation meant that the women at Visions spent large parts of their days in counseling
sessions and encounter groups. A typical day at Visions began with the inmates placing their children outside the facility, either in the adjacent day care center or the
nearby public school. The women then headed off to groups and classes—which
included classes in art therapy, drama therapy, anger management, and various
twelve-step programs. Interspersed throughout the day were staff-supervised yoga
classes and individual therapy sessions. Days ended with a house meeting to allow
women to connect with their "sisters" and share their "feelings."

Given the centrality of reflection and introspection in the Visions program, we
assumed that its environment would be conducive to creative writing. In a sense,
it was: from our first class, the women were eager to tell their "stories." Indeed, it
often appeared as though they had been practicing and perfecting these stories for
some time. They seemed to have immediate access to narratives about themselves
and were ready to divulge quite intimate details of their lives. Without exception,
the Visions inmates were very adept at "self talk" and could recount memories of
trauma openly and honestly. Or, in the program's vernacular, they could "go deep."
Furthermore, in their recountings, the women seemed unphased by the public nature of the classroom setting: we never had a shortage of volunteers willing to read
their stories. No matter how unsettling or disturbing the tale, hands would shoot
up when we asked for volunteers to share their work. They wanted to see the reactions to their texts and the shock their words prompted in their audience. "Let me
go first," Maria yelled out one morning after we asked for volunteers to read. "My
story is off the hook . . . You just wait."

Indeed, many of their stories were off the hook. After six months of working with
three groups of women, we remained amazed by the power and honesty of their
texts. Like Tamika's account of her experiences of incest, followed by years of abuse
as a prostitute. Or Rhonda's narrative of her first drug arrest, written from her perspective as well as that of her five-year-old daughter, who watched the whole event
unfold. Or Devon's narrative of how her son "parented" her for years due to her
crack addiction. Or Mildred's account of the first time she tried to leave her abusive husband—how she sat at a nearby bus stop, crying, until he pulled up and forced
her back into his car.

Then we had Tracy's story of giving birth in the state's largest women's prison.
Hers was a harrowing account that began when prison officials transferred her to
the ward for mentally ill inmates just before her due date. Convinced that her cell
mate was in for incest, she spent the week before the birth in a corner, refusing to
move or speak to anyone. After her water broke, she waited in terror for hours before calling the medical staff.

When that crazy woman [cell mate] heard I was givin' birth, she came at me. Like she lunged at me, and all I could think about was how I needed to protect my baby from this maniac. All I could think of was how she was gonna take him and abuse him. Then I became like a crazed animal who'd do anything to protect her young. I started to growl at that woman, to warn her off. Maybe I was even drooling from my mouth. When the medical staff arrived, they found me in the corner, all bloody and convulsing on the floor. They tied me up to get me out of the cell. Like a crazy animal, they had to rope me up. That's what I became. An animal giving birth.

Tracy's story always captivated the other women in the class: whenever she read parts of it, they listened with unparalleled interest. But Tracy never finished her story. In fact, she was the only inmate to drop out of our class. With time, we began to see her experience as indicative of one of the main limitations of "self talk": For many women, this form of expression became its own prison. Initially, we hoped we could offer the women at Visions a respite from the perils of prison life, an avenue of escape from their problems. Yet we quickly realized that the women could not use writing as an escape. The narrative form available to them brought their problems right back—often with a vengeance. Moreover, this confessional mode became inescapable; despite our attempts, the Visions women resisted any other writing style. Some claimed that a refusal to "go deep" in their writing was a "defense mechanism" or "avoidance strategy," terms appropriated from the Visions clinical staff. Others applied twelve-step logic to explain such refusals, suggesting that they were distractions from the painful work of recovery and redemption.

In effect, the writers at Visions were unable or unwilling to narrate outside the self; their stories were always personal and only personal. This focus persisted despite the obvious overlaps in their accounts; the women wrote about strikingly similar issues and experiences. Yet we had to be very careful in bringing up this similarity. The one time we pointed it out in class, the women took our comment as an insult—as if we were negating the originality of their stories. Freda articulated this reaction explicitly during a class when we tried to get her to experiment with different voices in her writing. Freda was having a hard time with her text; she thought it sounded too repetitive, with every sentence beginning with "I." So we asked her to take one paragraph and switch from first to third person. She resisted: "I can't do that cause I'm talking about me." We explained that it was her prerogative as a writer to use whatever voice she wanted, so she tried rewriting the paragraph. When she finished, she looked up from the page in disgust. The others didn't like it either. "That just ain't right," Malika argued. " 'Cause the story is about Freda, no one else." The others agreed, expressing outright resistance to the idea of writing in third person. In the end, Freda restored all the "I"s to her text.

Although Freda's desire to speak in her own voice is understandable, remaining in the "I mode" had several downsides for Visions writers. Not only did it block them from using writing to distance themselves from their problems, but it often turned writing into a competition. Early on in our classes, a battle of one-upmanship began to develop, with some women feuding over who had lived the hardest life. Two women, Brandee and Keisha, even began to write dueling accounts of their lives. They had quite similar backgrounds: both had been orphaned at young ages, abused by foster parents, and kicked onto the streets as teenagers, and both had turned to prostitution to support themselves and their drug habits. However, instead of allying, Brandee and Keisha seemed threatened by each other; they thought that finding someone with a similar "I" story negated their own accounts. So they turned their commonalities into an intense rivalry. Whenever one of them wrote about a memory, the other countered in the next class with a similar memory with slightly more detail about past abuse. This exchange went on for weeks. Finally, Brandee conceded defeat and decided to focus her writing on how she lost her children to child protective services—something that had never happened to Keisha.

Whereas Brandee and Keisha's feud devolved into a sort of competitive confessional, Tracy's struggle was internal. She labored long and hard over her prison birthing story. The process started to take its toll; she began to have nightmares and panic attacks. We wondered if the experience was just too painful for her to revisit while incarcerated. But whenever we suggested that she write a different story, or write her story as a fictional account of another woman giving birth, she resisted. She claimed that these approaches would be a "cop-out"—and she wasn't a "wimp." After weeks of battling with her story, she stopped coming to class; eventually, she stopped writing altogether.

After watching Tracy's struggles, we realized that part of the problem was related to the scripts available to her at Visions. As Maria noted on the first day of class, the facility was all about "depression" and "guilt"; the narratives it offered to the women emphasized their need to free themselves from addiction and pathology. This emphasis left them with little room for a social imagination. It restricted them from thinking outside the self. And it undermined their ability to use writing to contextualize the self or to dialogue with other selves—either of which might have given them a respite from confinement. Thus, we were left wondering whether this "alternative" program designed to empower women was fulfilling its promise. By psychologizing women's social problems, and transforming collective struggles into personal demons, it may have done just the opposite.

WRITING THE "OTHER" IN HUNGARIAN PRISONS

One can hardly imagine a prison environment more dissimilar from Visions than the Keleti Fegyhaz es Borton (KFB), Hungary's only maximum-security facility for women. Its history was totally different from that of the California prison: inherited from the communist system, the facility was under the official control of the military. Its staff had military designations and ranks; its budget came from the armed services. Thus, there was not even a semblance of alternative corrections or promises of inmate empowerment. On the surface, the prison adhered to a strict hierarchy and code of formality. When staff passed by, inmates had to stand at attention. We were always escorted to and from our classroom by guards. And before and after the class, our students lined up in front of the classroom and stood in silence until the guards came to escort them back to their cells.

Not surprisingly, KFB's daily rhythm was entirely different from the Visions routine. The women woke at dawn, had a hearty breakfast, and then went off to work for eight hours. After a late-afternoon meal, they rested and prepared for the next day's work. The staff allowed no exceptions to this schedule; all other prison activities revolved around the workday. In fact, work was so central that it determined the inmates' clothing: KFB women wore blue, green, or black-and-white–striped uniforms, depending on where they worked. Most had jobs related to the prison's maintenance and upkeep; they did everything from kitchen work to cleaning to office work. Others landed jobs making industrial apparel for a private company that operated out of the prison. The KFB world had no time for therapy or yoga, no counselors on staff, and no twelve-step programs available to inmates.

When we began our KFB classes, we worried that the environment would not be conducive to writing. In a sense, we were right: the inmates came to our late-afternoon classes completely exhausted. After eight hours of grueling labor, they were burnt out. Moreover, they often believed they were being watched and observed. The prison library was adjacent to our classroom, and everyone knew the librarians were snitches. They seemed to listen in on our classes, poking their heads in whenever the discussion got animated—as if to remind the women that they were under surveillance. Despite this scrutiny, something fascinating happened in our classes: from the first writing exercise, the women used the space to block out the problems surrounding them. They came to class eager to tell stories that took them away from the harsh realities of KFB. They used writing to distance themselves from the perils of prison life. "When I'm here, I forget about this place," Timea once announced, smiling and gesturing with her hands, which were covered with lotion to soothe the burns she got that day during her long kitchen shift.

In part, these women could use writing as an escape because of the scripts they had access to. The KFB inmates entered writing through a different mode than the Visions inmates did: instead of approaching writing through personal narratives, they did so through images of the other. For them, writing a "story" meant taking the role of the other. And they were adept at imagining the other and constructing story lines. They were also willing to help each other tap into their imaginations and fantasize about other worlds. Our classes often involved brainstorming about how to develop a character portrayed in an inmate's text. Sometimes the writers appeared to appreciate one another for taking them on imaginary journeys and offering them routes to escape prison life, if only for a few minutes.

This approach does not mean that their surroundings never entered the stories they wrote. Prison life, and their preprison lives, followed the writers into their fictional worlds as metaphors and turns in the narrative. For example, Henrietta wrote a story about a journalist who visited a cloister while working on a story. The description of the cloister—with its wooden gates, dark corridors, small windows, and tiny unfurnished cells—evoked the prison's atmosphere. And in the first chapter of Timea's novel, an underpaid computer programmer becomes entangled with the Budapest mob when he accepts a friend's offer to "make extra money on the side." And Kinga wrote a startling story about the interruption of a pleasant summer morning by a "large, black butterfly" landing on the main character's face. The stories revolved around themes of failure, confinement, and, sometimes, redemption.

Entirely absent from these texts were direct references to the women's own lives. Without exception, the KFB writers never engaged in self-talk; they never used the confessional "I." In fact, after months of working with them, we realized that we knew very little about their backgrounds. Occasionally, they referred to bits and pieces of their lives—mentioning how much they missed their children or how they dreamed of eating a particular food at family gatherings. But they were silent about the nature of those familial relations or the dynamics at those family gatherings. They also seemed silent with each other; they knew almost nothing about their fellow inmates' past relationships, personal traumas, or emotional turmoil. Often, they didn't even know where the others came from: after sitting next to each other for months, one day Timea and Hermina suddenly realized that they came from the same small town and had lived in the same neighborhood for decades.

Of course, this reticence does not mean that the KFB writers never wrote in the first person. Clearly, they did. But the voice was a different kind of "I": it was more abstract, less confessional, and more fictional. A poem by Zsuzsa exemplifies this voice:

> If not that day and that way,
> Not there and not then,
> If I had done what I did not,
> Or had not done what I did,
> Then, perhaps, it would be otherwise,
> And the otherwise would also be otherwise.

Lest we idealize the inmates' rejection of the personal "I," it ended up posing problems for them. At times, their refusal to "go deep" was itself imprisoning. Whereas the U.S. women had difficulty finding a way outside their selves, the Hungarian women had a hard time finding a way into their selves. As a result, they often were unable to reach out to others or to grapple with their pasts. Although they rarely spoke about their pasts, they had led extremely hard lives that were not very different from those of the women at Visions. All of them were poor, many of them faced racism as Romani women, and some had long histories of drug use and prostitution. And most of them had endured years of domestic violence because roughly 75 percent of female inmates in Hungary are victims of domestic abuse. We can only imagine the many traumatic memories they carried. But these traumas remained hidden beneath imaginary characters who were guilty of imaginary crimes.

On the rare occasions when personal feelings crept into the discussion, the KFB inmates became uncomfortable—acting as if they couldn't process such emotions. For instance, one afternoon Hermina came to class nervous and anxious. Midway through the first writing assignment, she dropped her pen and announced that she could not write. Fidgeting in her seat, she began to discuss the nightmares she had been having and her sense of extreme depression. The other women remained silent. Hermina continued that she often fantasized about jumping off the prison balcony and falling to her death. The others looked at one another, speechless. When Hermina's eyes teared up, Maria began to comfort her by stroking her arm. No words were spoken—they didn't seem to have the language to soothe her or a framework to take care of the self.

Without the personal "I," the KFB women had a hard time reaching out to others. In fact, many of them seemed quite masterful at repressing what was happening around them. Whenever the topic of confinement came up, the women nervously changed the subject. Few of them spoke to their families about prison life. "When I go home on a visit, I never talk about my life here," Kati declared. "That's a life they won't understand and I don't want anyone to know about." Eva claimed that her three kids did not know she was in prison, even though she was serving a ten-year sentence for human trafficking. "They think I'm away for work or something," she explained. "I will never tell them any different." Emotional turmoil often seemed to simmer under the surface of everyday life. There was a heaviness in the air at KFB, and it weighed everyone down. These repressed emotions seemed likely to erupt at any moment—an eruption the women could have avoided if they had had ways to interpret and represent the self.

Perhaps the best example of the repression at KFB occurred when the inmates openly resisted one of our writing exercises. In an effort to get them to reflect on their surroundings, we asked them to write about how an outsider would perceive the prison. Without hesitation, the inmates rejected the idea. "I'm not doing it," Timea declared. "I'm not either," Maria said. A discussion ensued in which the KFB writers made clear that they found an outsider's gaze, even the imagined gaze of an imagined outsider, too discomforting. They did not want their lives as prisoners to be revealed, and perhaps judged, even by a character of their own imagination. They also had a pragmatic reason for their resistance. "What if they hold a search and find my manuscript?" Zsuzsa worried. "They will send me to solitary confinement if they read what I have to say." The others nodded in agreement. Her response underscored the limitations of their escape through writing, for them as well as for us. In the end, we changed the assignment.

Thus, the challenges confronting the KFB women were almost the reverse of those facing the Visions inmates. This Hungarian prison was not meant to empower or prompt self-discovery. The downside of this regime was clear: its hierarchy and formalism often led to harsh, distanced treatment and surveillance. Yet it also came with other, unexpected possibilities: it left room for the women to maintain and develop a social imagination. Unlike the Visions confessional mode, which allowed for only one story line of introspection and redemption, the KFB writers could imagine different ways of being. They could think outside the self and fantasize about worlds outside their own. These imaginings gave them an escape, albeit brief, from the perils of prison. But it also left them unable to acknowledge the toll that prison life was taking on them. It enabled them to hide behind their imaginary characters—even when they could have benefited from a bit of "self talk."

We do not argue that one of these modes of expression is better than the other. Throughout this paper, we have pointed out that both modes encompass possibilities and limitations. Our goal has been to expose these possibilities and limitations and to link them to the surrounding prison environment. Clearly, one can find many ways to understand and explain the differences in how U.S. and Hungarian inmates expressed themselves. These women came from vastly different cultures and were exposed to vastly different educational systems and media. Yet the consistency with which the U.S. and Hungarian inmates reverted to these expressive modes suggests that they were at least in part connected to the surrounding prison cultures. Through our experiences teaching creative writing, we have come to appreciate how prison cultures not only shape inmates' life choices and options, but also their imaginations. And we have come to see just how consequential these aspects of prison culture can be—how they influence the kinds of relationships inmates can form as well as the space they can carve out for meaningful creative and intellectual lives.

My Art

Kinnari Jivani

My art is my voice
my vision, my passion, my meditation
my expression, my existence
my sanity walk
my devotional desire
my art is a part of me
      sobbing, fussing
      changing, growing
      dancing, playing, living . . .
      part of me
            dropped, draped in colors
            slowly emerging in details.

Art teaches me to keep flowing
flowing is my dharma

My art is my voice
if you listen closely
you will hear it whisper

My Window

Michele Molina

Isolation—Desperation—The hours become days
        And the days become weeks.
I look up and the leaves are turning colors once again.
Bright and sunny days make no difference when
      my mind is clouded and every heartbeat is like a
  thunderbolt of pain.
I tread through the months and the years.
At times I have to scrape up the energy to greet each day.
I see the light out of my window, but only feel the darkness
  around me.
My body is listless and my features betray my true age.
It is time to open the window to my soul and let the light in.

They Talked

Kinnari Jivani

Come to the workshop next week
bring your writing on 'Why I love me'
They heard
It frowned them into the silence
They sat on the metal bunk
beside the glass window view
enveloped by dirty-gray blue cloudy sky
They talked   I and me
I asked me
why is it so difficult for you to write it
Me said
therapists have theories attached to it
affected by all that makes you
brown, unrich, youth, immigrant, inmate
most important of all a woman
I said   Yes! I know that
but don't you see the beauty in all that
only the seasonable can be seasoned
Me looked at I   from front page to youth page and
towards the blank   middle and end page
I opened her bookish flashback   out of which flowed
smile, cheer, zeal, art, lovesome energy of
youth full of dreams and passion and quest
Me observed I through her tinted colored glasses

then said   remember   in a matter of moments
everything that bloomed and was loved
got stolen and stored   not on uneven scale but
within the dark folds of blindfold
tied on the eyes of the lady of justice.
What I saw was
fragile but strong wheatish body, brown eyes, jet-black hair
cut short, oval ingenuous face without a forced nose ring
the brine tear in me's eyes
reflected that I was lovely
flesh-wise soul-wise unique
but then why the struggle exists?

For a moment   I and me stopped arguing
they stepped out in the
nose-ear-shaped-ice frigid wind   as they walked
a cloudy window flared   flashing the sun
Together they stood there in awe and bliss
breathing in   the rainbow
glowing like a spectrum   coming out of prison

40

I Never Knew

Darlene Dixon

I never knew . . .

> how much I loved my family,
> until they wouldn't accept my calls, or even visit;

> how reassuring a hug could be, until I had to risk confine-
>   ment to enjoy   even one;

> the joy in watching children, until it was years since I
>   heard their laughter.

I never knew . . .

> how priceless my quiet time could be, until it no long ex-
>   isted in my world;

> the warmth of a sofa, until I spent years on cold steel and
>   cement;

> the beauty in a horizon, until all I saw was the razor wire
>   around me.

I never knew . . .

the value of a friend, until I was locked away, afraid to trust
   anyone;

what a privilege to speak my mind, until I was forced to bite
   my tongue;

the enormity of being free,

until I lost it all . . .

      I never knew.

41

Wise Women

Critical Citizenship in a Women's Prison

Tanya Erzen

During the first day of a college history class called Women, Politics, and Citizenship at the Bayview Correctional facility in New York City, the nine women in the class wrote down their definitions of citizenship and politics: "Belonging to a country"; "A person born in the United States, no matter what their ethnic background or cultural beliefs"; "My view of citizenship is closely related to freedom. As a citizen, I would be able to vote, protest, and have the right to practice my religion. I would be a resident not an occupant"; "A place of belonging. A part of a culture or group that wants to gain entry into unfamiliar grounds"; "A forum to enable citizens to have a voice in what goes on in their country."

During the next fourteen weeks, we read the Bill of Rights and the U.S. Patriot Act, articles and primary sources about racial restrictions on legal citizenship, the suffrage and antilynching movements, the Ku Klux Klan, the American Indian Movement, feminism, and civil rights. Throughout, we explored the questions of who is a citizen, what citizenship is, and how people excluded from citizenship have found ways to assert alternate meanings of citizenship through participation in politics and movements. We analyzed theories of racial formation and of legal, cultural, gendered, sexual, and social citizenship, but one question permeated everything we did: What did citizenship mean in a place where my students were not counted as citizens, and in some cases, did not count themselves as citizens?

This chapter looks at how the ideas of citizenship enabled the women at Bayview to speak to the conditions within the prison, at their prison jobs, and to the wider socioeconomic circumstances behind their imprisonment. Scholar and activist Ruthie Gilmore eloquently poses the question, "Who becomes a prisoner, what does a prisoner become?" The process by which the women at the prison related their lives to the material was not merely relational. In many ways, the ideas of citizenship provided a means to see their experiences as fundamentally social and political. Marlene, Wanda, Charlene, Daniele, Iris, Vanessa, Diane, and Ann were taking college courses because they had graduated from every other prison program available to them. They were conversant in the therapeutic language of anger management, parenting, and twelve-step groups, many of which they credited for helping them with severe issues. At the same time, the language of the prison was that of the state. The women spoke of being "stated down" and "drafted." Instead of relying on the redemption narrative central to their dealings with the parole board, in which they had to express remorse for their crimes and prove that they had become someone else, or on the language of the state they heard all around them, they found ways to situate their lives within a different language of citizenship and power, surveillance and vulnerability. To do so, they did not have to repudiate their former selves entirely or even the reasons they had come to be at Bayview. They could shift from the narrative of remorse to a critical voice to social critique and even express forms of personal agency often denied in the space of the prison.

The material in the course become a frame for their lives, just as their lives became a manner of filtering the material. Diane, who had been HIV positive for many years, wrote of her experience, "I have survived by refusing to hide in silence. By fight[ing] those who would divide me into risk groups and manipulate me as a political category." Before she was paroled toward the end of the course, and we discussed racial restrictions on citizenship, Daniele wrote, "I have come to realize that the rhetoric of the government is not about the immediate needs of the incarcerated men and women but about ways to continue to build capital." When we discussed how African American women went from three-fifths to zero as a result of the Thirteenth, Fourteenth, and Fifteenth amendments, Iris wrote,

> As America expanded, women of color continued to bear the double burden of racism and sexism. Long after the civil war ended, black women were politically and socially discriminated against because of their color and also because they were females. Shortly after Northern troops were withdrawn from the south, whites set out to intimidate blacks and to create a segregated society. Blacks began to see the gradual loss of their hard-won liberty. Various laws were enacted to ensure that blacks, "kept their places."

At the end of the paper, she concluded, "Being able to obtain a college education while in prison is similar to emancipation."

However, the class provided only one kind of knowledge; the women had already taken other classes, read voraciously, and had their own sets of knowledge and expertise that they brought to bear critically on the material we read and talked about. The single window in the sixth-floor classroom at Bayview faced out toward lower Manhattan and beyond to the growing skyline of Jersey City. The most visible landmark was the Statue of Liberty. "You can see the Statue of Liberty," said Vanessa, who used to live in Jersey City. "Thanks a lot," replied Charlene sarcastically. "Actually," Vanessa mused as she continued to stare, "the statue of liberty is modeled after a black woman, didn't you know that history?" At one point during the semester, Iris, a student who had taken college courses at another prison, had an altercation with a correctional officer over contraband. After exchanging heated words, he told her "You're an inmate." She responded, "No, I'm a woman. I know who I am." After we discussed the origins of the idea of the Panopticon one week, the next week they told of using the word at the job and with each other as a language only they could understand. Diane exclaimed, "Even in the mess hall, I'm being panopticoned." When they read articles about the history of sweatshops, they spoke of their work at the Department of Motor Vehicles, where they answered phones. Their sense of constant surveillance, from the limitations on bathroom breaks to monitoring of their calls, resonated with their sense of the lives of the women in Jamaica and Mexico in the sweatshop articles.

The college program and the class itself created a sense of affiliation and community in which students were linked to each other, to historical figures and movements, and to the world outside Bayview. The students commented that their experience of incarceration forced them to focus on the self—for safety, survival, and processing their circumstances—but the class enabled them to "forget myself for awhile and think about someone like Leonard Peltier," as Marlene explained. After watching the film *Incident at Oglala,* Marlene urged the students to write letters advocating the release of Leonard Peltier. They felt they could imaginatively connect to him, and in doing so, could move beyond their own circumstances to see the injustice of his.

Immersion in a community of scholars also altered their relationships to other women at Bayview. The college program of which this class was part emerged from the efforts of four women in the class, who came together and formed a prospective student government. Daniele had written, "The women of Bayview Correctional Facility (which we have dubbed the forgotten prison) have come together as a unit, a sisterhood, to implement a student government, where strategies and ideas will be and have been discussed." The college program, first called Wise-Women and later the Learning Center for Women in Prison, began as a collaborative project between the student government, a group of academics, and a member of the prison advisory board. As part of the student government board, the women at Bayview took part in an intensive seminar in leadership training, and the student board determined the program objectives, decided what courses to provide, and provided a mechanism for the students to expand the program and interest other women in the facility, especially those in the GED classes. Toward the end of the class, we conducted joint classes with the GED students so they could see what a college class entailed. The members of the student board were clear from the onset that they did not want to take the program for granted or assume its permanence. Thus, they collectively donated $1,500 to the project for books and materials, using their prison pay, which averaged $2.50 per day.

The goal of the college program is "to create opportunities for women prisoners in New York City to successfully reenter the community by offering a rigorous college curriculum and transitional academic counseling." The college preparatory program, only recently accredited by Bard, would offer sixteen nonmatriculated college coursework credits. When I taught Women, Politics, and Citizenship, the program was still searching for accreditation, but students took it and other classes even though they would not receive official credit. Without accreditation, students will not be eligible for a degree through the program. However, they may formally fulfill the application and admissions requirements of the sponsoring university, or transfer credits to another degree-granting program upon release from incarceration. Most of the women at Bayview, a medium-security facility, have come from maximum-security facilities like Bedford Hills, which has a college program in place, or Albion, which does not. They are all eligible for parole, and all of them will eventually be released, but the process can take up to three years. Students who complete the program gain skills and resources that could enable them to organize and facilitate change when they reenter their communities.

Education, especially college education, in the space of the prison at this moment in history is a radical and highly fraught endeavor. In an article by incarcerated women, the coauthors wrote, "Rehabilitation looks like radical language now that punishment is the explicit project of incarceration." This article also seeks to envision prisons as college campuses, and explores how that development might transform the idea of the university and that of the prison. It also asks what it means to have the public imagine prisoners as college students. The class and program, while cognizant of the constraints of teaching in a correctional facility, treated the course with the academic rigor of any other college course. Students studied together and complained about reading and exams, but they were acutely vocal about and conscious of wanting to be treated as college students would. In one of the most successful parts of the class, students at Barnard College who were taking the same class came in during the week to participate in discussion sections. At the end of the class, the students, inspired by the ten-point platform of the Black Panthers, created their own set of ten "Women's Commandments," which they brought into class. In doing so, they were able to mark the ways in which their conceptions of citizenship had changed since they started the class and find ways to lay claim to citizenship despite the fact that the prison denies it to them.

WOMEN'S COMMANDMENTS

1. Equal pay for equal work.
2. Free health care for children up to the age of eighteen.
3. Free lunches for children up to the age of eighteen.

4. Freedom for women to express their sexuality.
5. Equal representation in the media.
6. Protection of women's reproductive rights, right of abortion, right to insurance-covered birth control, and right to responsible sexual choices.
7. State-provided childcare for children under thirteen.
8. State-funded shelters for domestic violence victims. Serious policing of and more severe penalties for violations of restraining protection orders.
9. Free health care, prescription drugs, and transportation for elderly single women.
10. Education and community activities that empower women to be self-sufficient and self-satisfied.

42

Women of Wisdom

An Alternative Community of Faith

Suzanne Jabro and Kelly Kester-Smith

Once a month, a group of women living at the California Institution for Women in Corona, California, and women from the community "outside" gather to breathe in a sense of peace and sisterhood and breathe out the burdens that wear heavy on the heart. Some of the women in the circle are serving lengthy sentences—most of them are lifers. Some of the women in the circle travel from their homes and busy lives to take an equal part in forming an unlikely community. The sum of the group transcends life circumstances to reach a space, and a place, far beyond the walls that separate women in prison from their sisters in the community.

> The Spirit is powerfully present to us when we gather. Everyone feels the connection, inspiration. There is no preparation, only presence. There is no homework, only inspiration. There is no black-brown-white, just people. There is no preferential seating between "insiders" or "outsiders," just women joined in an unbroken circle. No Catholic-Protestant-Muslim-Jewish–Native American, just women of faith drawing upon their common wellspring as women.
>
> *Suzanne*

The Women of Wisdom circle began gathering in 2004. Several women from the "outside" and a small group of women from the "inside" were invited for a conversation around the following questions: What difference would it make if a group of women joined together from the inside/outside and drew upon their common feminine Spirit-Wisdom? What difference would it make to each of us, to all of us?

> For me the circle means togetherness, confidence, empowerment, and safety. The circle is symbolic of our interdependence—our connectedness and dependency.
>
> *Romarilyn*

Initially the group seemed to be intrigued, but resistance quickly moved in. The women inside wanted to know what the group was going to do. The response was simple: we don't know yet. We are going to sit together and let Spirit-Wisdom lead us. The women inside then explained why this concept was unsettling. When you are incarcerated, someone tells you everything that you are going to do every minute of the day. You are told when to wake up and when to eat. When it's OK to visit and when it's not. The women inside insisted that they had to know what they were doing and that someone was supposed to tell them. The women from outside replied that this experiment wasn't about one group leading and one group following but about all of the women joining in circle to *set the direction together*, with each woman listening and discerning the nudging of Spirit of Wisdom. While wary, the women inside agreed to at least try the approach of waiting, listening, and seeing.

It is spiritual, inspirational, a safe place to speak the truth.

Connie

A second thread of resistance wove itself into the conversation. Who would be in the circle? When the women outside explained that they wanted the circle to be open to anyone, the women inside expressed yet another reality of life in prison: in prison, you do not trust each other, and you don't really even know one another. This issue, above all, threatened the forward movement of the concept.

I find that my ability to exercise compassion has increased through this positive exposure. My heart goes out more readily to the peers I have shared sacred moments with, and when I see the "outside" women again, my heart leaps to greet them.

Vonda

Ultimately, the women in the group collectively determined that they would form a core group, and as requests for involvement emerged, the group would decide how and if to expand. The women inside hesitantly agreed to give the group a try. The group that started with four women on the outside and eight women on the inside has grown into eight women on the outside and sixty women on the inside.

The circle of women is very empowering to me. I see the faces of my sisters and I see them as the Amazon women they are. This is a special place where there are no bars, just the power of our femininity.

Tania

The group met for months and months without a name or prepared agenda. One evening, the group decided that the time had come to name the circle. Participants broke into small circles and began discerning through images. The images that surfaced were circle, women, conversation, spirit, inside, outside, feminine, spirituality. One group enthusiastically reported to the whole that they had the name. "We are Women of Wisdom," they shouted out. One woman gasped from across the room, "WOW!" Another said, "Yes, we are Women of Wisdom, WOW." It was done. It was unanimous. We knew who we were.

> Not being defined as an inmate but being recognized as a woman whose life experience, while greatly different than half the group, gives me the right to have a voice and valuable insights to share. WOW is an affirmation of the female spirit to survive and remain compassionate.
>
> *Leslie*

As the group grew and began to dream together, the women decided that a couple of hours once a month wasn't enough time to go as deep as they needed to go together. Thus, they planned a full-day retreat. And not just any retreat. A retreat that fed the spirit, mind, and body. The WOW group received special permission to bring in food, flowers, art supplies, and music—everything needed to nourish the spirit and celebrate at the table, to create an environment in which the feminine could thrive and find solace.

Women on the inside had the task of creating a ritual and designing a sacred space. Women on the outside were to take care of food and other care details. When the food committee asked the women inside for menu ideas, the women asked for the following: Starbucks coffee and Krispy Kreme donuts. They had all heard about these things but had never experienced them, because the products had entered the popular culture after these women were incarcerated.

The mantra for the day was, "This is my first retreat." The women inside outdid themselves by removing all of the chapel furniture and replacing it with sheets on the floor and pillows gathered from their cells. They placed a bouquet of flowers in the middle of the room surrounded by streaming ribbons. The opening song was a rousing Beatles tune, and everyone danced around the circle. Every woman was partnered with another, with each partner holding one end of a ribbon, and the pairs danced around each other until the whole room was woven together in a web of sisterhood and joy. In the corners of the room were stations: one for facials, one for foot massages. Women practitioners from the inside offered their services for a day in order to provide healing touch. Before breaking for lunch, a woman who had brought gourmet sandwiches told everyone that the caterer who prepared the meal had asked her to tell the women that the food had been prepared with great love. The women cried to think that someone who did not even know them was thinking of them. The retreat day, like every other WOW gathering, ended with a silent circle—women standing arm in arm embracing the energy that flowed from and between them; women possessing the courage to be their most authentic selves.

> Through WOW, I get the opportunity to talk to other wise women, to share and gain insight and to be the women I want to become.
>
> *Susan*

The retreat has become an annual event. It is a sacred time to look forward to and a time to savor for months in memory. The women inside have said that during the retreat, they feel that the prison walls do not exist. The day takes them over the wall. It is a day of freedom.

> In your visions, in your dreams, you can leave your baggage behind. Once I discovered that I was worthy of forgiveness, and I was able to forgive myself, and knowing that God forgave me, this opened up everything for me to accept myself and accept God's love. I'm from a very religious family. I distinguish religion from spirituality because I found spirituality here in this prison.
>
> *Sandra*

> The incredible circle of women is my faith community. I am at home here; my spirit feels connected; my soul is nourished; my energy births new life, light and love. This is a circle with no preferential seating. The presence of Wisdom is tangible, creating insight and inspiring us to experience the truth: WE ARE ONE.
>
> *Suzanne*

Women of Wisdom was one of eleven California faith communities featured in Golden States of Grace: Prayers of the Disinherited, an exhibit that premiered at the Fullerton Museum Center in 2006 and then traveled around the United States. Featuring photographs and text by artist Rick Nahmias, the exhibit documents alternative forms of spiritual expression practiced by diverse groups in California. It aims to give image and voice to groups of people who, because of the world, society, or themselves, have become marginalized. Nahmias says of the exhibit:

> I cast a wide net to show the diversity of communities worshipping outside the secure confines of middle class America. This ultimately included a range that runs from the elderly to the executable. In the years since I began this work, it has felt as if our world has drawn even starker divisions between "us" and "them." National and international events demonstrate we live in a fundamentally faith-based society with a greater intolerance for those not clearly embracing narrowly defined codes to live and worship by. Ultimately this is a study of otherness—the otherness out there, the otherness within each of us, the otherness which begs us to bind together as human beings to celebrate, contemplate, and find meaning in our lives.

The photographs in the exhibit captured the grace, strength, and beauty of the women who participate in WOW. Unfortunately, only women on the outside were able to attend the opening night to see for themselves the spirit of the group shining through the life-size photographs.

The gatherings of the Women of Wisdom have an essentially feminine numinous quality. They are a source of hope that lights up one's heart with anticipation, appreciation, self-love, and love of others . . . even when life holds pain or regrets that many of us can't imagine. They are a source of bliss, telling every woman's story and making it glow with purpose and strength. What else can you say but WOW?

43

Chain of Command

Kinnari Jivani

Do you know how it feels
to live in a big cigarette?
I do
'cause i am trapped in one
hand rolled
thick
rusted
chewed
filthy
groomed cancer

Clinching inside are
loud tobacco flakes
their tongue roll
good morning ugly hoe,
my bitch, your bitch,
Mm babies' daddy's bitch,
can't wait to fuck that nigger,
shit, let's get high,
u do u, i do i,
you m. . . . f. . . . .get at me salty.
All nonsense
will get-them-no-where talk

Weary inside are
quiet tobacco flakes
hankering to be green leaves again
we sob our choky lungs
murmur our sigh
something must be done
i get voted to vocalize

so i raise objection to gray-black clouds
they blow smoke back at me
smoke dance amuse them
they are friends with match-seller
to keep their salaries

i raise objection to acting gods
they offer to lock me up
in a collar cigar
cold cloudy
where flakes have been
stripped strapped on bed
I raise object to small gods
to them we are all tobacco
one rusty-blue print
difference doesn't matter
as long as the cigarette is filled
they are friends with tobacconist
keep their pockets full

i raise object to big gods
our tragedy entertain them
They talk roller-coaster
from seed plant branch leaf to seed
no mention of leaves to tobacco
or tobacco to health

Do you know how it feels
to live in a big cigarette?
i do
'cause i am trapped in one
hand rolled
thick

rusted
chewed
filthy
groomed cancer

I sit and ponder over All Mighty God
fly kite summoning rescue
and
wait
until. . . . .

PART FIVE

Struggling for Health Care

while Nancy finished serving her time Baby is 2 Day old

Nancy Bunke - an inmate @ Bedford Hills corrections facility - gave birth while serving time for Drug charges -The baby was released to a conven

A TRAGIC FACT OF LIFE FOR ALL AMERICANS is that basic health care is available in this rich country for consumer purchase, not as a human right. Because prisoners have little or no status as consumers, they have scant access to decent health care. Many incarcerated persons in this country have lost their freedom and also their health. (Because incarcerated persons are typically poor when they enter jail and prison, many of them already have health problems when they begin their sentences.)

The essays, reports, stories, and fact sheets in this section chronicle the varieties of deteriorating health that women prisoners suffer and also the various degradations of living locked up and ill. Johanna Hoffman of Justice Now describes three consequences of deficient health care in California prisons and elsewhere: insufficient treatment and containment of the epidemic of hepatitis C, insufficient and ineffective use of Pap smears to detect cervical cancer, and the rising number of incarcerated persons with broken and irreparable health. The excerpt from a larger piece by Nancy Stoller captures the most hideous consequence of terrible health care in prison: death. Rachel Roth reveals that prison authorities frequently suspend the constitutionally protected right to privacy of pregnant prisoners, denying or granting them reproductive autonomy according to the whim or the predilections of current prison authorities.

This section, like the others in this book, makes space for the important voices of incarcerated women, most strikingly here in the form of a story, "A Dazzling Tale

Moya and her two-day-old baby, T.J., 2001. Bedford Hills Correction Facility, New York. Photograph by Brenda Ann Kenneally

of Two Teeth," in which Tracy Lynn Hardin, incarcerated in Iowa, tells the absur-
dist saga of dental misery inside.

The chapters in this section show that incarcerated women are constructing and
pursuing goals such as claiming the right to decent health care, learning how to speak
for themselves, and collaborating with allies to help meet the medical needs of the
community. Sheila Enders writes about her work developing the language and tools
that incarcerated women need to speak on their own behalf about their medical
needs. Johanna Hoffman articulates the Justice Now commitment to nurturing self-
advocacy among women with medical needs. Various materials in this section are
models of information dissemination and strategic markers in the effort to draw
the attention of insiders, allies, and authorities. In this section, we encounter two
health care bills of rights: first, a manifesto about the elements of health care that
pregnant incarcerated women need and deserve; second, a demand by incarcerated
girls for safety, dignified services, and also the most basic resources, such as wholesome food. The section ends with a trio of "fact sheets" detailing some of the most
horrible health challenges that plague incarcerated women—and that define the
gruesome distance between American ideals and American practices in this domain.

44

Hep C, Pap Smears, and Basic Care

Justice Now and the Right to Family

Johanna Hoffman

In 2005, Stacy Stevens (a pseudonym), a thirty-year-old mother of two young children, was sentenced to two years in state prison on a marijuana-related charge. After moving her from one institution to another, prison officials noticed signs of mental illness, which prompted them to transfer Stacy from a rehabilitation facility to the California Institution for Women (CIW). There, she was supposed to receive mental-health services while serving her prison term. Stacy did not receive these services. Instead, doctors responded to her clear expressions of suicidal intent by giving her sleeping medication and leaving her alone in a cell. Within days, Stacy attempted suicide by hanging, using readily available materials. She survived, but suffered significant brain damage and is currently in a permanent vegetative state. Not only will Stacy be deprived of the opportunity to raise her children, but these young children, who originally expected to experience a short-term absence from Stacy, will never know what it's like to be nurtured and cared for by their mother.

INTRODUCTION

Modeled after a military structure that assumes its subjects are healthy young men, the prison system is fundamentally ill equipped to meet the needs of women. Every woman enters the prison with gender-specific health concerns, and many enter with already compromised health. Uniquely affected by imprisonment, many women establish health problems or experience exacerbations of preexisting conditions. Many suffer harm to their reproductive capacity through a variety of violent and negligent medical practices, such as forced and unnecessary hysterectomies. Many die prematurely because medical staffs in prisons do not provide timely test results for serious illnesses.

228228228882288228228228228

88882282288222288228882288228

22822882282288228228228

The response of the California Department of Corrections and Rehabilitation (CDCR) to the specific needs of women is to furnish more beds in "gender-responsive prisons." In the 2006 legislative session, the CDCR's Gender Responsive Strategies Commission recommended the construction of forty-five hundred of these beds, thus expanding the capacity of the women's prison system by 40 percent in two years. This "remedy" channels resources into locking up more women and diverts resources from dismantling the system that is, itself, deadly to the health and families of its victims.[1]

Justice Now is a human rights organization working with people in women's prisons to end violence inflicted by the prison-industrial complex against individuals and families.[2] In this essay, I discuss the ways in which prison practices violate prisoners' basic rights by denying reproductive and other health care.[3] I also describe the approaches that Justice Now has adopted to meet the immediate needs of people in prison, especially the need to advocate for themselves.

In 2004, Judge Thelton Henderson, a Federal District Court judge, stated that the current system for delivering medical care in California prisons is "broken beyond repair."[4] Justice Now agrees, but our organization goes further, suggesting that the entire prison system is a failure. Inadequate health care is just one manifestation—albeit a pervasive and deadly one—of this failed system. This manifestation produces, and is sustained by, the destruction of prisoners' right to family. Justice Now has worked to address—among other grave violences of the prison system—three health care crises that are inextricably bound to the denial of the human right of family to imprisoned persons: the prevalence and inadequate treatment of hepatitis C, prison procedures for Pap smear examinations, and the permanent physical and/or mental incapacitation of the incarcerated that results from a broken health care system.

Justice Now and the Human Right to Family

The population of people in women's prisons has grown over the past two decades, causing more children to undergo forced separation from their mothers. Currently, 2.4 million American children have a mother or father in jail or prison.

Because poor people and people of color are targeted by police and locked up more often than are white people and people with higher incomes, children in poor communities and communities of color disproportionately suffer the loss of parents, role models, and support networks. In addition, all fifty U.S. states have laws permitting the termination of parental rights of parents who are imprisoned, causing permanent separation of families.

Most prisons in California are in rural areas, far from children and families. The distance makes contact with children and families difficult while a parent is in prison. The high cost of telephone calls from prisons makes regular communication difficult, impeding parents' and other family members' ability to forge family bonds once they are released. The destruction of the family through mass imprisonment is a human rights violation that mainstream media have ignored for decades. Now, more than ever, with an expanding number of people being sent to women's prisons for longer periods of time, we need to highlight this violation so that we may begin to eliminate it.

An understanding of human rights law is vital in examining the harm done to people in women's prisons, particularly with respect to violations of the right to family. Modern human rights law began in 1948 when members of the United Nations signed the Universal Declaration of Human Rights. This document recognized that dignity and equal and inalienable access to rights for all people is the foundation of justice, freedom, and peace. In addition to being the foundation document for all human rights, the declaration is an authoritative guide for countries' behavior. However, this declaration is not currently legally binding.

International human rights laws often offer greater protection for people in general, and prisoners in particular, than do current U.S. laws. Many international covenants recognize rights to make decisions about one's body, especially decisions relating to family and reproduction.

The CDCR violates this human right to family in many ways, and the prison health care system is a significant one. When the CDCR fails to care adequately for people in its custody, it limits, harms, or destroys their reproductive health and capacity both during and after the period of incarceration. For example, the lack of a systemwide procedure for providing examination results and follow-up care causes people in prison to live for years unaware of serious medical conditions, which harms not only the people living with the illness but also those close to them. For people living with contagious conditions, the disease may spread because they are unaware of the need to take precautions. Further, serious health problems, including loss of reproductive capacity, permanent incapacitation, or death, may result. When the prison health care system harms or actively destroys the reproductive capacity of those for whom it is responsible, it directly violates the right to family.

Because U.S. law limits advocacy options for adequate medical treatment for people in prison, a different framework is required. International human rights law provides this alternative framework by focusing on the intersection of racism, sexism, and classism that—especially within the prison—denies the right to bodily integrity and health, often impairing the possibility of conception and birth as well as familial connections and relationships.

Although the right to family is a relatively undeveloped area of law, it is recognized in Article 23 of the International Covenant on Civil and Political Rights, which the United States has ratified. Article 23 states, "The family is the natural and fundamental group unit of society and is entitled to protection by society and the State." By failing to recognize the importance of the right to family as part of women's rights, officials and medical personnel often ignore reproductive rights both within and outside the prison setting. Further, as reproductive rights are being eroded more broadly in the United States, international human rights may become the only protection for women and their families.

Some of the most powerful human rights protections for women are found in the Convention on the Elimination of All Forms of Discrimination against Women (CEDAW). The United States has not ratified CEDAW, leaving women in the United States with little protection against sex-based discrimination. This lack of protection combined with CDCR's inadequate medical care leave people in California's women's prisons without basic rights to determine when, how, and if to have a family.

CEDAW recognizes the rights of women to "decide freely and responsibly the number and spacing of their children and to have access to this information, education and means to enable them to exercise these rights." People in women's prisons are often unable to obtain abortions, cannot access preventive care for cervical cancer, and suffer unique harm if they carry the hepatitis C virus (HCV) or become incapacitated. As a result of California's failed system for delivering medical care and lengthy prison sentences, many women are locked up during their reproductive years or are unable to birth children upon their release.

The prisoner-rights movement has not adequately addressed the impact of prisons and policing on families and communities of color nor concerns specific to people in women's prisons, especially issues of reproductive capacity and freedom. The mainstream women's reproductive-rights movement has focused narrowly on access to abortion, ignoring broader issues of reproductive justice. Although the human rights movement offers a framework for understanding the nature of violations stemming from inadequate health care, it has lacked the grassroots structure to allow the people who suffer the abuses to participate in documenting human rights abuses. This exclusion of their voice replicates an elitism that often supports the very systems of oppression it challenges.

Justice Now responds to this situation by exposing violations of the right to family. First, we put people in women's prisons in the forefront of the dialogue by using participatory documentation. Second, we build coalitions committed to progressive human rights work and create a replicable model of participatory human rights documentation. Finally, we promote organizing and leadership among people in women's prisons.

HCV-POSITIVE PEOPLE IN PRISON

I am frightened and I will explain why. On November 6, 2003, I had a needle puncture biopsy—the surgeon said I had stage II fibrosis. Supposedly, the biopsy was to enable me to begin treatment. I have asked for treatment and at my last telemed appointment, Dr. James told me I was "not sick enough" to get the treatment. For three weeks now I have been experiencing a swollen abdomen in the liver area, plus very severe pain. It hurts badly to bend, or even sit down. It is distended a lot. I wrote to the telemed nurse and asked to see a doctor. I included a copayment but I have had no reply.[5] I lost my husband to Hep C and I watched him die in steps. I have children and grandchildren I want to see, and I don't get out until 2010.

The death rate for people with the hepatitis C virus, currently estimated at eight thousand to ten thousand deaths a year, is expected to triple in the next two decades. CDCR maintains inadequate policies and procedures for screening and detection, which means that many cases of HCV go undiagnosed. This inattention is particularly damaging for the population of high-risk people in women's prisons because, without adequate practices and information, the infection spreads.

Through interviews with people locked up at the Valley State Prison for Women (VSPW) and the Central California Women's Facility (CCWF), Justice Now has identified lack of testing, lack of treatment, and grossly negligent medical care as significant problems for HCV-positive people.

CDCR has no consistent and effective testing policy for HCV. In some cases, people in prison are tested without giving their informed consent; others are required to pay a five dollar copayment for the test, and many never receive results. Upon incarceration in a California prison, every person is given a blood test. Some people in prison suspect that they were tested for HCV at this time—but without informed consent and without access to test results. Often, people in prison learn of their HCV-positive status years after detection as a result of an unrelated review of their medical file. Failing to inform patients of test results falls below the community standard of care and violates the state's duty to prevent, treat, and control epidemic diseases. These practices constitute a violation of the right to health care.

Even among people aware of their HCV-positive status, obtaining and maintaining treatment while in prison is almost impossible. For those who obtain treatment, side effects are often debilitating but ignored by the medical staff. Frequently, under these circumstances, the patient abandons treatment, seriously compromising both her present condition and her future treatment options. Institutions also maintain inconsistent policies and procedures in the handling of prescriptions, often resulting in delays of weeks or months between refills. Interviewees reported that when they found out about their HCV-positive status, they were given very little information or educational materials about the disease, and they were rarely informed of the risks associated with HIV-HCV co-infections. Without information, in a context in which medical personnel and procedures are untrustworthy and in which obtaining any care is a struggle, many people in women's prisons refuse treatment while they are locked up.

Without procedures for mandatory and confidential testing and with no informed consent for such testing, no procedures for informing patients of test results, and a general lack of treatment and education for HCV-positive patients, the

California women's prisons violate the right to family, often causing unnecessary health complications and sometimes premature death. Further, people in women's prisons are often unable to maintain family relationships while inside or are unable to reunify with family upon release because of the deterioration of their health or their premature death while in prison.

THE PAP-SMEAR EXPERIENCE FOR PEOPLE IN PRISON

I don't believe that my experience was unique, I have talked to several women who have complained about the way that their exams were done, who did them, just the issue in general. Women have talked about leaving the table bleeding because they have been treated so roughly; women who had abnormal results from Pap smears and other examinations aren't treated properly. And so their concern is, "Am I going to die from cervical cancer?"

People in women's prisons are at a high risk for cervical cancer because they are often exposed to multiple risk factors such as human papillomavirus, sex at an early age, multiple sex partners, sex with uncircumcised males, smoking, human immunodeficiency virus (HIV), chlamydia infection, diets low in fruits and vegetables, excess body weight, oral contraceptives, multiple pregnancies, low socioeconomic status, use of diethylkstillbesterol, and family histories of health problems.

Also, social and psychological factors affect a woman's decision to get a Pap smear, such as childhood sexual abuse and insufficient information about cervical cancer risks and the purpose of this test, which is the primary preventive measure for detecting and identifying abnormal cervical cells. CDCR has yet to meet the American Medical Association and other recognized standards of care or to provide any policies or procedures to ensure provision of this essential preventive care.

In the absence of proper Pap-smear testing, many people in women's prisons are denied early detection of one of the factors leading to the effective treatment of cervical cancer. Mandatory sentencing minimums and three-strikes laws continue to expand the population serving lengthy prison sentences, including life terms. Therefore, an individual may go years, decades, or her entire adult life without proper medical treatment or preventive care. Too often, this absence of care results in loss of reproductive capacity.

Participants in the Justice Now's assessment project reported that tests are provided in small, unclean rooms, without privacy, and that staff often inflict pain while administering the tests. One woman stated, "[The physician] was cramming the speculum in like a Roto Rooter." Many participants reported feeling sexually abused or violated during their Pap-smear examination. Many connected these feelings to previous histories of sexual or physical abuse. Participants voiced a preference for female care providers, who they believed would be more compassionate and understanding than male personnel.

Participants reported that a number of the physicians offered no explanation of the examination, the results, or follow-up care, including prescription drugs. When participants asked questions about these matters, physicians were not receptive.

As a result of these barriers, many people locked up at CCWF avoid or refuse subsequent treatment by prison medical providers. One participant, terrified by her experience with a physician, said, "I would refuse another Pap by him. I just couldn't do it, couldn't go through that again." Others said they made excuses, including menstruation, to avoid an examination.

Many people in women's prisons are aware of the potential health risks of refusing medical appointments but believe that this risk is outweighed by the value of avoiding violation by physicians and maintaining their integrity, right to privacy, and personal autonomy. In maintaining this system, the CDCR blatantly violates the patients' right to family.

INCAPACITATED PEOPLE IN PRISON

On February 03, 2001, while locked up at Centinela State Prison, Michael Smith (pseudonym) was attacked by another prisoner using a knife. As a result of this attack, Mr. Smith sustained a neck injury, rendering him instantly quadriplegic. Thereafter, he was transferred from a community hospital to several prisons, until he was transferred to the California Institution for Men on May 19, 2001. To date, Mr. Smith is only able to move his head minimally. He cannot move his arms or legs, is incontinent, his breathing is compromised, and he has suffered extensive weight loss, muscle atrophy and bone loss. Mr. Smith's injury is so devastating that he cannot benefit from rehabilitation and has no opportunity for physical improvement, yet he remains in the custody of CDCR, serving the remainder of his prison term.

As of April 2005, CDCR prisons contained over two dozen permanently incapacitated people, a population with urgent and immediate needs unaddressed by the system. Unable to advocate for themselves and stuck within a prison facility where medical care is ineffective and inadequate, these people are especially vulnerable to neglect and suffer more acutely from the substandard care than do many other people in prison.

Recent efforts to draw attention to medically incapacitated and terminally ill prisoners have been unsuccessful. Justice Now recently cosponsored a bill to expand the class of people in prison eligible for early release due to medical incapacitation and terminal illness, but Governor Schwarzenegger vetoed the bill, even though people in this category pose no threat to the public.

In spring 2006, the CDCR approached Justice Now, reporting that it was holding approximately thirteen medically incapacitated people in prison past their release dates because the department had been unable to find transitional living or medical facilities for them. CDCR was willing, under these circumstances, to violate the liberty, rights, and freedom of these people. Justice Now offered to help the CDCR find placements for and gain the release of all medically incapacitated people, but so far, the CDCR has provided information about only one incapacitated person in this situation.

In October 2007, California AB 1643—which Justice Now worked for—was signed into law. This legislation expedites the release of the terminally ill and medically incapacitated.[6]

The Imperative for Individual and Community Advocacy

I would also like to see more empowerment for the women inside. It would be nice to see prisoner self-advocacy that doesn't equate to having conflict with one's doctor or being confrontational, but by gaining power through negotiation.

Despite the obstacles, people locked up in women's prisons have formed strategies for individual and community advocacy. Interviewees at CCWF and VSPW said that they rely on peer health educators and members of the Women's Advisory Council, not on the prison health care system, for support in advocating for better health care. Many participate in informal peer education by teaching one another how best to navigate the health care system at CCWF. They also reported that individual advocacy and peer education are empowering for people in prison.

Justice Now provides educational materials about numerous concerns to people in women's prisons. Through this work, we provide resources to train and educate one another, thereby empowering people in prison to advocate for themselves and one another. In response to this work, people locked up in CCWF and VSPW have expressed a better understanding and appreciation of their health conditions as well as increased self-confidence when asking medical care providers for specific treatment or when assisting their peers. Given the prison system's pervasive denial of information and care, the empowerment through education and community is indispensable to the survival of imprisoned persons. Promoting an understanding of the rights to health and family as human rights is an essential first step in developing relevant education and building an informed community capable of self-advocacy.

NOTES

1. In October 2007, California AB 76 was signed into law. This legislation requires the CDCR to develop a gender-responsive plan, including a community-based female-offender program for housing female offenders who have committed nonviolent or nonserious offenses together during their term of imprisonment and while participating in a residential after-care program during parole. The text of the law is available at http://info.sen.ca.gov/pub/07-08/bill/asm/ab_0051-0100/ab_76_cfa_20070226_094043_asm_comm.html. I mention this legislation for informational purposes, not to suggest that it represents an unproblematic "victory" or that it reflects the political and philosophical perspective of

our organization. Indeed, Justice Now does not regard "gender-responsive" prisons as solutions to the human rights violations of people in women's prisons.

2. The designation "people in women's prisons" includes many people locked up in women's prisons who are transgendered and gender variant and do not identify as women.

3. The *right to family* is a human rights term that refers to the significance given to the family unit. Human rights law defines the right to family as the right to have children, the right to determine when to have children and how many, and the right to define one's family unit in order to build relationships with one's close relatives.

4. In June 2006, the California prison health care system was placed under federal receivership; www.cprinc.org/about.htm.

5. A copayment is a medical request form that requires a five dollar payment, which is virtually impossible for people in prison to come up with unless they receive financial assistance from outside family or friends. Prisoners generally earn only seven to ten cents an hour at prison jobs. Coming up with the money for a copayment is especially difficult for a lifer prisoner, who is more likely to have lost ties with friends and family who might provide financial support during lengthy sentences.

6. For information on California AB 1643, see www.leginfo.ca.gov/pub/07–08/bill/asm/ab_1501–1550/ab_1539_bill_20070223_introduced.pdf.

45

A Dazzling Tale of Two Teeth

Tracy Lynn Hardin

I have always been a freak about teeth. I guess you could say I'm very obsessive when it comes to the human grill. It might have started when I got my braces off. I had worn them from the time I was ten until I was fifteen years old. Braces are a pain in the ass. They cut up the inside of your mouth and are practically impossible to keep clean. Then they get tightened at least once a month and your mouth hurts so bad you can't eat anything but soup and mushy food. So when I finally got those suckers off, I became unnaturally preoccupied with teeth, and not just my own. I insisted on keeping my teeth white and sparkly clean. My teeth were so straight and perfect back then that even dentists complimented me on them. Of course, this just fed into my fetish even more! I resented the few cavities I had received before I realized how important it is to have good teeth, but I vowed not to get anymore. Believe me, this fetish went way past me; I also made sure to check out my boyfriends' teeth way before any of them ever became my boyfriends.

Don't ask how I ended up in prison; that's only the backdrop of this story. Let me tell you about my teeth! In prison I noticed that a lot of the women had horrid grills. A good majority didn't have any teeth at all. Some only had half of their God-given teeth left. And some had gaps every few teeth; they were usually the fighters who'd been knocked around one too many times and went back for more. Then you had some whose teeth were just rotted clear through like their mamas taught them that toothbrushes were solely for scrubbing the mud off your Air Jordans. There were teeth colored from yellow to brown and even some black. You could always tell the women who smoked crack, because their teeth were awful; some had holes smoked straight through them. Somehow, I ended up in a clique of women that had most all of their teeth. This fact didn't escape my attention and made me all the more proud of my own. We used to joke that no one could befriend or hang out with us unless they had all their teeth and that we'd do a mouth check before we'd even start socializing with anyone. We said it was all in good fun, but like I said before, we all had our teeth.

With this explained, let me get on with my story. The first year I got here I had a lot of problems. One of them was sleeping. I could not sleep at night. I was haunted by too many nightmares. This was very unfortunate for my bunkmate because as I tossed and turned throughout the night, she suffered through it with me. When it got so bad that I started fighting, punching, and flopping like a fish, my roommates finally spoke up. I had to get something to knock me out at night, so I went to "Death Services" and got on some Trazedone. This crap knocked me out cold. It worked for a while, but tended to wear off at around three A.M. When I started hanging off the side of my bed as I fought my nightly aggressors, it was decided I needed a bottom bunk restriction for my own good. So I went back to Death Services. When I told them why I needed a bottom bunk restriction, they looked at me real funny. In not so many words they said that was the dumbest reason they'd every heard of to get a bottom bunk. Bottom bunks were reserved for people with "real" problems, like bad backs, rearranged knees, arthritis, and the really hubulicious-fat-girls who couldn't seem to propel themselves up the ladder. They were not giving me a bottom bunk restriction for having nightmares. And so my nightly pandemonium continued.

Not too long after this, I had a particularly dreadful nightmare. Anytime my ex-husband is in my dreams, it's dreadful. This time he was chasing me down the street. As I tried in vain to escape him, my legs melted into the cement and every time I lifted my foot to run it was like going slo-mo through a street made of already-chewed Doublemint Gum. Just when he was gaining on me, my two little boys suddenly appeared, one on each side. We were holding hands so tightly that it looked as if they were welded together. They kept saying, "Run faster, mama, run faster!" But I couldn't go any faster and I could feel his breath on the back of my neck. I turned around screaming as his fist cracked into my jaw, catapulting me through the air, leaving my children to sink like quicksand into the street. He was on top of me trying to strangle me and I started punching and kicking as hard as I could. Somehow, I got him off me and instantly jumped up into a hard fast run.

This is when it happened . . . slam!! I woke up to the sound of my face hitting the tile. As I fought in my sleep and got up to run from my ex-husband, I dive-bombed from the top bunk landing onto my face. It felt as if my face cracked in half, and I felt my two front teeth break and shatter. My nose was fractured and blood gushed out, down my chest and in rivulets all over the floor. I gasped for breath and then screamed again as the cool air hit the exposed nerves in my two front teeth. It was like an electric shock of pain starting in my mouth and running down my spine.

Everyone was awake now and yelling for the CO [corrections officer]. She came in and frantically called the nurse. It seemed like forever before he got there, and it was just my luck to get the cocky punk nurse. He looked at me with a mixture of resentment and pity, asking what had happened. I driveled out the scenario between sobs. He gave me a huge wad of toilet paper and told me to lean my head back and then he left. A few minutes later, he returned with a big ice pack that had a towel wrapped around it and told me to sit in a chair. He said that the next shift would have to deal with me because he was off in a half-hour. As he left he told me not to go back to sleep because I might choke to death on my own blood. So there I sat bawling like a baby, oozing blood, holding the wrapped ice pack to my face and keeping my mouth shut so no air would hit the nerves of my broken teeth.

Because of this it was hard to breathe at all. My nose was fractured, swollen, and bleeding, and if I tried to breathe through my mouth, it became an electrical hot box.

I stayed that way for about two hours, when I was finally loaded up and taken to the county hospital in Des Moines. They took me to the dental department in handcuffs and chains, and the dentists began to patch up my two front teeth. They said there wasn't anything they could do for my nose, it would have to heal on its own. My teeth were still broke in half, but the dentist packed and sealed them so that the nerves were no longer exposed and even did a root canal on one of them. Then they sent me on my way, saying the prison could rebuild my teeth. This alarmed me. Our medical department was bad enough, but a girl had recently died from an abscessed tooth due to the negligence of our dental department.

When I got back to the prison, I had to walk around for two days with my two front teeth broke in half looking like one of the bimbos popped straight off of *Hee Haw*. I couldn't believe they'd left me with teeth looking like this.

I tried to talk with my lips closed over my teeth, but it didn't work, much to the delight of the other women, who busted up laughing every time they saw my new smile. I didn't find this at all funny. Now I was like all the other riffraff in this place with missing, cracked-up teeth!

I was livid and I was devastated, but even more than that, I was mad! I wanted my teeth back and I wanted them back exactly like they were! All I could think of was that I had told those bastards I needed a bottom bunk restriction!

A couple days later, the dentist called me into his office. He told me he was going to make my teeth look as good as new, and I prayed he was telling the truth. Evidently, there was a new method for restoring broken and chipped teeth called "laser bonding." Basically, they take this goo and glob it onto the broken area. Then they take a brush and shape it into the missing part of your tooth. This was similar in process to the way acrylic nails are made, only they use a laser to superheat the goo until it's hard. This was kinda cool. I suspect it would have been all right had our state dentist been more of an artist. But since he was far from having any artistic abilities, my teeth looked bad.

Needless to say, I had to make do. About a year later, the laser bonding broke off. The dentist put it back on again. About a year after that, the laser bonding chipped.

I couldn't even get into the dentist then. Then about a year or so after that, the laser bonding broke off yet again. It was then repaired yet again.

A week later, it broke for the fourth time. Now, remember, I am very careful with my teeth, so it's not like I was crunching up Jolly Ranchers or anything. This time when I went to the dentist I asked him why my teeth kept falling off. I knew a lot of people who had chipped or broken teeth and they never had these problems; theirs were fixed once and they were done with it. This is when he told me that laser bonding is a "temporary fix," that I really needed veneers or crowns, which were a more permanent solution. I was like, "What??!!" Laser bonding was pawned off on me as the "new technology." Hell, I didn't know any different! I was mad, mad, mad! I asked him how come they didn't do veneers or crowns if that's what they knew I needed? He said, "Because D.O.C. [the Department of Corrections] won't allow it. They're too expensive."

I ask how expensive, and he says it's about seven hundred dollars a tooth. I told him that was too bad! It was their freakin' fault my teeth were broken to begin with! I told him to get permission to fix my teeth right. He said there is no way I was getting crowns or veneers. I was like, "Oh, yeah? Just watch me!"

So I file a grievance. I tell the whole story about how my teeth got broke to begin with and that I had perfect teeth from wearing braces and a headgear for five years. I tell them how my teeth keep breaking off and how I have to be careful about what foods I eat, etc. Then I break it to them that they are responsible and liable for the damage and I want my damn teeth fixed and I'm ready to go to court to make them fix them if that's what it takes! I wait two weeks and the grievance comes back denied, as usual. The grievance officer actually had the nerve to say, "I went over your medical record with the head nurse and it isn't written anywhere that the prison is liable."

Now this really pissed me off! So in my appeal to the warden, I wrote about the same thing, but then at the end I added, "I found it very humorous that the grievance officer would actually go over my record with the head nurse looking for where it was written that the institution was liable. I don't need a nurse to write that they're liable, nor do I need the institution to admit that they are liable! Iowa code says the institution is liable!!"

A week later the grievance comes back from the warden. After two paragraphs of telling me off and telling me how the procedure I need isn't allowed, she ends it saying how she's going to approve the procedure anyway in the interest of the institution (saving money in the long run I guess!). Now, this was totally unexpected! I just wrote a half-assed appeal to her totally expecting it to get denied. I was just trying to get through the grievance procedures so I could get to court, because I knew I'd win my teeth! Maybe she knew, too, because it is totally unlike anything to actually win a grievance. Needless to say I was elated! I was finally getting my teeth! Yee-haw!

So, a couple of weeks later I get called to the dentist's office. He's shocked that I am actually getting some crowns, and he's also happy to be doing them. I guess he considers them some actual and real dentistry or something. So he puts me in the chair and numbs me up real good. Then he stuck me two or three times with the Novocain needle and so I couldn't feel anything. But, man, could I ever hear it! He starts drilling. And drilling . . . on, and on, and on, and on. By now I am getting really nervous and all tensed up! No one has that much tooth to drill in two teeth! You know that feeling you get when you go to the beautician and tell them all you want is a little trim; so they start cutting and you keep seeing these big hunks of hair falling to the floor? And then they keep cutting and cutting? Well, hair grows back!!! Teeth don't!! Just when I'm ready to jump out of the seat screaming . . . he stops. He says, "There we go, we're halfway through."

What? I'm thinking that there is no way we're only halfway through, because there is no way I have that much tooth left. I tell him to give me a mirror 'cuz I want to see my teeth. He says, "Oh, you don't want to see your teeth." I look at him like he's crazy and say, "Yes, I do want to see my teeth!" So he gets the mirror and hands it to me, reminding me that things are only half done. My teeth were two freakin' stumps!!! I couldn't believe it! They'd set me up in retaliation! Just as I started getting tears in my eyes and freaking out, the dentist tells me to calm down. He says he's going to make a mold and send away for two brand new teeth that will be just as pretty as my real ones.

But he pulls out these two teeth from a drawer and says, "Now I'm gonna put these on." And he holds them up, explaining, "They're temporaries. I put glue inside and slip them right over your stumps." And he has the guts to be all smiley.

So he proceeds. No more than two minutes later he says, "See," and hands me the mirror.

I look like a freakin' bucked-tooth beaver!! And to top it off, they're yellow!!

The dentist says, "I need to shave them down a bit."

And I'm thinking, "You're damn right and more than a bit!" I've never had even a close resemblance to Bugs Bunny!

So he gets the drill back out and gets to shaving them down even more.

This time they look more like two yellow teeth instead of two huge yellow Chiclets, and I have no choice but to be all right with it.

As I get up to leave, he tells me my permanent teeth should be back in a week.

A week later, I'm more than glad to hear my name called back to dental. I go in and get into the chair. He takes pliers and pulls the temporaries off. Then he pulls out the two newly made, permanent teeth and shows them off all proudly. He says they just came back from the lab and aren't they pretty. I have to admit, they do look nice. They look like my real teeth did, and they're just as white, too.

So he goes to put them in my mouth, saying, "Open."

And I'm like, "Wait up! Aren't you forgetting the Novocain?"

He says he won't need it.

I say, "Well, I hope you don't think you're bolting those things into my jaw without it!"

This is when he tells me that they aren't being bolted into my jaw. And I ask how it's going to be then. He says he just puts glue on the inside and slips them on my stubs!

I'm like, "Say what??" You mean to tell me you're giving me some permanent slip-covers??!!" Here I go feeling my temper rising again. All this and I'm getting some stupid ol' slipcovers??!!!! Even I know that slipcovers are temporary, but now my teeth are drilled down to stubs! I ask what happens when they fall off.

He says, "They won't."

But I'm not taking this well and I says, "Humor me. What if they do?"

He says that if it happens, we'll take care of it then.

You think I believe that? Hell no! But it's too late now! So I ask, "Exactly how long these are supposed to last?"

He answers calmly, "Oh, about fifteen to twenty years."

I point out that he won't even be around by then. And he tells me that they will have to fix them. And I'm like, "Yeah, just like they did all the other times, huh?"

I hate this place.

46

Women's Rights Don't Stop
at the Jailhouse Door

Rachel Roth

Imprisoned women won an important victory when a state court of appeals ruled against a county sheriff's unwritten policy requiring women to obtain a court order in order to be transported from jail to a clinic for an abortion.

The unconstitutional policy was that of Sheriff Joe Arpaio, the self-proclaimed "toughest sheriff in America," who oversees the jails in Maricopa County, Arizona.

Arpaio boasts of forcing prisoners to work on chain gangs, housing hundreds in tents under the hot Phoenix sun, exposing them on the Internet via his "jail cam," and making men wear pink underwear.

Although Arpaio's persona may be unique, his restrictive abortion policy, unfortunately, is not. Across the country, correctional authorities make it difficult for women to obtain abortions, by forcing them to jump through bureaucratic hoops and refusing to pay for the abortion or even to take them to a clinic.

Arpaio told the *Arizona Daily Sun,* "You lose a lot of rights when you're in jail, whether it's trying to get an abortion or watching R-rated movies or sex movies or smoking or coffee."

But as the judges in this and every other similar case make clear, women don't automatically lose their rights just because they are behind bars.

TWO CONSTITUTIONAL RIGHTS

Two important constitutional rights protect women's decisions about pregnancy and abortion. The right to choose abortion applies to all American women, and the right to adequate medical care is guaranteed specifically to people in prison, as part of the right to be free from cruel and unusual punishment.

Moreover, the U.S. Supreme Court has held that government policies cannot "unduly burden" a woman's exercise of her abortion rights. Forcing women to hire an attorney, appeal to a judge for a court order authorizing the abortion, and risk delays of such magnitude that an abortion becomes impossible constitute precisely such undue burdens.

"Jane Doe," who brought the lawsuit against Sheriff Arpaio, decided early on to have an abortion and paid the clinic's fee in advance, but she still spent eight long weeks trying to get a court order so that the jail would take her to the clinic.

She succeeded only when the American Civil Liberties Union stepped in to represent her. She had an abortion shortly before her fourteenth week of pregnancy, after which she would have needed a more expensive, more complicated procedure.

Women in Houston, St. Louis, and other communities have experienced similar problems and have succeeded in obtaining abortions only because they have had legal assistance.

Although no one knows precisely how often these conflicts occur, advocates say they have been going on for a long time and continue to crop up in different parts of the country.

PLENTY OF LOST FIGHTS

There are also plenty of women who lost their fights, or for whom justice came too late.

One woman in Wilkes-Barre, Pennsylvania, was so far along by the time she prevailed in court that she decided to continue the pregnancy. Another woman in southeastern Louisiana, who could not obtain a court order and whose pregnancy was too advanced by the time she got out of jail, wound up needing an emergency caesarean section to deliver her baby, whom she placed for adoption.

An especially troubling feature of the Maricopa County policy and others around the country is that they are unwritten, subjecting women to the whims of jail and prison authorities and corrections officers. Where medical care has been contracted out to private companies, nongovernmental employees might also be in a position to obstruct women's access.

Although most imprisoned women are poor, jails and prisons deny abortion funding, leaving women to find the money themselves. Grassroots abortion funds, lawyers, and clinics often provide the funding that women need; if they did not, many would find the financial obstacles insurmountable.

UNCERTAIN FUTURES

Women in jail and prison decide to have abortions for the same reasons that women everywhere do: because they have weighed the impact of having a child (or having another child) on their lives. Yet arguably the consequences are even greater for women who face either uncertain futures or the certainty of long prison sentences.

Women who must place their children in foster care risk losing them forever because of federal and state laws that impose strict time limits on foster care and allow no exceptions for parents who are in prison.

In practice, child welfare agencies may not bring children to visit or provide mandated reunification services when a parent is imprisoned because they assume that her parental rights will be terminated.

In addition, pregnancy within prison walls can be extremely stressful. Many women and advocates report that health care is inadequate, and they express concern about high rates of miscarriage and stillbirth. Moreover, even when women bring their pregnancies to term, they may experience degrading treatment.

Karen Shain of San Francisco–based Legal Services for Prisoners with Children testified to the California state legislature about a woman who was hospitalized for the last three weeks of her pregnancy—and was shackled to the bed for every minute of those three weeks. She had to ask every time she wanted to turn over or needed to use the bathroom.

With so much attention focused on the Supreme Court and presidential politics, we can too easily forget that for many women, the right to abortion is already very tenuous. The experiences of imprisoned women remind us of the complex circumstances in which women make reproductive decisions and of the need to ensure access to reproductive health care if women's rights are to be meaningful in practice as well as in theory.

YOUR RIGHT TO PREGNANCY-RELATED HEALTH CARE IN PRISON OR JAIL

FACT: If you are pregnant, being in prison or jail does not mean you lose your right to decide whether to continue your pregnancy or have an abortion.

Your constitutional rights are being violated if:

1. You are told that you must have an abortion that you do not want.
2. You are told that you are not allowed to have an abortion that you do want.
3. You cannot get prenatal or other medical care for your pregnancy.
4. You are forced to pay before you can get the medical care you need.

If you are not getting the medical care you need, you should:

1. Ask yourself if it is just one particular nurse or guard who's giving you a hard time. If it is, then ask other medical staff or officials to help you.

2. Document everything that happens. Put your request for an abortion or other medical care in writing and keep a copy. Also, keep a list of the people you've spoken to or contacted. Be sure to write down what they've told you and the dates and times you've spoken to them.

3. In addition to your request for medical care, you should also file a grievance (an official complaint). If your grievance is denied or rejected, you must file an appeal. *It is very important that you file all appeals that are allowed in your jail's or prison's grievance system. It is also very important that you follow all the rules and deadlines of the grievance system.* These rules and deadlines are usually written in the inmate handbook. If officials will not give you the grievance forms you need, will not let you file or appeal a grievance, or are interfering with your use of the grievance system in any way, you should immediately contact your lawyer or the ACLU (see contact information below).

If you are still told that you must have an abortion even though you don't want to, or you are unable to get an abortion or the prenatal care you want, you should contact your lawyer or the ACLU.

Whether you decide to continue the pregnancy or have an abortion, it is important to act quickly. Early prenatal care is very important for you to have a healthy pregnancy and a healthy baby. If you decide to have an abortion, it is also important to act quickly. While abortions are extremely safe, the costs and risks increase with time. The longer you wait, the harder it may be to find a doctor able to provide the service.

For assistance or more information:

American Civil Liberties Union Reproductive Freedom Project; for contact information, see "Your Right to Pregnancy-Related Health Care in Prison or Jail," available at www.aclu.org/pdfs/prison/reprorightsad20060816.pdf.

National Network of Abortion Funds

Doe v. Arpaio, 150 P.3d 1258 (Ariz. Ct. App. 2007).

R. Roth, "Searching for the State: Who Governs Prisoners' Reproductive Rights?" Special Issue on Gender, Welfare, and States of Punishment (2004), *Social Politics* 11 (3): 411–38. R. Roth, "Do Prisoners Have Abortion Rights?" Special Issue on Prisons (2004), *Feminist Studies* 30 (2): 353–81.

NOTES

This article was originally published in 2008 by Women's ENews, Inc. Grateful acknowledgment is made for permission to reprint.

47

The Death of Luisa Montalvo

Nancy Stoller

It was Thursday, August 28, 1997, in C Hall, cell 347, at the Women's Facility in Hot Springs. Luisa Montalvo, a thirty-six-year-old woman with a five-year sentence, had been vomiting since Tuesday morning. She had been unable to keep anything down, not even water. This day she was too weak to do her usual job of mopping the C Hall floors. She had difficulty pulling herself up to her assigned top bunk, and as a prisoner, she was not allowed to trade her sleeping space even temporarily. Her five cell mates were worried.

On Friday, under a blazing hot sun, she walked over to sick hall at the clinic, which was about three hundred yards from C Hall. At first, Dr. Dao thought she might have the flu, but he decided that she did not because she had no fever. He gave her a two-day "lay-in," excusing her from her housecleaning job. The nurse wrote the lay-in for five days, to extend through Labor Day weekend to Tuesday evening. Another staff member ordered antinausea medicine, a prescription that would not arrive at the "pill line" until three days later. Today, therefore, Luisa went slowly back to her cell with nothing.

Luisa's weeklong struggle to reach the health care that could save her life was almost half over.

In prisons, access to health care requires that prisoners move from their residential units to clinics or other sites of care where they can see a nurse or a physician. The prisoner's movement through the geographical space of the prison is intensively controlled by custody policies, routines, economies, and spur-of-the-moment decisions. These policies and practices, primarily determined by custodial priorities, can create significant delays, roadblocks, and detours on the routes to care.

Attention to the specific nature of a prison as a "place" illuminates the ways in which features such as architecture, acoustics, and larger sociopolitical forces penetrate correctional institutions and create a unique kind of total institution in which the presence of medical care and access to it are continually negotiated. Space/place analyses of prison environments can provide new insights into health care barriers in correctional environments.

An examination of health care providers within a correctional setting exposes such challenges as potential ethical conflicts for health care practitioners in the areas of trust, consent, and confidentiality. Trust is weakened by limits on the ability of practitioners to provide follow-up for necessary care and by correctional demands for information in the interest of close supervision. Consent for treatment, while technically available, is limited by the fact that prisoners have no say in the selection of a care provider. It is either this one or none. And confidentiality is compromised by the presence of guards during clinical interactions, the fact that most prison and jail administrators have the authority to requisition or simply open files, and the common practice of situating medical services and administration under the authority of the corrections department. In addition, the prisoner must navigate and move through the prison to reach health care services, whether they are at a clinic, a nurse's station, a pill line, or an infirmary. Sometimes the care is located outside the prison, requiring additional guards, special vehicles for transport, or even telemedicine if movement is too much of a threat or is an inconvenience to the authorities. Because movement control is an essential feature of prison life, the prisoner who seeks care faces unique obstacles.

In their accounts, incarcerated women who sought health care repeatedly reported lost laboratory results and the need to wait days for urgent prescriptions or months for important appointments. Several were forced to take improperly labeled medication intended for other patients. Many never had the tests or appointments that were ordered.

One way that policy makers sometimes view these errors and inadequate services is to think of them as moments in which the prison health care system breaks down. They then attempt to "fix" the system in order to avoid the breakdowns. Yet the breakdowns are the result of systemic barriers to care. Fixing them requires systemic change. Prisoner narratives are attempts to "explain" the functioning—or nonfunctioning—of the system. In them, the prisoners and their advocates reformulate the construction of the prison and the health care system from a subaltern perspective.

The following extended case of Luisa Montalvo, a woman with HIV, demonstrates the magnitude of the difficulty of locating and receiving the benefits of health services in a prison. At the start of this chapter, we left Luisa waiting for nausea medicine on the Friday evening before Labor Day weekend. Her story is constructed from interviews with her cell mates and from medical records.

The daily high temperatures in Hot Springs that weekend were over one hundred degrees. Friday evening the cooling system in C Hall broke down, blowing hot air into every room. Even after midnight, the unit's temperature was still in the low eighties. The guards unlocked the solid metal cell doors for part of each night to admit a small amount of air to the rooms. Luisa's cell was stiflingly hot.

August 30, 1997

Luisa was so weak over the weekend that she lay resting on the floor most of each day. Later her roommate remembered that she had to sit on a chair to take a shower. Her skin was blotchy, her lips parched. Although her skin felt cool to one of her roommates, she complained that it burned. Despite her requests and those of her five roommates, the correctional staff refused to bring her any meals, saying she could go to the dining hall if she were hungry. A roommate stole some dry toast and punch for her, but she couldn't keep the food down. Luisa continued to grow weaker.

September 1, Labor Day

By Labor Day, Luisa had been without significant food or water for six days and was still experiencing dry heaves. Luisa's roommate Mary went to the pill line at the clinic and spoke to the medical technical assistant (MTA) on duty, telling her that Luisa needed help but was too weak to walk over to the clinic. The MTA responded that even if Montalvo were able to get there, no nurses or doctors were at the clinic because of the holiday, so she should come the next day. That same morning, another roommate, Bettina, told Luisa that the medications ordered for her the previous Friday for her nausea had now arrived at the pill line. However, the MTA could not give them to anyone except Montalvo herself. But how would Luisa get to the pill line, three hundred yards from her unit, in her weakened condition? The MTA had said that there were no wheelchairs available to bring her over. With the physical help and encouragement of Bettina and Mary, Luisa tried to walk to C-Clinic. The three were able to get only about a third of the way before Luisa became so weak that her friends had to half-lift and carry her back to her cell, exhausted and shaking.

Bettina immediately returned to the clinic and told the MTA what had happened. The MTA agreed to bring the medicine to Montalvo. At one o'clock, MTA Green brought Montalvo one small white pill in a paper cup and a prescription bag with twenty small royal blue capsules to be taken twice a day as needed. Green told Montalvo that the white pill would increase her appetite. She should come to the clinic tomorrow. She did not examine Montalvo but did ask Janice, one of Luisa's roommates, to feel her skin. Janice told the MTA that Luisa's skin was cool, almost clammy. Later Janice realized Luisa's skin felt almost waxy. Green told Montalvo to come to pill line at dinner for another white pill.

One of Luisa's roommates asked the correctional officer (CO) in charge of their hall if they could have a Labor Day dinner tray delivered to Montalvo. After joking that Montalvo would not be able to eat it and might end up with a box lunch (i.e., vomit), the guard agreed to call his supervisor for permission. The request was approved, and the food was sent over. However, Luisa was only able to eat a couple of bites of watermelon, which she then did vomit. Neither could she walk to the clinic for another white pill.

September 2

Tuesday morning Luisa's roommates were able to borrow a wheelchair to transport her to morning sick call. She saw another MTA, who told her she was very dehydrated. He told her to come back at 1:00 P.M. She was wheeled back to her room. But at noon, the MTA sent a message to Montalvo, saying that they were too busy to see her. She should come back the next day instead. Meanwhile, Correctional Officer White, who was in charge of C Hall housekeeping, was angry with Montalvo. "You better fucking get it taken care of today or fucking be back to work tomorrow," he threatened. As a porter, Luisa was supposed to be cleaning the halls. If she did not have a new lay-in permission, she would be disciplined for missing work.

At 7:00 P.M., while the cell doors were still open, Luisa begged her roommate Carrie to get the evening guard in charge, CO Brown. "I have to get out of here," she whispered. Carrie came back down the hall saying CO Brown would come when he finished laundry sign-up. At 8:00 P.M., Carrie went to remind Brown about Luisa's plea for help. Brown came down to the room and lectured Montalvo: "You had all day to take care of this [seeing a doctor] . . . There's nothing I can do now," he added. He told her there was no one he could call because she was awake and breathing. A roommate remembered hearing him say she should just lie there. Luisa told him he did not understand: she felt like she was going to die.

Brown agreed to call the MTA on duty but told her not to expect anything. At about 8:15, another CO came to collect Montalvo's lay-in request for another day off from work. The system was still proceeding in a normal manner. A minute or so later, Brown returned and reported that the MTA he called "really pissed me off" because he would not come over to the unit. Brown could see that Luisa was indeed ill, and he was becoming angry. He called his superiors at the C Unit Program Office to ask for help. They phoned central control, which then ordered the prison's Fire Rescue Team to go to the unit immediately.

Twenty minutes later, the in-prison emergency rescue team arrived. The team supervisor was short with Brown, wanting to know why she was told to pick up Montalvo "ASAP." She did not think Montalvo looked that sick. Luisa and her roommates explained her symptoms once again and repeated that no one from medical would help her. Luisa told the rescue team leader she felt the same as she had once before when something was wrong with her lungs and she was in the prison's skilled-nursing facility for a month. (She had had pneumocystis pneumonia, a sign of HIV infection.) Her roommates gave Luisa's pills to the rescue-team supervisor. Luisa walked slowly to the gurney. The rescue team wheeled her down the hall and out the door.

September 3

After an hour at the prison's emergency room, Luisa was transferred by ambulance to the local hospital, where she was diagnosed with acute septicemia and HIV/AIDS (a diagnosis already in her medical record). She passed away at 3 a.m. the next morning. Her roommates discovered her fate only by reading the Daily Movement Sheet on September 4: "Luisa Montalvo W6000 died September 3, 1997."

When we examine the last week of Luisa Montalvo's life, we can see that the obstacles before her were certainly socio-structural (the clinic, which has limited hours, and the rules of distribution of medication), but they were also embedded in a geography (the distance to be crossed on foot or in a wheelchair to get to a doctor) and the social organization of space.

THE SOCIAL ORGANIZATION OF SPACE

The following section examines Luisa's story and considers some of the ways that the organization of space in prison impedes movement and prisoners' strategies to overcome barriers to effective health care.

The physical layout of the prison shaped Luisa's walking with difficulty to the clinic, lying on the floor in exhaustion, ability to get around the living unit, and difficulty traversing the distance to the clinic and emergency room. Space is tightly regulated in the prison, for example, by the requirement that a prisoner pick up her own medications and that she do it at the pill line. In this case, Luisa's inability to cross the distance between her room and the pill line caused dangerous delays in her access to the medicine that could have slowed her dehydration. MTA Green had to decide to bring the meds to Luisa, crossing the distance herself in an act of generosity that was not part of her job description for this shift.

The objects in a prison space—the bed, the keys, the doors, and ducats (movement passes), the wheelchair, the equipment for emergencies, and the pill envelopes—played crucial roles in the story: because Luisa was too weak to climb into her upper bunk, she lay on the floor most of the time. It is forbidden to lie on another inmate's bed. Because all prisoners must be locked in their rooms at night, the door to Luisa's cell was shut most of the time, despite the 100+-degree weather. No wheelchair was officially available to inmates who had not been ruled in need; the stretcher was brought only when the rescue team finally came, when Luisa was only hours from death. Pills arrived at the clinic but not at the cell.

The *economics of space* in Luisa's prison mandated that a prisoner authorize a five dollar copay deduction from her corrections bank account to receive permission to cross the distance from cell to clinic. Also, Luisa was pressured to return to her job cleaning floors. Prisoners who cannot prove their illnesses or disabilities with a "lay-in" (which authorizes the prisoner to stay in her cell and rest while ill) or a "chrono" (for an ongoing problem) must go to work or lose "good days," which reduce their time in prison. The day before her death, Luisa struggled to get her medically approved lay-in for the next day in order to stay out of trouble with her prison employee boss.

Because of the ways that prison space is organized, creating a space in which efforts are made to prevent the prisoner from creating a sense of place that is beyond the planners' intended use, one can see the prison as an "antiplace."

Nevertheless, as long as people are alive and located somewhere, they tend to create a sense of place, whether through unthinking practice or through the creative use of materials, memories, and interactions within their grasp or view. The story of Luisa Montalvo's attempt to get to care can be seen as her attempt to negotiate this antispace where her particularity did not fit the imposed order. Her cell mates brought the comradeship and culture of life they had created within their six-person room to the task of getting Luisa to a doctor and to treatment.

Prisoners often argue that sociostructural barriers are compounded by indifference. They say that the indifference is embedded in the view of prisoners as undeserving, in the staff's alienation from their positions, and in anger toward prisoners who challenge the quality of their care. To understand the treatment of Luisa and other women, we also need to recognize the impact of gender stereotypes that depict women in general as emotional, irrational overseekers of health care who have inadequate knowledge of their own bodies. Racism is also a powerful determinant of prison conditions and staff attitudes. Not only are women of color and especially African American women incarcerated more frequently than white women, the language of prison guards is often tinged with racial insults. The stereotypes of these groups, gender expectations, and cultural differences between prisoners and staff further reduce the potential for empathy by physicians and medical staff, who may share one or two characteristics with their prisoner/patients but rarely more.

Emmanuel Lévinas, a French philosopher and ethicist, writes that suffering is found precisely in the inability to escape and that suffering at its most intense opens up into death, a place that is by definition unknowable. Luisa's case tells us important things about the disciplinary regulation of space, the micromanagement of movement, and the creation of an environment where care seekers and caregivers are institutionally thwarted in their attempts to reach each other. In Luisa Montalvo's story and her death, we see that failure of connection at its most untenable level.

Rights for Imprisoned People
with Psychiatric Disabilities

RIPPD

We must end the discrimination and dehumanization in the criminal justice system!

We are a grassroots, direct-action organization united to demand justice and social change for imprisoned people with disabilities.

Our membership is made up of people with psychiatric disabilities who have been in jail or prison, who have suffered in the system. Our membership also includes family members and friends of people with psychiatric disabilities who are, or who have been, imprisoned.

We believe in humane treatment for all regardless of race, class, or sexual identity. We want to end the discrimination and dehumanization in the criminal justice system.

We fight the stigma against people with mental illness by demonstrating our courage and empowerment. We are outraged and disgusted by the deplorable treatment by the people controlling the current system.

We confront all those who have the responsibility to make changes by strategizing, protesting, negotiating, collaborating with other groups, and by any creative means necessary.

RIPPD confronts a system set up to oppress people who have a mental illness and who have been in jail or prison. Despite the existing power structure, our organization has been able to gain respect from the "powers that be" and meet with judges, politicians, and other government officials and begin to achieve the policy changes that we seek. Through this work, members develop leadership skills along with a greater understanding of the process involved in organizing for social change. Organizing is about more than the tasks at hand and the projected outcomes. It is also about the process that membership goes through as individuals unite and take action together. It is this process that empowers members and makes this work possible.

OUR FIVE MAIN ISSUES

1. **Increasing the availability of alternatives to incarceration for people with mental illness in the criminal justice system.** We know that people with mental illness belong in treatment, not in jail or prison.

2. **Eliminating the use of solitary confinement for people with psychiatric disabilities in prison.** No more SHUs ("Special Housing Units") for people with mental illness in prison! An SHU is a small cell used as a disciplinary measure. People with mental illness are locked up twenty-three out of twenty-four hours each day.

3. **Improving mental health treatment inside jails and prisons.** We demand that consumers receive quality mental health treatment—a constitutional right of those imprisoned by the government.

4. **Guaranteeing discharge planning for people with mental illness released from jails and prisons.** People treated for mental illness in jail and prison are entitled to have a discharge plan and services in place when they are released. Despite the Brad H. settlement, this is not happening to the extent it is required. Few people with psychiatric disabilities leaving the state prisons receive adequate discharge planning.

5. **Ensuring more accountability and training for correction officers.** We know that correction officers need training in order to better understand imprisoned people who have mental illness. Even training cannot guarantee that officers will be dealt with appropriately when they abuse individuals in their custody; this is why we insist on accountability as well.

49

A Plea for Rosemary

Beverly (Chopper) Henry

Rosemary (Rosie) Willeby died on October 22, 1999. Rosie was one of many female prisoners diagnosed with both HIV and the hepatitis C virus (HCV). On February 28, 1998, Rosie came here (the Central California Women's Facility, or CCWF) to serve a short sentence and then return to her mother and children.

My peers and I watched as, earlier this year, Rosie's health began to decline: her abdomen was swelling inch by inch, which gave her the appearance of being nine months pregnant. Her legs and feet were swollen tight; walking became a task, and regular shoes no longer fit on her feet. Rosie went from dressing herself to being assisted by friends in her cell.

During my talks with Rosie, I learned that she needed the fluid in her abdomen drained. She was confident that if she could get to Madera Hospital in a timely manner, treatment and a compassionate release were in order—but her fear was "they may take too long getting me out of here." Well, Rosie was right; she finally left here for Madera Hospital, but it was too late! Anyone could easily see that Rosie needed emergency care and a compassionate release, but for reasons unknown/inhumane (or whatever), no one in CCWF's Medical Department could find it in their hearts to request emergency treatment or expedite a compassionate release for Rosie!!!

So how many more with chronic HCV do we add to the HIV/AIDS quilt panel before doctors and CMOs (chief medical officers) within the prison system understand that HIV/AIDS and HCV are life-threatening diseases?

Watching Rosie's life slip away is very personal to me. We need better medical treatment and compassionate releases for every prisoner in need of such, and they must be granted in a timely manner.

To Rosie's mom and family, Rosie was an absolute joy; her spirits stayed high, and she fought for better care for herself and her peers. I will not rest my pen or quiet my voice because Rosie would want "the next Rosie" to receive what CCWF Medical Department denied her—the dignity of dying at home. Not alone!

The Thing Called Love Virus

Tiffany Jackson

You didn't tell me you were sick,
You didn't tell me I'd get it . . .
You never said you'd soon die
You never told me it could happen one night
Oh God what will my family think,
Will they still want to be around me . . .
A is for   Always living inside,
I is for   It never dies
D is for   Deadly weapon
S is for   She caught me slippin' . . .
Why, my love, did you do this to me, the one you loved?
I guess we'll go together to the heavens above.
Love virus is its name,
And unprotected sex is to blame . . .
I'm lonely without you
Stuck and sick at C.I.W. . . .

Bill of Health Rights for Incarcerated Girls

Residents of the Cook County Juvenile Detention Center

A right is defined as something that all people deserve, simply because they are human beings. This bill of rights was created by young women who are or have been incarcerated in Cook County's Juvenile Temporary Detention Center. These are rights that all young women deserve, regardless of their involvement with the juvenile justice system.

1. *Family Contact.* We believe girls should be able to see their children more than once a week and without a judge's special permission. Girls should be allowed to see their immediate family members regardless of age.
2. *Accurate Information.* We believe girls should have access to information about their health records and their court case details.
3. *Personal Privacy and Confidentiality.* We believe girls have a right to privacy that includes their personal information as well as their bodies and personal space.
4. *Food, Water, and Exercise.* We believe girls should have access to nutritious food, sufficient water, and daily exercise.
5. *Proper Hygiene.* We believe girls should have more time to bathe, quality, bathing products, as well as clean clothes and towels more often.
6. *Adequate and Respectful Mental Health Care.* We believe girls should have access to counseling services for their mental health.
7. *Another Chance.* We believe girls have the right not to be treated as criminals upon their release from detention and to be connected with community resources prior to release.
8. *Medical Care.* We believe girls have a right to receive medical attention and medicine when they are ill.

9. *Gender-specific Care.* We believe young women struggle with issues that are specifically related to their experience as girls and deserve support in doing so from people who understand those issues.

10. *Freedom from Discrimination and Verbal and Physical Abuse.* We believe girls have a right to be respected by both staff and peers.

52

Working to Improve Health Care
for Incarcerated Women

Sheila R. Enders

*This is my body. I got only one. I put myself here and I'm gonna be here, but
I don't feel my body parts should have to do time.*

INCARCERATED FEMALE VOLUNTEER AT A CALIFORNIA PRISON

Gathering in groups, expressing their fears, frustrations, and hopes, one hundred
and thirteen incarcerated females at the nation's largest women's prison described
their need for adequate health care inside prison walls. Twenty focus groups met
at Central California Women's Facility (CCWF) over a ten-month period in 2001
and 2002. I helped organize the groups so that incarcerated women could define
ways to reduce their health and medical vulnerabilities inside the prison. The
women's comments resulted in the compilation and publication of a handbook, *Simple Answers to Difficult Healthcare Questions—Choice*.

While providing technical assistance for the prison staff, and training hospice in-
mate-volunteers at CCWF, I learned from many of the incarcerated women that they
had difficulty talking about and expressing their health care needs to their medical
providers. Like most of us, they seemed to lack basic knowledge and understanding
of illness and disease, and these women feared reprisal if they asked for more information or asked too many questions. Like many people in the general population,
the women reported they did not know what to ask or how to ask what they wanted
to know. Few women inside understood the meaning of advance health care planning or knew about a health care directive. Few were aware that they had the right to
complete one. Although most had seen the advance-directive forms, and some had
completed one, those with limited reading skills did not understand their purpose.

. . .

"I guess because I feel they are superior, I forget everything I went in there for. I can
speak my mind to the next person, but when I sit in that doctor's office, I'm just little."

Many women echoed this woman's comment. They felt that because the doctors had diplomas on their walls, they must be smarter and have all the right answers.

Another woman, a brave one, said, "I always have to have them break it down, get straight to the point. Put it in layman's terms. I didn't go to school with you, and I don't understand what that word was you just said. Could you please tell me in basic English, what are we going to do and what's going to happen?"

Others said they wished they could question their doctors more. But sometimes, if they did, the physicians initiated disciplinary action against them. However, as one of the incarcerated women said, "More punishment is not going to make what the doctor says more clear; it's just more punishment."

Women in the groups expressed the problem in basic terms: "You sometimes gotta talk to me like a child. Don't talk to me like I'm a professor. Break it down, be simple with me. I'm a simple person with a complicated disease."

Simple Answers to Difficult Healthcare Questions—Choice grew out of comments like these. Meeting participants defined the kinds of information and resources they needed to improve their health care. This material formed the backbone of the handbook. Once I completed a draft, I reconvened several focus groups to review and field-test it and to make suggestions or revisions.

The participants shared one desire: to understand more about their illnesses or conditions. One said, "I just wish you could step into my body for a minute and see what I'm feeling and then you would understand the helplessness I feel."

Another expressed her desire for care and collaboration: "I look for someone who will talk to me and tell me, 'I don't know all the answers, but we'll find out together.'"

And another woman defined her vision of proper, dignified health care: "I like my doctor to be my teammate . . . I just want him to know I'm smart and we can talk about this . . . getting him to recognize that I'm a person and I have a problem that I would like him to hear."

Conducting the focus groups gave me a clearer understanding of what incarcerated women face in making decisions about medical care and treatment. For example, incarcerated women pay five dollars for every doctor visit yet earn only eleven cents per hour of work. They are allowed to list only one health problem or issue even if they have several. They wait for long periods in the clinical area and may not get in to see a doctor. They face language barriers in seeking to communicate with health care providers. They are given orders for laboratory tests or medical procedures without receiving a clear explanation of their purpose.

Our focus group discussions followed a predetermined set of questions in four areas: knowledge/information, experience/process, barriers, and outcomes.

We asked, "Who do you trust with your questions about health care? Women cited a number of sources of trust, but they did not name the medical staff in the prison. They tried to get good information by:

- Talking to family members and friends outside the institution
- Having family members or friends send materials from the Internet
- Talking to other inmates (peer counselors, WAC)
- Using resources in the medical library such as medical dictionaries and the *Physicians' Desk Reference*
- Watching medical programs and commercials on TV

Many of the women had been inside for so long that they were not aware of something called "managed care." They learn about medical issues on television or via information that family and friends mail to them. A significant number of women reported being afraid to take some of the medications that had been prescribed because the advertisements on television talked about "bad side effects."

In summary, the women named the following obstacles or barriers to receiving health care in the institution:

- Feelings of helplessness, intimidation, confusion, shame, guilt, or embarrassment
- Fear of finding out what's wrong
- The sense that asking questions is not culturally appropriate
- Terminology they do not understand
- Fear of being perceived as "dumb"
- Fear of further punishment if they assert themselves
- Uncertainty about what or how to ask

The participants wanted the health care handbook to include information about these matters:

- Definition of common terminology and how to use it
- Descriptions of types of specialists and specialties
- Specific examples of diagnostic tests and procedures
- Descriptions of the risks of common tests and procedures
- Information on where to find information and how to use it
- Frequently asked questions and how to ask them
- A list of informational resources
- Description of what will happen to their bodies
- Information about advance health care directives and hospice services

While conducting the focus groups, working with the participants, and listening to how they expressed their needs, I learned that the women at CCWF support each other and have a bond that goes beyond race, ethnicity, and educational level. These women form "families" to take care of and advocate for each other. Older women are the "grandmas," "mothers," or "aunties" to the younger women. Race or ethnicity, at least among those who took part in the groups, was not an issue for taking care of each other.

These women were supportive of each other. For example, African Americans spoke up for their Hispanic/Latina counterparts (for example, supporting the translation of information into Spanish if necessary). They found ways to get around language barriers and to stand up for and protect one another. Some of the women of varying races/ethnicities had developmental disabilities. Other group members consistently assisted them in the consent process or helped answer their questions. In several groups, I heard essentially the same message: "I worry about my Hispanic sisters. If I don't understand it, how can they?"

I learned that these women are resilient. They are determined to survive in this environment despite the most difficult circumstances. I learned that they want to ask questions about their illnesses and conditions, yet many have a hard time expressing themselves or are fearful of "looking stupid."

Here are examples of what the participants want from their doctors.

- "Can you just stop for a moment and look at me? Maybe if you look in my face you will hear me better."
- "I want him to look me in the eye. He can look in my chart, but then put the thing down. Look me in the eye and answer me the best he can."

People facing illness, whether on the outside or inside the walls, wish their physicians would look them in the eye. But those on the inside are fighting a special uphill battle.

My work on this project showed me that these women are skillful problem solvers who find creative ways to get their needs met. One woman offered her method of remembering the doctor's statements: "Always take a paper and pencil, write down as much as possible to look over later . . . The faintest of ink is better than the best memory." She had just completed chemotherapy and radiation for breast cancer.

Another woman reported using a technique she calls "trick-o-lation" with her doctor. When we asked her to define that word, she explained that she has both HIV and hepatitis C. Sometimes she has new, strange, or unusual symptoms. She asks her mother or sisters to look them up on the Internet and then send her any articles that relate to her symptoms or possible treatment. She gives them to her doctor at her next appointment. The doctor puts the articles aside and proceeds with the medical appointment. The next time she sees her doctor, he says, "I found this article [the one she had brought in], and it seems to match your symptoms. Perhaps we can try this treatment and see how you do." She said, "You have to trick-o-late him into thinking it was his own idea."

Although some of the women felt they might be perceived as "stupid" if they asked questions, one was self-assured enough to report, "Like I said, I'm a hands-on person; not really smart when it comes to words, but I know how to get what I need."

Each time I leave the prison setting, I feel an overwhelming sense of liberation. I can walk to my car; listen to my radio; drive home to my family; watch TV; eat what, where, and when I want; go to the movies; and talk on my cell phone. I cannot imagine being unable to step outside into the "free" world; fearing I will not get the medical care I need, being afraid to ask questions about my diagnosis or treatments, or going through a serious illness with no family nearby to care for me.

Finally, through the process of developing *Choice,* I learned that I am more of an activist/advocate than I ever imagined, though my methods may be less vocal than some. I have a strong desire to improve care for vulnerable people through this small contribution. My next steps will be to reconnect with CCWF and make *Choice* available to the wonderful women whose perspectives helped make it possible.

NOTES

This article appeared in slightly different form as "End-of-Life Care in the Prison System: Implications for Social Work" in *Living with Dying: A Handbook for End-of-Life Healthcare Practitioners,* ed. Joan Berzoff and Phyllis Silverman (New York: Columbia University Press, 2004) and as "An Approach to Stimulate Effective Decision Making in Medical Treatment, Advance Care Planning, and End-of-Life Care for Women in Prison" in *Journal of Palliative Medicine* 8, no. 2 (2005): 432–39.

53

Women in Prison Project

Fact Sheets

Correctional Association of New York

SURVIVORS OF ABUSE IN PRISON FACT SHEET
In Prison

A study conducted in 1999 found that 82 percent of women incarcerated
at New York's Bedford Hills Correctional Facility had a childhood history
of severe physical and/or sexual abuse and that more than 90 percent had
endured physical or sexual violence in their lifetimes. This study also found
that 75 percent of the women had experienced severe physical violence by
an intimate partner during adulthood.

Nationwide, more than 57 percent of women in state prisons and 55 percent
of women in local jails report having been physically and/or sexually
abused in the past. Two-thirds of female state inmates with histories of
abuse and 68 percent of female jail inmates with histories of abuse report
that the abuse was perpetrated by an intimate partner.

The U.S. Bureau of Justice Statistics reports that more than 37 percent of
women in state prisons have been raped before their incarceration. The
Bureau also reports that female inmates are at least three times more likely
than male inmates to have been physically or sexually abused in their past.

Women in prisons are at least twice as likely as women in the general public
to report childhood histories of physical or sexual abuse.

A 1996 government study found that 93 percent of women convicted of killing
sexual intimates, current or former husbands, boyfriends or girlfriends had
been physically or sexually abused by an intimate.

Eighty-nine percent of women prisoners who report having been abused before arrest state that they used drugs regularly before their imprisonment.

A 1996 study found that a majority of women incarcerated in the New York
City jail system reported engaging in illegal activity in response to experiences of abuse, the threat of violence, or coercion by their male partners.

Counseling programs that assist women in dealing with issues surrounding
abuse have proven to reduce recidivism rates: women jail inmates participating in the Trauma, Addiction, Mental Health, and Recovery (TAMAR)
Project in Maryland had a recidivism rate of less than 3 percent; women
who participated for more than six months in the Family Violence
Program at New York's Bedford Hills Correctional Facility had a recidivism
rate of just over 10 percent versus nearly 24 percent for nonparticipants.

Survivors of violence incarcerated for defending themselves against abusers
pose little threat to public safety: they have extremely low rates of recidivism, and, most often, no criminal records and no history of violence other
than the offense for which they are in prison.

In the general population

One and a half million women in the United States are raped or physically
assaulted by an intimate partner each year; more than 50 percent have been
assaulted at some point during their lives. It is estimated that only one in
seven domestic assaults come to the attention of the police.

The financial costs of intimate partner abuse are estimated to be more than
$5.8 billion each year. More than $4 billion annually is spent on direct
medical and mental health care services for survivors.

Battering is the number one cause of injury to women in the United States.
Attacks by abusers result in more injuries requiring medical treatment than
rapes, muggings, and auto accidents combined.

Since 1976, about 30 percent of all female murder victims nationwide have
been killed by an intimate partner.

Studies show that women in substance abuse treatment programs are significantly more likely to report histories of physical or sexual abuse—
especially childhood abuse—than women not in treatment. Studies also
show that girls who have been sexually abused are more likely to be
arrested as adults for prostitution.

Over three million children nationwide witness domestic violence each year.

Women of all cultures, races, sexual orientations, gender identities, income
levels, and ages experience abuse. Nevertheless, socioeconomic status and
cultural background significantly influence the impact of domestic violence:

low-income women, for example, often have fewer options than women with more financially stable support networks, such as the option to leave an abusive relationship and still have the ability to afford to take care of children; women who are not fluent in English may be even more hesitant than English-speaking women to reach out for help or call the police.

March 2007

WOMEN AND HIV/HEPATITIS C FACT SHEET

The high rates of HIV and hepatitis C among incarcerated women in New York State spotlight the need both for expanded gender-specific services and programs and for heightened attention from correctional administrators, elected officials, service providers, and community advocates.

HIV/AIDS

Experiences that often lead to women's incarceration—sex work, drug abuse, poverty, unemployment, and physical, emotional, and sexual victimization—are also experiences that put women at risk for HIV and hepatitis C infection. An important indicator of HIV risk for women is a history of trauma associated with poverty and sexual abuse; such histories are pervasive among women incarcerated in New York.

At year-end 2004, New York State had 4,500 inmates living with HIV—the largest number of HIV-infected inmates in the country. New York's prisons house one-fifth of all inmates known to be HIV positive in the United States.

New York State also has the largest number of HIV-positive women inmates of all prison systems in the United States: 400 women at year-end 2004.

Some 14.2 percent of women in New York's prisons are HIV positive. The rate of infection among women inmates in New York is more than double the rate for male inmates (6.7 percent) and almost 100 times higher than the rate in the general public (.15 percent).

As rates of HIV are disproportionately high among African American and Latina women in the general public, HIV disproportionately impacts women inmates of color.

New York has the largest number of HIV-positive jail inmates in the country—1,359 in 1999. A 1999 New York City Department of Health study found that more than 18 percent of women entering the New York City jail system were living with HIV compared to 7.6 percent of men. This study also found that African American women accounted for over 21 percent of HIV-positive cases; almost 14 percent were Latina and about 12 percent were Caucasian.

The number of AIDS-related deaths in New York's prisons dropped 92 percent from 1994 (244) to 2004 (20).

Hepatitis C

Hepatitis C (HCV) is a viral disease that attacks the liver. People infected with HIV are often co-infected with HCV: approximately 30 percent of all people living with HIV in the general public are co-infected with HCV. Effective HIV prevention must also include a focus on HCV.

The New York State Department of Correctional Services (DOCS) estimates that more than 15 percent of HIV-positive inmates are known to be co-infected with HCV.

A State Department of Health seroprevalence study of 4,000 inmates admitted to DOCS custody from September 2000 to March 2001 found that 23.1 percent of female inmates and 13.6 percent of male inmates were infected with HCV.

The rate of HCV infection among New York's women prisoners is more than 14 times higher than the HCV infection rate in the general public (1.0 percent).

HCV is especially prevalent among women incarcerated for crimes related to sex work and drug addiction.

Because HIV and HCV have shared routes of infection (blood), the U.S. Department of Health and Human Services and the Infectious Disease Society of America recommend screening all people living with HIV for HCV.

Identification and Treatment in Prison

Many women in New York's prisons either do not know or have not revealed their HIV and/or hepatitis C status: of the combined female inmate population in four of the five all-women's correctional facilities in New York State (Bedford Hills, Albion, Taconic, and Bayview), only 8.5 percent (compared to the estimated 14.2 percent) had been determined to be HIV positive and only 11.5 percent (compared to the estimated 23.1 percent) had been determined to be infected with HCV.

Just under 62 percent of the women identified as being HIV positive at Bedford Hills, Albion, Taconic and Bayview are on an HIV treatment regimen. Only 4 percent of women inmates identified as living with HCV at these facilities are on treatment for HCV. (Note: *not all people infected with HCV are appropriate candidates for treatment.*)

WOMEN IN PRISON AND
SUBSTANCE ABUSE FACT SHEET

The 2004 and 2005 modifications to New York's drug laws reduced the length of some mandatory minimum prison sentences; made certain offenders eligible for resentencing; made all sentences for drug offenses determinate (flat, e.g., eight years) with a period of postrelease supervision; increased the amount of narcotics that one must possess in order to trigger a particular charge; and made certain drug offenders eligible to earn additional merit time. These changes represent a small step in the right direction.

Even with these changes, however, the harshest aspects of the drug laws remain intact: though reduced, prison terms are still too long; judges still do not have discretion to consider mitigating factors when sentencing drug offenders, such as the individual's character, or whether she is a first-time offender, had a minor role in the drug transaction, has a substance abuse problem, or is a parent.

The main criterion for guilt under the laws remains the amount of drugs a person has in her possession at the time of her arrest, not her role in the transaction. In addition, the reforms did not allocate any additional funding to expand drug treatment or other alternatives to incarceration programs.

The provision of the drug laws that applies to the most serious category of drug offenders—the AI provision—now requires a judge to impose a term of no less than eight to twenty years for first-time, nonviolent offenders convicted of selling two or possessing eight ounces of a narcotic substance. For AI offenders with a prior violent felony, the sentence range is from fifteen to thirty years.

As of February 2006, of the 1,023 inmates eligible for resentencing under the drug law reforms, only 294 people have actually been resentenced. Because there are a very small number of women in New York's prisons for AI (4) and AII (44) drug offenses, the recent amendments have provided only limited relief for female drug offenders.

In 2006, more than 38 percent of women sent to prison for drug offenses were convicted of B-level drug crimes. More than 58 percent were convicted of one of the three lowest categories of drug offenses (C, D, or E offenses).

As of January 2007, 2,859 women were incarcerated in New York State prisons, 33 percent (943) of whom were drug offenders. As of January 2007, 21 percent of male inmates (12,985) were incarcerated for drug offenses.

Almost eight in ten women who entered New York's prisons in 2006 were convicted of nonviolent drug or property offenses—more than 18 percent of the women were sent to prison for drug possession only.

In 1973, when New York enacted the Rockefeller Drug Laws, there were 384 women in the state's prisons, 102 of whom were drug offenders. Since 1973, the number of women in prison for drug crimes has increased by 825 percent.

Almost the entire increase (91 percent) in women sentenced to prison in New York from 1986 to 1995 resulted from drug offenses. From 1987 to 2001, the number of women under custody for drug offenses in New York State increased at almost double the rate of the number of men under custody for drug offenses.

As of January 2007, almost 80 percent of women in prison and more than 91 percent of men in prison for drug offenses were African American or Latina, even though studies show that Caucasians use, sell, and buy drugs in greater numbers than people of color.

Almost 60 percent of women in New York State prisons are from New York City and its suburbs. Most women in prison lived in low-income communities before their arrest.

About 82 percent of women in New York's prisons report having an alcohol or substance abuse problem prior to arrest; 70 percent of women in treatment report having been abused as children compared with 12 percent of men.

The National Center on Addiction and Substance Abuse at Columbia University reports that drug and alcohol abuse play a role in the incarceration of 80 percent of the individuals imprisoned in U.S. jails and prisons.

A 1997 RAND Drug Policy Research Center study concluded that drug treatment reduces serious crime (against persons as well as property) by as much as fifteen times more than incarceration.

A five-year evaluation of the Kings County Drug Treatment Alternative to Prison (DTAP) Program found that participants were 67 percent less likely to recidivate two years after leaving the program than nonparticipants. The study also found that DTAP graduates were three and a half times more likely to be employed than they were before arrest. DTAP achieved these results at about half the average cost of incarceration.

It costs almost $37,000 to incarcerate a person in a New York State prison for one year, and more than $66,000 to incarcerate a person in a New York City jail for one year. The cost of outpatient drug treatment ranges from $4,300 to $7,500 per person per year, and residential treatment is generally less than $20,000 per person per year.

There are not enough women-specific treatment programs in New York. In 2006, just over 5 percent of the total number of drug treatment programs certified by the State Office of Alcoholism and Substance Abuse Services

(OASAS) were women only. More than 62 percent of women admitted to OASAS-certified treatment programs in 2006 either had children or were pregnant at the time of admission. Nevertheless, only a small number of programs allow women to live with their children during treatment.

Many drug treatment programs are designed to respond to the experiences of male substance abusers and, as a result, are often ineffective for women participants. In addition, because women's substance abuse is often tied to their histories of trauma and abuse, addiction treatment methods that are not women-centered (such as confrontational group sessions) can reignite past trauma and have harmful consequences.

Children of incarcerated parents often suffer from anxiety and depression and low self-esteem. They are also at high risk for acting out in school and getting caught up in the criminal justice system.

March 2007
WOMEN IN PRISON PROJECT
Correctional Association of New York
135 East 15th St., NY York, NY 10003
Tel 212-254-5700
Fax 212-473-2807

PART SIX

Serving Time, Sentenced and Unsentenced

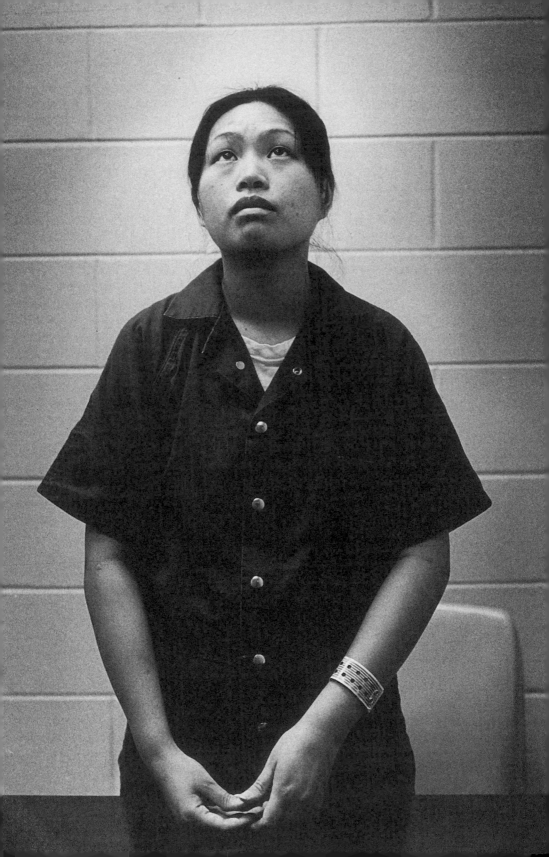

MANY INCARCERATED PEOPLE DESCRIBE the "criminal justice" system, including prison, as an arena where logic doesn't obtain. This section begins with a trio of essays that explore the experiences of women who have encountered particular and deeply consequential versions of illogic, especially in the realms of sentencing and detention. Irum Shiekh writes about "Zihada," an eighteen-year-old Muslim woman from Pakistan, who, caught in post-9/11 passions and without apparent legal grounds, was incarcerated, moved from site to site, held for varying lengths of time, and eventually deported. Leticia Saucedo tells us the story of "Mae," a Chinese woman who, like Zihada, was hideously vulnerable because of her immigrant status, her gender and youth, her poverty, and her distance from allies and family and familiar culture and language. She had the bad luck of being in the United States at a time when being an immigrant was too often conflated with being a criminal. Marleine Bastien and Rosta Telfort highlight the experiences of women detainees across Florida and describe the conditions in the detention centers in the Miami Department of Homeland Security District; some of the women Bastien and Telfort encountered are suffering indefinite detention, denied due process.

A second group of essays in this section grapple with the special physical, medical, and ethical problems associated with holding women in prison for very long periods, sometimes long past the time they could possibly be a danger to society. Kathy Boudin reviews the reasons for the increasing number of women in prison and for their sentencing to ever-longer terms, despite the tiny number of recidivists

---

Chen in Detention, 2001. Riverside Regional Jail, Hopewell, Virginia. Photograph by Steven Rubin

among this population. Boudin concludes, "The long sentences, the parole denials, the many ways of rendering invisible or dehumanizing women in prison who have committed violent crimes offer another window into the criminal justice system. Punishment: Is it solely about revenge? What happened to ideas of people changing, of prison being a place for rehabilitation? How did our prisons become a dead-end road?"

Erline Bibbs, an incarcerated woman, describes the kind of leadership that "experienced" incarcerated women in Alabama and Louisiana have been willing— and determined—to exercise in the interests of their community. Bibbs shows how the Longtimers/Insiders Activist Group at Tutwiler Prison in Alabama claimed a voice in decision making about a number of issues, especially about the new women's prison under construction. The participants in this group believe fervently that they can offer important, seasoned insights about the proper size of the new facility, its location, and its programs. Bibbs shows that even in a domain governed by crude practicalities and politics, a group of incarcerated women can act on the powerful urge to introduce logic and lay claim to the dignity of experience.

54

Reading Gender in September 11 Detentions

Zihada: The Journey from a Young
Pakistani Wife to an Anthrax Suspect

Irum Shiekh

Since September 11, the state's war on terror has primarily targeted Muslim males. For the most part, women have been spared from detention. In the spring of 2005, however, two teenage girls from New York, Tashnuba Hayder and Adama Bah, were arrested on suspicion of a suicide bombing. Months later, Tashnuba was deported to Bangladesh and Adama was released on bail for immigration violations. Their cases convinced many activists that the government was widening the fish net for Muslims. Yet the number of detained Muslim women has remained considerably low.

Below I tell the story of "Zihada," an eighteen-year-old Pakistani Muslim woman arrested with her husband, Ali, in October 2001 for an expired visa and a fictitious identity card. Even though she and her husband were arrested for immigration violations, their religious identity put them under suspicion of terrorism. Authorities' suspicion lingered throughout their detentions as they stayed in jails for months for a first-time immigration violation. If not for 9/11, neither might have even experienced detention.

I met Zihada in Pakistan in March 2003 and stayed in her house overnight. In talking with her, I learned about the emotional effects of incarceration on women. Through narratives such as hers, I am reading, tracing, and locating gender in a male-dominated discourse. Her narrative and those of other women detainees are important resources for scholars and activists who generally have to work in areas in which the overwhelming majority of subjects are males. Here is the story Zihada told me.

On a beautiful evening on October 9, 2001, Zihada accompanied her husband, Ali, as he made deliveries for Domino's Pizza. Driving back, Ali noticed the sky glowing red over the fields below the road. He looked at Zihada and said, "The sky is red and angry today. May God protect us."

Around eight in the evening, Ali called from the store, sounding a bit concerned. "The police are looking for Javed. I am not sure about the situation. Just pray and be mentally prepared." Javed was a childhood friend of her brother's and had been instrumental in finding a job for Ali in Hudson, New York. A few hours later, she called Ali's cell phone. No one picked up. She called Javed, but his phone was shut off. Then she called Shaoib, the owner of Domino's Pizza. He replied, "The police have arrested Ali and Javed. I am driving to the station to find out why."

Zihada unrolled the prayer rug, prayed, and waited. Around two in the morning, a few uniformed officers knocked at the door. They showed her their badges and said, "We are with the FBI. Ali has given us permission to search the house. We want to search." Zihada stepped aside, and three officers went upstairs to the apartment, while a few stayed outside with her. Half an hour later, one officer came down and told Zihada to come upstairs. She sat down on the chair in her living room and broke into sobs.

"Why are you crying?" the officer asked.

"You have arrested my husband," Zihada replied.

"He is fine at the police station. Just tell us the truth and you will be fine also." After a quick interview about her background, the officer asked,

"Who is Osama bin Laden?"

"I don't know who he is."

"Did you ever go to Afghanistan?"

"No."

"What is your opinion about the attacks on the World Trade Center?"

"I am very sad that happened. No matter what, whether a Muslim or whoever did it, it should not have happened."

Officers continued to search the apartment. Zihada noticed that the officers were especially interested in the spices in the kitchen. Wearing gloves and masks, they picked up bottles from the shelves and inquired about each one. Then an officer found garam masala (a mixture of Pakistani spices) and got suspicious. Zihada told him the ingredients and offered him a taste. The officer put it back on the shelf. Then he found Zihada's medicines, which had a different name printed on them. Zihada had obtained the medicine in New York. Zihada clarified quickly, "It belongs to my friend. She just left it here."

Zihada's cousin's son had given her a drawing when she had left Brooklyn a few months before. The child had drawn a car speeding down a roadway and had written "Danger" at the end of the road. The officers were suspicious. "Why did the child write 'Danger'?" one asked. Zihada was surprised at the obvious question. "This is just a child's drawing. He gave it to me as a going-away gift. I don't know why he wrote 'Danger.'"

Two hours later, officers told her to come with them. Zihada thought that she would return home in a few hours. She picked up a light sweater and slippers and arrived at the police station, where she found Ali handcuffed in a room. He told her in English, "I have told them everything. Don't hide anything." After seeing Ali handcuffed, Zihada broke out in sobs again. "Don't worry. They will just deport us back to Pakistan. It is not a big deal," he reassured her.

It had been a year since Zihada and Ali had come from Pakistan to the United States on a visitor visa. Ali sold his mobile business, collected his savings, and headed to and stayed in Brooklyn for a few months. At the invitation of their childhood friend Javed, Zihada and Ali moved to Hudson and rented an apartment. Ali got a job with the Domino's Pizza store where Javed worked. The week before the arrest, they had celebrated their first wedding anniversary. Sitting on a cold iron bench with handcuffs in a police station was a sudden, harsh change. Zihada spent that night with Ali in the small room.

In the morning, immigration officers took them to the Albany court, where the judge gave them a court date of October 24. Zihada had expected an immediate departure and now was going to have to spend the next fourteen days in jail. The thought of staying in jail was devastating. Ali understood her pain and felt guilty that he could not do anything.

Marshals took Zihada to Schenectady County jail and placed her in a cell for processing. Zihada was menstruating at that time and was feeling sharp pains. Waiting on a bench for hours made the pain worse. Finally, a guard came and asked her to strip. Zihada squatted, coughed, and went through a cavity search. After the shower, Zihada put on an orange shirt and pants. While an officer was recording her biographical data, another young officer walked in, saw Zihada, and said, "Wow." He watched Zihada during this data-entry process. Later, he asked, "What is a way that you can stay in the U.S.?" Zihada thought that a marriage was the only way to stop her deportation.

"I think marriage is the only way to stop deportation."

"Marry me," the officer said.

"I am already married," Zihada replied, furious.

Guards placed her in a cell alone to determine her classification. This part of the jail had six or seven cells, and women from the other cells were allowed to come to a central lobby area to chat, watch television, or make telephone calls. Zihada's cell was locked. She watched them from a distance.

The first morning, a few women came to her cell and asked, "Did you put anything in the water?" Zihada was confused. They told her to watch the news on the television, which reported that Zihada, Ali, and Javed had been taken into custody under suspicion of throwing anthrax in the water-treatment plant. Zihada was speechless. The women continued to tease, "You wanted to kill us? You wanted to throw anthrax in the water? All you Muslims want to do this?" Hurt and tearful, Zihada replied, "I have not done anything." Until then, she thought that she was there because of her expired visa.

On October 9, Javed had gone near the water-treatment plant in Hudson to take a photograph of a scenic view. Someone had become suspicious and reported him. The FBI arrested all three of them. Within hours, the FBI cleared them of any terrorist activity; however, immigration officials arrested Zihada and Ali for expired visas and fictitious identification cards. Javed had a green card, but he was coerced into stating that he knew about Zihada and Ali's expired visas. Javed was charged with "harboring illegal aliens" and was later deported. The local television news continued to sensationalize the initial anthrax suspicion.

The next morning, Zihada entered the central lobby area. A few women asked about her case, and Zihada explained. As they talked, they slowly built a friendship. One told her how to make collect calls, and Zihada called her cousin in New York. Both of them cried. She was happy to hear her cousin's voice.

The first week in jail was very hard. There were so many rules to get used to. Food was available only at certain times. Many times, Zihada felt hunger pangs in the middle of the night and had no choice but to wait till the morning. Storing food in the cell was not allowed. One of the women told her, "If you keep anything with you, they will lock you up for the next twenty-four hours." Zihada lost seventeen pounds in the first month.

On October 25, she appeared before the judge in shackles. He postponed the hearing for two weeks because Zihada needed an FBI clearance. She was surprised because the FBI had already cleared her. Later she learned that after 9/11, many Muslims with immigration violations had to undergo the FBI clearance process, which unnecessarily extended their detentions. Disappointed, Zihada returned to her cell and started to get accustomed to her life in jail.

Javed had been temporarily released on bail, and Zihada called him. Javed made her laugh, which lifted her spirits. Soon, Javed's public defender advised him not to talk with Zihada. He was afraid that the FBI was recording their conversations. When Zihada heard this, she felt hurt and lonely. Javed was the only person she could call from jail. The rest of her family in the United States was either scared or indifferent.

Zihada's uncle had a green card and lived in New York. He came once but left quickly. He was cold and did not even offer his phone number. Zihada's cousin was concerned about the phone expenses. Once she told Zihada, "My husband told me that the collect call was very expensive."

"I will be careful in the future," Zihada said.

"You can make a quick call to tell us how you are doing." Zihada stopped calling. Ali was in a different jail and Zihada had no way to call him, so she wrote letters instead. Sometimes, he wrote back and described his daily routine. Zihada sent poems and descriptions of her life in jail. His letters made her feel that she was with him, and they gave her courage.

Zihada received a Koran from a Christian priest who visited the jail. Reading the Koran gave her the strength to pass the time. After the second court hearing, she had learned her rights and knew how to request someone for religious services. An Indian Muslim man came and gave her a book about Islam in Urdu. Ramadan was coming, and she wanted to fast. He requested that the food be delivered to her before dawn and after sunset. She also joined the school in the jail; she did very well and enjoyed it. If she had stayed another three weeks, she would have received her GED.

She spent a month and a half in that jail. Everyone, including her fellow prisoners and guards, were nice and respectful to her. Their interactions with her changed their attitudes toward Muslims. Many of the women suggested that she fight her deportation case and stay in the United States. She was happy to receive a kind response.

For reasons undisclosed to her, marshals moved her to another jail. Here they placed her in the section for minors. She told them about Ramadan and received her food before dawn and after sunset. While she was there, her period started, but she didn't tell the jail authorities that Islamic rules forbade fasting during menstruation. She felt that the jail personnel wouldn't understand. She stayed in that jail for seven days.

On December 5, Zihada and Ali had a court date. The Judge gave them five years probation, which meant that the criminal case for her fictitious identity card had ended. If the immigration officers had agreed, they could have stayed in the United States. However, the immigration officers were waiting outside and immediately took them to Albany jail. The public defender told Zihada that the deportation proceedings would take a week. She did not trust that information.

In Albany, guards locked her up in a small cell at 5:00 P.M. She was very cold sitting on the iron bench, and the cell was dirty. After six hours of waiting, guards started processing her case. "You look so worried," one officer commented. Zihada explained, "I am concerned about the classification and the solitary confinement. I have been in two jails already and they have classified me, so please don't put me in solitary confinement." The officer replied, "We don't know about the previous classification, and we have to give you a new classification." Around one in the morning, guards moved her to the classification cell, which was separate from the rest of the jail.

"I am a Muslim. I need food to observe Ramadan."

"We don't have anything to do with it. You will get your breakfast at seven and dinner at five." Zihada fasted by not eating in the morning and eating only after sunset. She had brought a copy of the Koran that one of the Black Muslim imams at the Schenectady County Jail had given her. She read it during her solitary confinement and found strength in it. She stayed alone in the cell for seven days again and was allowed out only for a few hours to make a telephone call, but she did not have anyone to call anymore. Although twenty to twenty-five Muslims were in that jail, including two or three women, she could not talk to anyone during the classification process.

Spending time in solitary confinement was torturous. The only items in the cell were a small bed, a toilet, and a bench. There was nothing to do in the small and dirty cell, nothing at all. There was no light during the day and only one lamp at night. Zihada constantly prayed for the end of her confinement.

At the end of her seven-day confinement, guards told her to pack her things. She saw Ali when she came out. Marshals allowed the two of them to sit in the same car. Each of them was relieved to see that the other was all right. The marshals dropped Zihada in Madison County jail and took Ali to the Buffalo detention center in Batavia.

At Madison, the jail authorities were nicer. Here they did not put Zihada through the classification process and did not strip-search her. She did not tell them about fasting. School was available, but Zihada no longer had the courage to sign up for classes. The authorities kept moving her around. The lawyer had also told her that she was going to be deported soon, and she was looking forward to it. At the Madison County jail, she played cards and talked with the other women.

Most of the guards were fine, except for one who continued to call her "Ms. Laden" despite her clarification. One day, she got angry and told him coldly, "Don't call me Ms. Laden." He apologized and stopped.

After seven days, she was moved to Warsaw County jail and had to endure classification again, but she didn't care anymore. She had become used to waiting in solitary confinement. Her English had improved also.

During the processing at Warsaw, someone noted that she was Muslim.

"Oh Muslim, Afghani? Do you know Osama bin Laden?" Zihada shook her head and the officer continued, "I don't speak Urdu or Afghani."

"I can speak English well."

"Thank God," he replied.

In this jail, Zihada stayed in the minor section from December 18 to January 15 and spent time watching television. She was supposed to leave in the middle of December, but the Christmas holidays and a snowstorm delayed her deportation.

On January 16, two deportation officers came to pick her up. After she changed her jail clothes, deportation officers placed handcuffs on her, which she hid beneath her scarf. After she arrived at JFK Airport, the female deportation officer asked if Zihada was going to give them trouble. Zihada replied, "No, I am eager to leave the country." They unlocked her handcuffs.

While waiting, Zihada conversed with the deportation officers and criticized the

American justice system, especially the changes after 9/11. She criticized the delays in her deportation proceedings and her constant transfer from one jail to another. She also felt that her case, as well as Ali's and Javed's, was closely monitored because of her religious and ethnic background. The deportation officers listened. They told her that they were sorry that she had had to experience this treatment.

Zihada had a safe and uneventful flight back home. Looking back, she believes that the American justice system became vengeful after 9/11 and expressed the country's anger by throwing people out. She regularly heard reports about the deportation of large numbers of Pakistanis from the United States. She believes that these deportations resulted from religious discrimination and could escalate the existing anti-American sentiment. Right after her return, she was happy to find her freedom, but she began noting the losses in her life. Ali was unemployed, and they had to start their lives all over again. However, this experience has made her stronger, and she is ready to experience anything now.

55

Victim or Criminal

The Experiences of a Human-Trafficking Survivor in the U.S. Immigration System

Leticia M. Saucedo

In 2004, "Mae," a Chinese woman who was exploited by human traffickers, was detained by the U.S. federal government for passport fraud as she tried to enter the United States through an international airport in the Southwest. Mae was incarcerated for several months in a contract detention center run by the local police department. I joined forces with students at the Thomas and Mack Legal Clinic in the law school at the University of Nevada, Las Vegas, to represent Mae in her claims for asylum and release from detention. All of us witnessed the ways in which U.S. society increasingly equates the immigrant experience with criminality. The restrictive parameters and hostile attitudes of the immigration system encourage prosecution of immigrants rather than determination of asylee status. Mae's story illustrates these realities, particularly the experiences of many women who are coerced into human trafficking for purposes of involuntary labor and/or sexual servitude.

We learned Mae's story one hour at a time, over countless visits, due to visiting restrictions. Before Mae was released after fifteen months, she had to tell her story piece by piece to people she hardly knew, within the context of a legal system she didn't understand, under totally unpredictable conditions. Here is Mae's story.

MAE'S STORY

Mae was an eighteen-year-old Chinese woman from a rural, desolate part of China, where employment was scarce and salaries were meager. She appeared to be no more than fourteen years old when we first met. She had gone to school in China only until she was eleven. She spoke no English, and she knew very little about the United

States or where she had landed in the country. In China, Mae's father had physically and emotionally abused her and her mother. Her father called Mae stupid and told her that she was not worth his financial support; he eventually sold his only child to an older man from the city. As this man's second wife, Mae explained, she was expected to be a concubine and also do housekeeping for the first wife. Mae resisted this fate and tried to escape. Her father and the would-be husband found her and forced her to return. Mae begged her mother to help her. Mae's mother turned to her own brother, Mae's uncle, for help. This man had sent his own daughter to the United States earlier.

Mae's uncle put her mother in contact with the "snakeheads," or traffickers, who had arranged his daughter's trip. Mae said that she did not know how much her mother paid the snakeheads as a down payment. When her mother arranged the trip, neither she nor Mae knew what her final destination would be. Mae's mother sent her daughter out of the country so that she could escape her fate of forced marriage, not knowing what other dangers Mae would face when she arrived at her destination. For Mae's mother, this was the only choice. For Mae, following her mother's directive to leave the country seemed like a better choice than becoming someone's house slave.

Mae traveled in fear of both the traffickers and the unknown every step of her trip. Following the instructions of her contacts, Mae went from Hong Kong to Mandalay to Tokyo and finally to the United States. She did not know where she was going until the last minute. At one point, the snakeheads took Mae's passport and gave her a passport belonging to a Singapore citizen, because Singaporeans do not require visas to enter the United States. They also gave her the phone number of her snakehead contact in the United States.

When Mae got to the airport in the United States, government officials looked at her passport and refused to let her enter. They arrested her and put her in jail. Mae called the snakehead's number, and the man who answered the phone told her she was a stupid girl for not getting rid of the passport before she got off the plane. He told her she would have to pay "a snakehead lawyer" over five thousand dollars to get out of jail, but of course Mae did not have such funds.

The court appointed a federal public defender to Mae's case. She was charged with a felony for attempting to enter the country with a false passport. Mae was detained for more than a year before she pled guilty to passport fraud. Mae had no choice but to plead guilty: if she didn't cooperate, she risked more time in jail or deportation.

Mae remained in detention after her guilty plea for another four months, this time awaiting an immigration removal hearing. The immigration clinic, having been contacted by the federal public defender's office, agreed to take Mae's case and defend her in immigration court. As Mae's immigration lawyers, my students and I helped Mae seek asylum and apply for a trafficking visa. We spent months meeting with her during visiting hours and preparing the documentation for her asylum and trafficking applications. Because Mae spoke no English when she arrived, she talked to us through an interpreter. After a few weeks, she made friends with some of the other female detainees, some of whom were themselves trafficking victims. They communicated in Chinese for the most part, but they also began to teach her English. One of them left her a Chinese-English dictionary before she moved to another detention facility, and Mae started to study it every day. She also took some English classes, but they were not offered very regularly. These few classes were the extent of the learning opportunities in the detention center, and Mae learned little from them.

The longer Mae was detained, the more the detention staff became accustomed to the shy, unassuming, hardworking young woman. They started allowing Mae to help prepare the dining room before meals and clean up after the meals, among other routine tasks, to help her fight the boredom of detention. Mae told us she communicated with staff and other detainees through sign language until she learned a few English phrases to get her through a day. She hated the food, and she lost weight.

After a few months, Mae became restless and depressed, and my students felt powerless to help her through this long period of uncertainty. They tried to do what they could within the legal system to obtain her release. They tried to obtain a bond for her, but the judge refused to grant it. Mae maintained sporadic correspondence with her mother in China and with her cousin and best friend in the United States. She also phoned them, although not often because the calling cards sold at the detention center were expensive. Through her correspondence with her cousin and best friend, she learned that, had she not been detained, she likely would be living like they were: housed in dormitory quarters with other women and girls from China who worked in Chinese restaurants throughout the country. As she explained to us, the girls were paid about two thousand dollars in cash every month but were obliged to return fifteen hundred dollars of their salary each month to the restaurant owners to pay off the snakehead fee.

Despite what she learned about the economic exploitation of these girls, Mae decided that if she were released and allowed to stay in the United States, she would take this work, because returning to China and the slavery of a forced marriage was not an option.

Finally, about fifteen months after she was arrested, Mae was able to tell her story in immigration court. The court let her go free and granted her asylum status in January 2006. She was granted asylum status in part because of her fear of further persecution for resisting a forced marriage and in part because the court recognized that she was trafficked into the United States. Mae immediately moved to New York to work in a restaurant that paid Mae's passage from Nevada to New York.

Mae's obligations to the snakeheads and the terms of repayment are unknown. Presumably, Mae continues to pay off an enormous debt to the traffickers despite her legal status, because, in the end, they know where her family lives in China. Even with legal status, Mae told us, she had to find a way to pay off the traffickers because she feared for her mother's safety.

REFLECTIONS ON MAE'S STORY:
CRIMINALIZATION OF THE VICTIM

Mae's story and circumstances fit the classic experience of a human-trafficking victim in that she was caught before she was able to start her debt-peonage arrangement. Her story reveals the unwillingness of the immigration enforcement system to readily accept the realities of forced marriage, domestic violence, and other oppressive conditions that cause women to flee. More important, the system is devoted to defining each individual's immigration story as an instance of "economic necessity." This explanation eclipses the fact that even when economic circumstances are part of the reason for leaving home, many immigrants fall prey to exploitative, dangerous, and coercively powerful human-trafficking rings. This fate especially falls to women and girls from poor countries, because they lack economic self-sufficiency and are vulnerable to traffickers' promises to save them from desperate situations at home.

Mae was willing and able to provide prosecutors with details about her trip, her contacts with the snakeheads, their control over her travels, and the labor ring into which the snakeheads delivered her. But the sophisticated trafficking ring made sure that she did not possess sufficient details to give prosecutors ammunition for a successful trafficking conviction. FBI investigators could accept her story and open a federal—and possibly national and international—investigation, or reject her story and move forward with a much more limited prosecution investigation. Confronted with limited resources and staff, as well as the inability to mount a coordinated investigation with other offices facing similar cases, the FBI chose the less costly option. The result was a long negotiation and jail time for Mae. In the end, Mae pled guilty to carrying a false passport.

The U.S. attorney in charge of the case also had strong incentives to prosecute. She recognized that Mae might have a trafficking claim but did not consider the claim to cancel out her wrongdoing. In other words, the facts that Mae feared persecution in her home country and that an organized ring took advantage of her fear did not matter. She could still apply for asylum or other relief even though she had a conviction for passport fraud. The prosecution, a relatively simple one, kept the government's objectives in mind, sent a message, and the government hoped, prevented similar instances of illegal entry.

Mae and others in her predicament will continue to navigate life in the United States as perpetrators, with all of the consequences of being labeled a criminal in the United States. Thus, although Mae was granted asylum status, her adjustment to legal permanent residency (LPR) status will require her to disclose her conviction and may even bar her from adjustment, depending on the discretion of the adjudicating immigration officer. Under the statute, Mae is subject to deportation once she asks to change her status from asylee to LPR. Under the Immigration and Nationality Act, conviction of a crime of moral turpitude, such as fraud, is considered grounds for removal.

If Mae seeks adjustment, she will have to retell her story and risk (again) that an officer will not credit her story or her existing status as an asylee. She may not win a waiver of her conviction even though, if the system had worked appropriately, she would not have been charged once officials recognized that she was a potential asylum applicant.

The same result would occur had Mae been deemed a trafficking victim instead of an asylee. Mae could not overcome the presumption of her criminal status through any of the immigration routes available to her.

Throughout this ordeal, did Mae fully understand the nuances of a legal system that labels her a criminal? More likely, she understood that she dare not choose any course of action that could send her back to China. Although Mae never considered herself a criminal, and she is clearly more a victim than a lawbreaker, the legal system has given her a criminal identity. This label will have consequences for Mae as she assumes a range of identities in the United States: as worker, young woman, survivor, Chinese person, and, finally, immigrant. Ultimately, Mae's story reveals that the government is implementing a harsh, punitive enforcement strategy, mixing immigration law with criminal law, and that the legal system turns a blind eye to the legitimate attempts of trafficking survivors to enter this country with safety, dignity, and appropriate legal status.

56

Detention of Women Asylum Seekers in the United States: A Disgrace

Marleine Bastien and Rosta Telfort

INTRODUCTION

Every day, women flee their countries of origin to come to the United States for safe haven. Many of the 135,000 to 150,000 refugees in removal proceedings at any given time in the United States are women who are forced to flee their countries of origin as a result of war, political instability, and other societal conflicts related to their gender, including state repression, politically unstable in-country conditions, female genital mutilation, political rapes, sexual slavery, prostitution, and planned and forced marriages. Instead of receiving the protection for which they travel many miles, sometimes in the most horrible conditions, women detainees frequently report physical and sexual abuse, overcrowded facilities, inadequate or nonexistent medical care, and illegal, arbitrary, insensitive discipline and solitary confinement. This chapter highlights the experiences of women detainees across Florida and the conditions in the detention centers in the Miami Department of Homeland Security District.

U.S. REFUGEE POLICY AND DETENTION SYSTEM

In 1965, Congress passed an amendment to the 1952 Immigration and Naturalization Act that defined a refugee as someone who had "fled his/her country of origin because of political persecution." The provision placed the heavy burden of proof of persecution on the refugee. Aliens who were in exclusionary proceedings because they "have not entered the U.S." (because they did not make it to land) could not benefit from deportation hearings. Around this period, the United States welcomed about 600,000 Cubans who got permission from Fidel Castro to leave. Later, in 1980, 125,000 Cuban refugees landed in south Florida at the same time that 13,000 Haitian refugees arrived. While the Cubans received red-carpet treatment, the Haitians were kept in detention for months and sometimes years. Most were arbitrarily deported back to Haiti, where they risked imprisonment and even death.

In May 1992, President George H. W. Bush issued an Executive Order to directly repatriate all Haitians intercepted at sea outside U.S. territorial waters. President Clinton continued this policy when he took office in 1993, despite campaign promises to end it. Under the policy, Haitians intercepted by the U.S. Coast Guard were returned to Haiti without even a cursory attempt to identify those who might be at risk—a policy that was in violation of international rules and the obligations of the United States under Article 33 of the 1951 Convention Relating to the Status of Refugees. The U.S. government claimed that while some Haitians deserved political asylum, most attempted the difficult 750-mile voyage for economic reasons, and allowing them to remain in the United States would encourage others to risk their lives to come to the United States in search of better economic opportunities. In a landmark case, *Haitian Refugee Center v. Civiletti*, filed by the Haitian Refugee Center in 1979, Haitian advocates successfully argued that the so-called "Haitian program violated the most basic rights of the Haitian refugees and that it was both unconstitutional and illegal."

Twenty-five years later, asylum seekers, not only Haitians, are still being detained, although they have not committed any crime. Asylum seekers detained by U.S. Citizenship and Immigration Services in the Department of Homeland Security, formerly the Immigration and Nationalization Service, can be found in immigration processing centers run by private corporations, U.S. Bureau of Prisons Facilities, local jails, and maximum-security prisons. No logical standards are in place to regulate the placement of asylum seekers.

With the passage of the Illegal Immigration Reform and Immigration Responsibility Act (IIRIRA) in 1996, followed by the Antiterrorism and Effective Death Penalty Act, which amended certain provisions in IIRIRA, the U.S. Congress enacted and called for immediate implementation of expedited removal, a provision that gives the department full authority to detain refugees who enter the country illegally. If the refugee is unable to prove to the immigration officer a bona fide fear of persecution upon return to his/her country of origin, he/she is immediately deported without a hearing or an appeal in front of an immigration judge. This policy is highly unfair because most people who flee their countries to seek refuge in the United States have to leave very fast, with no time for planning or strategizing. Many have to go into hiding and are forced to live in dangerous conditions for months before they get a chance to flee. Refugees who are able to articulate an asylum request by showing a credible fear of persecution are allowed to stay to present their cases in a court of law, but under IIRIRA they can be detained throughout the process, which can last months or even years. In recent history, no other groups have been victimized by these unfair policies more than Haitian refugees.

WOMEN IN DETENTION IN THE UNITED STATES

County jails and other detention facilities received millions of dollars from the federal government to detain refugees and immigrants, but the conditions under which authorities keep these vulnerable individuals are, in fact, shameful.

In Florida, refugees are held at the Krome Service Processing Center (better known as the Krome camp), the Turner Gilford Knight Center (TGK), area motels and hospitals, Sarasota County jails, the Palmetto Mental Health Center, the Federal Detention Center in Miami, Fort Lauderdale jails, the Palm Beach County Stockade and County Jail, the Hernando County Jail, and the Monroe County Jail. The conditions in all these institutions are deplorable. The facilities lack the basic infrastructure to treat these women in a humane and dignified manner. They lack adequate health care, telephones, education, recreation and exercise, and a decent law library. Women are denied a balanced diet, the ability to practice their religion, and access to family, visitors, and the press.

TURNER GILFORD KNIGHT CENTER

TGK is a maximum-security prison that opened in 1989 to relieve the jail overcrowding in Miami-Dade County. It has the capacity to hold fifteen hundred inmates. TGK entered into a contract with the Department of Homeland Security to house the women detainees in a separate section of the jail. After arriving at TGK, women detainees are photographed, fingerprinted, and given uniforms just like other criminal inmates. The women have cited many problems at the facility, including language barriers, lack of access to legal advocates and telephones, an inadequate room for meeting with their attorneys, an inability to communicate with family members abroad, lack of activities and medical care, inedible food and food products, and the lack of sanitary services and personal-hygiene items such as deodorant, toothbrushes, toothpaste, sanitary pads, and other necessities.

Women detainees at TGK have many problems communicating with their family members and others on the outside. Despite the right to private legal visitation seven days a week, asylum seekers also have difficulty communicating with their lawyers. One woman said, "There is no confidentiality at TGK for the asylum seekers to speak with their attorneys because the Department and TGK offices are right next to the small attorney room."

Most of the women can only make collect calls, which are extremely expensive, and most families do not have telephone setups that allow them to receive collect calls. Haiti and some other countries have automatic blocks that prevent exchanges among the detainees and their family members. One detainee was able to call home after spending months in detention only to find out that her mother had died. When she called four weeks later to find out about her mother's funeral, using a calling card donated by a Haitian doctor, she found out that her father had also died. This woman was inconsolable and became suicidal.

Women detainees at TGK are allowed only one contact visit per month and two noncontact visits a week. The contact visits often take place in the busy hallway used by guards and other personnel to enter and exit the area. Noncontact visits are even worse. Women detainees are able to see their relatives through a Plexiglas window, but because the small holes that allow the detainees to communicate with family members are below the glass and at waist level, the women and their visitors have to bend and twist their heads in order to hear each other. A Colombian woman detainee told a worker at the Florida Immigrant Advocacy Center (FIAC), "I truly believe that once I get out of here, I'll have to see a psychologist because it's too much. The psychological abuse here, with no access to our family, it is so cruel. At least we could talk to our family by phone [at Krome]. One officer said even if we complain, nothing is going to change. It will be worse for us." A Nigerian woman added, "Does INS understand that they are not only destroying our lives but destroying our children's lives as well?"

Most women prefer to remain inside instead of going to the restricted recreation area for fresh air and sun because they have to be strip-searched when they come inside, even if they did not leave the compound. Except for sporadic religious activities programmed by area volunteers, the facility has none of the types of educational activities available in the rest of the prison. The detainees are not allowed to receive books or magazines from anyone. They're not even given local newspapers. Each unit has only one television set, which restricts choices and forces everybody to watch the same thing. When interviewed by FANM (an advocacy group for Haitian women and their families) and FIAC personnel, the women complained that they feel "useless, helpless and hopeless sitting around all day with nothing to do." Many expressed thoughts of suicide. A Haitian woman detainee told a Miami business delegation, "We came here in search of freedom and liberty. If I knew I would be treated so bad, disrespected and humiliated, I would [have] throw[n] myself overboard."

Many of the women at TGK lack access to medical care. During numerous visits by human rights groups with participation by FIAC and FANM, some women detainees complained about the quality of the medical attention they received at the center. Medical complaints are ignored for days, and often, the women's lawyers must complain to higher authorities to force the detention staff to intervene. A young Haitian woman who was throwing up blood due to a bleeding ulcer wasn't taken to the hospital until an FIAC paralegal and her lawyer intervened. The women also report abrupt medication changes, with medical personnel reducing or discontinuing their medication without notification. Women reported, "TGK cut back my medications. They keep messing up my levels of medication at TGK and I had seizures coming and going all the time." "I can't eat the food. . . . I was told that I would get special food and medications . . . but I only got it on the 19th." "At TGK, we are put in a fish-bowl. I was never supposed to be shackled or handcuffed because of my seizures. I have acute grand seizures. I can break my bones if I'm shackled like that and start seizing. They are not supposed to leave me alone like that but at TGK, all the girls were locked in like that . . . I kept telling them I did not have my meds."

Many women are victims of abuse and racial slurs by guards. Women are punished, punched, pushed around, and placed in isolation or lockdown for minor infractions such as asking repeatedly for an item like a sanitary pad or reacting too slowly to commands because of language barriers. According to a Colombian detainee, "Sometimes an officer, for whatever reason, decides to punish us and locks us down for a long period of time. I have gotten to a point of desperation locked up in that tiny room, and I have desperately cried. I have also consoled some of my cell mates when I have seen them affected by this. It is a large psychological harm which they are doing to us."

INDEFINITE DETENTION AND LACK OF DUE PROCESS

At TGK and the Broward Transitional Center (BTC) and Wakulla County Jail, Haitian women who have passed their credible-fear interview have had to prepare their political asylum applications, a very complicated process, on their own or sometimes with the help of a security guard who is clueless about the asylum request. Most of the women have been receiving one- or two-sentence responses from the Board of Immigration Appeals and now face deportation to turbulent Haiti, where their lives will be in danger. By keeping these women in detention, the department denies them the right to due process in a court of law.

On March 28, 2007, one hundred three Haitian refugees arrived from Hallandale Beach Boulevard. The fifty women in the group are very young. Their ages range from seventeen to thirty-seven, and fourteen of them are unaccompanied minors; nine of them are eleven to seventeen years old. Despite the fact that all of them have passed their credible-fear interviews, none have been released. The women all show signs of depression. Most of them have children in Haiti, and they suffer greatly from the long separation from their loved ones. The anguish of not knowing their fate or when they might see their children again places an unbearable emotional burden on these women. Many have suffered in their personal relationships and are victims of domestic violence, conditions that compound the tragedies that forced them out of their homeland in the first place. FANM, FIAC, the Haitian Lawyers Association, the Haitian-American Grassroots Coalition, and Church World Services have all called for the release of these desperate women, to no avail.

After months of fighting against the detention of women at the Krome camp, the women and their children as young as six months were moved to the Comfort Suites Hotel in South Miami. The Department of Homeland Security contracted with the hotel, which turned its entire fifth floor into a prison. The women and their children were held in secured rooms monitored by armed guards. The asylum seekers were locked in their rooms for twenty-four hours a day, seven days a week, without fresh air or exercise. The children became so distraught that several started to exhibit strange behaviors such as banging their heads on the walls, making strange sounds, and refusing to eat. FANM, FIAC, and the Haitian-American Grassroots Coalition fought and organized for months to have the women and children transferred from the "Hotel in Hell."

NIGHTLY RAIDS AND INCARCERATION

The United States continues to build prisons and is contracting with businesses nationwide to detain undocumented immigrants and refugees. The number of detained individuals jumped from 19,718 in 2005 to about 26,500 in 2006 and is projected to go much higher.

In recent years, women from Haiti and other Caribbean and Latin American countries who have been living in the United States for an average of ten years and have exhausted all their legal avenues have been subjected to raids during which they are hauled off in the early morning hours, in front of their children, to jails where it costs taxpayers ninety-five dollars a day to lock up each woman. Most of these women have worked in the United States for years, paying taxes and contributing to the U.S. economy, and they want to stay. They have no criminal records. When they are arrested, no provision is made for their children, who often end up in state custody.

For Mrs. H., a twenty-seven-year-old Honduran woman with two young boys who were born in the United States, the nightmare began on December 15, 2006, when she and her husband were arrested in a bus on their way to Miami to visit friends. A traffic stop ended with their arrest when they were unable to show immigration papers. They were both undocumented. She was sent to BTC, and her husband was sent to the Krome camp. She later learned that her husband was deported back to Honduras. No one told her what happened to her children despite her repeated requests to see them. She saw her children for the first time on February 14, 2007, when she learned that they had been placed in foster care. Mrs. H. was lucky to get help from the lawyers of the Florida Immigrant Advocacy Center. But many other women have no one to assist them. They are faceless, without documents and without rights.

U.S. policies are creating a vicious cycle. Haitians, for example, send about $1.17 billion a year in remittances to relatives in Haiti. When U.S. immigration authorities remove Haitian immigrants from their employment and place them in detention for deportation, they cut off the families' only lifeline and thus encourage additional asylum seekers to leave Haiti in search of hope and a better life. The U.S. government's forcible repatriation of Haitians is a racist policy that denies their basic rights. It destroys Haitian families and creates hopelessness and despair.

CONCLUSION

Women who are fleeing wars, persecution, and political instability to save their lives and search for freedom deserve fair, dignified, and humane treatment. The Department of Homeland Security has failed miserably to protect the women detainees in its custody and has sadly relegated them to the same status they had in their own country and for which they sought our protection: degraded and endangered persons. The United States can do better to protect the rights of women asylum seekers.

57

"Did you see no potential in me?"

The Story of Women Serving Long Sentences in Prison

Kathy Boudin

INTRODUCTION

Conversations about prison reform are beginning. The buzzword is *reentry*. The enormous expansion of prisons and the high recidivism rates are raising questions about mass incarceration as a solution to social problems. The conversation usually centers around drugs, the war on drugs, and nonviolent offenders. This chapter, however, takes the reader to a harder space: reform for women who have been convicted of a violent crime.

Women in prison are known as "talkers." Sometimes the prison "COs" (aka correctional officers, guards) complain about working in a women's prison. They'd rather work with men than have to listen to women talk all the time. "Talk, talk, talk," they say, "it makes you crazy." Sometimes I think that women in prison talk to stop themselves from going crazy. They tell stories about their lives: what happened, how they ended up in prison, their men, their mothers, their kids. *Maybe it will make sense. Maybe someone will listen. Maybe someone will understand.*

CASES/SITUATIONS

Many women are in prison for a crime that in one way or another relates to a relationship with a man. In a writing group, Maria began by telling a secret. She read her work aloud, haltingly. She had been raped by her cousins as a child. She had graduated from high school as a special ed student and was proud that she had graduated. As a young woman of twenty-one, she was raped again, this time by her best guy friend, with whom she and her family had grown up. Violated, feeling betrayed, she confronted him a few days later to ask him why he would do that to her, and she took a gun to help her feel safe. He laughed at her, and she saw the flash of a knife. She shot, and he died. His knife was found by his body. She received a twenty-five-year sentence. Had she ever shared with her family or police anything about that rape or the earlier one? No. Her mother had a hard enough time accepting that she was not a virgin, and Maria had never seen the police as her allies.

Most women in prison have a ranking of crimes. Women who are there for a child-related crime are low on the totem pole. Behind their backs, or outright in arguments, these women are referred to as "baby killers." Before joining a parenting class in which the women explore how they could have left their kids, they had to answer the question "Can you listen to the story of a woman who is here for the death of her child? Can you listen and suspend judgment?"

Many of the women in the group had been abused as children, but when Kendra told her story—her broken bones, her experience being locked in a closet, her inability to protect her own child who died—the women listened, felt the horror of the child she had been and also of the mother she was, the woman who could not protect either herself or her child, who died from neglect. Kendra is doing fifteen years to life.

Drugs are another major reason why women end up in prison. Anna, raised by a mother who used crack, in a home with no guidance, got pregnant and dropped out of high school in the tenth grade. Her world became the streets, and she was a fast learner who figured out how to make fast money. Selling drugs led to turf wars, which led to violence. Anna and another drug dealer got into a fight; Anna survived the fight but the dealer did not, and she is serving twenty years to life. For some women, like Tanya, childhood abuse was followed by drug addiction, leading to her constant need for money, which in turn led to armed robberies. Tanya is serving twenty-five years to life.

Many women are convicted of murder under the felony murder law that holds people responsible for a death that happens during a felony, such as an armed robbery, regardless of the fact that their role may have been that of an unarmed accomplice who was not present at the scene of the crime. Rosie was eighteen and served as a lookout for her twenty-nine-year-old boyfriend. Although Rosie was not at the robbery itself, was not armed, and did not kill anyone, the law makes her responsible for the murder. Rosie is serving thirty years to life and will have to complete thirty years before she goes to a parole board.

WHO'S IN FOR VIOLENT CRIMES

The women in these stories are all in prison for crimes that led to someone's death. Among the rising group of women in prison, approximately 20 percent have been convicted of violent crimes. Although, overall, women represent about 6 percent of state prisoners, they make up the fastest-growing segment of the prison population. Since 1980, both in New York State and nationally, the number of women imprisoned in the United States has increased at nearly double the rate of men (Beck 2000). The vast majority of women (and men) are in prison for nonviolent crimes, often related to drugs. But, regardless of the kind of crime, the stories behind the women's actions reveal social problems. A significant number of mothers in prisons had been struggling with drug use before their arrests. Close to 75 percent of women in prison had been using drugs regularly before their arrest, and 40 percent of women in the state prisons report being under the influence of drugs when they committed the crime for which they were last arrested (Mumola 1999). In addition, women who end up incarcerated commonly have endured abusive families and/or battering relationships. According to some studies cited by Covington (2003, 9), as many as 80 percent of incarcerated women were abused either as children or adults. Therefore, it is no surprise that women in prison face many mental health issues. Estimates suggest that from 25 percent to more than 60 percent of the women in prison need mental health support (Owen 2004). Studies show that a history of abuse frequently coexists with substance abuse and mental health problems (Covington 2003). Finally, economic survival has been a major issue for most women in prison: 30 percent of incarcerated women had been receiving welfare assistance before their arrest; fewer than 50 percent of them have graduated from high school or have a high school diploma. Race and class and disintegrating urban neighborhoods intertwine to become the defining elements of who ends up in prison: In New York State, 50 percent of the women in prison are black, 27 percent are Latina, and 25 percent are white (New York State Department of Correctional Services 1999).

THE COMMUNITY OF WOMEN
PRISONERS: WHO ARE THEY?

As a result of enormous efforts by women to draw attention to the issue of battered women, a public consciousness exists about women who have been victims of domestic violence. Some states have legal options that aid women who killed their abusers in self-defense. However, usually these legal options are narrow and apply to a limited group of women whose crimes fit narrow facts, even though a large number of women in prison have been victims of violence either as children or adults. Women incarcerated for crimes of violence are most often reduced, through labels and headlines, to their crime: "murderer," "baby killer," "man-hating bitch." However, for the vast majority of women in prison, their humanity and identities are hidden behind these labels; in prison, they are most likely to be rendered disposable. For example, in Alabama, three hundred women long-termers with the best institutional records were moved out of Alabama, away from their children, families, and community support, and sent to a private prison in Louisiana. Across the nation, as more prisons are built and people who are in for nonviolent crimes begin to get out, the long-termers are at the greatest risk of being kept in and rendered invisible. The policy is to keep the women long-termers in prison for as long as possible. Sometimes exceptions are made in the law and in public opinion for a woman who killed her batterer. In most states, women with crimes that led to the death of a person are having trouble getting out of prison, even if they can obtain a date with the parole board. In New York State, women who have committed violent crimes in which someone died and who have sentences of fifteen, eighteen, or twenty years to life become eligible for parole at the minimum sentence of fifteen, eighteen, or twenty that the judge has determined. At this point, the parole board usually tells them, "We recognize your growth and participation in programs, but because of the nature of the crime that you committed twenty-five years ago, parole is denied."

Shauna, sentenced to seventeen years to life, who was eighteen at her arrest, received her bachelor's and master's degrees in prison, taught parenting programs, developed printing skills, and thought that she would serve her minimum sentence of seventeen years. She dreamed that she would be able to begin life as a mature woman and have a child. She is now forty-two and has been "hit" by the parole board four times; she is waiting for her fifth parole board. Shauna has served eight more years than the judge's minimum sentence of seventeen years. This extended sentence amounts to a practice and policy of resentencing by the parole boards.

HOW WOMEN SPEAK ABOUT THEMSELVES AND THEIR CRIMES

Women are receiving longer and longer sentences: life without parole; forty years to life; seventy-five years to life—meaning that they will spend forty or seventy-five years in prison before they have even a possibility of going home. What happens to the women who see a future with no exit? The human spirit struggles. Some women are filled with guilt, remorse, a sense of responsibility, and they try to use groups in the prison to help them sort out their lives:

> I don't know what my truth is. I go from one thing to blaming my husband for everything, then I go to the other blaming myself. I have no in-between, I can't find no middle, I say it was the drugs, I say it was the abuse and then I blame it all on him, and then I'll go, it's my fault, you weren't good enough, you didn't stop it, so I don't know the truth. This person's life was taken in vain. I beat myself up every year it [the anniversary of the crime] comes around. I beat myself up, relive it. I feel like I have to, if I don't remember this person's face, then I'm saying his life wasn't worth anything, then I'm not honoring him . . . I never had the heart to tell my mother, hey you know I'm partly responsible for this, and at some point I know I have to take responsibility.

Many incarcerated women feel an injustice was done to them because their own life story was never heard, and they are determined to survive: Roslyn, sentenced to a minimum of fifty years for a crime she committed at seventeen, wrote a letter in a writing group that she imagined she would send to the judge who had sentenced her if he were still alive:

> Did you see no potential in me? You noted my high IQ, how "articulate" I was, how "mature." I'd run away from home because I refused to let my mother keep hurting me. You put me in a home for bad kids; my roommate wasn't even sane. I left there, too, so you put me in a group home. You call that help? No matter who I tried to tell, no one got it. So then you sentenced me, said no hope for rehabilitation, said I'm as good as dead. Just like my mother: kicks, flights of stairs, words that made me flinch. Well, you were both wrong. I have a life. I have a beautiful daughter, a college education. I teach parenting skills. I make a difference in people's lives. You never gave me a chance, so I made my own. My poverty, skin color, background, past—who at age seventeen can't change, won't grow? You robbed me of my youth, of my belief in justice. But from the graveyard, the barbed wire, and the cinderblock, I'm resurrected. I'm worthy. I'm somebody.

A SAD IRONY

Being in prison for a long time usually brings a lot of growth: reflection, education, maturing. Some women prisoners in Alabama saw the need to improve conditions for all the women in Alabama prisons and instituted a class action lawsuit to do so. They had the highest level of education and the ability to work together. They were punished by being removed to Louisiana (see chapter 59). But if one looks at the public safety risk, these women were the least likely to come back to prison. Moreover, the state of Alabama has spent over $10 million dollars to keep them in the private prison in Louisiana.

The women in New York State who go to the parole board and who are turned down because of an "instant offense" they committed fifteen, twenty, or twenty-five years ago are the least likely to ever return to prison. Of the ninety-two women convicted of a violent felony who were released and followed over a twenty-four-month period between 2000 and 2004, only one woman returned for a new offense (a robbery), which amounts to a recidivism rate of 1.1 percent. None of the twenty-four women who served fifteen years or more returned to prison. None of the forty-two women who served ten to fifteen years committed a new offense, and only one woman was returned to prison for a parole violation (Fine and Clear 2007). This record is in contrast to the 30-plus percent recidivism rate over a thirty-six-month period of all women released between 1985 and 1995 in New York State (Fine et al. 2001).

The sad irony lies not only in the recidivism rate but also in the nature of the women who cannot get out of prison. They are generally the ones who are role models for the younger and newer prisoners. They teach the AIDS and health programs, are the key tutors for GED classes, and teach parenting skills. They have spent so many years in prison that they symbolize the ability to survive, grow, and become "somebody." When the prison population sees these role models turned down by the parole board over and over again, hopelessness and demoralization cloud the prison yards.

The overuse of incarceration as a response to drugs in the community—their use and sale—has created a situation referred to as "mass incarceration." As a strategy, it does not address the underlying social issues, which is clear from the recidivism rate. The long sentences, the parole denials, the many ways of rendering invisible or dehumanizing women in prison who have committed violent crimes offer another window into the criminal justice system. Punishment: Is it solely about revenge? What happened to ideas of people changing, of prison being a place for rehabilitation? How did our prisons become a dead-end road?

From the classroom windows on the school building's second floor, we can watch when women leave. It's the Waving Goodbye Ritual. Just before the visitor's parking lot sits a small building. The departing prisoners enter one door of it. Five minutes later, they come out another door, free women. We watch our friends walk from the main entrance of the prison buildings into the small structure, then out into freedom. Today three women are leaving. They have lived with us for more than fifteen years each. We wave. They can't see our heads or bodies—just our hands sticking out. Waving our love and support. Waving our own dreams. Now, as I crane to catch a glimpse of my friends, I look into the sun's rays bouncing off the razor wire. Row on row, circle on circle, silver, gleaming. I wonder what happens to birds and butterflies— do they get caught in the wire? Do our dreams ultimately get caught in it? I can barely see my friends. Now I can't see them at all. My gaze is caught in the wire.

Can you recognize us yet? Can you *notice* us, phantom shapes shimmering behind you in your mirrors?

Women. Human. Like you.

REFERENCES

Beck, A. J. *Prisoners in 1999.* August 2002. Washington, DC: Bureau of Justice Statistics, U.S. Department of Justice.

Covington, S. C. 2003. A woman's journey home: Challenges for female offenders. In *Prisoners once removed: The impact of incarceration and reentry on children, families, and communities,* ed. J. Travis and M. Waul, 67–103. Washington, DC: Urban Institute Press.

Fine, M., and T. Clear. 2007. *Policy brief on long-term incarceration: An analysis by gender and crime in New York State.* New York: Graduate Center, City University of New York.

Fine, M., M. Torre, K. Boudin, I. Bowen, J. H. Clark, D. J. Hylton, M. Martinez et al. 2001. *Changing minds: The impact of college in a maximum security prison.* New York: Graduate Center, City University of New York.

Mumola, C. J. 1999. *Substance abuse and treatment, state and federal prisoners, 1997.* Washington, DC: Bureau of Justice Statistics, U.S. Department of Justice.

New York State Department of Correctional Services. 1999. *Men and women under custody 1987–1998.* New York: Department of Correctional Services.

Owen, B. 2004. Women and imprisonment in the United States: The gendered consequences of the U.S. imprisonment binge. In *The criminal justice system and women: Offenders, prisoners, victims, and workers,* 3rd ed., ed. B. R. Price and N. J. Sokoloff, 195–206. Boston: McGraw Hill.

58

Dignity Denied

The Price of Imprisoning Older Women in California

Legal Services for Prisoners with Children

Elder prisoners are costly to care for, yet research indicates that many of these older inmates represent a relatively low risk of reoffending and show high rates of parole success. A 2003 estimate by the Legislative Analyst's Office suggests that releasing nonviolent prisoners over fifty-five would result in state savings of approximately 9 million in the budget year and significantly more in the out-years without jeopardizing public safety.[1]

Some older inmates may be good candidates for community placement. Perhaps some who committed murder a long time ago truly no longer pose a threat to society.[2]

Prisons are alien and intimidating places to people struggling with the sensitivities and vulnerabilities of old age and illness. In short, providing care in prison settings poses significant challenges to ethical and effective medical practice.[3]

> Staff says all inmates are to be treated just alike. There is no differentiation, whether you're old, crippled or whatever.
>
> *Myrtle Green, seventy-three*

> The only fear I've got is dying in prison.
>
> *Martha Roberts, eighty-two*

AGING PRISONER CRISIS

California legislators currently face an urgent fiscal crisis generated by the graying of the state's prison population. Because of "tough on crime" policies such as mandatory minimum sentences, the "Three Strikes" law, and a general reluctance to release long-term prisoners on parole, more Californians are growing older in prison than ever before. Moreover, prisons are not geared to the specific needs and vulnerabilities of older people.

The continued incarceration of frail elders—who represent the smallest threat to public safety but the largest cost to incarcerate—embodies failed public policy. California policy makers have an opportunity to create meaningful solutions to this crisis by taking measures to ensure the rights and dignity of older prisoners and creating community-based alternatives to their incarceration. Such measures are in accordance with a social commitment to ensuring that society's elders live out their lives in dignity, and they are ultimately in the interest of building a safer California.

SCOPE OF THE PROBLEM

According to the most recent statistics, the state incarcerated approximately 7,550 persons over the age of fifty-five. Estimates indicate that by 2022, more than 30,000 older people will be incarcerated in California.

The annual cost of incarcerating an older prisoner is approximately $70,000 a year, nearly double that of a younger prisoner.

Older prisoners have the lowest rates of recidivism of any segment of the prison population and have the highest rates of parole success.

Older prisoners face a unique set of health and safety concerns as they grow old in a system not designed to address their specific needs.

Concerned about this situation, Legal Services for Prisoners with Children (LSPC), a prisoner advocacy organization, spent nearly two years investigating the health and safety concerns of older women prisoners. As part of the investigation, LSPC surveyed 120 women prisoners over fifty-five who are incarcerated in the California state prison system, which represents approximately 34 percent of the female prison population that is over fifty-five. In addition, LSPC conducted a series of semistructured interviews with older women prisoners and their families and friends. The results of this investigation as well as policy recommendations appear in our report *Dignity Denied: The Price of Imprisoning Older Women in California*.

SUMMARY OF FINDINGS

Older prisoners must contend with prison rules that require them to drop to the ground for alarms, climb onto top bunks, and undress for strip-searches. In addition, the built environment (for example, the limited number of bottom bunks, cells without handrails, and long-distance walks to the dining hall) contributes to making life difficult for older people.

Most older women live eight to a cell, with only minimal consideration to cell mates' ages, health status, or physical limitations. Though many older women articulate the frustrations of overcrowding, noise, lack of privacy, and intergenerational tensions, they also reaffirm the importance of maintaining social relationships with younger prisoners.

The California Department of Corrections and Rehabilitation (CDCR) sets no retirement age for prisoners; all but the most ill and disabled prisoners are required to work or participate in a prison program. Failure by prison staff to adequately consider an individual's age, abilities, health status, and physical limitations when issuing job assignments routinely puts older prisoners at risk for injury.

The CDCR's systemic failure to provide humane medical care was a prominent theme in our surveys. Respondents cited several issues: the barrier to care imposed by the five dollar copay, long delays in receiving treatment, difficulties in obtaining medication in a timely manner, lack of preventive care, inadequate nutrition, and lack of mental health services.

Nearly half of older women responded "yes" to questions that are indicators of depression. The majority identified the outside help of family and friends as their greatest source of support during their incarceration.

STATISTICS AT A GLANCE

Three out of four respondents are serving sentences of either life or life without parole.

Almost half of respondents have been in prison more than sixteen years.

Half of respondents identified domestic violence as a factor in their crime.

Over half of respondents reported falling in the previous year. Nearly half of respondents reported being injured while performing a prison routine, such as climbing onto top bunks, dropping to the ground for alarms, or undressing for strip-searches.

One out of four respondents reported difficulty getting help during an emergency.

Two out of three respondents reported being assigned to a prison job that was difficult to perform, such as a janitorial position, work on a yard crew, and kitchen duty.

Nearly half of respondents experienced difficulties paying the five dollar copay.

RECOMMENDATIONS

LSPC's report presents two categories of recommendations: measures to reduce the number of older prisoners, and short-term recommendations to ameliorate the conditions of confinement faced by older prisoners. Geriatric prisons are not a recommended solution because of CDCR's troubled history of providing specific and specialized care to its most vulnerable prisoners. Highlights of the recommendations follow.

Reduce the Number of Older Prisoners

Implement the Legislative Analyst's Office recommendation to save the state over $9 million dollars in a single year by releasing all nonviolent prisoners over fifty-five on geriatric parole.

Expand the compassionate release law to include older and disabled prisoners.

Establish a home-monitoring program that allows older prisoners to serve the remainder of their sentences on home confinement.

Reform current parole policies to ensure release for eligible prisoners serving indeterminate sentences.

Repeal California's "Three Strikes Law" to curb the exponential increase of the elderly prisoner population.

Improve the Lives of Older Prisoners

Establish training for correctional staff working with older prisoners.

Appoint an ombudsperson who reports directly to the legislature about CDCR's progress in enforcing new policies aimed at meeting the specific needs of older prisoners.

Establish a yearly comprehensive geriatric assessment for prisoners over fifty-five.

Establish an "over fifty-five" status that affords older prisoners age-specific consideration and assistance in housing, programming, and the activities of daily life.

Designate a certain number of cells within the general-population housing units as "over fifty-five" cells.

Establish a retirement policy for prisoners and couple it with the development of age-appropriate activities.

Work with community volunteers and organizations to establish age-appropriate programs and activities specially geared to seniors.

Conduct health-education classes for prisoners that focus on aging and include information about the unique health and psychosocial issues faced by older people.

Eliminate the five dollar copay for prisoners' for medical visits.

Allow prerelease prisoners to apply for MediCal benefits before their release to ensure that benefits begin immediately upon their departure.

Establish case managers to coordinate prerelease planning and postrelease services that address the specific concerns of elderly parolees.

NOTES

1. Legislative Analyst's Office, 2003.
2. California Department of Corrections, 1999.
3. National Institute of Corrections, 2004.

59

The Longtimers/Insiders Activist Group at Tutwiler Prison for Women

Erline Bibbs

The Longtimers/Insiders group grew out of the *Laube v. Campbell* lawsuit, which a group of women prisoners, of which I was a part, filed in August 2002 against the Alabama Department of Corrections and the State of Alabama. When we sued, Tutwiler Prison for Women housed more than 1,000 women in a decrepit facility built in 1942 to hold 365 women. Every dormitory was filled front to back with bunkbeds. The weather gets extremely hot in the summers—the heat index regularly rises over 100 degrees in the facility—and cold in the winters. Designed to cross-ventilate through large open windows, the physical structure is now so old that all the windows have been braced so that they open only a few inches at the top. Personal space is nonexistent, and security is very poor. The medical system was in chaos at the time of the case, contracted out to a private for-profit company that operated with no oversight.

In December 2002, after a preliminary injunction hearing that lasted five days, federal district court judge Myron Thompson declared Tutwiler Prison constitutionally unsafe. He ruled that the prison was a "ticking time bomb." He gave state officials thirty days to develop a plan to remedy the conditions.

In April 2003, as part of the state's plan to reduce overcrowding at Tutwiler, it sent 140 of us from Tutwiler out of state to a prison run by Louisiana Correctional Services, a private prison company. We were shipped off in the middle of the night to Basile, Louisiana, a small town in the swamps of southwest Louisiana. In June 2003, another 100 were sent, and what we now call the "Tutwiler/Louisiana shuffle" began. The Alabama Department of Corrections (ADOC), trying to stay ahead of the game and keep its numbers down at Tutwiler, would sometimes ship a woman two or three times back and forth without regard to her personal situation. The most important thing to the prison authorities was the numbers, not the women.

Many of us pointed out that women being sent to Louisiana were being pulled out of educational and treatment programs. Though Tutwiler did not have enough programs, it had some, but the private prison in Louisiana did not offer *any* educational opportunities. Some women had court orders stating that they could not be paroled or released until they had completed certain drug treatment or educational programs. Ironically, we were told that the ADOC chose prisoners for transfer based on our good conduct at Tutwiler.

A few months after the first rounds of transfers, a group of us who were serving long sentences got together and formed the Longtimers/Insiders. The group wanted to have a voice in the decision making. We feared that once in Louisiana, we would be "out of sight, out of mind." We felt as if Alabama had sent us off to the wolves to be used, abused, and mistreated by strangers who were being paid to care for us . . . and failing. We had been taken away from our children and family members. We felt it was time to speak up, make a stand, and be heard.

The number of women in prison is growing very fast. In Alabama, the number of women and girls in the prison has grown 645 percent since the late 1970s. Women are the backbone of society, and there needs to be a lot of study into why women are the fastest-growing segment of the prison population.

The Southern Center for Human Rights had represented the women of Tutwiler as class counsel in the *Laube* case. Now the center helped those of us in Louisiana start to organize and learn how to make a difference in the right way. Since that time, we have worked together on our own to develop the skills to collectively produce a platform, write articles for the newspapers, write letters to our representatives in the legislature, discuss legislation and have people lobby on our behalf at the legislature, and challenge the parole board on its "certificate of due diligence" policies. We have increased public awareness of our cause and are continually striving to give input to a system that has not allowed us to be heard.

One of our biggest achievements happened the first time we had lobbying representation in the legislature. The 2006 legislature passed Joint Resolution 15, establishing the Commission on Girls and Women in the Criminal Justice System. The commission is charged with studying the conditions, needs, and problems of the criminal justice system in Alabama for girls and women. Since we have not been able to thank the women who fought for us in person, we want to thank them publicly in this article: thanks to Representative Barbara Boyd and Representative Laura Hall for caring and believing in us enough to carry this resolution for us.

Ann Jacobs of the Women's Prison Association and Phyllis Modley of the National Institute of Justice came to Alabama in September 2006 to speak with the Commission on Girls and Women about the need for gender-responsive risk assessment. From the beginning, we have wanted to make clear to the outside world that women are different from men in the area of crime and in the ways in which they get tangled up in the criminal justice system. We believe that classification and parole decisions should be gender responsive. All the studies show that women go to prison for different reasons than men do, and women have different needs than men in programs designed to keep them out of prison. It doesn't make sense to pretend we are the same as men when we're not. Treating us differently is not being discriminatory, it's being fair.

(We have been told that the ADOC intends to start using gender-specific criteria for its classification. This step is a start, but only a start. The parole board should also use gender-responsive risk assessment to determine who can safely be released. Also, *dynamic* risk assessment is best for both classification and release decisions, since it pays attention to the things that can be changed—housing, employment, and so on—to keep women from ending up in prison.)

The state of Alabama does not yet recognize the need to help women rather than lock them up, especially the women who are in trouble because of drug addiction, mental illness, or domestic violence. None of the state's self-defense statutes take into account the fact that some women in prison are there because they had to act to protect themselves and their children. Another problem is that Alabama's "accessory to a crime" laws make a person sitting in the car just as guilty as the person who goes into a store and shoots the store clerk. Many of the women who are deemed violent offenders and are serving long sentences actually had no idea that their boyfriend or boyfriend's buddy was going to go into a store and rob it or kill someone.

For women in our group who had a good public defender, some of these issues came out. Most of us, however, had no public defenders, just part-time lawyers appointed from a list of lawyers who thought of our cases as ways to earn some extra cash, but who had no real interest in helping us understand what was going on. These lawyers saw us as their clients and knew that the easiest thing to do was to pressure us to take a plea bargain. Just sit down in any dormitory and ask how many women were "promised" by their appointed lawyers that they would "be out in three years" or "walk out the door in seven years" if they would take the plea and stay out of trouble while in prison. These women *have* stayed out of trouble but are now going on ten, fifteen, or more years.

The Longertimers/Insiders group is raising concerns about the new women's prison that the state is considering building. One of our major concerns is the size of the prison. We would like to see a 700- or 800-bed facility instead of a 1,600- or 2,200-bed prison. When we look around and see who is in here with us, it is obvious that most of the women should be in drug treatment or work release rather than in prison. We believe that if the state were to spend the money it wants to spend on a new prison on developing work release opportunities and building drug treatment programs around the state instead, the new prison could be a small one. The benefit of a small prison is that it can work to rehabilitate rather than just warehouse women.

Another concern about the new prison is the location. It is hard enough as it is to get good nurses and doctors out to Tutwiler, which is thirty minutes from Montgomery. The state has made some improvements in the medical system at Tutwiler, but the medical care will deteriorate very quickly if the state places the new prison in one of the many rural towns trying to attract it. Of course, the new prison should contain enough staffing and space for education, recreation, and programs.

Instead of building a large-capacity prison, the state could spend the money in a lot of better ways. Building another work release site for women would allow those of us who are serving long sentences to stay connected to the free world and to come out of prison with enough savings to get housing and have time to find a job. The state needs to be able to identify women who are low risk (rather than simply relying on the current categories of "violent" and "nonviolent" prisoners) and send them out the door. Most important, having well-run drug treatment facilities—ones that understand that women especially need to deal with low self-esteem, lack of job skills, child care, and mental health issues all at the same time—would help all the women who really want a better life, for themselves and their families.

The Longtimers/Insiders group is looking to the commission to make its recommendations to the governor, the legislature, and the judiciary about what needs to be done to improve Alabama. We are working to make sure the recommendations will downsize the present population and find a better way than prison to deal with the problems faced by women in Alabama.

60

The Forgotten Population

*A Look at Death Row in the United States
through the Experiences of Women*

Capital Punishment Project, Women's Rights Project, National
Prison Project, National Criminal Justice Program, and the
National Clearinghouse for the Defense of Battered Women

Since 1973, 148 women have been sentenced to death in the United States. As of December 2004, when we conducted our study, there were 50 women on death row. These women varied in age from twenty-two to seventy-three years old and had been on death row for periods ranging from a few months to nearly twenty years. While much attention has been paid to women who have already been executed, such as Aileen Wournos and Karla Faye Tucker, little is known about the experiences of women who are living on death row.

Our report, The Forgotten Population, reviews the cases of sixty-six women, including the fifty-six women who lived on death row at some time between April 2002 and December 2003 and the ten women who were executed between 1984 and 2002. It marks the first time anyone has surveyed women about their experiences on death row. The Forgotten Population was produced by three programs of the American Civil Liberties Union—the Capital Punishment Project, Women's Rights Project, and National Prison Project—along with the National Criminal Justice Program of the American Friends Service Committee and the National Clearinghouse for the Defense of Battered Women.

The project team found that women's experiences on death row mirror many of the problems that have been documented in the cases of men condemned to death, such as inadequate defense counsel, official misconduct, poverty, alcoholism, drug abuse, mental retardation, and mental illness. However, in addition to facing these problems, numerous women on Death Row have also suffered abuse and domestic violence. Moreover, once incarcerated, women face unique challenges living on death row, including mistreatment and lack of access to necessary services that are generally available to their male counterparts. A particularly disturbing finding of the report is the degree to which many of these women live in virtual isolation, which often leads to psychosis or exacerbates existing mental illnesses.

The Forgotten Population makes thirteen recommendations to improve conditions for women living on death row and to ensure that women receive fair and adequate defense counsel when charged with capital offenses. The recommendations include:

- establishing programs to train defense counsel to litigate issues of abuse
- providing adequate support and assistance to abused women
- integrating women on death row into regular prison units
- providing women on death row with opportunities to work
- adopting prison staffing policies to prevent abuse
- amending the Prison Litigation Reform Act to provide access to the courts for women who are sexually abused while in prison

Following are some of the highlights from the report:

- Women on death row are likely to have received ineffective defense counsel or to have been subjected to official misconduct by prosecutors during their trials. Because of such unfair and inadequate defense, two death-sentenced women were found innocent and exonerated. A third woman, Frances Newton, awaited execution in Texas at the time of the study. Her trial attorney did not interview any witnesses in preparation for trial. The majority of the evidence against her was forensic evidence processed at the thoroughly discredited Houston crime lab. She has always maintained her innocence.
- Nearly two-thirds of the women had experienced regular, ongoing abuse as children and as adults. In many cases, independent evidence was available to verify these claims, but some defense attorneys failed to present this information during trial, and juries were unable to take this history into consideration before sentencing the women to death.
- Of the cases reviewed, thirty-three women acted with at least one other person. In twenty-two of those cases, the codefendant received a sentence other than death—even in cases in which defendants appeared to be equally culpable.
- Nearly two-thirds of the women on death row were convicted of killing family members or people they knew. No one has calculated how many of the men on death row are there for killing family members, but from what we know of the general prison population, women who are in prison are more likely than men prisoners to have killed family members or intimates.
- In nearly one-third of the sixty-six cases reviewed, women on death row were

accused of committing homicide by their intimate partner, usually a man (six-teen were accused by a man, and one was accused by a woman), whose self-interest was served by blaming the woman for the crime. Eleven of the women were sentenced to death for a homicide that they claimed to have committed under threat of coercion by a male perpetrator in order to protect themselves or their children.

· In addition to enduring the harsh conditions of prison life, most women on death row live in almost complete isolation, rarely leaving their cells, and most of their infrequent human contact is with sometimes-hostile guards.

· One in five women in our survey reported that she had been assaulted or sexually harassed while in prison. A third of the respondents said that corrections officers observed them when they used the toilet, showered, or dressed.

· Although nearly all of the women who responded to our survey reported that they had been addicted to drugs or alcohol at the time of their arrest, two-thirds said that no drug or alcohol treatment was available at their prison. In addition, although more than half reported that they had been victims of physical or sexual abuse, fewer than half of the facilities offered counseling for sexual, physical, or emotional abuse.

PART SEVEN

Struggling for Rights

UNDER A REGIME OF MASS INCARCERATION, what is the definition of "prisoners' rights?" How are rights protected, asserted, lost, and gained? In this section, we provide examples of the ways that incarcerated women and their allies are approaching matters of rights and developing rights claims in a variety of domains.

Here we encounter another "bill of rights," this time, the Incarcerated Young Mothers' Bill of Rights, a ten-point visionary document that codifies what must not be left to chance. This document seeks to draw a thick, bright line that prison authorities dare not cross, even though the incarcerated females in question are young and particularly vulnerable. The incarcerated young mothers have identified respect, information, and access to advocates as conditions of their lives in prison that they cannot do without. They want to keep or regain their health. They take their status as mothers very seriously and want the prison authorities to do the same. Despite their status as incarcerated persons, these young women, perhaps especially because they are mothers, see reason to live for and plan for the future.

For many incarcerated persons, "rights" must include the right to communicate with family and allies on the outside, free of the outrageous surcharges that telephone companies, in collusion with the governments of some states, have tacked on to calls into and out of prisons. Annette Dickerson and Lauren Melodia explain the damage these practices have caused families and describe the campaigns that prisoners, their families, and allies have organized for "telephone justice."

Three excerpts from a prisoners' newspaper, *The Fire Inside*, lay out a critique of

---

Escort, 2002. Women's Community Correctional Center, Kailua, Hawaii. Photograph by Cindy Ellen Russell labor conditions inside the Central California Women's Facility in Chowchilla. The pieces also offer an opportunity to educate the public about practices that violate prisoner-worker dignity and health and lay down a set of principles for protecting prisoner-workers' rights inside.

Two pieces in this section see a core "rights" problem in the way that prosecutorial and incarceration systems fail to distinguish between victims and perpetrators. Several women write about their journeys as battered women, and the testimony of Kemba Smith, who had never handled, used, or sold any drugs when she was sentenced as a first-time nonviolent drug offender to almost twenty-five years in prison, defines the contours of "the girlfriend problem."

Five additional writers in this section observe their personal situations from a rights perspective. In turn, Justice Now director, Cynthia Chandler, and others address the complicated issue of "gender responsiveness," a concept that is shaping debates about where and to what ends women should be incarcerated in California and, by example, elsewhere.

61

Incarcerated Young Mothers' Bill of Rights

From A Vision to a Policy at San Francisco Juvenile Hall

Sophia Sanchez

In November 2006, there was a ribbon-cutting ceremony at the new Juvenile Justice Center in San Francisco, and planners asked the Center for Young Women's Development (CYWD) to provide a speaker on the Incarcerated Young Mothers' Bill of Rights, which had recently become policy for the new facility. I and others at the center wanted to make clear that CYWD was not there to celebrate the opening of a new prison to house young people, but that if the city was going to open a new jail, it needed to have a policy and procedure to protect the rights of the young parents who would be housed in the facility. The Incarcerated Young Mothers' Bill of Rights is now policy and aims to protect the rights of pregnant and parenting young mothers at San Francisco's new juvenile hall.

In the center's effort to break the cycle of incarceration, we knew we had to do something with the Incarcerated Young Mothers' Bill of Rights to keep our families together. In July 2005, the Young Mothers Organizing project here at CYWD, along with the Girls Justice Initiative, came to San Francisco's chief juvenile probation officer, Bill Sifferman, with our stories of inhumane treatment and hopes for making the bill of rights a policy. He embraced the project and promised to put together a work group to build a policy around the bill of rights for San Francisco's juvenile hall. At the table with CYWD in the meetings to develop the policy were the heads of Juvenile Probation, the director of the Juvenile Justice Center, detention staff and counselors, nurse practitioners and doctors from the Department of Public Health Special Programs for Youth, and Julie Posadas Guzman, director of the Girls Justice Initiative, whose guidance and direction were crucial to making this policy a reality.

We met once a month for a year to hammer out a policy that could protect the rights of incarcerated parents and function realistically for each department. The process was difficult, and we seemed to be speaking different languages. But in the end, not only did we come up with a great new policy but we had established strong relationships with folks at juvenile hall that would improve our ability to advocate for the young women locked up there.

With the new policy, mothers can visit with their children during normal visiting hours and they can do so unshackled. Young women must be treated with respect by probation and detention staff at all times. Young women can call to check on their children every day. Parents are allowed extra phone calls when they first enter jail so that they can make sure their children are safe. Young women who give birth while in custody or who have a medical emergency or miscarriage now have the right to have support people at the hospital with them. They have the right to give birth unshackled. Young women have the right to continue parenting their children. These are just a few of the highlights of a policy that will dramatically improve conditions for young mothers at San Francisco's Juvenile Justice Center.

However, the policy is one thing, and the practice is another. We are keeping a close watch on mothers locked up at juvenile hall to make sure that this policy is put into practice. We plan to educate all young women about this new policy and to walk them through the grievance procedure if the policy is not followed. We hope that all parties who helped make this policy a reality will live up to their commitments.

Though we celebrate a victory as our Incarcerated Young Mothers' Bill of Rights becomes policy, we still have so much work to do. Mothers in virtually every other California county outside of San Francisco are still fighting to be recognized as parents, for the right to visit their children. Just on the other side of town is a county jail in which many parents never get to touch or visit with their children. In the California Youth Authority, mothers are still fighting for proper prenatal care and education and for their right to recover and nurse their babies in the hospital. We must reflect as a society, and more importantly as a community, about why we do not have policies and legislation to protect the rights of incarcerated parents. Why, in 2006, is this the first policy of its kind?

The Center for Young Women's Development would like to thank Bill Sifferman and members of the work group for having the courage to realize and admit that things did in fact need to change and for being willing to be the first city and county in the entire nation to design a policy jointly with the community specifically to protect the rights of young parents.

It also is necessary and important to honor the young women who challenged the status quo and who inspired this project; their voices should not be forgotten. These amazing women include Delma Valencia, Elisa Talavera, Karla Pena, Esmeralda Urquilla, Cherise McClendon, Kimberly Butler, Patty Rincon, and Veronica Araiba. The progress we have made has stemmed from the courage and vision of these young mothers.

To support the implementation of this policy, the Young Mothers Organizing Project has completed a young mother's survival guide, *My Life Chose Me: A Young Mother's Guide to Surviving the System.* The sixty-page guide explains not only how to navigate the family-court system while in detention but also how young mothers who are incarcerated can work with Child Protective Services to establish guardianship for their children with family members or loved ones. In addition, it offers step-by-step guidance on how to reunify with their children when they are released. The guide has grown to incorporate "10 ways to show your child you love them" and "Making the truth fit to tell: How to talk to your child about your incarceration." The manual, which has been in the making for a year, includes perforated letters to family court and probation officers and is the most recent effort of CYWD to continue the fight to keep this system from tearing our families apart.

Though today we celebrate this policy and our newest advocacy tool, we have so much more to do. In the meantime, the ones who are suffering the most are our children, who have done nothing wrong. CYWD will continue fighting for the rights of all pregnant and parenting incarcerated mothers, until we as a community are able to keep our families together, even beyond the walls.

PREFACE TO THE INCARCERATED YOUNG MOTHERS' BILL OF RIGHTS

At the Center for Young Women's Development, young mothers came together to create the Young Incarcerated Mothers' Bill of Rights. This bill is modeled after the Children of Incarcerated Parents Bill of Rights, created by the San Francisco Partnership for Incarcerated Parents.

Please know as you read this ten-point declaration that these are not in fact your rights. It is our hope that someday, someday soon, these will in fact be the rights of all mothers in the state of California, and throughout the nation. Baby Mammas United, who created the Bill of Rights, is fighting to make these rights a reality for all young mothers. To join the fight, please log on to www.cywd.org.

INCARCERATED YOUNG MOTHERS' BILL OF RIGHTS

1. We have the right to be treated with dignity and respect.
2. We have the right to be mothers and not be discriminated against because of our age and status of offense.
3. We have the right to regular check-ups and proper prenatal care and nutrition.
4. We have the right to have somebody with us while we're having our babies.

5. We have the right to not be handcuffed and shackled during labor.
6. We have the right to recovery in the hospital after birth.
7. We have the right to see, touch, and speak with our children.
8. We have the right to be informed about our children's well-being and safety.
9. We have the right to have support and advocacy while incarcerated and the right to know our rights as parents.
10. We have the right to have access to information and education, such as prenatal and parenting classes, so that we have the ability to be the best parents we can be.

62
___

Slaving in Prison

A Three-Part Indictment

These three pieces are from The Fire Inside, *a publication of the California Coalition for Women Prisoners, Issue 34, Fall 2006/Winter 2007.*

I. NEW MILLENNIUM SLAVERY
by shawnna d. and the Fire Inside Editorial Collective

Just as newly freed Africans were convicted of minor offenses and then, as prisoners or indentured servants, used as cheap (free) labor for industrial capitalists, poor people and people of color are similarly targeted and incarcerated at disproportionate rates today. Once incarcerated, California prison laborers are paid almost nothing for their labor. In addition they are regularly exposed to extreme weather conditions, abusive supervisors, and unsafe work environments.

Over the past two decades incarceration has become one of America's top growth industries—an industry replete with Wall Street investors, trade exhibitions, conventions, and scholarly journals. Most prisoners work as clerks, porters, or kitchen and yard workers and earn nothing or as little as 8 cents an hour.

Prison Industry Authority (PIA), the state agency operating California's prison industries, employs approximately 6,000 California prisoners and provides over 60 types of goods and services. Prisoners working for PIA make dentures, glasses, American flags, clothing, and office furniture used by state institutions. They earn from 30 to 95 cents per hour.

A few prisoners work for Joint Ventures—a collaboration between California prisons and private corporations—and they earn the "prevailing wages." These prisoners are required to pay toward their room and board, restitution, and mandatory savings. Only a small portion can be used for purchasing needed items from canteen. The corporations earn huge profits. Allwire Electronics operating out of CCWF [Central California Women's Facility], for example, reports $10–15 million in annual sales, yet pays most prisoner laborers a minimum wage.

The job skills acquired by those participating in prison labor programs, for the most part, are not marketable in today's workplace. Prisoners working for PIA are using obsolete equipment and outdated techniques. Those few who do acquire a marketable skill, may still not get a job because of the stigma of being a former prisoner.

Although prisoner work assignments are supposed to be voluntary, prisoners who either refuse or are unable to work suffer significant consequences: they can be out of their cells for only 2 hours per day, they are allowed to spend a maximum of $35, and they are ineligible to earn half-time credit.

Workplace injuries are common. Yet neither PIA nor Joint Ventures provides any insurance. If a prisoner insists on receiving medical attention, she will risk possible retaliation from CO's and free world staff.

A History of Prison Labor

Prior to the emancipation of the enslaved African, penal institutions were to rehabilitate criminal offenders based on a belief that the offender could be reformed. At the close of the American Civil War, the purpose changed from rehabilitation to providing a virtually free labor source for capital. Emancipation of the slaves created a demand for cheap labor.

The link between slavery and incarceration is clear. The Thirteenth Amendment to the U.S. Constitution states: "Neither slavery nor involuntary servitude, except as punishment for a crime whereof the party shall have been duly convicted, shall exist in the United States. . . . " Still, today's penitentiary is nothing more than a new millennium plantation and prison laborers are the new millennium slaves.

The ever-increasing incarceration rates could be reduced by investing in programs that prevent incarceration as well as those that promote successful re-entry to society. Shockingly, California spends over $30,000 per capita for incarceration and less than $6,000 per student for education. The average level of education for California's prison population is 7th grade.

CDCR's [California Department of Corrections and Rehabilitation's] premise for prison labor is "to reduce prisoner idleness and violence, and increase successful re-entry for prisoners." The reality is that in California, on any given day, the number of parole violators can easily exceed that of new commitments, which speaks to the failure of that goal and shows the ways poor people and people of color are targeted under America's newest form of enslavement. The prison system remains complicit in this evolving form of new millennium slavery.

II. PRISON LABOR HIERARCHY

Joint Ventures [assignments] are at the "top" of the jobs for prisoners. Here are a few facts about Joint Ventures: Proposition 139, passed by California voters in 1990, allows private businesses to contract with the CDCR to hire people incarcerated in CA state prisons to produce on prison grounds goods for sale. Participating businesses get a 10% tax credit. Businesses do not have to pay overtime, worker's compensation, vacation, or sick leave. Wages are comparable to wages earned on the outside. However, deductions are made for taxes, room and board, restitution, and family support. The prisoner only receives 20% of wages. Training is unpaid. In 2004, only 150 people incarcerated in California state prisons were employed though Joint Ventures and only 6 out of the 32 prisons have a Joint Ventures program. Both CCWF and VSPW [Valley State Prison for Women] have Joint Ventures. CCWF's is with Allwire Corp., which manufactures cables, circuit boards, and other electronic components.

In 2002, 167 prisoners at Donovan State Correctional Facility won a class action lawsuit against CMT Blues, which produces clothing for brands including Mecca, Seattle Cotton Works, Lee Jeans, No Fear, and Trinidad Tees, and were awarded $841,000 in back pay because of the company's violations of wage and hour requirements.

In 2004, a San Diego Superior Court judge assumed control over the Joint Ventures program in response to complaints that employed prisoners were not paid fairly or even at all. The stipulated injunction required that the director of the CDCR Joint Ventures program report to this judge on the status of compliance for two years.

Prison Industry Authority [jobs] are the second "layer" of jobs for prisoners. Pay starts at 30 cents per hour and goes up to 95 cents. At CCWF, for example, PIA jobs consist of:

PIA farm: cultivate almond trees and grow alfalfa.

PIA warehouse: warehouse for prison supplies.

PIA fabric: sew jumpsuits for county jails, men's underwear, men's T-shirts (for men's prisons), flags, silk screening. The shop looks like a 19th century sweatshop, no A/C in summer, no heating in winter, lots of lint, which has caused fires when it gets into the machines, the preservative on the fabric causes women's hands to break out in hives, etc.

PIA dental lab: make dentures, partials, night-guards for state prisons and some veteran homes. It is a good skill. People are able to get a job outside after working there and getting experience. There used to be a training program, but it was cut a few years ago.

Bottom of the pyramid: the mostly unpaid, though sometimes paying 8 cents to 37 cents per hour, jobs such as:

Central kitchen: various aspects of food preparation.

Dining room: serving food, cleaning after meals, etc. Women in those jobs are sometimes burned by the heavy hot pans.

Porters: mop, sweep, clean cop-shops.

Yard crew: maintain the outside: have to work in all kinds of weather with no protection (no sun-screen in the summer, little protection from the cold and rain in the winter).

Maintenance of electrical appliances: lights, fans, washers and dryers.

. . .

III. WORKING FOR THE PIA
by Edaleen Smith "Mama Sherrie," Central California Women's Facility

I'm writing from behind the wall in Chowchilla, CCWF. For the record, incarcerated women have no equal opportunity or support working in Prison Industry Authority.

It's no secret that they slave drive inmates all day long in uncomfortable positions. Spending 8 to 10 hours a day on the sewing machine, in chairs that are not up to date, at the end of the day you hurt so bad. On other stations you find women on their feet working physically so hard that they bleed from the pressure on the body, which must burn out.

It's a disgraceful business, you work so hard on the sewing machines and you don't even get minimum wage. You don't feel your work is valued, because all you get is chump change. My pay is 30 cents per hour or $2.40 per day. I work my tail off for a little bit of nothing. The state takes out 44 (now 55) percent for restitution. It's a form of abuse.

For real, we have no rights here. One day I had such a bad headache I felt dizzy. But I could not leave to get medication. My supervisor said I was needed on the sewing machine. There is no mercy or grace.

And you better not get sick or get hurt because they will find a way to say you are in the wrong, write you a 115 [a citation for bad conduct], and you may be out of a job. I had a stroke on the job, and the only thing that mattered to them was that I stopped putting out the product according to their quota.

We don't have any control over the working conditions, which are unbearable. It's real dusty in the shop. The fabric is treated with chemicals that irritate your skin, cause itching, redness and bumps, which develop into sores and lesions.

You come in here with a sentence to do your prison time. But being a PIA slave you pick up other charges. The money you earn is so little, it's not enough for basic hygiene items or food you may need from the canteen—the prison does not supply enough of either. So you end up taking the boxer shorts, or anything, to trade for things to take care of yourself. When caught, you get more charges against you and you lose your job. You feel guilty all over again.

I don't understand, what are they teaching us? That it's OK to work in sweatshops, be underpaid, and get new charges against you, otherwise you're selfish? They make it as though PIA is so great—they hold job interviews, etc., as though it was an important position. But the pay is so little you might as well stay in and not work. The only real incentive to work is to earn half-time if you're eligible.

I don't see how it's benefiting the women to work for the PIA. If they ever see the free world they won't be good for anything in society. Their bodies are used up: swollen feet, misshapen behinds, irritated skin. Their minds are broken, too, from the mental abuse suffered every day. They walk around like human robots, machines waiting to fall apart. They are scared to put up a fight. I have no patience to deal with PIA again. The inmates don't help one another. It's a disgrace. This is the reason the state keeps getting away with the things they do to us.

This is my story. Is anybody listening?

63

Freedom Gon' Come

Cassandra Adams

Freedom . . . the word was a constant in my world for 11 years
What I cried about
dream about
prayed for
schemed for
got mad and wanted to fight about

What motivated me to go to college
What made me mentor little girls
because I knew I could help some body because I had a story
    to tell
Freedom was going to let me do that

but it's just a word—one that has no true meaning because each
    individual defines the word freedom

Foolish I thought freedom would come with parole
but instead I realize I was freer inside the gate at least I knew
    my captors

Now I'm constrained by the negative stereotypes of a world that
    preaches one thing but does another . . .

Held by the bars WE DON'T HIRE FELONS!!!

WE DON'T RENT TO FELONS!!!

I cry about it . . . dream about it . . . pray for it . . . get mad and
    want to fight about it . . . but I wait . . . because
my Freedom gon' come!!

64

Reducing the Number of People in California's Women's Prisons

How "Gender-Responsive Prisons" Harm Women, Children, and Families

Californians United for a Responsible Budget

In April 2007, Californians United for a Responsible Budget (CURB) published a report titled Reducing the Number of People in California's Women's Prisons: How "Gender Responsive Prisons" Harm Women, Children, and Families. *CURB describes this report as responding "to a dangerous and controversial policy that would expand the capacity of California's women's prison system—already the largest prison system for women in the world—by up to 40% in two years."*

Below is a summary of the CURB report. Following this piece is an interview with Cynthia Chandler, founder and codirector of Justice Now, a California-based organization dedicated to ending violence against women and stopping their incarceration. Chandler explains the dangers many see in the "gender-responsive" concept at the heart of growing numbers of "prison reform" plans around the country.

The California prison expansion plan was first publicly proposed by the Gender Responsive Strategies Commission (GRSC), established in February 2005 as an advisory committee to the California Department of Corrections and Rehabilitation (CDCR) "to assess and make recommendations on proposed strategies, policies, and plans specific to women offenders." In January 2006, the GRSC identified 4,500 people serving time for offenses classified as nonviolent and "low-risk" who were candidates for release from the state's women's prisons. But rather than advising the CDCR to release these 4,500 prisoners and to reunify them with their families and communities, the GRSC proposed building 4,500 new prison beds in female rehabilitative community correctional centers (FRCCCs) to house them, thereby expanding the CDCR's capacity to imprison people in California's women's prisons by almost 40 percent in two years.

After listening to the concerns of advocates who have long worked to address the needs of people in women's prisons and their children and to the over 2,000 people currently imprisoned at the Central California Women's Facility, the Valley State Prison for Women, the California Institution for Women, and other prisons for women in California—who registered their opposition to the 4,500-bed and other prison expansion proposals with a twenty-five-foot-long petition to the governor and legislature—policy makers and advocates who had originally been drawn to the proposal's purported intent of providing services and the author's language of "community-based alternatives to incarceration" began joining the opposition.

Susan Burton, a member of the GRSC and executive director of A New Way of Life, a reentry program in Los Angeles often cited as a model by proponents of the miniprison expansion proposal, also registered her opposition to the proposal, asserting that the CDCR "has demonstrated its failure to use resources already available to provide services. Expanding the CDCR in the name of services and on the back of taxpayers is a gross exploitation of power." By the end of February 2007, over 2,800 people in California's women's prisons had submitted letters opposing the expansion plan.

The FRCCC prison expansion proposal comes at a time when fewer than 3 percent of Californians believe that prison construction is an infrastructure priority. In fact, prisons are the "only area in which the majority of adults, and voters in both parties, prefer to have either less or the same spending."

Over 80 percent of people in women's prisons are serving time for actions classified as nonviolent or for property- or drug-related crimes—"crimes of survival." People of color are represented disproportionately in prison systems across the nation, comprising around 60 percent of people in women's prisons. African Americans make up nearly 30 percent of the people in California's women's prisons but constitute only about 7 percent of women in the state.

In contrast to policies to reduce the number of people in women's prisons, the FRCCC prison expansion proposal uses the grave needs of people in women's prisons to manipulate public sentiment in favor of rehabilitation and services to expand a failing system at the same time that Californians overwhelmingly oppose prison expansion and increased spending.

Increasingly, the state's only and ubiquitous answer to any problem within the prison system—whether it be the need for more and better programming, disastrous physical and mental health care, or overcrowding in prisons—is bricks, mortar, and expansion.

In response to overwhelming evidence of unaddressed violence, medical neglect, and abuse, the CDCR, federal courts, and watchdogs are working to centralize control of California's prison system to increase oversight, address the myriad scandals within it, and ensure that people are treated equally no matter where they are imprisoned. Counter to this objective, the expansion proposal scatters prisoners throughout the state in miniprisons unaccounted for in any oversight plan.

Because the CDCR has been unable to guarantee even basic constitutional and human rights, advocates and people in prison spend a lot of their time monitoring and exposing abuses. By scattering people throughout a system of new miniprisons, maintaining even the limited oversight that advocates have won would be nearly impossible to maintain, and people in prison would be rendered invisible to policymakers, increasing barriers to ongoing litigation aimed at prison reform.

We all agree about the urgent need for change. This prison expansion plan is neither an imperfect proposal that will improve the lives of women, nor is it a good first step: it takes us backward by expanding an already failed and costly system—the CDCR. It is a rehash of the state's failed experiment with community corrections centers, now dressed up in "gender-responsive" language.

RECOMMENDATIONS

1. Reduce the number of people in women's prisons by discharging the 4,500 people CDCR identified as no longer needing to be in prison.
2. Provide six months of housing to the people discharged. The state has proposed spending approximately $36,591 per person per year—or $3,049 per person per month—in operational costs alone to contract our prison beds for 4,350 people in women's prisons whom it has identified as "nonserious, nonviolent" and not in need of "high security measures." This figure does not include facility-use costs and medical costs. Alternatively, the state could discharge the identified 4,350 people and provide a "kinship subsidy" at $500 per month for six months housing upon discharge. Taxpayers would save over $2500 per person per month. Extrapolated to 4,350 people, the total savings would be over $11 million per month. Moreover, the state would directly provide the "linchpin" (housing) to parolee success.
3. Close one women's prison in two years.
4. Reapportion funds saved from prison construction and operation to social services independent of the criminal legal system, including women's community health care, education, job placement, and skill training.
5. Reduce barriers to women's reunification with families and communities.

CONCLUSION

As the California Performance Review Commission on Prisons, headed by former governor George Deukmejian, has concluded, the "key to reforming the system lies in reducing the numbers."

The FRCCC expansion proposal puts expansion before reform. We will never reduce the number of people in prison by expanding the capacity of the system to imprison them. Increasing the number of cells will only increase the number of people in prison.

Real reform demands a true reduction in the number of people in prison, beginning with a moratorium on new prison construction. We can then redirect funds saved from prison expansion into the local services that women and transgendered people need, including housing, health care, education, and employment independent of the criminal legal system.

65

The Gender-Responsive
Prison Expansion Movement

Cynthia Chandler

On April 4, 2007, Cynthia Chandler of Justice Now participated in a conversation with Cara Page, then executive director of the Committee on Women, Population, and the Environment; Loretta Ross, executive director of Sister Song; and Rickie Solinger, coeditor of Interrupted Life. *This chapter is an edited version of Cynthia's critique of what Justice Now and others are calling "the gender-responsive prison expansion movement," a development that Chandler explains must be opposed. Loretta Ross provides a perspective on the relationship between the work of the reproductive justice and prison abolition movements.*

Cynthia Chandler

California is the first state to adopt a commission on gender-responsive strategies as part of its Department of Corrections, whose purpose is to directly inform the programming in women's prisons at the state level. At this point, the National Institute for Corrections—and other proponents of the gender-responsive prison expansion rubric—considers the California model appropriate for expanding to other states.

This model is dangerous to incarcerated women because it embeds a mix of paternalism and imperialism, racism and classism—all promoting the idea that prisons can be safe, respectful, dignified places where we can do what's best for our "downtrodden" sisters. The model includes no critique of prisons or of the role prisons have played in dominating poor women and women of color.

The model is also dangerous because it promotes a deeply homophobic, transphobic element. When folks say "gender" in "gender-responsive policies," they mean a white, middle-class heterosexual woman. And when they refer to "women's needs," they often mean the needs of women having problems in their relationships with men. They make no mention of trans women, ever. The assumption is that all women want to be treated with gender-rigid chivalry. The gender rhetoric in this campaign throws us back more than three decades to a very antiquated feminist analysis and feminist theory, a feminism linked to paternalism that lacks understandings of the intersection of gender, race, and class.

The California Gender Responsive Strategies Commission issued a press release with lots of fanfare saying that the Department of Corrections and its gender-responsive task force have identified 4,500 women in California's prisons who should go home because they don't pose a threat to society. The press release indicated that these women, in prison for poverty crimes and domestic-violence–related crimes, really just need programming and assistance to be pulled out of poverty and to get their relationships in order. This press release sounded as if 4,500 women were going to be sent home and provided with services in their community. But the actual policy program was to create 4,500 locked prison beds for women who previously would not have received a custodial sentence at all, and none of the other 11,000 to 12,000 beds would be closed.

This program would create a *massive* expansion of the prison system. Rather than sending 4,500 women home, the new system would actually pull 4,500 women out of their communities, women who would not have gotten a custodial sentence at all but who now would be sentenced to these new prisons that would be "good for them." The programming would be designed to help women with their troubled relationships with men and provide them with vocational training and parenting training.

We've asked repeatedly for information on model programs, so that we can understand the content of the proposal. But there are no models, anywhere. We're just told that these programs will help women with their troubled relationships with men and help them be better mothers, whatever that means.

Then, last July [2006], the Health Subcommittee of the Gender Responsive Strategies Commission made a formal recommendation for programming that would address women's special health concerns. The first recommendation was to change the language describing sterilization during labor and delivery so that this procedure is defined as an *essential, necessary, medical practice*. In California, as in almost every state, only "necessary" medical procedures can be provided to prisoners. So with this redefinition, sterilization could be offered during labor and delivery.

The subcommittee also recommended investigating the implantation of intrauterine devices, again as a "necessary" medical procedure. This proposal helps us understand exactly how the subcommittee defines the health needs of incarcerated women. The subcommittee wants a clear, eugenicist, paternalistic, imperialistic policy that will stop poor women and women of color from having children to endorse abuse in these prisons under the guise of helping women.

When these clearly eugenic policies were proposed in the subcommittee, not a single person objected. The consensus appeared to be that women in prison should not be having children, period, so optimally, their reproductive capacity should be terminated. Even in the mainstream women's rights community, and certainly among the legislators who've been supporting the Gender Responsive Strategies Commission, the replies to our critique have been, "Well, shouldn't women in prison have the choice to be sterilized?"

The fact is, in a coercive environment, women rarely can give informed consent for *anything*, even for something so permanent and potentially devastating as sterilization. These folks on the commission aren't talking about giving women access to in vitro fertilization or about allowing conjugal visits so that women can choose to bear children. Such policies certainly exist in other countries, where women are allowed to bear children in prison. Here in California, sterilization is the only reproductive, "medically necessary option" that's on the table.

The Gender Responsive Strategies Commission is saying that we should recognize that women in prison are mothers, and because they are almost certainly bad mothers, they need parenting skills. Plus, prison authorities can use the motherhood of incarcerated women in incentive programming: if people want to be near their children, they will comply with treatment and other programming demands. How horrible, to use a woman's child as her reward or punishment in prison.

Loretta Ross

These developments profoundly violate the concept of reproductive justice (RJ). They clarify the intersections between the work of the RJ movement and the prison abolition movement. RJ depends on a framework with three core principles: the right not to have a child, the right to have a child, and the right to parent one's children. The second and third principles are the ones that relate immediately to the commission's proposal because the right to have a child and raise a child is obstructed by so-called gender-responsive policies. Using the RJ framework, we tend to separate three aspects of the reproductive justice movement. First is the reproductive health aspect—that is, the provision of services—which of course gender-responsive policies do not address. The second is reproductive rights, the affirmation of constitutionally protected rights held by women who are incarcerated, which are not affirmed by these principles either. And, third, reproductive justice refers to the concept of embedding a woman in the community context in which she makes her decisions. This principle also seems to be neglected by gender-responsive policies. So in just about every way I can think of, the gender-responsive policies I've heard discussed are in violation of the principles of reproductive justice.

Cynthia Chandler

As Justice Now does its work—for example, on human rights reports about how prison destroys the right to family—we have learned so much from the reproductive justice community about how prisons are functioning as institutions of reproductive oppression. Even before this gender-responsive strategies stuff came up, we were already hearing from women on a regular basis about how prisons were destroying their dreams of being mothers, whether for the first time or to expand their families, because of the length of their sentences.

Numerous people contacted us, and we were able to determine that they had been sterilized without their knowledge during exploratory surgery or other medical procedures. And we worked with people who never got to have families because of gross medical neglect that caused sterilization and learned of some who died as the result of such neglect. Now we really understand that this society cannot remove women from their communities, from their children, from their families, put them in a controlled punishment environment, and have that environment be conducive to women's reproductive health or to their human rights in general. In gender-responsive prison expansion work, folks claim that you can have a safe, respectful, dignified prison. Using the reproductive justice framework, we're clear that a prison is never safe and respectful and dignified. It's fundamentally not so.

In response to the new gender strategies, Justice Now has been developing an affirmative gender justice platform. It's not that we think there shouldn't be a gender lens through which we can view prisons, or that we can't pay attention to the distinct needs of people in women's prisons—that's not what we're saying. We think it's really important to reduce barriers for reentry for people coming out of women's prisons, and actually all prisons, and returning to their communities.

We need to get rid of the horrible welfare reform laws that deny access to basic benefits to people with drug convictions and make it very difficult for them to reunify with their families and that also deny them access to housing and education.

We want cash incentives for counties that are able to keep their residents out of jail and prison. Counties can be rewarded with funds for non-correctionally controlled, county-based services, in proportion to the amount of money they save the state by not sending people into the prison system. Californians United for a Responsible Budget put together a list of fifty ways to do decarceration and give money back to counties for public services.

We think there should be a moratorium on prison construction and also on prison staffing. We shouldn't be funneling more and more money into these broken institutions. We need to create incentives and services to support people in their communities and reduce the number of people in prison and reduce the barriers to reentry. And then we need to develop ideas for repurposing prison sites and give communities the opportunity to figure out how to use those sites productively. That's our gender justice platform.

In the meantime, the gender-responsive prison expansion commission has accrued enormous power. Its model is politically enticing: the state can look like it's helping women while being tough on crime. Every single liberal in the state legislature put his or her name on the first rendition of the bill to build 4,500 new women's prison beds.

We were finally able to kill the bill, but the bill has come back this legislative session and is expected to pass, so we're fighting hard against it. The public has to understand that people in women's prisons are not in favor of these prison expansion plans, despite what the proponents say. Justice Now has worked with a group of women in prison who wrote a petition in response to the bill, outlining their arguments in opposition. In just a month and a half, we've already collected over 3,000 signatures from about 11,500 women in prison in California.

We took the first 2,500 signatures and made a thirty-five-foot-long scroll that we've been taking to legislators' offices and legislative hearings, but also to organizations that were supporting the bill. The California American Civil Liberties Union (ACLU) originally signed on in support of the bill when it saw all these liberal legislators signing on. And I asked, how can the ACLU be signing on to something that is about prison expansion? But we brought the petition to the organization, and it has now abstained. The NAACP is currently a cosponsor of this bill. We brought the petition to the organization and the policy person got down on his hands and knees and almost cried when he started to read the names.

It's really important to understand that people in women's prisons are absolutely opposed to the bill because they understand more than anyone else that prison expansion means ripping apart communities and families and hurting families' ability to come together.

I want to stress that women in prison made clear to us, and included the point in their petition, that if more of them go to prison, more families will be ripped apart. Under the new prison expansion and so-called gender sensitive program, we'll see the same number of people in large institutions in rural communities, away from their families, because the authorities aren't talking about closing any of those. The folks who are put in prisons in urban centers, closer to their families, are people who would not have been in prison at all before this "gender sensitive" bill. And so we need to ask whether the state is really helping their families and communities. We think not.

I also think there's a lack of understanding of just how impoverished the average family is when the mother's in prison. Even a distance of ten miles can create insurmountable difficulties for visiting. The person caring for the children may be on a fixed income, yet she may be trying to pay for three or four outlandish collect-call prices for phone calls that the mother's making to her kids every month. The caretaker's ability to muster up a car or public transportation and pay for everyone to visit the prison can be really, really hard. We don't have a lot of confidence in the idea that that the new facilities will be close enough to make visits easy. And many of these women would have been at home anyway, or on probation, not in facilities at all, without this bill.

People also need to understand how this "reform" movement is replicating history. In the early twentieth century, the big push to reform women's prisons created "nicer, gender-responsive" women's penitentiaries. But all the people in those "nicer" facilities were white. Black women and brown women remained in the harsher, larger institutions.

We also know that the conditions in those so-called nicer prisons were extremely gender normative and very abusive. The "nicer" prison incarcerated thousands of women who would not have been put in prison before the reforms but were now there for status offenses like adultery or fornication. This development marked the first major imprisonment of women in our country. At the end of the progressive era, all those penitentiaries reverted to the purely custodial, harsh model. Today we're replicating this massive mistake. And I think that anyone who cares about racial justice and women's rights in the United States ought not let this happen again. We need to recognize that we're headed for another tragedy, massively expanding the women's prison system in the biggest prison system in the world.

66

Free Battered Women

Linda Field and Andrea Bible

ABOUT THE ORGANIZATION

Of the nearly 12,000 women incarcerated in California's state prisons in 2007, the vast majority have survived physical, sexual, emotional, and economic abuse by an intimate partner before entering prison. Hundreds of abuse survivors are serving life sentences after defending themselves and/or their children from abusive partners, being forced by batterers to commit or confess to crimes, or being held responsible for their abusive partners' violence against their children. A disproportionate number are women of color whose efforts to gain and maintain a sense of safety for themselves and their children were systematically blocked by the institutional racism and other forms of oppression that they had experienced throughout their lives. Once convicted, survivors go from the prison created by their abusive partners to one run by the state, where staff members' tactics of control mirror the abuse the women experienced by their batterers.

Free Battered Women (FBW) works to end the revictimization of incarcerated survivors of domestic violence as part of the movement for racial justice and the struggle to resist all forms of intimate partner violence against women and transgendered people. Between 2000 and 2007, Free Battered Women has been instrumental in successful efforts to win the release of twenty-seven survivors serving life terms—eighteen through parole and nine through other legal processes. We determine our priorities in collaboration with domestic violence survivors in California's state prisons, and our work includes public education and media campaigns about unjustly imprisoned survivors of battering; grassroots advocacy; promotion of just public policies for domestic violence survivors who have been charged with and convicted of crimes; and development of leadership capacity among women inside and outside prison. In addition, FBW collaborates with four organizations (the California Women's Law Center, Legal Services for Prisoners with Children, the Los Angeles County Public Defender's Office, and the University of Southern California's Post-Conviction Justice Project) to implement a unique California law (Penal Code section 1473.5) that allows domestic violence survivors to challenge their convictions in court if their legal defense did not introduce expert testimony on domestic violence at the time their cases were prosecuted.

. . .

ABOUT BATTERED WOMEN AND THE SYSTEM

For too long, society had turned a blind eye to the plight of women who experience domestic violence. After surviving generations of abuse, many women have resisted their abusive partners' violence and control. Far too many are showing up in prison after they have become their own advocates and, as a last resort, stopped the abuse of their children and themselves. Battered women who enter the prison system often have no previous criminal record. Some have spent their lives as mothers, wives, homemakers, and career women. Now many are receiving life sentences. Society, male oriented and dominated, cannot sanction women's violent actions, which violate women's roles. As a result, women are dealt with harshly and swiftly, locked away for life. This policy creates more chaos: children who have already been punished by an abusive father are now punished by a vengeful society as well.

Laws slowly have changed to allow expert testimony on "battered women's syndrome" (now referred to in California as "expert testimony on intimate partner battering and its effects"), but women who were convicted before the law went into effect are in limbo. Although the parole board once handed out release dates to some men, it historically has been reluctant to give dates to women. Women who have committed only one crime in their lives have ended up serving decades for protecting themselves.

After many years, society finally has recognized the experiences of battered women in prison. The legislature in California and in many other states now acknowledge that something has to be done for battered women who were incarcerated before the present laws came into effect. The California Habeas Project has become a light in the darkness for wrongfully imprisoned women. Attorneys are working *pro bono* to bring justice to those who thought justice no longer existed for them.

After serving almost nineteen years of my sentence of twenty-five years to life for killing my abusive husband, I, Linda Field, had my conviction reversed due to the law that the California Habeas Project works to implement (California Penal Code section 1473.5). My *pro bono* attorney filed a *habeas* petition presenting the expert testimony that would be introduced at trial if I were charged with first-degree murder today. When this petition was granted, I was recharged with voluntary manslaughter and given credit for time served and released with no parole. Although this outcome was wonderful, it threw me back into a society I was not prepared for. Due to health and mental problems, I cannot work. I am having problems getting to a doctor because of lack of transportation. I know that these difficulties too will pass; however, in the meantime, I am trying to pick up the pieces of my shattered life and mesh my life with those of my children and grandchildren.

Free Battered Women has worked relentlessly to bring our problems to light and to recruit attorneys to help us. My attorney was a corporate attorney who took on the challenge and rose to the occasion and won my freedom for me. I can only pray that more attorneys like her will be moved after hearing our stories and will join the ranks of volunteers seeking to bring freedom to the sisters still held within the razor wired walls of prison.

Life's Imprint

Michele Molina

Abuse takes the color out of life.
All that is left is a gray and bleak existence.
The pain struggles to come to the surface while it searches
   for an outlet
to express itself.
The world says the pain is a lie, because no outward scars
   are visible.
Look into her eyes, and they won't lie to you.
There's the abuser standing at the doorway to her soul.
No amount of years will ever erase that memory.
Help her believe in herself and become whole again.

Testimony of Kemba Smith before the Inter-American Commission on Human Rights

March 3, 2006

Members of the Commission, my name is Kemba Smith, and only a little over five years ago, I was identified by an inmate number, and today I am speaking on behalf of those currently incarcerated, those who are in district court today, and for those in the future who are being sentenced under federal mandatory minimum drug sentences.

Three days before Christmas 2000, President Bill Clinton commuted my sentence of 24.5 years for [a] drug conspiracy charge. If he had not done so, this morning, instead of talking to you, I would still be in federal prison until the year 2016. If my parents had not waged a campaign in the news media, in the churches, and among the criminal justice reform community, I would not have been freed from prison to raise my eleven-year-old son.

I grew up as the only child of professional parents in a Richmond, Virginia, suburb, leading an advantaged and sheltered childhood. After graduating from high school in 1989, I left the security of my family to continue my education at Hampton University in Hampton, Virginia. I was not a drug trafficker. I was a college student and at the age of nineteen, away from the protective watch of my mother and father and in an attempt to "fit in," I met a man while a sophomore in college who I became romantically involved with and, unbeknownst to me at the time, according to the government, he was head of a violent 4 million dollar crack cocaine ring. He eventually became verbally and physically abusive in which I had to seek medical attention. I continued to be in a relationship with him for over three and a half years in which during this time he increasingly drew me into his drug activities.

The prosecutor stated during my court hearings that I never handled, used or sold any of the drugs involved in the conspiracy. Yet, I was sentenced as a first-time nonviolent drug offender to 24.5 years, one for every year of my life. I remained in prison from the moment I turned myself in September 1994, seven months pregnant with my first child, until December 22, 2000. My boyfriend at the time did not do any time; he was killed.

After my boyfriend was murdered, the U.S. government came after me and held me accountable for the total amount of drugs within the conspiracy, which was 255 kilograms of crack cocaine, even though according to the government's investigation, the drug dealing started two years before I even met him. I did not traffic in drugs, but I knew my boyfriend did. I knew that while living with him that he did not have a job and we were living off of the proceeds of his drug crimes.

I never claimed total innocence and this is the reason why I pled guilty. The prosecutor added extra incentive in negotiating the guilty plea, stating that he would allow me a bond so that I could go home until sentencing to give birth to my son and that I would only receive a two-year sentence.

Unfortunately, due to his unethical conduct, after pleading guilty I remained in jail. Minutes after giving birth in a hospital, guarded by two prison officials, [an officer of] the U.S. Marshall Service walked into my room and ordered that I be shackled to the bed, and two days later my son was taken away. I was sent back to a cold jail cell with my breast gorging and in extreme pain. If my parents had not been able to take and raise my son, my parental rights would have been terminated.

Since being released from prison in 2000, I graduated from Virginia Union University with a bachelor's degree in social work, worked at a law firm for over four years, bought a home, and I am currently a first-year law student at Howard University. I have spoken across the country to youth audiences, inspiring them to become educated about injustices in the U.S. criminal justice system and hoping that they will recognize that there are consequences to their life choices. But most importantly, I am raising my only child, who is now eleven years old. Unfortunately, my burden is that I represent the thousands of others still currently incarcerated, some my friends who I left behind, that deserve an opportunity to raise their children as well.

. . .

U.S. law provides that any person who is an accessory to a crime or who aids or abets the commission of a crime is a principal and is treated and punished exactly like the principal perpetrator of an offense. . . .[1] The consequence is that the most minor participants in the activities of a drug trafficker are charged with all of the crimes of the drug trafficker. This means they are facing the equivalent punishment. The threat of imprisonment for twenty or thirty years or more leads many to plead guilty and seek a departure below the mandatory minimum sentence. In 1986, the U.S. Department of Justice insisted on a provision to the mandatory minimums to permit the government to move the court to sentence below the statutory mandatory minimum if the government found that the defendant had provided "substantial assistance in the investigation or prosecution of another person who has committed an offense."[2]

Many women are unwilling to provide this "substantial assistance" in order to be loyal to the man they love, even if they are not married. This results in what has been called, "the girlfriend problem." The drug trafficker pleads guilty, cooperates in the prosecution of his colleagues, and is sentenced below the mandatory minimum. His girlfriend, having no information about the criminal organization other than the acts of her boyfriend, feels morally and emotionally compelled not to testify against him. Therefore she is unable to qualify for the "substantial assistance" departure and receives the full mandatory minimum sentence even though, in fact, her culpability is substantially less than that of the principal offender.

Aside from mandatory minimum sentencing, various features of drug enforcement in the United States have a racially disparate impact.

The United States Housing Act of 1937 was amended by section 5101 of the Anti-Drug Abuse Act of 1988 to permit the termination of a lease in a public housing facility "if any member of the tenant's household, or a guest or other person under the tenant's control . . . engage[s] in criminal activity, including drug-related criminal activity, on or near public housing premises, while the tenant is a tenant in public housing."[3] This has been implemented as the "one strike and you're out" public housing provision that has resulted in the eviction of public housing tenants. This policy was recently unanimously upheld by the United States Supreme Court in *Department of Housing and Urban Development v. Rucker.*[4] Mrs. Rucker's daughter was found with cocaine and a crack pipe three blocks away from her apartment, and Mrs. Rucker was evicted.

A person with a drug conviction has a lifetime ban from food assistance and temporary assistance to needy families.[5] Any student convicted of any drug offense (even a summary citation for simple possession) shall be denied federal higher education financial aid.[6] Such sanctions are not applied to convicted murderers, rapists, or child molesters.

A non-U.S. citizen convicted of a drug offense (other than one involving less than thirty grams of marijuana) must be barred from entry into the United States, or deported from the United States, no matter when the offense took place.[7]

It is evident that the people who are disproportionately impacted by these federal drug sentencing laws are people of color, and I am not ashamed to say again that I represent those who are currently incarcerated, people just like me who are capable of being productive taxpaying citizens. When the U.S. Congress created the mandatory minimum sentences and collateral consequences for drug offenses, they may not have been acting with the intent to inflict special punishment upon people of color, but that has unquestionably been the effect.

NOTES

1. Title 18 U.S. Code (U.S.C.) sec. 2, Principals.
2. Title 18 U.S.C. sec. 3553(e), carried forward in the sentencing guidelines as a section 5K1.1 departure. Quote from Public Law 100–690, 102 Statute 4300.
3. Title 42 U.S.C. sec. 1437d(l)(6).
4. Title 535 U.S.C. sec. 125 (2002).
5. Public Law 104–193, sec. 115.
6. Public Law 105–244, sec. 483(f); title 20 U.S.C. sec. 1091(r).
7. Title 8 U.S.C. sec. 1227(a)(2)(B).

69

Keeping Families Connected

*Women Organizing for Telephone Justice
in the Face of Corporate-State Greed*

Lauren Melodia and Annette Warren Dickerson

When a woman is incarcerated, how does she maintain contact with loved ones? When an incarcerated woman is a mother, where do her children go and how does she continue to play a role in their lives? In New York, under the Adoption and Safe Families Act, a woman who is forced to place her children in foster care during her incarceration can lose her parental rights in as little as fifteen months if she cannot maintain consistent contact with her children or adequately "plan for their future." However, maintaining consistent contact is physically impossible for the majority of incarcerated women who hail from New York City but are housed in prisons up to eight hours away from where their children reside. The web of unwise policy and planning is punctuated by the social role of women as primary caretakers and the dehumanization of imprisoned people, and makes it extremely challenging for imprisoned women to play a significant role in their children's and families' lives. It also makes the price of a collect call from prison a critical issue for women who are incarcerated.

Since the mid-1980s, single-carrier collect-call systems have become the norm for telephone service in prisons across the United States. Under these monopolistic systems, incarcerated individuals may only call people collect, and loved ones who accept the calls must accept the terms and rates dictated by the phone company. In all but two states—Nebraska and more recently, New York—the government receives a whopping commission from the phone companies that receive the exclusive contract, creating an incentive for the state and company to collude to set inflated collect-call rates and generate millions of dollars in revenues. Historically, New York State generated some of the highest revenue nationally from its prison-telephone commissions. However, due to intensive activist pressure on the state from the New York Campaign for Telephone Justice (NYCTJ), New York State governor Eliot Spitzer eliminated the commission on January 8, 2007.

In 1996, the New York State Department of Correctional Services (DOCS) entered into a contract with MCI to provide telephone service to state prisons. Under the deal, MCI paid a major up-front signing bonus to acquire the monopoly contract and agreed to deliver 60 percent of the profits from the contract to DOCS in the form of a commission. MCI, DOCS, and the state's Public Service Commission set the collect-call rates at sixteen cents per minute with an additional three dollar connection fee. The average prison phone call logs at nineteen minutes. Thus, under this contract, a call recipient pays over six dollars for an average call—a markup of more that 630 percent! In contrast, MCI's advertised collect-call rates to the general public are as low as five dollars per month for service and five cents per minute. The phone companies and prison officials argue that the high rates are justified by the need for added security measures. But evidence does not support this claim because calls from all federal prisons—which have identical security needs—cost just seven cents per minute with no connection fee.

Regardless of any stated justification, the companies and states reap millions of dollars in profits from these contracts at great hardship and expense to families. Since 1996, DOCS has made at least $200 million off its contract's commission. At the same time, families have endured monthly phone bills totaling hundreds of dollars and abusive treatment by customer service. Disproportionately, people in prison come from poor communities, and the burden of staying in touch falls heaviest on those with the least ability to pay. Often, those who accept calls must choose between basic necessities and the chance to speak with their loved ones. Incarcerated mothers and women on the outside are struggling to keep their families together. The collect-call rates place an enormous strain on families' financial resources and on the relationships themselves, both of which are already stressed by the trauma of incarceration:

> *Diane:* I have a son who has been incarcerated for almost eight years. He's five hours away from home, and it is a hardship to make that trip. I work and can only visit on the weekend. I have a granddaughter who comes over on the weekend to talk to her father. I once paid a bill for one month in the amount of $666.00. I nearly passed out when I saw my bill. I think it is a shame how we are being taken advantage of. This action causes my son to become very frustrated. I am constantly telling him to be patient. I feel that the government we have put into office needs a wake-up call. This is so unfair to people who are struggling in their everyday life. The majority of us are poor. You can tell by the population of prisoners.

> *Patricia:* The MCI phone rates are really all about business and killing the inmate's family structure. The company has no pity for the family and no remorse for the type of price gouging it engages in. My husband has been incarcerated for eighteen and a half years in the DOCS prisons of New York State and believe me, MCI has been my

biggest pimp. Our children could only speak to him maybe once a week because the costs are so high. On average I pay $650 to $700 a month in phone bills. This is more than my rent and food. My husband is in brain-cancer remission so I must have contact with him almost daily. [Governor] Pataki gets a kickback from inmate phone [calls]. This must be stopped! We need to send a clear message to him and [State Senate Majority Leader] Joseph Bruno, that WE HAVE HAD ENOUGH!

The New York Campaign for Telephone Justice arose out of conversations among the women and men in prison, their loved ones on the outside, and people in the community. Women on the outside, for example, shared their frustrations with one another on buses to upstate prisons, in waiting rooms, on online message boards, and through family support groups. These conversations made one thing clear: if people had to rely on the phone to keep their families together, they had to fight to change the system and demand fair treatment and prices. Mothers and wives on the outside began organizing for action to change the circumstances of their family communication.

In October 2004, the Center for Constitutional Rights, in partnership with Prison Families of New York and the Prison Families Community Forum, officially launched the New York Campaign for Telephone Justice.[1] The campaign made three basic demands. The first goal was to end New York State's prison-telephone commissions. The profits made by DOCS were treated as state income. The state used them to pay for basic prisoner services such as health care and release clothes. Thus, the commissions essentially served as unlegislated and illegal taxes, under which families bore the financial burdens that are the proper responsibility of the state. By imposing such burdens on the families of prisoners, the practice acts as a form of collective punishment.

Second, families demanded affordable rates for phone service. Although families were willing to pay a reasonable fee for security features, New York State at times made more than $26 million in annual profits due to the inflated rates. The campaign demanded that DOCS aggressively seek contractors that provide the lowest rates possible for consumers, not the highest commissions to the state.

Third, the campaign insisted that the state and its contractors provide options for calling and billing. For example, other states developed debit calling systems, which are cheaper to maintain than operator-assisted, collect-call systems and drastically reduce the rates that consumers must pay. Furthermore, MCI and New York State consistently abused their monopoly by arbitrarily forcing some call recipients to prepay for their collect calls, blocking people's phones from receiving collect calls when they see "extra activity" on the account, placing limits on how much money a call recipient can spend per month, and blocking people's phones when they are unable to pay on time. The campaign called for an end to these discriminatory business practices, and calling and billing options would eliminate the devastating impact such redlining has on families:

Norma: I do not like MCI. Not only do they charge outrageous prices, but they have an illegal block on my phone and have had for over a year. They claim I owe them money, I do not agree. I have called repeatedly and told them to take the block off. I am not and have not been with them for over a year! The block is why I left them. I have a very ill sister incarcerated, and this has caused her and I enormous worry, because she cannot call me. Their prices for prison/inmate calls are a deplorable price gouge, in my opinion. I hope the system is changed to a carrier that is more considerate of the plight of inmates' and families' need for connecting by phone.

Liz: My phone was blocked yesterday without notice. I only know because my husband sent word through his friend's wife. I called MCI this morning only to be treated with attitude and told by the customer service rep that she wasn't "obligated" to give me a name, number, or address to complain to. She was rude and unsympathetic. I gave up my car, cable, eating out, any extras that I can live without just so my son and I could stay connected to my husband. My payments have always been paid in full and on time. There is no reason for them to put us families through this. They treat us with no respect, and yet the bulk of their profit is made off of us. It's a disgrace. Do their long-distance customers have to go prepaid too? Of course not. This is all just another way for DOCS and the government to get over on us. Their actions are criminal, but they won't own up to it. Unfortunately, they have us where they want us. I beg everyone to *please* join the boycott in November, don't let them make a penny that day and let them feel the loss, like we have to deal with ours.

Outraged at the profiteering from their misfortune, the families and organizations involved in the New York Campaign for Telephone Justice took on MCI and New York State. For years, the Center for Constitutional Rights had challenged these monopolistic contracts in the courts. As the lawsuits proceeded, the NYCTJ also used leaflets, rallies, street theater, billboard ads, public service announcements, and other public education tactics. The point was to elevate this issue in the public's attention, stimulate press coverage, mobilize opposition, build solidarity among families and allied organizations, and end the contract by pressuring the governor and state legislature to cancel the contract and replace it with one that enabled families to stay connected.

Since its inception, NYCTJ has focused most of its organizing efforts on reaching out to other families directly affected by the contract. NYCTJ members have handed out information sheets and answered questions during regular visits to the bus stops where families meet each Friday and Saturday evening to visit their loved ones upstate. Women and families joined NYCTJ's efforts in whatever way they could: signing petitions, going to meetings and rallies, and distributing leaflets in waiting rooms, at neighborhood hair salons, and to family and friends. Fear of retaliation against their loved ones prompted many women to participate in the campaign anonymously rather than publicly. NYCTJ received hundreds of letters from women and men in New York's state prisons who became active in the campaign after hearing about it in a newsletter, from a friend, or from a loved one. They, in turn, shared the information with their loved ones and friends and, as a result, many new women joined NYCTJ for monthly meetings because their incarcerated loved ones encouraged them to get involved.

Families have always been the driving force and primary spokespeople of the campaign. Although many families were initially concerned about speaking out because of the stress of trying to explain why their loved ones are incarcerated, NYCTJ media training helped them realize that they did not have to share anything they did not want to, that it did not matter what circumstances had led to the incarceration of their loved ones, and that they did not deserve to be punished with high phone bills for anything. Empowering family members, and primarily women, to feel in control of their stories and opinions in the face of media professionals has strengthened the entire campaign.

With an ever-expanding base of support, the campaign organized larger actions targeting the profiteers of the contract, including letter writing and call-ins to key elected officials. In 2004, NYCTJ organized a trip to MCI's shareholder meeting in Virginia to protest the company's practices. Then, on November 16, 2005, we organized a boycott against MCI. On that day, families across New York State and around the country refused to receive collect calls from their incarcerated loved ones. Refusing a call was emotionally difficult for many families to consider, especially knowing that their loved ones have little contact with the outside world aside from the telephone. Still, many families spoke with their loved ones before the boycott, excited to unite in taking a stand against the contract. Many women on the outside were notified about the boycott by their incarcerated love ones who had heard about other families' plans to participate. Organizing from the inside and outside, families overwhelmingly joined us in refusing to give MCI and DOCS any money on that day, and many continue to boycott MCI on the 16th of every month.

Governor George Pataki was consistently unresponsive to the concerns of families and to calls for criminal justice reform in general, but his tenure ended in 2006. Our unrelenting pressure from 2004 until that time had led to extensive press and public awareness around the state and broadened the public's understanding of the issue. As a result, we made prison-telephone rates an issue in the statewide election, targeting individuals running for office in New York State. On January 8, 2007, on his eighth day in office, New York State's new governor, Eliot Spitzer, ended the state's commission arrangement and immediately reduced the collect-call rates by 50 percent. Furthermore, he committed to maintaining the programs that had been financed by the illegal commissions by earmarking funds in the general state budget. On June 21, 2007, the state legislature followed suit and passed the Family Connections bill, which cemented Governor Spitzer's decision in state law.

In many ways, the fire of our campaign has been ignited, reignited, and sustained through the personal relationships and support networks that families, especially women—inside and outside of prison—built during this fight. Although many of our active members are located in New York City, many are scattered and isolated across the state and beyond. Yet, through our website, action alerts, and monthly toll-free conference calls for families, women have shared stories, built friendships, found common ground, and learned that they are not alone and that their struggles are a collective source of power and justice.

NOTES

1. The **Center for Constitutional Rights** is a nonprofit legal and educational organization dedicated to protecting and advancing the rights guaranteed by the U.S. Constitution and the Universal Declaration of Human Rights through the creative use of law as a positive force for social change for poor communities and communities of color. Based in Albany, **Prison Families of New York** is run by the family members of people incarcerated in New York prisons. It provides information about jail, prison, parole, and physical and mental health issues for prison families, ex-prisoners, prisoners' children, people of conscience, educators, ministries, agencies, and social-change groups. **Prison Families Community Forum** (PFCF), based in New York City, is a membership-led organization whose core membership is people, primarily women, dealing with the incarceration of a loved one. However, it also involves individuals who have themselves come into contact with the system, as well as volunteer allies. The organization provides a space for people with loved ones in prison to find support and community, and to learn advocacy skills for themselves and their loved ones through grassroots organizing toward structural change.

70

Prick Poison

Kinnari Jivani

So . . .
you're listening through the wall
listen carefully
I am speaking directly to you
and if you need visual
of what I look like
I look like you
      may be shade lighter or darker
      a gender on left or right
With culture from north or west
             south or east
but I look like you
laugh, sob, breathe, grow like you
you see, I am human, too
society labels me "criminal"
if you too   keep seeing me distantly
then this wall will grow
            tall and fat
So you're listening through the wall
listen carefully
my life clogged when January snowed in 2000
I froze.   I killed.   I died.
I slowly melt to live. And if you were me
A young legal immigrant

fresh from plane, not speaking fluent English
not knowing 911 or U.S. laws
            or how and whom to ask for help
and made atrocious mistake
not as choice or last resolution
but out of utter confusion, helplessness
            depression and desperation
                in firey moments
you won't get bail with foreigner label
your interpreter will sleep
                while court proceeds
your rights will be stolen from you
                empty pockets will bring losses
your American dreams will
            crumble to deportable trash
wall will suck you in deep
            dark wild forest
humiliation will strip your identity
            label you with number
give you a cube to sleep
same routine to slowly wither and fade into
you will cry, write letters asking for help
but society will exhale you like carbon-die-oxide
leaving you alone with bundles of battles

so you listening through the wall
listen carefully
I made my mistakes, ate my guilt
repented, learned and matured
completed given recommendations and extras
but bureaucracy is still chewing me
not just me
hundreds and hundreds like me
                I won't tell you about
grade less food and drugs
harassments and rapes
or how women cry for their children at night
            die because of healthcare neglect
or what happens to children that come in
or elders that need aid to move around

because that will fill a book
and may bore you
       or prick your conscience
              I won't drain you with details
but I want to ask
       if it matters to you
that Pluto is not considered
a planet anymore
because scientist changed the definition of planet?
       the same thing happened to
Michigan's parolable lifers
who have served much more than
       their judge imposed
but are still caged hostage passed their outdates
because parole board changed the definition of life?
does it matter to you?
       would it if we were your
           mother, sister, daughter, wife, or lover?
Does it matter to you
if scientist tomorrow decide that Homo sapiens are
monkeys not human beings?
       Would it?
WHY   ARE   You listening through the wall?
My life is clogged
       your flaws on
world is full of creepy politics and wicked wars
       warnings and warmings
at local, community, country, and global level
you hear it, see it, live it

the question drools
will you keep flowing
       in your comfort zones?
or will you plunge into
what matters to you as a human being
and do something?

71

The Prison-Industrial Complex in Indigenous California

Stormy Ogden

I write this essay from the position of a California Indian woman, a tribal woman, recognized as a member of the Tule River Yokuts tribe, also Kashaya Pomo. I also write as an ex-prisoner of the state of California housed at the California Rehabilitation Center, located in Norco. While there, I was influential in forming the prison's first American Indian women's support group, along with the first women's sweat lodge built at a state prison in California. I am also a survivor of colonization by the European powers, against the original peoples of these lands and especially the indigenous nations of the state of California. This history of colonization is a tragic one, and native people still suffer the ramifications to this day.

The colonizers brought with them two tools of mass destruction, the bottle and the Bible, both of which were forced upon Native people. The outcome of this was the erosion of Native peoples' language, culture, lifeways, religion, land base, and lives. Even their traditional ways of behavior and conduct became illegal. Since the beginning of colonization, Native people of these lands were imprisoned as a form of social control, which can only be described as deliberate genocide.

With these increased attacks on Indian sovereignty and culture, imprisonment became the government's principal means of intimidation and punishment. Enforcing "foreign laws," Europeans locked up Native people in military forts, missions, reservations, boarding schools, and today, increasingly, in state and federal prisons. For American Indians, incarceration is an extension of the history and violent mechanisms of colonization.

Angela Davis argues that the prison-industrial complex (PIC) is about racism, social control, and profit. This mechanism/process/reality is not new to the Native people of these lands, as illustrated in the numerous laws that have been passed against them without their knowledge or their consent. In this article, I will show that the PIC was built right on the ancestral lands and the very lives of the indigenous people of this continent.

MY PEOPLE/OUR LANDS

My Indian heritage is Yokuts and Pomo. Both of these tribes are indigenous to some of the most beautiful and fertile of the lands now known as California. The Indians of precolonial California were the most highly skilled explorers of North America and extremely knowledgeable about the natural environment. They developed cultural lives in California over thousands of years. We have creation stories that will always connect us to these lands of our ancestors. We continue to live on these lands.

The Natives of California lived in a well-ordered society before the encroachment of the Europeans. The people were guided by relationships that fixed the status and the position of every member. Every part of the tribal society was enriched and maintained through religious laws and traditions; the indigenous nations of California were nations of laws. They had no police force and no courts to enforce these laws and obligations because the people strongly believed in and supported the law, knowing its key role in survival. Violations were addressed by restitution, not retribution. Exile from the tribe was an extreme penalty.

OUT OF SIGHT/OUT OF MIND

In the warmth of my fantasy
I awake to the cold gray walls
Of my reality

These words thundered in my mind as the judge read the sentence: "Ms. Ogden, you are sentenced to five years, which will be served at the California Rehabilitation Center in Norco." The reality of incarceration is especially likely to be yours if you are a poor woman, a woman of color, or an American Indian woman.

I tried to find out how many American Indians are in prison, especially numbers of women. But I found it almost impossible to obtain an accurate count. The number is buried and lost in the prison classification system that considers prisoners to be White, Black, Hispanic, or Other.

Outside the door to my room was a small white 8 x 5 card that listed my last name, Ogden; my state number, W-20170; and my ethnic classification, Other. Every morning as I left for my job assignment, I would cross out "Other" and write "American Indian." Each afternoon when I returned for count, there would be a new card with "Other" written on it. After this had gone on for a few days, the correctional officer approached me: "Next time, Ogden, it will be a writeup and a loss of good time." The next morning, before work, I found a permanent laundry marker, tore the card off the wall, and wrote "American Indian."

All women in prison are fighting to maintain a sense of self within a system that isolates and degrades, a system that is designed to punish, but we American Indians must also fight for our identity, on the very lands of our ancestors.

Another problem I had while incarcerated was the inability to get reliable health care or mental health care. Mental health is a major concern for all female prisoners. Psychiatry in prison has everything to do with control and management and nothing to do with effective treatment.

Most of the women I knew while I was in prison were on some sort of medication "to calm them down." Prescribing these medications is a dangerous practice considering that many of these women were addicted to drugs and alcohol before they were locked up. In addition, giving a woman such medication when she is going through alcohol or drug withdrawal is very dangerous.

I was medicated on Elavil and Mellaril the entire time I was in county jail, before I was sentenced. These medications made me sleep most of the day and night. I woke up only to go to "chow hall" and to take a shower. County jail never allows yard time. The only daylight we saw was when we were transported back and forth to court. The meds were given to me for the nine months that I was there. By the time I left for prison, the pills had affected my speech. I had a hard time speaking: the thoughts were there, but I had a difficult time getting the words out. My mouth and skin were dry, and I was weak from constant sleep. Upon arriving at prison, I was given Thorazine for two weeks. I was a walking zombie from these medications. Speaking with the other Indian women, I found out that many of them were also given high doses of these medications. When I returned to jail after my sentencing to five years at the California Rehabilitation Center, I was given a med packet with a small pill inside. "What is this for?" I asked the guard as she locked my cell door. "It came from the doctor this morning when he found out that you were being sentenced; take it, Stormy, it's just to calm down." The next thing I remember was my cellie shaking me as I was sitting on the floor watching my cigarette burn a hole into my nightgown. "What did they give you, Storm?" "I'm not sure what it was," I said to her with slurred speech, "all I know is that it was small." "Must have been Thorazine," was her reply. "The doctor gives that to all of us women, especially the Sisters that get sentenced to prison."

My younger Sister was incarcerated at Northern California Women's Facility in Stockton. When she wrote me, she told me about her fear of going to counseling, even though she knew that she needed it, because she didn't want to take medication that would make her a zombie, especially when her kids come to see her.

I am sure that many women feel this way and choose to suffer in silence instead of becoming "zombies in a house of madness."

IN THE UTMOST GOOD FAITH

The American criminal justice system in Indian country is complex and highly difficult to understand, let alone explain. Its governing principles are contained in hundreds of statutes and court decisions that have been issued randomly without the knowledge or consent of the Indian nations. Almost every aspect of the internal and external relations of Indian people has been subjected to the unrestricted jurisdiction of the U.S. government. As a result, the Native people of these lands have more frequent contact with the criminal justice system, and at a much earlier age, than other Americans.

Indian tribes had their own systems of criminal justice long before the non-Indian came to these lands. Until 1855, the federal government did not interfere with these traditional tribal systems. Criminal justice was left solely in tribal hands. Then in 1855, Congress passed the Major Crimes Act (title 18 U.S. Code section 1153), which rejected tribal sovereignty for reservation Indians, imposing instead a policy of forced assimilation, backed by the extension of federal law to tribal Indians for serious offenses. The Major Crimes Act of 1885 has arguably had a greater impact on Indian people than that of all other laws, giving federal courts jurisdiction over crimes committed by Indians against Indians in Indian country, in utter disregard for international law, treaty law, and Article VI of the U.S. Constitution.

Even as late as the 1930s, the Bureau of Indian Affairs had openly promulgated the Indian Offenses Act, a law forbidding the practice of Indian religion. Indians were assigned English names to replace their Indian names, and the law even established a penalty for wearing Indian hairstyles.

The U.S. government relied on three central arguments to justify its control over Indian nations.

1. The Plenary Power Doctrine, which holds that Congress has absolute power. This power clearly contradicts internal law as well as Article VI of the U.S. Constitution, which recognized the legitimacy of treaties between the U.S. and Indian nations and the supremacy of these treaties over laws passed by Congress: "All treaties between Indian nations and the United States government have supremacy over any law congress might enact which unilaterally abrogates a treaty within the consent of the nations-parties to the treaties."

2. The Federal-Indian Trust Doctrine, which holds that the U.S. government has the moral and legal duty to "help" Indians protect their lands and their rights. This "Great White Father" doctrine justifies U.S. control over Indian nations, in their "best interests," and has been devastating for Indian nations, denying Indians the right to make our own decisions.

3. The Doctrine of Geographical Incorporation has led the courts to determine that because Indian lands (i.e., reservations) lie within the boundaries of the

United States, the United States holds title to all of the land and thus has the absolute right to assert legal jurisdiction over Indian country.

These doctrines together created a powerful, racist implement of social control that has ultimately filled prisons with Indians and Alaskan natives convicted in the white man's courts for hunting and fishing and subsistence gathering in accordance with their customs and with prevailing treaties. Others have been convicted for political activism.

THE PRISONIFICATION OF THE NATIVE PEOPLE

Just as alcoholism has touched the life of every Indian person, so has the U.S. criminal justice system, in particular the prison system. It is common for Native people to be involved on some level with the system, to have been incarcerated at some point in their lives, and/or to have relatives who are or have been locked up. Because we are a colonized people, the experiences of imprisonment are exceedingly familiar.

Beginning with "foreign" laws that criminalized traditional Indian ways of dance, speaking, hunting, and gathering, Indians were imprisoned and fined. The outcome of this system can only be described as genocide, given its impact on the Native people of these lands. The Native world has been devastated by the laws that have been forced upon it; the number of jailed Natives is a chilling reminder of this fact.

Native people are being locked up at alarming numbers on their own ancestral homelands. The criminalization and imprisonment of Native people amount to another attempt to control Indian lands and deny Indian sovereignty.

For the American Indian people, federal and state prisons are part of the violent colonial mechanism. Indians have been colonized on their own lands, the lands to which they trace their social, cultural, and religious origins.

Criminalization joins the bottle and the Bible as a tool of the American colonial power to control Indian lands and deny Indian sovereignty. One devastating outcome of land dispossession today is the disproportionate rates of incarceration of Native adults and children. For American Indians, U.S. correctional facilities are part of the violent colonial apparatus. These facilities commit human rights abuses on prisoners and exploit them for government and private profit.

> We have been degraded to criminal status in our homeland
>   and become a people incarcerated.
> What was my crime, why 5 years in prison?
> Less than $2,000 of welfare fraud
>   What was my crime?

Being a survivor of molestation and rapes
What was my crime?
Being addicted to alcohol and drugs
What was my crime?
Being a survivor of domestic violence
What was my crime?
Being an American Indian woman

72

A Prison Journal

Tammica Summers

JANUARY 2007: THE "FEEDING" EXPERIENCE

I walk into the chow hall, and the usual and familiar stench of a dead animal of some sort slaps me in the face. I squinch my face up and make that ugly face that I've become so accustomed to making. The ladies who are serving on the line look exhausted and seriously perturbed because of it. The sergeant on seating and feeding patrol is his usual arrogant, pompous self, frantically screaming out various commands: "There should be no talking in the chow line . . . There shouldn't be any talking on that serving line . . . There is absolutely no talking in the chow hall . . . If you're talking that means you're done and you need to get up and dump your tray!"

I'm thinking, talking or no talking; per state-mandated rules and regulations, we are still entitled to twenty minutes to consume our food in the chow hall. Being forced to eat within five to seven minutes with no talking is barbaric! As I continue to think how ridiculous this is, and how over this I am, the commands continue to drone on.

I finally pick up my tray and quickly find out that there are no available tables. Mr. Tyrannical has been so engrossed in barking commands that he failed to pay attention to how many inmates were coming into the chow hall versus coming out of the chow hall. He has messed up, but, of course, this rocket scientist would never admit to that.

My only alternative is to walk over to a nearby wall with a ledge on it and eat right there. The sergeant walks toward me and sees that I am standing while eating, and he gives me a "What do you think you're doing, are you stupid?" look. So in answer to his thoughts and the look on his face, I say, "There was no place to sit."

Someone had just gotten up as he walked in and someone else was waiting to sit. So being the smart guy that he is, he says, "There's a seat right there, why can't you sit there?" And just as he says it, the girl waiting for that seat sits down. And I then say, "Because she was going to sit there!"

Needless to say, I find a seat all by myself, although I practically have to dive for it when someone gets up. In the overall scheme of things, the seat doesn't matter much because my appetite was ruined the minute I got here and has been further ruined by this appalling man who might as well have been a Nazi concentration camp guard. He rudely and abruptly tells inmates who are still eating that they are "done." "You done, yeah, you done. Get up and dump yo tray, bye," as he so crudely puts it. I'm telling you, after he says that to the person sitting in front of me, I most certainly am "done"! I bite my tongue and swallow the words. I force myself to chew and get up and dump my tray. I exit the chow hall, and the only taste in my mouth is disgust.

PART EIGHT

Being Out

IN HER GLOSSARY OF TERMS IN THE FIRST SECTION of this volume, Tina Reynolds describes profound problems with the now-ubiquitous term *reentry*. Reynolds points out that this word is typically employed in a way that does not pay attention to "how the person who has been in conflict with the law is perceived by society. Most important," Reynolds points out, "*reentry* does not acknowledge this truth: a person needs to know that she is welcomed and invited in order to reenter successfully."

The pieces in this section circle around the consequences that plague women who leave prison only to find themselves grappling with a society, a community, a family that may be, at best, ambivalent about their return. And even when the woman coming home is loved and welcomed, most receiving communities and families do not possess the resources to offer generosity and opportunity.

First, reclaiming space in the loving family is often horribly complicated by a mother's need to establish the bases for love, trust, and authority—profoundly difficult tasks under the best of circumstances. Margaret Hayes presents the experiences of "Maria" and "Sylvia" to show how hard going home can be. Even under the much better circumstances that Tina Reynolds writes about, the process of mending parent-child relations after incarceration is slow and heartbreaking and requires deep wells of fortitude and imagination.

"The Child of a Convicted Felon" tells the other side of the story, a narrative the author of the piece will "proudly stick to" about losing and refinding her mother. Life hasn't been easy, but this writer focuses on what it means to be a girl who has

Home of Mine, 1990. Photograph by Melissa Springer

a mother, again. "It feels good," she says "to be able to say, 'I'm going to my mother's house,' or to ask her, 'Ma, can I have $20?'"

A number of the writers in this section report that they have emerged from incarcerated life armed with political insights and the energy to work for the interests of other incarcerated and formerly incarcerated persons. A battered woman who spent years in prison and a woman inside for eight and a half years on a "drug conspiracy" both face stunning obstacles, yet, as one of them, Alfreda Robinson-Dawkins, writes, "Life was interrupted, but I'm still invigorated about surviving and making a difference!"

Joanne Archibald, in the concluding section of her prison autobiography, recognizes that as a mother and a person trying to remake her life, she is "paying and paying and paying," financially, emotionally, professionally, years later—"still paying for those ten months" inside. But Archibald also credits her hard experience with waking her up to "politics" and to the way the world works. She no longer relies on the mass media or on others to explain things, to fix things. Now Archibald is an activist in Chicago who invites other formerly incarcerated women and allies to do important work with her.

Half a continent away, in Southern California, Setsu Shigematsu, Gwen D'Arcangelis, and Melissa Burch describe the LEAD project, which "creates a space in which women who have recently been released from prison can temporarily step outside conventional recovery programs' emphasis on the personal and look critically at the larger social and political systems that perpetuate the prison-industrial complex." Using terms that Tina Reynolds surely honors, they explain, "This program offers a vision of justice that is based on the well-being of entire communities." And drawing on a vision that many writers in this volume share, Shigematsu and her coauthors are working toward the empowerment of formerly incarcerated women as they reimagine their "place in the world and the possibility of a future without prisons."

73

A Former Battered Woman
Celebrating Life After

Lorrie Sue McClary

June 2005

"All right, thank you. I want to note for the record that everyone who was previously in the room and identified themselves have returned to the room. And Ms. McClary, the panel has reviewed all of the following circumstances including that you are suitable for parole and would not pose an unreasonable risk of danger to society or a threat to public safety if released from prison . . . "

September 2005

"Inmate McClary, you have legal mail. The full Board of Prison Terms has decided that you are suitable for parole and is in agreement with the Panel's decision. The decision has been sent to the Governors office for final review."

October 2005

"Inmate McClary, you are wanted in the counselor's office. Sit down and read this please and tell me what it means."

"Governor Schwarzenegger has decided not to review the decision of the Board of Prison Terms."

With a smile on my face I said, "This means, sir, that I am finally going home to my family after thirty years in prison. What I need to know now is when, tomorrow, this afternoon, when?"

"I was told by the records office that you will be released in about two and a half weeks as soon as all the paperwork is finalized. The parole officer has already been to your home and checked things out and he will be the one picking you up and driving you home. So I suggest that you stay in your room and not be out among the other inmates unless you have to because there are some who will be jealous that you are going home and who will try to take your release date. I will let you know as soon as I hear the date of your release."

October 18, 2005

"McClary, you are wanted in the Program office to see your counselor."

As I walked to the Program office I felt dread in my heart, and it was hard to breathe. The last time I took this walk to the Program office they called me to tell me that Governor Pete Wilson had pulled my release date. Lord Jesus, please, not again, I don't know if I could survive it if anything happened to my family because the Governor decided to pull my date again. I almost lost my mom last time from the stress. Please, Lord Jesus, help me.

"I'm here to see the counselor."

"Yeah, McClary, come on in. I finally got the word from the records office, and you will be leaving to go home on Friday the twenty-first of October. Your parole officer will be here to pick you up around eight in the morning. All I can say is good luck. Know this, though, if you come back I will personally kick you in the rear and there will be a line of people after me, so you better do good out there."

Oh my God, thank you. Thank you, Lord Jesus, for not only hearing my prayer but for giving me such a prompt and absolutely wonderful answer.

"Mom, dad, I finally got the word that I will be coming home on, of all things, my birthday. Can you believe that? My parole officer will be picking me up and driving me home."

October 20, 2005

"McClary, you are wanted at the Program office."

Oh Lord, I know you are with me and hopefully this will be just to sign some parole papers or something, not bad news, not after all this.

As I approached the Program office I could see a bunch of inmates standing around the gate area and an officer with them. Oh my God! All these lifers came to say good-bye to me.

"Lorrie Sue, finally one of us gets to go home. Do good out there and let them know how Free Battered Women has helped you. Tell them there are more of us in here that need help. Your being released gives us hope. You are our hope. Show them that we are not all bad and that there are lifers who are one-time-only inmates, that we are asking for a second chance. Remember you give so many of us hope who have long ago lost hope in the system."

How powerful is that! Me, of all people! And they came to say good-bye to me. But, to be their hope, that puts so much pressure on my shoulders. I don't want that kind of pressure. I just want to go home to my family and get to know them again and to fade into the background. I just want to go home. So much pressure!

"No, McClary, there is no parole ducat for you this morning. Maybe the prison just doesn't want a bunch of people knowing you are leaving. I'd just be ready because R&R will be calling for you probably at eight in the morning. If you don't get called you can go see your counselor in the morning and maybe he can straighten things out for you."

Seeing my counselor will do no good since he only works ten hours a day for four days a week and is off on Fridays.

October 21, 2005

"No, McClary, you are not leaving today. There is some problem with paperwork, and we haven't been able to get hold of your parole officer; he is out of the office."

Help me not to cry, please, Lord, help me not to cry.

"Mom, dad, I just got out of the Program office and they said that they couldn't locate the parole officer and something about the paperwork so I won't be coming home 'til Monday. I am sorry, I can't get them to change it, and I asked, they won't let you come get me either."

October 23, 2005

"McClary, this time I do have a parole ducat for you. Have a good life and don't come back. Do some good out there if you can, and remember, if you talk to Governor Schwarzenegger, let him know what some of us officers think needs to be done to fix this system."

October 24, 2005

What I want to take home is packed in a little bag. I have to get a cart to take the mattress and pillow over to R&R. I want to try and slip out without seeing too many people if I can, but it will be work and school release at the same time. God give me strength.

Eight o'clock

Walking down to the work exchange to leave the yard, I did my best to hide behind the cart and not attract too much attention. But that didn't do much good. There must be more than a hundred inmates calling my name. Oh God, here we go.

Finally, R&R. Another lifer is paroling also. Can you believe that two female first-degree lifers are being released and on the same day and from the same prison? This must be making history for the prison.

Nine o'clock

"Do you see anyone out there who looks like a parole officer? My mom said mine was tall and had silver hair." "No, not yet."

Nine forty-five

"Anyone out there look like a parole officer yet?" "Nothing yet."

Ten o'clock.

"McClary, you have a phone call in the Sergeant's office. It's the Correctional Counselor III."

Wow! That was something, a phone call to wish me good luck and good life from someone so high up in prison.

Ten thirty

"McClary, there is no paperwork yet for your release. I don't know what to tell you. Records is working on it."

Lord Jesus, I am on my knees in this dirty nasty cell asking you to please intercede. I can't call home and tell my parents that I can't come home again. After the last call it will kill them. Mom has the house full of friends, family, Don (the victims' last remaining son), and my attorneys, Rachel, Steven, and Jessica are there. I ask for my family as well for myself, please Lord, help us.

Ten forty-five

"McClary, you have a visitor."

The Captain came to say good-bye. This is so strange to have all these inmates, officers, and officials wishing me luck and personally coming to say good-bye to me. I pray that I can get home to tell my parents about this because no one would believe that an inmate could get this much attention and respect. A peon, of all people.

Eleven o'clock

"McClary there are a couple of guys over there that could be parole officers. That one has silver hair and is tall. Listen to them talking with the Sergeant. Wait, she told them that there is no paperwork for your release. That must be your parole officer. He just said that he was going to the administration building to talk to them in Records. Who is that other guy with them?"

Eleven thirty

"McClary, you have a phone call in the Sergeant's office again. I don't know who you think you are, but don't stay on the phone long. We do have other duties around here if you haven't noticed."

"Hello! Yes, Warden. Well, thank you for calling to wish me good luck, but it doesn't look like I am going anywhere. Apparently the records office can't locate the paperwork to release me and my parole officer just left here about a half hour ago with another guy and they were headed to the records office. Think you have any pull with them?"

Twelve o'clock

"McClary, time to change into your parole clothes. The paperwork has finally come through, and your parole officer and his boss are on their way back down here to R&R to pick you up."

Twelve thirty

Parole officer Steve said that we would be stopping by his office to drop off his boss and for me to sign some paperwork and call home to let everyone know that I am finally on my way.

The entire ride was not handcuffed, and someone body-snatched me because I couldn't stop talking about the dumbest things. Boy, was I nervous. At every stop sign in the foothills I wanted to ask, "Are we there yet? Are we there yet?" But I never did, I just kept on with this incessant chatter about stupid stuff.

"Okay, this is the turn off to your folks' place."

I became silent as I took in every detail of the road. Then I started noticing, from the mailboxes on, yellow ribbons lining both sides of the road tied to oak trees, telephone poles, and fence posts. It was more than a mile down the road and [I saw] more yellow ribbons, a blue house, a metal building, a green house. The parole officer is slowing down . . . there a yellow house with a welcome home sign, balloons, cars, mom, dad, my wonderful sister Cydne Ann, Don, my attorneys Rachel, Steven, and Jessica, my best friend Caroline (who was a lifer in the inside until Free Battered Women helped to get her home to my uncle, who she married nearly six years before coming home herself; she is my best friend, sister, and aunt all rolled up into one), my brother Dennis, so many people.

Hugs, tears, kisses, and more tears, a big dog, inside the house. Pizza, Pepsi, and peanut butter fudge ice cream. Gifts for my birthday and more people. I am so nervous I don't know what to do, who to talk to, hug, where to sit, where the bathroom is; the bathroom, I need to pee and catch my breath. This is so unreal and yet so wonderful.

My parole officer watched as I opened the birthday gifts for my forty-sixth birthday from my friends and family; I felt strange, gifts for me. Being home is my greatest gift. Why are people giving me gifts for coming home? Oh yes, it's my birthday celebration too!

A large heavy package, my brother Dennis helped me to open, as my uncle Lew tells me he wants the hand-painted stein I gave him back once it is emptied. Dennis dumps the stein out on the rug. It is filled with hundreds of coins from pennies to quarters. A total of $344 my uncle had been saving for me.

I bent down to pick up the coins and jerked my hand back as though I had touched fire. Then I remembered that I was at home, not in the prison, and it was okay for me to touch money without getting in trouble.

Sleep. Not this night. I need to be here, and I can't afford to fall asleep and wake up back in the prison. I can't sleep. This bed is so soft. The night light, good, I can see the room and know where I am. Please, Lord Jesus, don't let me fall asleep and wake up back in prison.

I can open my window and hear crickets, an owl, coyotes howling, they sound so close. The air is so fresh. I can open my door and the bathroom has a night light also. In the living room, moonlight is shining through the sliding glass doors and windows. The shape of the trees lining the tops of the mountains around us in contrast to the night sky. God, thank you, I am home.

There is a gurgling sound coming from the kitchen, like boiling water, and something thumping in the refrigerator. Investigation reveals a coffeepot beginning to make coffee. It smells like heaven. The thumping noise is not important. Back to my room, dress, and wait for sounds of movement in the house. My chest is tight, I am really home, aren't I? Please Lord, tell me this isn't a dream. If it is, I don't ever want to wake up.

Sounds coming from the bedroom down the hall. The door is opening and someone is walking down the hall. I open my door to find the glowing face of my mother looking at me from the hallway. "I love you mom," and a kiss. I will never be able to say that enough.

March 22, 2007

I am sitting in front of my computer listening to mom and dad work on the stove vent in the kitchen. The dogs are outside lying in the sun, the sky is clear blue and oh so fresh after the rain we just had.

I have been home a year and five months now. It took months to get my Social Security card, California ID card, driver's license, savings account, and ATM card. If I had not come home to my family, I would have been lost in this world.

I write to a couple of people on the inside, Ellen, Linda, and Nora, an aunt by marriage. I try to keep in contact with those on the outside as well who helped me come home both mentally and physically.

I have been adopted by two beautiful dogs, Chunky and Missy, that moved in with us shortly after I got home. My neighbor has finally given them to me officially, now that he has another dog that hasn't decided to adopt me (of course, I haven't met the new dog yet either). And I have a new puppy, the son of Chunky; his name is Pretzel. Now if they will all just get along.

On my forty-seventh birthday last year I spoke at Free Battered Women's "Our Voices Within" event. During the time that I was there I gave interviews to all who asked and did two radio interviews to let people know that there are still more people who need help from those on the outside.

I have always had tremendous family support and love, [and I had] the victims' son testifying on my behalf for my release and DNA testing that in the end proved I did not commit the murder and that I was only in prison for being involved in a robbery that I *never* would have been involved in had I had not been forced into it by my batterer.

Without groups like Free Battered Women, I truly believe that I would still be on the inside looking out.

They are the ones who found the law firm that was willing to take on my case pro bono before the Parole Board, prove that I experienced intimate partner battering and its effects and that in fact I was not in prison for killing the victim, as the DA's office had told the Parole Board every year.

As for me, I am enjoying life and its little speed bumps (I am dealing with PTSD after thirty years on the inside), here at home with my family.

Pssst! Guess what? *I'm Home!!!*

74

Life on the Outside—of What?

Alfreda Robinson-Dawkins

When I think back to the nine and a half years that the federal government snatched from me, seeking to enforce a "conspiracy" charge, I still get a little mad! There was a conspiracy all right, one that the government has against people who seek an honest trial by a jury of their peers, an attorney who actually uses ethics and principles to guide decisions, and a judge who can accurately mete out a sentence based on the actual role one may have played, and other pertinent life factors. How silly to think there was "justice," as I watched them sentence me, and my twenty-one-year-old son, to forty-five years for a drug conspiracy. They tore my heart out and then stomped on it. Anyway, my life has been interrupted, and now I seek some semblance of "catching up" and making the pieces fit, to live a life of normalcy despite a "felon" afterthought every time I want to pass "Go" and do something that is *lifelike*. Like applying for a new apartment, or obtaining a credit line, or a grant for school, or certification to use my counseling degree. Just the little things that would allow me to assimilate back into society, earn a decent salary, and live like everyone else. After all, every one talks about "reentry."

Forgiveness. Do people forgive you once you have been incarcerated? Do church people forgive you? Do people feel uncomfortable around me once they know I served time in prison? Do they think I can act sociably *and* civilized after being treated like an animal for so long?

After being rejected from so many jobs and trying to maintain my self-esteem and faith, I realized I was not alone out here. So many women feel the same thing and think the same thoughts. Women all want the same things—to belong, to feel needed, to nurture those we love, to be financially secure, to have our children feel safe with us, to survive. Simple things, right? Well, for me, after having so many doors closed, I realized I had to take more assertive responsibility for my own course of action, to help cement my destiny.

I had a strong desire to help other women who were facing the same obstacles, so I founded the National Women's Prison Project (NWPP) in Baltimore, Maryland. Building partnerships and relationships with health, recovery, housing, counseling, and job agencies, NWPP now assists more than five hundred women a year. And guess what happens for me? I continue to heal from my incarceration by helping other women like me heal. The many mentors I've found along the way have helped me define and design my passion, and the rest is now NWPP.

Yet I see so many women who allow drugs to rob them of their future. I see pain embedded so deep that only drugs can keep them from feeling, because they cannot see the sense in trying to work it out. I see and feel the thick cancer of depression, of suicidal ideations, of this plague of hopelessness. I see the need for housing and dignity for women who just want a second chance. I see the pain that has spread to the next generation as the children stand on the other side of the fence shouting, "Bye Mommy, I love you," and get on the bus and hide the tears while riding back to town. I see the children who think it's a rite of passage—or a route to getting somebody's love—when they have their first arrest or pregnancy at thirteen or fourteen, 'cause Mommy was not there. I watch the babies take their first steps in the prison gym during a Saturday session. I see the employers who don't want to risk hiring a "felon," thinking it may destroy the reputation of the business, when the applicant only wants to prove she can be a great employee. I see the legislators look down at the group of ex-prisoners assembled in Annapolis to fight for their right to vote and be heard. When will society just call us "people"?

Our lives have been interrupted, and I've heard women inside say that this "bit" saved their lives, the way they were going. Why can't we address the ills before incarceration? Why can't we heal the addiction and provide treatment for those who need it without making them jump through hoops to get clean? Why can't we provide jobs for people who want and need them? Why can't we provide a worship experience for all? Why not provide health care for all, without the criminal background check? Why not give us forgiveness and redemption once we return?

Though my life was interrupted, I believe I am a better person today. I am not shallow today, nor do I take things for granted. I appreciate a breeze on my face and the swaying of the trees. I remember when I did not see trees, or cars, or the hustle and bustle of life. The Internet—how amazing—and cell phones and iPods. Whoever would have thought? Life was interrupted, but I'm still invigorated about surviving and making a difference! Intercepted at the crossroad—to survive or to fail, which way shall we go? Oh, we have to press our way!

But for those still incarcerated—how must you encourage another sista' to keep hope alive? To know in your soul and spirit that this system will not break your innate spirit to survive? To keep the faith and pray till your answer comes—knowing it is coming! How do you tell your sista' who you love and are leaving behind that you will never forget her? You just do because you have to. You find a way to do it in your own way, through a letter, a magazine, a money order, a prayer. You just do. And that is what will provide that bridge over our interrupted lives.

75

California and the Welfare
and Food Stamps Ban

All of Us or None

Adopt a resolution that California should opt out of the lifetime
welfare and food stamps ban. State legislators should sponsor
comprehensive bills opting out of the welfare and food stamps ban.

California is one of seventeen states that deny welfare and food stamps for life to
people who were convicted of a drug felony after August 22, 1996. As a result of this
policy, more than 2,289 people in need in Alameda County who have applied for
food stamps have been denied. An unacceptable 77.8 percent of people denied these
benefits are African American.

The lifetime ban on welfare and food stamps for people convicted of a drug
felony harms our community. By taking away the supports that former prisoners
need to make the transition from prison, our government encourages recidivism,
breaks up families, and perpetuates a discriminatory system of imprisoning the
poor, who are disproportionately people of color. Our state also loses out economically. The California Legislative Analyst's Office estimates that California residents
lose out on $25 million in federal food stamps each year due to the ban. This is
money that would be spent directly in our communities and contribute to the economic development of our neighborhoods.

- California's drug felony exclusion policy is harmful and unnecessary. The 1996
  federal welfare act allows states to opt out of the ban. Not only have thirty-four
  states already done so, but six states have recently changed their policies. Even
  in California, the state legislature is currently considering changes to the blanket ban on food stamps eligibility. Nationwide the trend is toward more effective policies that enable people who have been in prison to rebuild their lives.
  We call on our local leaders to join us in urging state legislators to opt out of
  the lifetime welfare and food stamps ban that unfairly targets former prisoners.

- In California, 37,825 women became ineligible for benefits for the rest of their lives between 1996 and 1999 due to the welfare ban.
- Some 24,100 California adults would be eligible for food stamps if the state opted out of the ban, including 16,300 parents with children.
- Women of color and their families in California are disproportionately hurt by the ban because of racially biased drug policies and drug law enforcement.
- Nationally, 30 percent of women in prison were receiving welfare in the month prior to their arrest, and these women are likely to require public assistance after their release.
- Only seventeen states have adopted the federal lifetime ban on welfare and food stamps: Alabama, Alaska, Arizona, California, Georgia, Indiana, Kansas, Mississippi, Missouri, Montana, Nebraska, North Dakota, South Dakota, Texas, Virginia, West Virginia, and Wyoming.
- The California legislature is considering a bill that would restore food stamp eligibility to people who have prior felony convictions of drug possession.

76

Employment Resolution

Human Rights Commission of the
City and County of San Francisco

All of Us or None

WHEREAS people with criminal records suffer from pervasive discrimination in many areas of life—employment, housing, education, and eligibility for many forms of social benefits;

WHEREAS at least 13 million people nationwide experience lifelong discrimination because of past felony convictions, and California incarcerates and releases more people per capita than any other state, resulting in large numbers of people whose backgrounds include past criminal activity and/or imprisonment;

WHEREAS many people who have been convicted of offenses in other states have moved to California to begin their lives anew;

WHEREAS 55,000 people are booked into San Francisco County jails annually with an average daily population of 2,200 people—each one released with their life shattered and a criminal record to haunt them;

WHEREAS in 2003, 2,507 people were paroled from the California Department of Corrections to San Francisco County;

WHEREAS people of color in general are convicted and incarcerated in numbers disproportionate to their representation in the population as a whole, which disproportionately impacts their families and communities;

WHEREAS 70 to 80 percent of all formerly incarcerated people in California are unemployed, and people with felony records are twice as likely to be denied employment as people without past criminal records;

WHEREAS formerly incarcerated people represent a workforce experienced in disciplined, structured environments with the same range of work skills as any other group of job seekers, ready to add value to the community;

WHEREAS the application form for public employment by the City and County of San Francisco specifically requires an applicant to answer yes or no to the statement, "I have been convicted by a court," even if the applicant has received a Governor's pardon;

WHEREAS many companies being awarded contracts by the City and County of San Francisco have policies and application forms that discriminate against people with past criminal records;

WHEREAS the City and County of San Francisco seeks to assist the successful reintegration of formerly incarcerated people back into the community after their release from prison;

WHEREAS it is the policy of the City of San Francisco to prohibit discrimination on the basis of race, religion, creed, ethnicity, national origin, color, ancestry, age, sex, sexual orientation, gender identity, domestic partner status, marital status, disability, AIDS/HIV, weight and height;

WHEREAS a past criminal record may be used as a pretext to allow discrimination against people who would otherwise be protected, based on a person's membership in one of San Francisco's protected categories;

THEREFORE, in order to mitigate or eliminate discrimination against people who have been in prison or convicted of criminal activity in the past and to assist with their successful reintegration into the community after prison

BE IT RESOLVED that the Human Rights Commission supports the All of Us or None effort to eliminate the box requiring disclosure of past criminal records on applications for public employment and for employers doing business with the city and county; and

BE IT FURTHER RESOLVED that the Human Rights Commission of the City and County of San Francisco urge the State of California and other cities and counties to eliminate the box requiring disclosure of past criminal records on their public employment applications.

77

Only with Time

Tina Reynolds

I had turned another corner in my life. Before I could process what this meeting might mean for moving forward in my life, arrangements had been made. I was on my way to see Danielle, my third daughter, who lives in New Jersey. She was twenty-four; it had been twenty years since I'd seen her. I was in my Volkswagen, driving through the Holland Tunnel toward New Jersey, feeling this vast silence. I was trying to avoid feeling emotions, and then it dawned on me the car was silent too, so I turned on the radio, but the silence within me didn't go away. Stevie Wonder's "Isn't She Lovely" was playing. He'd dedicated this song to his daughter at her birth. Danielle had never had a song dedicated to her. We nicknamed her Dani when she was little. Dani disliked wearing dresses and having her hair braided, and she would not go anywhere without her favorite toy, a red pickup truck. I remember her little face; she was four years old, always bright eyed and easy to make laugh. She loved animals and often fell asleep on the big stuffed pillow next to Lizzy, a mixed shepherd pup I had bought the girls when they were little. Dani had been separated from her sisters and me when her father came and got her while we were living in New York City with an aunt.

Monisha, Aja, Danielle, and I were living the best way we could at the time, but it was not a safe place for them. Her father and I had agreed early in our relationship that if one of us fell too deep into our addiction, we would not separate the girls.

As I drove to my meeting with Danielle, it was the beginning of autumn, the sky was clear, and the sun that came through the driver's-side window was warm on my face and arms. A day that wasn't too warm or too cold. The leaves on the trees had not begun to change yet. Danielle and I had made arrangements to meet at her house. Aja, one of her older sisters, had begun searching for Dani during the time she was in college. She never gave up the search but was unable to retrieve an address under her name. Monisha and Aja had always wanted to find Dani. In September of 2006, Aja learned that Dani had lived in New Jersey all along. She was just a bridge or tunnel away, with nothing physically separating us but the Hudson River. I live in New York. Many times I had wanted to begin the search for Dani, but I clearly knew that during those times when Aja and I spoke about finding her, I was not ready to search for Dani myself. I blocked out thoughts about how we might have met sooner. Aja had reached out to Dani after finding her address on the Internet. She cross-referenced her sister's father's last name and decided there couldn't be many people with the same last name. She found her sister.

Once when I was talking with Aja after she had been successful in locating Danielle, she'd asked me to explore my memories of the time I removed her and her sisters from my boyfriend's house because I found them asleep naked in bed with my boyfriend. I must have been about twenty-six years old at the time it happened, it was 2:00 A.M., and I'd just come home from work. I stood for a second looking at what I had walked in on, not believing what I saw. I woke my children up, told Monisha to put her clothes on, and began to help her sisters get dressed. After they were dressed, we packed what little belongings we had and I told them we were leaving. They were disoriented and cranky. My boyfriend, David, woke up, and asked, *Where are you going?* I said *We're leaving*. My car was parked in front of the house. I walked the little ones to the car and told the oldest to follow me. She wasn't awake yet and was walking slowly. David lumbered to the door. He followed us outside and grabbed Monisha's hand and asked *Why are you leaving?* As calmly as I could, I said, *David, it's late. Let go of my daughter's hand, go in the house, and go back to sleep. We're leaving. I'm going over to my grandmother's. We can talk about this in the morning, but I have to leave here now.* I grabbed his arm and pulled his hand from my daughter's wrist and ran to the car with her, hoisted her into the front seat, and locked the door. *You can't go*, David said, *I love you and the girls.*

I wasn't afraid of David, I was thinking of my children, but I didn't know how desperate he would be. He had never been violent, but if he had tried to hurt me then, I'm sure things would have gotten out of hand. I walked to him, stared him in the face, and said, as directly as I could, *You're naked. You were naked in the bed with my girls. They were naked too! That's more than a little fucking strange. I am going home and you better let me fucking go right now because the longer I look at you the more you disgust me.* I turned away from him, closed my eyes for a moment. I held my breath, praying this man would not go crazy. I walked quickly to the car and got in. As I closed the door I exhaled and put my hands on the steering wheel, looking at my kids, the oldest in the front with me and the little ones in the back. I was shaking; every part of my body was trembling. As I turned my head and began to start the car, David was standing at the passenger side, and he began banging on the window pleading for us not to leave. My oldest, Monisha, who was in the front seat, startled from the noise at the window and moved closer to me. I quickly pulled away from the curb, tires screeching. I clung tightly to the steering wheel. I arrived at my grandmother's house safely.

My daughters had not been physically hurt, but they had endured many instances of bad judgment on my part in the past. I didn't want to revisit the memory. I was never proud of the decisions I made regarding my children. During this time in my life, I was running away from everything, and I was dragging them with me. After my account of that time in our lives, I apologized to Aja. These can be very difficult conversations. I can see that my children did not make the same decisions I made when I was their age because of what they experienced with me. My family had a difficult time upholding the love my children have for me. They were hurt and embarrassed by my choices, often not knowing how to cope with the burden of the crimes I committed due to drug use and addiction. They tried the best they could to support my children during my absence, but they did not know how to explain why I wasn't there.

During my conversation with Aja, I realized I had reopened a wound within me that I thought had been healed. It had been sewn up, and the scar was invisible. I had not fathomed how painful it would be to relive this incident with her. I was discussing the decisions I made when I was a twenty-six-year-old adult to a child who is now a twenty-eight-year-old adult. I've never made excuses. I was aware that she had taken a stand for herself, and I was overwhelmed with pride. I have a friend who describes emotional challenges as limps only visible to the people who love you. So here I was metaphorically limping, steadying myself to be the parent my child needed. I wasn't looking for a chair or a wall to lean on. I wanted to heal both of us. I wanted the wound to heal without the infection of denial.

I stated over and over again in my head that this was the right time. *It shouldn't have been any sooner or later. It is now and I'm okay with it being now.* I'd practiced this mantra five times before when reuniting with my other children for the first time. This made the sixth time I would have to reintroduce myself. My sense of worthiness as a person has been challenged by the emotional impact of child abuse, drug dependence, and incarceration, particularly in the way it has shaped the relationships I have with my children. Today, very different in mind and spirit than I was during those other introductions, I'm able to face my daughter Dani. I am at peace with my past.

During the drive, I thought about Danielle, that little girl so innocent, strong, and beautiful. She's an adult now, and I didn't know how she had been living these last twenty years. I didn't know how much she would be willing to tell me, but I wouldn't push. After all, I was the one who had to meet her where she was emotionally. I called Danielle's cell, because I had gotten off at the wrong exit. She told me to pass this exit, but I really don't follow directions well when I'm driving to an unfamiliar place. She knew exactly where I'd gotten off and instructed me to park in front of a local Pizza Hut. As I waited I wondered if I would have known her if she had ever passed me walking down a street. I remembered her young face, her smile, her soft touch, and all of that curly hair. I forgot to ask her what she was driving, so I began to look at the cars as they pulled in, wondering whether I would recognize her. About ten minutes went by and I saw a Volkswagen bug, one of the newer ones, pull up two spaces down from where I was. As I turned my head, a young woman got out of the car. She was thin, but not skinny, her eyes bright and clear, her mouth full with a wide smile. Her complexion was like honey, and she had her hair in a thick ponytail. I knew it was Danielle. My heart told me it was her. I got out of my car and neither of us said a word. We walked straight to each other and embraced. We stayed in each other's arms outside of the Pizza Hut for about two minutes, holding each other closely. I didn't hear a car go by, a door close, or people talking. It was like the world had stopped. I was holding my daughter again. All of these years of my being absent began to flash forward up to this point. This is the point that I had been waiting for. It was at this moment that our circle had been made complete. She was the missing voice when the other children and I planned holiday dinners. Hers was the missing face in many family pictures. I didn't want to let go, and she didn't seem to mind that I wanted to hold her. I felt her warmth, her chin rested within the crook of my neck; we weren't letting go of each other. The embrace was comfortable . . . it was right . . . it was forgiveness and love.

Reuniting with my children has been an uphill battle. I left when they were small children, expecting them to be the same when I returned and expecting that meeting them again would be an easy process. Aja's unshakable determination to have clarity in her life challenged me to look at my own choices. During those moments when clarity is needed, I offer my children an opportunity to see me as I am. I'm able to give this today.

78

Child of a Convicted Felon

Anonymous

At first I didn't notice or understand my parents' wrongdoings. To me they looked normal. I didn't see my father often, but when I did, I admired his flashiness and liked the presents he brought. My mom, on the other hand, was my best friend. She taught me everything from gymnastics to the catchy hand game "Down, Down, Baby." She braided my hair and painted my nails every Sunday.

I noticed the glares my grandmother gave my mom when she was with me and I heard her mumble that I would get hurt in the end, and I did get hurt. My mom would leave for days, and when she returned, she was a different person. I started to notice a smell on her return that was the same smell she left behind in the bathroom when she locked the door and wouldn't let me in. Like I said, the two of us did everything together, so I didn't understand this particular bathroom trip and the dazed look and scent I called "sweet burning." As I got older, I learned that my mother's absences were called "missions," and the "sweet burning" was the smell of a lit crack pipe.

My mother was an addict, but it was not noticeable because she kept herself well maintained. My mom was "Red" or "TC," and my dad was "Bullet." I was proud of them because they had respect. My father's occupation—a dealer—was no secret, and even now when people speak of him, I can feel pride for a second, but then I remember what has become of it all.

Like it's been said over and over, "What goes up must come down." When it came down, it hit hard. My father got locked up for reckless endangerment and grand larceny, and my mom stopped keeping her addiction a secret. My grandparents became my mother and father.

Over the years, my mother claimed she had had enough and turned herself in to the custody of Nassau County Correctional Facility about four different times. I guess this shows how much *rehabilitation* this prison had to offer. She tried other programs, too, but always relapsed.

During these periods, my second stepfather, a really good man, cared for the child he had with my mother and also for me and my brother. When my mother relapsed once again, he felt she needed to be in a new place, so they set out for Florida, leaving the three of us children behind. But then in 1997, my grandmother, the rock of the family, died. Ultimately all of us lived with my sad, lonely grandfather, and my mother went back to her old ways, which included using drugs while she was pregnant. The baby died, and the social worker said we kids had to live away from her. I was sad to leave my grandfather but very lucky not to have to go through foster care. I jumped from relative to relative and, eventually, when I was seventeen, the courts gave my father, now out of prison, custody of me. But the morning of my eighteenth birthday, I walked out his doors and never came back.

I had a goal to do it on my own, given the circumstances. My mother was incarcerated at Nassau County again. We hadn't stayed in contact, so I heard about her through other people. Suddenly, my grandfather was so sick that I had to put him in a nursing home—and my mother was charged with attempted forgery. I didn't go to visit my mother at all because I couldn't handle seeing her. Even though I was eighteen, I still wanted my mommy to come with me instead of walking in the other direction. And then my grandfather died. My mother was allowed to go to the funeral, but she couldn't comfort her own children.

My mother has recently come home. She was released in 2006 to a program that allowed her to come out and stay with me for the weekends, at first, and then eventually for an entire week. She was paroled to my apartment. It felt great to have her home. Of course I worried, but this time I had less fear. She had lost so much now and would be aced with a longer sentence and more consequences if she were to get into trouble again.

My mother finally began to realize the damage she was causing, not to me but to my younger brothers. After maintaining a steady job and income, my mother saved enough to move out on her own and take my younger brothers to live with her, fulfilling a promise she had made to them. Although the living arrangements weren't too spacious, my brothers didn't mind because they were simply happy she was home. Christmas 2006 was the first time we celebrated the holiday with her. My mother had missed most of my birthdays, so my twenty-first was the best just because she was there.

Two weeks ago, my mother moved into a three-bedroom apartment with space for her growing sons. She works at the Salvation Army as a shift supervisor. Every little thing she does, I'm proud of. It took her a while to get herself together, and now that she has, I have matured, but sometimes I feel ten years old when I'm with her. It feels good to be able to say, "I'm going to my mother's house," or to ask her, "Ma, can I have $20?"

I know my mother is doing wonderfully simply by her appearance, with her neck and wrists full of jewelry, and a size 14 fitting her snugly. Even after it all, my mother still remains my best friend. Since we both work and our schedules are different, we try to see each other at least once a week. If I am at school late, I sometimes wait for her to get off the train so that I can give her a ride, since we don't live far from each other. At times, I let my worries get the best of me. I fear that during one of her trips home, she will make a decision that causes her to throw away all that she has worked for. Part of me feels that she might have already faced this situation. I have to believe in my heart that my mother is stronger now and has made up her mind and knows what direction she wants to go in.

I do believe that all the problems with my mother and father have affected me and made me very antisocial; I definitely have difficulties opening up and building relationships with people. In my opinion, though, this is a small price to pay for the more valuable lessons I have learned. I am the daughter of a felony-convicted father as well as a recovering felony-convicted mother. That is my story, and I proudly stick to it.

79

Mothering after Imprisonment

Margaret Oot Hayes

A National Institute of Corrections study recently reported that nearly 85 percent of mothers in prison plan to live with their children when they are released. The fact is, the obstacles to this plan are huge for most women and include lack of support for substance abuse problems, unmet medical and mental health needs, unresolved issues related to trauma and abuse, a lack of educational and occupational opportunities, the need for safe and affordable housing, the impact of extended separation from their children, and specific challenges relating to intimate and family relationships, social functioning, physical and mental health status, and economic status. The two case studies below illustrate the terrible difficulties into which many formerly incarcerated women step when they reenter family life.

I interviewed the two mothers in the case studies, "Maria" and "Sylvia," about their experiences mothering after prison every month for four or five months after their release. The women had similar backgrounds. They had been teenage mothers before their incarceration, lived in poverty, had a history of mental illness, and were victims of domestic abuse. Maria also had a history of substance abuse. Both Maria and Sylvia described their mothers as former "crackheads" who were unable to provide adequate mothering to them during their childhoods. The following stories represent the mothers' journeys from prison to home with their children, and back to prison.

Maria

When Maria was released from prison, she was surprised that the reunification with her daughter was as positive as it was. The only contact she had had with her four-year-old daughter was through the mail during her two years of incarceration. As

Maria said, "So, it was just an experience, like, wow, ya know. She still knows who I am, and that was the greatest feeling in the world." Maria's mother was not as happy about the positive reunification. Maria said, "I was not expecting the baby to be as open as she was; I was actually expecting my mother to be more open, and it's totally the opposite." In fact, there was a great deal of friction between Maria and her mother. Maria said her mother thought she was going to mess up again and end up back in prison. Even more painful, Maria felt that her mother saw her as a threat because her return from prison interrupted the relationship Maria's mother had developed with her granddaughter.

Maria ended up moving into a "sober house" within a week of her release because she felt this tense situation was threatening her sobriety. She believed that the move represented good judgment and that she was doing what was best for her daughter and herself. Maria told me, "My daughter's in great care, she's in great hands. I need to focus on myself. And that's hard. Saying that you need to focus and take time on yourself, knowing that you have other responsibilities as far as your child." Throughout the interview, Maria emphasized how difficult it was for her to function with her mental health issues.

Maria was living in a sober house during our second interview. She reported that this living situation improved her relationship with her mother. She also said that her daughter loved visiting her. Maria told me how much it hurt to be separated from her daughter again but said that she needed to do what was best for her child. Maria was upset because her mother made her daughter call the older woman "mommy one" and call Maria "mommy two." Maria believed that her mother was trying to do for her granddaughter what she hadn't done for her own children.

Maria felt bad about this situation because her own mother clearly didn't realize that even though Maria was twenty-three years old, she still needed a mother. In fact, Maria became involved with a man while she was at the sober house, and she said she took up with him because she really needed love and affection at this time. Maria observed sadly, "I don't think my mom will ever fill that gap." But, according to Maria, "She's trying to fill that in with my daughter."

After Maria moved to the sober house, she felt that her little daughter didn't know who to listen to anymore. She said that she and her mother had very different styles of discipline and that she tended to be stricter than her mother. Maria described an instance in which her daughter was "throwing a fit": "My mom takes it lightly. But I'm sittin' there lookin' at my daughter, like, you need to stop. And my daughter's in a position where she doesn't know who to listen to." Complicating the situation, Maria found that the demands of parole took up a lot of her time. Between work, meetings, and counseling she was busy all day long and into the evening. She said she usually didn't get home from her meetings until 9 o'clock at night, but because her daughter stayed up late, she was able to be with her.

Maria said that she was receiving fewer visits and phone calls from her daughter during her second month at the sober house. The visits that did occur seemed to add to the friction between Maria and her mother. "She [the little girl] tells me, Mommy I don't wanna leave. I wanna stay here. And I see the look in my mother's eyes . . . 'Go.' She tells my mother to leave. She wants to be here alone with me, and that infuriates my mother."

During this interview, Maria reported, "I'm feeling like shit as a parent." She felt she had too many issues of her own to deal with and that these difficulties interfered with her ability to provide for her daughter. Maria's addictions were starting to haunt her through "drug dreams" and "stinking thinking," the experience of "not being able to deal with the thoughts that are going through my head, and drugs stop that."

During our last interview, Maria was fixated on the breakup of her recent relationship, mental health issues, stress, and her traumatic childhood. I tried to focus the interview on her experiences mothering after prison, but Maria seemed to have a difficult time talking about her daughter. Maria was upset that she was seeing her daughter less frequently, even though the reason was usually that Maria hadn't scheduled a visit. Her mother continued to insist that Maria's daughter call her grandmother "mommy one" and Maria "mommy two." "I don't like being called mommy number two! And when my daughter does that to me, I tell her, just call me mommy. And it confuses her, and that's what I hate. She shouldn't have confusion over who's who." During the following month, Maria lost three jobs and became pregnant. Before our next interview, Maria called me to let me know that she was using heroin again and was going back to prison for violating parole.

Sylvia

Like Maria, Sylvia was surprised that her reunification with her children was positive. Sylvia had been incarcerated for nearly six years and received biweekly visits from her children. Sylvia's mother had cared for her two granddaughters during Sylvia's incarceration. Sylvia described her reunification this way: "We had a bond that I don't even know where it came from. It was like I never left. It's like I've always been here."

But now that she was home again, Sylvia's daughters did not listen to her. She said that she was very lenient and was concerned that her daughters were testing her to see how far they could push her. Although Sylvia and her mother were trying not to contradict one another, Sylvia was letting "Nana" be the "bad guy."

Sylvia spoke lovingly about her original family. She believed that even though their life was "messed up," their mother always loved her children. Sylvia and her family don't believe that "tough love" works. They believe in supporting one another no matter what a family member does wrong.

Sylvia felt that the demands of parole were interfering with her reunification with her children. "You get of jail after five and a half years and, ya know, you been away from your kids and whatever, and they want you to have a job within two weeks. Your kids go to school, and by the time you get home from work, your kids are in bed. So it's like, hello, where's the reunion here? There was no time to bond. None at all. Thank God the bond was already there, because we wouldn't even have it. Because I was so busy. I had no time. And when I did get home, I was so aggravated that I didn't want to do anything. I didn't want to play games. I didn't wanna do nuthin.'"

During the second interview, Sylvia reported that her children were behaving a little better, although there were some problems. "They seem to be getting a little better, but they were playin' sides. Goin' to Nana and Nana will tell them 'no' and then they come to me and I'll say 'yes' and then they'll start doin' it, and Ma will be like, 'Well, I said no.'" However, Sylvia continued to "let Ma deal with the kids." Sylvia was pregnant, and she and her family were visibly happy about the pregnancy.

Sylvia was frustrated about the difficulty of making ends meet. "We went up to the church to get clothes. It sucks when you gotta go to the church and get food and clothes." Her daughters never wanted her to leave the house without them, so she had missed some of the meetings she was supposed to attend. Also, Sylvia was angry about all of the counseling sessions and group meetings she had to attend. "Ya know, I just miss appointments. It's like, how many things can one person do? I was in jail for five years. I did every group possible. What out here is gonna help me that didn't help me in there?"

During the third interview, Sylvia reported that the kids were worse. Her major complaint was that they were not listening. She said that her daughters were not playing sides anymore, but "They just don't listen. My oldest daughter's favorite word: No." Her daughters still didn't want to be separated from her. She also spoke about how protective her brothers were of her and how protective she is of her daughters.

Sylvia was battling with depression during this period and was hoping to be able to work soon so that she could get out of the house.

When I called to schedule my fourth interview, Sylvia's mother was very upset when she answered the phone. She said that Sylvia had recently absconded and that there was a warrant out for her arrest. According to Sylvia's mother, Sylvia was afraid that a parole officer was going to send her back to prison for a supposed parole violation. Sylvia did not want to have her baby in prison, so she left the state until her baby was born. She turned herself in after her son was born. Sylvia had a successful appeal after a short stay in prison. The parole board released her to her home under house arrest so that she could be with her children.

NOTES

This article was originally published in slightly different form as "The Lived Experience of Mothering after Prison: The Preliminary Study" in *Journal of Forensic Nursing* 4, no. 2 (2008): 61–67. Reproduced with permission of Blackwell Publishing, Ltd.

80

Being about It

Reflections on Advocacy after Incarceration

Martha L. Raimon, Luz Alvarez, Sunshine Brooks,
Casey Deas, and Lorrayne Patterson

*Our deepest fear is not that we are inadequate. Our deepest fear is that we are
powerful beyond words . . . Define success for yourself and live it.*
MARIANNE WILLIAMSON

The formerly incarcerated women that I, Martha, worked with in two advocacy
programs at the Women's Prison Association and Home (WPA) and at the Women
in Prison Project (WIPP) of the Correctional Association of New York dramatically demonstrate the power of Marianne Williamson's words through their commitment to personal and political change.

The two workshops seek similar outcomes. The goal of WPA's program, the
Women's Advocacy Project (WAP), is to develop leaders able to craft solutions to the
many-faceted challenges facing incarcerated and formerly incarcerated women.
Similarly, ReConnect, part of WIPP, trains women in advocacy and leadership, seeking to provide women who have come home from prison or jail the information and
tools they need to advocate effectively for themselves as they secure basic life needs,
such as housing, employment, and reunification with family. Both programs work
to enhance women's natural leadership skills so that they can engage in collective policy advocacy. The participants in both programs have had varying levels of involvement with the criminal justice system, but they share a desire to bring about improvements in criminal justice policies that affect women in and out of jail and prison.

My principal role in these workshops was to teach participants about family
law, especially laws relating to custody and foster care, and I loved the experience.
As a legal services lawyer, I often worked with complex issues that involved individually crafted strategies and plans. Success was measured in small increments.
Here, I was surrounded by a group of highly motivated women, interested in—to

put it simply—changing the world as they knew it. After a few months, I noticed a pattern. The group would begin with preliminaries, talking about personal experiences, triumphs, and difficulties: my son was arrested, my daughter is back in the residential program, my health is failing. Slowly, with very little input from the front of the room, the class would turn its attention to the larger political world. I witnessed the personal become the political in each classroom. This transformation astounded me and made me hopeful both for each class member's personal growth but also for the success of the changes they sought to make in the world.

In taping four of the women who participated in these workshops, my goal was to give each class member time to think and talk about how the ability to sharpen her advocacy skills had affected her in her personal and professional life. I also wanted to capture some of the excitement that was palpable in each class. Below are the women's chosen words of introduction, followed by their responses to questions I selected for them.

Luz Alvarez

I am a fifty-year-old Latina. I have an eighteen-year-old son, my only son. I served my time at Hopper Home, an Alternative to Incarceration program. I completed fifteen months there and was part of WAP while I was there. I am going for my B.A. in human services. I am a case manager at CASES [Center for Alternative Sentencing Employment Services], and I work with adults with mental illness who have had involvement with the criminal justice system.

Sunshine (aka Rita) Brooks

I am a forty-seven-year-old mother of seven sons. I was sentenced to three years in prison and am a formerly incarcerated woman. My children are now back in my life. I am a case manger working with women with HIV/AIDS. I am one of the founders of WAP and a three-time graduate [of the workshop].

Casey Deas

I am a fifty-four-year-old gay woman. I spent six years in prison. I have no children, but I raised my niece and nephew and the children of my significant others. I have an associate's degree in business and accounting. I came to WPA because I got tired of being ashamed of who I was, a formerly incarcerated woman. I said "let me get connected with my people. Who I am." Those open arms and support I got make me feel like I want to be an open arm for others. I am looking forward to graduating from ReConnect and starting WAP.

Lorrayne Patterson

I am forty-seven years old and on parole. I was sentenced to four and a half to nine. I have been on parole for a year. I came to ReConnect out of frustration. It seemed like there were no programs for me since I was not HIV positive and I have no children. When I was in prison, I had ideas that something needed to be changed. I am currently at John Jay School of Criminal Justice studying deviant behavior and social control. I work in the admissions office.

Why were you interested in an advocacy class?

SUNSHINE: Before WAP my idea of advocacy was getting involved with women to discuss issues that plagued women in prison and then getting out on the Senate floor and blaze away and make people hear what we had to say, me leading the pack. That was my idea of what advocacy was all about. I learned it wasn't like that. I learned a better way to do things, and I like having a voice in things that matter. There is power behind a pen. A lot of power behind some words. And we can be heard in the right places where it really matters. I had no idea until I went to prison that women were being sentenced to five [years] flat for a dime bag of crack. I heard a lot of women saying they got time just for standing at a bus stop and pointing in the wrong direction. I found out that Rockefeller rules from the grave.

LUZ: Going in and out of the criminal justice system, I observed a lot of Latinas, especially older women, having problems with language and obtaining information about their criminal or family court case regarding their children. I kept running back and forth to the law library translating documents for women because a lot of them were in worse situations than me. I joined WAP because I feel that my voice is not just my voice but all the voices of all the sisters I left behind when I was incarcerated.

LORRAYNE: My family members are professionals with degrees and stuff like that. My mother and father were very active in the civil rights movement. My father died trying to get black history in the public schools. So I know that the masses can have a voice. I grew up with that idea.

CASEY: Violence. I know inmates that died. I know inmates that got beat down. I got beat down with three broken ribs. And I was afraid to speak up. I was afraid to speak up all those years. Training will get me information, so when I help others, I'm educated. I can get on committees and change laws. Imagine that? Changing a law, a bill? A policy? This is the best way to be violent. I went to jail because I took a bribe as a housing inspector. I wanted to save the city from homelessness. What I did was take a bribe, and I had to pay for it. I can't justify it. I did my time for it. And I'm still paying for it.

What aspects of advocacy training were of interest to you? How did you apply what you learned?

SUNSHINE: When I did the class about foster care, I learned a lot, especially one specific thing: I had the right to be produced [to demand that the "system" follow mandated procedures to enable her appearance] every time I went to

family court! Nobody told me this! My attorney should have told me! When
I learned this, it brought tears to my eyes because for seven years I fought for
my kids. It literally brought tears to my eyes. I was angry. I wanted to rewind
the tape and punch somebody. Now I'm a better-equipped person for what
I'm going through with my granddaughter.

LUZ: One of the things I found interesting was learning what women go through
with children and family court cases in terms of their parental rights. When
I got to WAP, they trained me to properly assist somebody and guide them. It
gave me a lot of confidence personally and professionally, and it also made me
exercise patience, which is something that I have problems with. When you
advocate, you need patience. I use every little skill that I learned in the advocacy project now in my work [to get women] public assistance and SSI [Sup-
plemental Security Income]. WAP also gave me more confidence to advocate
for myself. My salary was being garnished by the Department of Education. I
won a fair hearing, and I'm no longer being garnished. Personally and professionally, advocacy training has done a lot for me.

LORRAYNE: I was a former abuser of crack cocaine. Through use of crack cocaine, I enlarged the left side of my heart, which caused me to have high blood
pressure. This was diagnosed while I was at Rikers Island. The state maintained me for two years. I was released with only one week's worth of medicine. It takes forty-five days to get Medicaid. I wondered, why can't they process this before release? I went to the emergency room. They couldn't help. I
went to another. My blood pressure was off the chart. Understand? I was diagnosed by the city and maintained by the state. Why release me with high blood
pressure with one week of medication? [Without ReConnect] I wouldn't have
known that I could stand up at a public hearing and vent these feelings in a
proper manner and people would understand. It costs more to have me go to
the emergency room than to give me sixty days worth of pills. It angered me
so bad. In ReConnect I learned I didn't have to take this. I can combat this.
Knowing things gives you a feeling of empowerment. Legislators need to see
the face behind the story. And I could talk about it honestly and passionately. It
was scary. I could have died. Seeing other people care also helps you care more.

CASEY: When I go to a housing class, I take what I learn back to the shelter. I
even pass it on to staff. I've looked into credit reports of women in the shelter.
It's amazing; these women on SSI, fixed incomes, they owe loans they don't
even know about. That's why they can't keep any money in the bank. I have an
associate's degree. I want to get a B.A. My strength is in human services. I have
a plan. I'm patient with it. I'm charged up. So I'm there, listening. I have the
information to take back and read. I want to make this my life's work.

What was your turning point, if you had one?

SUNSHINE: At my job, a young lady about to have her children taken away ran in the door screaming and crying. My boss asked me to please talk with her, so I did. I hadn't realized that I'd learned so much in advocacy class! I thought, damn, I'm scaring the hell out of myself! I was calm. I was giving her information and phone numbers. A sense of peace came over that cubicle when I was finished talking with her. It was really nice to be able to help somebody and know that the information was there that I could give. I was talking faster than my brain was working. But it was all correct stuff. I was proud of myself; it made me feel real good. And now I'm faced with the dilemma of using the same information to get my granddaughter. I'm grateful I have the information now.

LUZ: The turning point for me came when I finally said to myself, even though my son's father is a good father and a gentleman, this is my son too and I want to share custody of him. I want it in writing. There was an empty feeling inside me all those years. I had to stand up for myself. I was a heroin addict and a crack addict but I had been proving myself. I needed to prove to myself I could do it. Something one day in the WAP class clicked, like a Pandora's box. It just opened. No matter how good this looks—that he's the perfect father— this is something I want for myself. To pinpoint the feeling . . . it was like a spiritual experience, a feeling of awakening. The classes led up to it. I went to family court, got the documents, and sat my husband down. I told him I need this in writing for myself. I went through the motions and now we share custody.

LORRAYNE: It's been in little spurts more so with me. Every time I left the class I was armed with new information. All the places I was affiliated with nobody had any answers and that bothered me. How can you say you're a parole-based program helping ex-offenders? Having the answers was an ego burst; I started to say, yeah, I'm important. And my stature grows with these meetings. On the bus ride up to Albany for Advocacy Day, I realized that's where my transfer order came down from. I saw the long, tall ceilings and marble floors and nice polished oak doors and I absorbed everything. It was so empowering to be in Albany, for the first time in my life not in shackles, not in "greens," not with a nasty CO [correctional officer] and a brown bag with some nasty sandwich and some stale cookies. I had Dunkin' Donuts on the bus! It was an experience! I revisited in my mind what I said I would do when I was inside trying to fight for a law library or a drug program. I said, you all are going to hear from me. I kept it to myself. Advocacy Day was my chance to have a voice. Not sitting in the yard or the TV room talking about it, but *being* about it. Saying, I've arrived; I'm credible now. I didn't feel afraid to disclose. And that's the biggest thing that advocacy work has done for me. I'm a plus, an asset. It's a good feeling because when you're released, officers say stuff like: see you when you get back. No you won't, oh no you won't. I'll see you in there before you see me in there, how 'bout that? A human being deserves a second chance, and to move on from a mistake.

CASEY: My spiritual awakening—and I'm going to call it that—happened yesterday at the New York Telephone Justice rally. It's been building up, and I saw the flyer about MCI charging us 630 percent more than a regular customer. Then yesterday I was giving out flyers asking, "Do you have an incarcerated loved one? Listen to me." I found myself preaching. People were coming at me with questions. I was charged up. I kept going back for more and more flyers. I had everyone else giving out flyers. I thought, "Casey, you're back." I used to be a housing inspector. I used to walk the streets with my head held high. I used to walk these streets of New York and feel like I could make a difference and change things. And I lost that. I lost that. But I regained it yesterday. I gave away my thug coat. Why? I'm not a thug. I'm not a criminal. And that was my spiritual awakening.

81

The First Time Is a Mistake . . .

Patricia Zimmerman

"The first time is a mistake; the second time is intentional . . ."

This is a phrase that we often use within the prison community when we're talking about someone getting "locked up" again. I shared those thoughts while behind walls. Yet when I was released in December of 2002, I realized how serious parole supervision was, along with the whole process of reentry.

I have watched friends go back to jail and prison for so many reasons: problems at home, problems with the parole officer, problems with a spouse or lover. "The money wasn't flowing right," or "I can't get a job," or "This is all I know." I expected doom when I was released.

Women with criminal justice involvement do not normally talk about their issues. We are emotional beings trained to hide what we feel. So we show tough exteriors and persevere in spite of incredible odds. Also, we go through so much and don't seek the help we need. The sad thing is that many of us are in such denial that even if help were available, we would not get it because we deny that we need it. This causes us great harm.

It hurts me to see some of my sisters in so much pain. Am I really any different? Of course I'm not. My history, my own experiences, and my way of handling my life are unique but not different. All of us are dealing with the huge effects of incarceration—on us and on our families. Our children and our parents suffer so much while we are behind the wall, watching helplessly.

Being out, with all the weight on our shoulders, we wonder how we will get beyond all this. How do we get to the light at the end of the tunnel? How do we begin to rid ourselves of all the baggage that we've carried around for years? The abuse, misuse, the drugs and violence? How do we get people to believe in and support what little innocence we have left? How do we say that we are hurting or in trouble in a way that people can hear? How do we get help when our kids are out of control? How do we express that we do not want to use drugs, but that being high drowns out the fact that our partners are cheating on us and then beating us every chance they get? Whom do we tell that our parole officer is insane or that no one in our families will accept us in their homes? Is there anyone we can tell that we are HIV+ and even though we are not dying, we feel like we are? One person cannot come up with the answers to all these questions. The answers may lie in the unified efforts of an entire society, not in the heart of one troubled soul.

We need to be able to say things such as, "I need someone to talk to," or "I need counseling and other supports." "I need financial help." "I need a babysitter." We must learn to take better care of ourselves and, especially, express our need for love and affection in ways that are not detrimental to our well-being. We have to find ways of taking steps toward the type of change that is necessary for making wholesome and valuable lives for ourselves and our children.

We need our families, and we also need the parole-probation system to be supportive. Women who have had criminal justice involvement need counseling and other kinds of treatment. We need to know that there are understanding, supportive people we can count on, even if we fall short. We need to learn that we are each other's keepers and that no one has to be alone in her struggle. We need to learn to say "enough!" and mean it. Many of us have survived on hope. We stand on the shoulders of each other's strengths, especially the capacity to be persistent. If I am successful, we all are successful. I cannot remain silent when there are things that need to be said. We have the obligation to reach and teach and touch lives. We owe it to ourselves and each other.

82

What Life Has Been Like for Me
Since Being on the Outside

Freda Swinney

I served eight and a half years in prison, and I've been home ten months. There was so much for me to learn about life all over again. I had to learn how use modern technology; I had to learn how to cope with relationships.

Technology changes every day, but still I thought that things would not have changed very much by the time I got out of prison. Some things seem similar when it comes to technology; for instance, software programs have the same kinds of menus and editing tools. ATM machines are the same. But the Internet amazed me. A person can go all over the world, talk to people, shop. And cell phones—they have become like a second heartbeat for some people. I actually thought at first that people were walking the streets talking to themselves. People seem to be in relationships with all this advanced technology: men and women come home from work, and they go straight to their computers and consume themselves with work that they were not able to complete at the office. They get the company they work for to agree to allow them to work from home on their personal computers.

I had to catch myself. I did not realize that I had developed a relationship with my cell phone. One day it dawned on me that I did not do anything without my cell phone. But after only being home thirty days, and having a relationship only with my cell phone, I got involved with a young man who had also spent time in prison. After being out of society for so many years and not having contact with the opposite sex, I soon remembered: it is an *experience* to have to deal with the opposite sex.

Men can be so deceitful, especially when a woman has not been dealing with men for so long. It can be dangerous when you allow the wrong man into your space. It can be painful when the infatuation wears off, and you learn who the man really is. My heart was broken when I found out that this young man was leading a double life. I found a letter from a man that he was locked up with that explained that he and this man were very close friends; in fact, they were close in ways that men are not usually close to each other, and if that wasn't enough, there was another woman who came into our lives and caused total chaos between us. Relationships are not easy to maneuver when you are an introvert. What I am saying is, I had my mind set and focused, and I allowed a young man into my life. It seemed as if we started out very well, and we spent time together, and enjoyed each other's company, and then the sexual intimacy happened, and we became even closer. But because we had both been out of touch with dealing with the opposite sex, we were jealous and overprotective of each other.

I did not realize how time-consuming a relationship could be, and I also did not know that my loved ones, such as my son and my mother, who had been without me for so long, would be jealous of my relationship with this man. I was being pulled in many directions. My son would say little sly remarks, and my mom would do the same. The man I was dating would also say things like, "I need your time" and "You owe yourself some time for yourself."

Yes, I really do. I agree. Now I am taking the time I need to get to know me.

83

Alternatives

ATI in New York City

Alexandra Bell and Leche

When Leche and I first meet, it is a scorching hot day on the long strip that divides Allen Street on the Lower East Side of Manhattan—a strip known as "the island" to many drug users who frequent the Lower East Side Harm Reduction Center. The area is familiar to Leche, but today she visits as something of a graduate. She's been clean now for three years. She has squeezed me between appointments with her counselors—both mandated by her enrollment in an Alternative to Incarceration (ATI) program. On her last bid in prison, the conclusion of which would have marked seven years served, she was accepted into an ATI program at the Women's Prison Association (WPA).

ALEXANDRA: Before the ATI, what did you do when you got out?

LECHE: I went straight back to selling drugs. Only once did I put myself in a shelter, and that was after I did three years at Albion. The most I ever got [upon] leaving was a sheet of paper, and even that didn't refer me to places that could help; it was for welfare. I didn't want welfare.

ALEXANDRA: I found it interesting that WPA looked for you after you had served a number of sentences. Why so late?

LECHE: I don't know. I try and look at it as if they are still working out the kinks with the system in general. I also think it is just the way it is, considering ATIs aren't the norm.

ALEXANDRA: You were released into the custody of WPA. Are there comparisons to arriving at WPA and say somewhere like Rikers or Albion?

LECHE: Yeah, but not many. There are the basics, paperwork and rooms and things like that, but from the moment I got out, WPA worked with me to map out my goals for the entire time I was there. It looked as hard as it was. It was like getting a new long prison sentence in the beginning, but over time you get attached to the people who see you through.

ALEXANDRA: When we first spoke, you told me about some of the clashes between women at Rikers and at Albion. Did you find a better sense of community with the women at WPA?

LECHE: It was what it was. I worried about me. You got some women who are there just to stay out of prison. Fake it to make it. Some are serious about it and some don't really care. But that's everywhere you go. Moving me around wasn't going to make me stop. Hell, I could use [drugs] in Tibet and you sure could get hold of drugs in prison.

ALEXANDRA: Did you? What about the ATI helped you overcome your drug use?

LECHE: No. I never gave dirty urine, but plenty of women did. I can't say I didn't use because the ATIs stopped me, but there is more incentive to quit. There isn't really any [incentive] with prison—you're bored to death.

ALEXANDRA: What happened to the women who gave dirty urine? Did they go back to prison?

LECHE: For the most part, no. That's when the difference between the criminal justice system and ATI programs is obvious. One time [of drug use] on the outside and you're in jail for half your damn life; one time in an ATI and you have to go to an extra session or something, but prison was never the first option.

ALEXANDRA: It is common to think of WPA and ATIs as drug rehabilitation centers or family places. Why were you there?

LECHE: I saw it as an opportunity to get housing. I'm not really sure I looked at it as a means to get out of prison at the time; my sentence was practically over when I got accepted. I didn't really look at it to help me stop drugs either. Housing was key. The other times I'd been in prison I didn't have a place to go when I got out. Prisons don't address the homeless issue; they just give you your shit and open the gate.

ALEXANDRA: You talk a lot about housing. What else did you gain from your experience with WPA?

LECHE: Opportunity. Opportunity to stay clean. Opportunity to learn new things. Opportunity to be around people who cared about me, and by that I mean family. My mother died when I was at the ATI, and it worked out for me to be around to go and to have the support of my family. All that matters to recovery.

ALEXANDRA: I'm amazed you see it that way. Seems unfortunate that they didn't intervene earlier. Did you come to that opinion quickly? Did you ever think you should have just completed your sentence?

LECHE [laughs]: At times, yes. The Alternative to Incarceration is just that—an alternative. You ain't free! And it is more difficult on many levels. You have to really look at yourself. When I first got out, I had an escort go with me everywhere. That lasted about two months; and then there is the counseling. I had about three therapists and spent most of my day in some type of group therapy or rehabilitative meeting. When I was at Rikers I spent half the day in my cell. There was nothing established to put you on the track to making change. At an ATI, they'll program and counsel you to death!

ALEXANDRA: Given those activities, what do you believe to be the fundamental principle that separates WPA from prisons?

LECHE: There is something inspiring about people believing in you. True, the environment has women who aren't ready, but it also has women who would do better if the circumstances were different. Prison never demands the best of you.

ALEXANDRA: Three words to describe prison.

LECHE: Confined. Defeating. Mentally, physically, emotionally, psychologically defeating. It's a dungeon. There are no three words.

ALEXANDRA: And Alternatives to Incarceration?

LECHE: Shed of Light!

Leche and I met one more time, and during that meeting I learned more about her time in prison, or what she frequently refers to as "the Jungle." It is a place where recovery from a destructive life is the last option. In her depiction, prison "offers little change" from the social ills that women encountered on the outside. Leche entered prison a hustler and continued to hustle on the outside, returning to prison four more times.

For many, prison is a world that mirrors the world they once inhabited, but the drug of choice is just a cellblock away, the next fight is at the next meal, and your abusive partner is replaced by a corrupt corrections officer. Like Leche, more than 70 percent of New York's female inmates are women of Latina or African descent, and more than 80 percent of women who are incarcerated for drug offenses are women of color.

Despite studies showing that drug treatment and ATI programs are healthier and more cost-effective alternatives to imprisonment, women continue to be imprisoned at staggering rates. In the fifteen years after 1987, when Leche began serving her first sentence, one of five drug charges she would receive, the number of drug cases among women increased at almost double the rate of the number of cases among men. In fact, between 1973 and 2006, the number of women in New York State prisons increased by almost 645 percent.

Much of the increase in women's incarceration is due to the enactment of the Rockefeller Drug Laws in 1973. The Rockefeller Drug Laws require harsh prison terms for even minor drug convictions. Under one of the laws' harshest provisions, a judge must hand down a prison term of eight to twenty years for anyone convicted of selling two ounces or possessing eight ounces of a narcotic substance, regardless of the circumstances of the person's involvement. For many women, the inability of judges to consider their personal circumstances before imposing sentencing means irreparable damage. Many women have been coerced by abusive partners; many are struggling with addiction themselves; and a large number suffer from extreme poverty.

The Women's Prison Association supports women and prevents further damage by maintaining family and community ties. Leche's experiences at WPA point to the successes that are possible when women's problems are approached from a different direction. Women who complete ATI programs are less likely to go back to prison and are more likely to retain custody of their children, maintain healthy living arrangements, obtain job skills through training, and overcome addiction.

The next time I saw Leche was at the Correctional Association. She was working as an intern on the Lower East Side, taking computer classes, working as a peer educator, and working with WPA. That day, she was pacing frantically, trying to read over statistics about women in prison in preparation for the Annual Advocacy Day. "You ready?" I asked. "Yeah," she said. "It just sucks to go each year, the incarceration rate higher and to have to say the same thing, but if one more woman can get the opportunity I had, it is worth it."

84

Violent Interruptions

Noelle Paley and Joshua Price

"Three parole officers in a vehicle roll up on me; none of them was even my parole officer. When I looked in the truck, I saw a baby seat and asked what that was for. They told me, 'It's so when we violate you, we can take your daughter.' They have me off balance, unsure. I never know what is going to happen. I'm not going to run from parole, but I don't answer the door until after curfew." Candis Henderson, a young black parolee in our hometown, Binghamton, New York, then tells us of yet another time she was stopped in the street, this time as she was leaving the grocery store with her newborn daughter. Nowadays, Candis does not go to her mandatory parole meetings alone. She takes her mother or her sister so that if parole "violates" her and sends her back to jail, her family can take her daughter home in an attempt to keep child protective services from placing the baby in foster care.

For Candis and for us, the baby seat in the back of the parole car is a potent symbol of the ongoing attempts of the criminal justice system to interrupt the reproductive lives of poor women of color and poor white women; separate them from their offspring and their loved ones; and tear these women and their communities asunder. Our political work with incarcerated women at our local jail has exposed these interruptions, which are, we claim, acts of violence in opposition to any standard of reproductive justice.

The fact is, assaults on sources of community support for women of color when they come out of jail, on their reproductive processes and their child rearing, are orchestrated by institutional systems such as welfare-to-work mandates, social services, child protective services, the schools, hospitals, battered women's shelters, and the structure of child care itself. These institutions individually and collectively assess formerly incarcerated women and judge their fitness and their competence.

They can report unfitness and incompetence. They have the power to investigate. They extend the cage beyond the term of incarceration.

Candis Henderson started serving her first prison bid, five years at Albion, an adult prison, when she was sixteen and her first child was less than a year old. She lost custody of her son. Five years later, and less than one month after she was paroled, she was violated the first time and sent back to jail, at which point she found out she was pregnant with her second child. She was again paroled in her seventh month, but her parole officer violated her two months later for missing a meeting with the housing office and sent her back to jail.

Candis was paroled again just days before the delivery of her daughter. Now out, she continues to be threatened by parole officers, who actively follow, if not stalk, her and her children. "Parole officers seven deep came up in my crib," she tells us, "flipped over the bed, pulled apart radiators, and strip-searched me. My daughter and I were the only ones home." They demanded to know how and why Candis had two hundred dollars in cash, a gift that her father sent. The police treated the money as evidence that Candis was selling drugs. "My father doesn't have the right to help his daughter? They want to see me down, broke, humble and humiliated."

Incarceration, and the threat of reincarceration, is a way of separating, harassing, stalking, and sexualizing women of color, their children, and their friends, lovers, and communities. In our political work, we have encountered many examples of the ways in which incarceration "interrupts" the reproductive lives of women of color and the ways in which state policies and social practices compound these violent assaults or interruptions.

We are convinced that when a police officer sends a woman who is nine months pregnant back to jail for missing an appointment, this act is violent and intentional. Unfortunately, such acts have ripple effects that reshape the lives of the mothers, grandmothers, sisters, children, and grandchildren of the incarcerated woman. For example, Candis's mother, Gilletta Henderson, could not take her grandson to visit Candis in prison because the family did not have custody of the little boy, who had been sent to foster care. "I want my baby back," Gilletta Henderson told us. Gilletta Henderson sees her daughter's incarceration as a violent, institutional intrusion on her own ability to mother her daughter and as a violently traumatic event for Candis, who has nightmares about monsters on her back.

We met Candis Henderson and her mother through our political work with the Broome County Jail Project in New York, an independent organization we started in 2004 in response to complaints of incarcerated people to the local NAACP. Under the auspices of the NAACP, we have interviewed over one hundred incarcerated people, including over thirty women. We document testimonies and advocate for changes. The project is a participatory, nonhierarchical research and activist project made up of community members, formerly incarcerated people, family members of incarcerated people, students, and a professor. We have no external funding, and we have not yet sought funding. We do our work by word of mouth.

We see the many factors that undermine the ability of women of color to live healthy lives: the loss or potential loss of child custody; poor and inefficient prenatal care; dangerous contraceptives; forced adoption; limited, delayed, or denial of access to abortion, gynecological or other health care personnel, and hormonal treatments; and a near-total absence of routine preventive medical care. These factors prevent women from making decisions. They actively harm women and in some cases, thrust women in harm's way.

The women in the Broome County facility have no access to reproductive justice. They rarely receive Pap smears, breast exams, mammograms, or other basic services. The prevailing "medical system" requires each woman to have the medical expertise to perform self-diagnosis and request medical services. Women can and do diagnose themselves and share experiential information, but this is not equivalent to medical care.

Incarcerated women are routinely denied information about and care for pregnancy, pregnancy prevention, yeast infections, urinary tract infections, venereal disease, seizures, osteoporosis, menopausal and postmenopausal conditions, hormone replacement, high blood pressure, diabetes, and other illnesses. Some women, ill with asymptomatic conditions such as pelvic inflammatory disease (PID), will never be diagnosed without routine checkups. PID can lead to tubal pregnancy, chronic pelvic pain, abscesses, infertility, and death. In fact, one woman we followed, Felicia, had had several tubal pregnancies previously and was panicked because she could not get a sonogram that would diagnose whether her current pregnancy was healthy or not.

Even when a woman has accurately diagnosed her problem and requested treatment, including in an emergency, the authorities often refuse proper treatment or timely response. One incarcerated woman on a full HIV cocktail when she entered jail received no medication for the eight months she was inside, despite her pleading. Eventually this woman pled guilty to a crime she would have otherwise contested, knowing she would be sent to an upstate penitentiary where she was more likely to receive decent medical care. Another woman said that when she was in jail, she filed slip after slip asking for an abortion because she did not want and could not care for another baby. But by the time she was taken for the procedure, it was too late. She was forced to carry the pregnancy to term, and she gave the baby up for adoption.

Felicia was incarcerated for almost her entire pregnancy. Her mother, Noelle, asked us to interview her daughter because both women had good reason to think that Felicia had toxemia and was not receiving proper medical attention. Indeed, she delivered months early while she was incarcerated. In addition to denying Felicia medical care, the medical staff had not made a plan to avoid a C-section; in fact, they had no delivery plan. The staff did not discuss breastfeeding with Felicia because her incarceration made it impossible for her to handle her daughter. These policies and practices significantly interrupt these women's reproductive processes and prevent their access to even a semblance of reproductive justice.

On one of our visits, Felicia told us that, many months into her pregnancy, she had worn wrist and ankle shackles when the guards took her to her ob-gyn appointment. She was worried about falling and being unable to catch herself because of the shackles and her awkward shape. The female corrections officer with Felicia would not help her up the stairs because, she said, she was not wearing gloves. Felicia replied, "I'm pregnant, not diseased."

The Broome County Jail Project follows people once they leave jail, giving us the chance to determine the full range of assaults on women's reproductive and maternal lives, spearheaded by the foster care, educational, and juvenile justice systems. We work with incarcerated and formerly incarcerated people to design goals, tactics, and safeguards to respond to these assaults as well as with grandparents, children, and other relatives.

We have found that when Felicia and Candis and other women of color like them get out of jail, they are kept constantly "off balance and unsure," as Candis puts it. The women do not know whether their kids will be seized by child protective services, parole officers, school authorities, the police, substance abuse counselors, court personnel, or the numerous social workers and others who fill their lives and have the power to take their children away. These authorities and others put women of color at risk for reincarceration and for loss of their children and their right to stay with their kin, because felons can be banned from public housing.

Candis's mother observes, "The chains are gone," but still, she implies, the forcible separation of women of color from their children continues. Historically enslaved, women of color have been separated from their children throughout history to maximize labor efficiency and control. Today in Binghamton and elsewhere, women of color continue to be threatened with loss of their children as a strategy of control. Intentionally or not, separation disrupts communal and generational continuity, the transmission of family history, and opportunities for intergenerational teaching, learning, and spiritual life. Candis's mother sees the irony in the way she, her daughter, and grandchildren are patrolled and separated by the institutions that surround them. "They say you can't beat your children, but they take them away and beat the hell out of them. They put them in the hole for thirty days. [Candis was put in solitary confinement when she was pregnant]. Why isn't a [child protective services] worker in there to protect *them* like when they come into my home to protect her from *me?*"

Felicia and Candis became good friends while they were incarcerated. They are still good friends outside, supporting each other in making good lives and communities. Ironically, Candis's parole officer forbids her from seeing Felicia and will

violate her if she does for "fraternizing" with another ex-felon. For the same reason, both women are restricted from participating fully in our project because of
the possibility they would encounter other felons at our meetings or at our forums
at the YWCA or homeless shelters. They cannot go with us to interview inmates at
the jail. Such parole policies clearly fragment the community as well as the lives of
formerly incarcerated women, dictating their social relations and ensuring a degree of isolation. The mandates of parole force women of color into a constant state
of unease and insecurity, always fearful of losing their children.

Felicia has expressed many times during and after her incarceration that she does
not trust white people, particularly the white women who are in charge of her case
and in charge of distributing the services she receives. She has expressed ongoing
frustration with school officials, doctors, nurses, and social service workers because
of the power they have to take her children away. Why, she wants to know, do so
many outsiders have that power?

If one of Felicia's neighbors calls child protective services, the worker interviews
her teenage children at their schools. Even though the investigation turns up nothing, Felicia has to defend herself and justify the way she takes care of her children.
Several times when Felicia has gone to the store with her infant daughter, she has
been arrested or been served warrants meant for other women of color in cases of
"mistaken identity." Medical professionals have diagnosed her as bipolar even
though the degrees of stress, paranoia, and hostility she experiences seem completely
appropriate. The police, with their racist carelessness, the hypervigilant neighbors,
and the hypermedicalized physicians—and the potential consequences of their assessments of Felicia's fitness to keep her children—certainly sustain stress. These
assessments continuously threaten Felicia's emotional and economic well-being.
Each negative assessment raises the specter of reincarceration and all that it means:
ripping Felicia's children, and her, out of the social structure.

Women express continuing worry that their children will be seized, a concern
that persists long after release. They speak of their children as if they have no "own-
ership" or rights to them or right to be with them. Because welfare policies require employment, they are, in fact, often separated from their children. Also, many
women have family members who have assessed them as unfit mothers and have
interfered with the custody of the children. Some fathers abscond with the children,
for example, and grandmothers have taken charge of the grandchildren even when
the formerly incarcerated women have retained custody.

CONCLUSION: FIGHTING INJUSTICES

What can be done about these problems? For us, this question leads to another:
What is the utility of the Broome County Jail Project? As a matter of course, we ask
inmates, ex-inmates, and their families to help us assess our collective political work.

Does it make a difference, and if so, what kind? Does it put anyone at risk? Do the project results make it worth taking those risks? Is the project the best way for us to engage politically at the local level?

Gilletta Henderson said to us, "God is the number one protector, but here on earth we need you guys. We need people who will be the second ear and the second eye to show them up." Candis remarked that after talking with us, "I saw things from a different perspective—I never thought to do something about it. I did something, and I did it the right way." We include these comments not for self-vindication but rather as an indication of what participatory research can do.

We try to stave off the sense that the problems and forces we face are overwhelming. We live in a small, deindustrialized town, full of defeated people and aging, shrunken social services. The authorities who possess small-time power are accustomed to acting with impunity and operating outside of public or communal accountability. At its best, our project offers a vehicle for making a bona fide community, a community in action, to use Studs Terkel's phrase, for women of color under the thumb of the law, together with their allies who wish to hear women of color and to accompany them and support them in their agency. Through this tentative, ginger, modest venture, we attempt to discover our own larger collective agency, to recapture some hope or, at the very least, to sustain ourselves.

85

Prison Abolition in Practice

The LEAD Project, the Politics
of Healing, and A New Way of Life

Setsu Shigematsu, Gwen D'Arcangelis, and Melissa Burch

In 1982, in a residential neighborhood in Los Angeles, a speeding police car hit a five-year-old boy and killed him. Susan Burton, the mother of the little boy, experienced the agony of losing her son because of this preventable "police incident." Without a supportive family or community around her, and with a police force that failed to offer even an apology for killing her son, her loss, added to the already-difficult factors in Susan's life, had a devastating effect. Turning to means deemed illegal by the state to lessen her pain and grief resulted in Susan's imprisonment on drug-related charges. For the next decade, Susan was in and out of prison, her life becoming one of millions caught in the vicious cycle of the penal system. Fifteen years later, she was finally admitted to an effective rehabilitation program and began the road to her recovery.

How can women whose lives have been most adversely impacted by the penal system transform themselves and be transformed through a politics of prison abolition?[1]

In 1999, with her own recovery under way, Susan founded A New Way of Life (NWOL), a group of transition homes for women coming home from prison in the Watts district of Los Angeles. Susan's life reveals how an abolitionist perspective works to transform the lives of women impacted by the prison system. In our view, abolition is not only a political ideal but also a practice that creates new kinds of communities. This article elaborates how prison abolition works to transform and heal lives. We focus on the transformation of Susan Burton and the Leadership, Education, Action and Dialogue (LEAD) Project—a political education program that fosters critical analysis of the prison-industrial complex (PIC). The LEAD project grew out of a collaboration of A New Way of Life and the Los Angeles chapter of Critical Resistance, an abolitionist organization that Susan began working with in 2003.

FROM CAPTIVE TO FIGHTER: ONE WOMAN'S STORY

Soon after Susan became sober and began to work in her community to aid elderly African Americans who were suffering from health problems, she learned about the increase in the number of incarcerated women and realized that they faced the same daunting systemic conditions that she had confronted. She decided to do something about it. In 1999, Susan was able to obtain a home in Watts that she opened to women coming home from prison and women on probation and parole. This home was the beginning of the network that would become A New Way of Life, a group of nonprofit sober-living and transition homes.

On any given day in Los Angeles County, three thousand women are on parole. About half of them have the disease of drug addiction and live in South Central Los Angeles. Close to 70 percent will go back to prison, either convicted of a new crime or failing to meet the conditions of parole within a year of their release. Often unable or unwilling to obtain assistance from agencies perceived as insensitive and judgmental and that have highly structured programs that restrict individual choice, the women struggle to stay out of prison, to find legal income, and to remain sober in isolation.

In contrast, Susan's homes offer clean, safe, supportive environments for women coming home from jail or prison. One resident describes the environment at NWOL:

> She [Susan] helped me get a job, and now I have a steady job . . . She made me feel welcome, I can't explain it, she just taught me so much and made me feel comfortable; it's really hard for me to open up to people, but she really made me feel like she cared about me and wanted me to get clean, instead of just trying to make money off of me.

While supporting women's struggle to put their lives back together, Susan repeatedly saw them lose their children to the foster care system because they couldn't meet the state's requirements for reunification. Susan experienced their pain and felt her loss all over again:

> It was devastating to watch women lose their children when they were doing everything they possibly could . . . But to see that happen and understand what it felt like to lose a child, I felt it over and over again, and that was enough to give me the fire, the determination, the commitment to address it and it was against all odds . . . I was so angry at the system that I was going to walk through hell and high water in order to make a difference.

Susan has been able to work out of her pain, anger, and grief to create a remarkable home where women can reunite with their children after suffering from the multifaceted disruption and breakup of their families imposed through the prison and police system. In addition to providing the necessities of housing, food, clothing, transportation, and health care, NWOL has added programs to help women access case management services, job training, skill building, and community advocacy opportunities. In developing NWOL, Susan became increasingly involved in working toward systemic changes to address the injustices she had been witnessing on a daily basis, and she soon became a leading advocate in California for the rights of former prisoners.

In 2003, Susan participated in the Critical Resistance South conference in New Orleans, Louisiana. Her encounter with Critical Resistance (CR) proved to be a pivotal experience. Founded in 1998, Critical Resistance is a member-led organization that seeks to abolish the prison-industrial complex—in other words, to end the use of prisons and policing as ineffective and dehumanizing responses to social and economic problems. Through grassroots campaigns and projects, CR works to challenge the notion that caging and controlling people makes us safer and to build a national movement—guided by those most affected by the system—to promote and realize genuine forms of safety and security.

Recalling when she first met CR members and came to understand their abolitionist stance, she says,

> I didn't have a concept as wonderful as that . . . I had never heard anyone challenge prisons in the way that CR challenges the existence of prisons, period. To understand and to know that a prison is not a solution, what a prison does to people is torture—this should be prohibited. It should not be able to function. . . . And then to begin to imagine a world without prisons . . . there's so many other ways to treat people.

Susan readily states that when she first became involved in community activism, she did not fully understand the interconnections between the prison-industrial complex and the other systemic forms of oppression. Her exposure to CR's analysis of the PIC and her own development of an abolitionist perspective set the stage for the formation of the LEAD project.

THE VISION AND PRACTICE OF LEAD

In 2004, Susan met Critical Resistance organizer Melissa Burch through mutual anti-PIC activism in Los Angeles. As they began to share their political visions, Melissa conceived of the idea of starting a political education program at A New Way of Life. Susan wholeheartedly collaborated. Melissa, along with a few other CR members, began to design workshops to critically analyze the PIC with A New Way of Life residents.

The women who live at A New Way of Life and participate in the LEAD project have all experienced the effects of the criminal justice system on their lives and on the lives of their loved ones. Most of the women at NWOL are low-income African American women, a population increasingly affected by the PIC. Although the number of imprisoned men is much higher, African American women are the fastest-growing population of prisoners in the United States today. Over the past eighteen years, we have witnessed an astounding 800 percent increase in rates of imprisonment for women of color. Largely because of the so-called war on drugs, the majority of these women remain behind bars on small-scale drug charges, the result of a system less interested in treating addiction than in punishing those who do not have the social, economic, and political clout to keep themselves out of prison. Through education about the history and politics of the prison-industrial complex, LEAD exposes how the system operates—not to prosecute all forms of "crime" but to target and entrap only certain groups of people. One woman tells her story:

> I was at the can place, at the recycling, and this girl was going to do the recycling for me, because I couldn't go in, because me and the recycling lady didn't get along, so she took the cans and bottles in there for me, she took my cans and bottles in there, she came outside and gave me two dollars and five cents. A police car drives by and sees her handing me the money, it made a U-turn and came back, and then a bunch more police cars came and jacked me up, and said I have "possession of sales." I couldn't argue the case because they said they seen her hand me the money. It was two dollars and five cents for my cans and bottles. I'm right in front of the can place! The people at the can place even tried to tell them [that I was recycling cans], but they [the police] said, "No, she was buying dope!" So I went to jail with two dollars and five cents on my books for possession of sales.

Through biweekly participatory workshops, the LEAD project creates a space in which women who have recently been released from prison can temporarily step outside conventional recovery programs' emphasis on the personal and look critically at the larger social and political systems that perpetuate the prison-industrial complex. Drawing on the women's experiences with the system, the LEAD project further exposes how the penal system labels certain groups of people as "convicts" or "felons," a status that simultaneously affects one's sense of self-worth and cuts off opportunities to lead a healthy, economically self-sustaining life.

The LEAD project works toward a women-of-color–centered critique of the PIC, emphasizing its role within the interlocking racist, heterosexist, and classist forms of systemic oppression. The workshops offer a critique of various interconnected aspects of the PIC, such as the "war on drugs" and the arbitrary construction of "crime." In each workshop, LEAD organizers facilitate activities such as role playing, films, guided discussion, small-group work, guest speakers, journal writing, and life history exercises to help participants make the connections between the PIC and the systemic conditions of their own imprisonment and their probation/parole status. Other LEAD projects that foster political education and leadership development include the maintenance of a political education media library and a grassroots organizing internship that focuses on collective engagement in community actions.

In this way, LEAD offers an organic extension of Susan's own experience and politicization, as well as an extension of CR's abolitionist vision in practice. By emphasizing learning about, envisioning, and practicing alternative forms of justice and safety, LEAD instantiates abolition in the present, resisting a narrow reliance on the state that dictates punitive forms of justice. Instead, LEAD seeks to implement restorative forms of community-based justice and rehabilitation. By collectively imagining what changes would be necessary to create truly safe and secure communities, the LEAD project offers a vision of justice that is based on the well-being of entire communities.

HEALING, TRANSFORMATION, AND ABOLITION

It takes quite a bit of energy and belief in yourself and willingness to open your mind to make that transition from *captive* to *someone who is going to fight.* . . . It takes a bit of commitment and force within yourself to come out and do that, after living in that place of less than and not-good-enough.

As exemplified in Susan's story, a new understanding of the system is integral to the process of reevaluating the conditions of one's incarceration and vital to the process of healing and the determination to fight an oppressive system. The LEAD project offers women this space to engage in critical dialogue about their experiences. Many of the women at A New Way of Life describe the particularities of a criminal justice system that keep them in an incarceration cycle. Instead of offering treatment, the system penalizes these women who lack the resources to escape such entrapment. As one of these women has said, "Don't just drag [in] twenty-five people where the only crime they had was getting high, and then give them four years in prison, and then release them out into society with nothing. . . . You're just making it a revolving door. You let them out with nothing."

Susan emphasizes that healing from the denigration, abuse, and dehumanization inflicted by the system requires new forms of knowledge and the time and space for each person to recover. The LEAD project helps push the women through the very difficult but essential transition that shifts the blame from "it's me" to "it's the system." Susan believes that this understanding is necessary to move oneself away from the self-destructive tendencies that lead to addictions and "self-abuse." The opportunity and ability to reevaluate oneself from this political perspective can be key to rebuilding self-worth and making a successful transition to a healthy life.

One woman says that NWOL and her education in the LEAD workshops have been key to her empowerment and transition to healthier living: "I didn't realize things like CR actually existed. I didn't know that there were people out there trying to stop it or reform it . . . people who have never been incarcerated, never been in trouble, and they're out there fighting against something that's wrong. So CR, all of that showed me something different, that I do have a say and that my voice can make a difference in a lot of things."

BUILDING A MOVEMENT

For Susan and for many women at A New Way of Life, a new understanding of the system has allowed them to reevaluate the conditions of their incarceration and begin the healing process. In the seven years since its opening, Susan's program has touched the lives of over 250 women. Through their experience at NWOL and the political education provided by the LEAD project, many women have not only begun to feel more empowered to stand up and fight but are now also able to view the problems of the PIC and envision alternatives.

One resident says, "I think that the way that it is right now . . . just needs to be completely abolished. I am not saying that we do not need some kind of system in place, but the one that we have we do not need." Another resident speaks to her vision of safe communities:

> They should build more of these [NWOL homes] than prisons. Because when I got here it was like a new world to me. I was glad. . . . It wasn't like being locked in; there were restrictions, but still, I wasn't locked in. I could go outside and smoke a cigarette. I could do this, I could do that. I was gonna go back to school. She [Susan] showed me a school, got me an ID and Social Security card; things I didn't have, she showed me how to get them. It was like starting all over again in a new world. If they had more places like A New Way of Life, they would have better communities, I believe.

Many of the women at NWOL homes have taken the political education further and, like Susan, are transforming themselves into leaders in the movement against the PIC. Several are active in the local chapter of All of Us or None, an initiative led by former prisoners to end discrimination in jobs, education, and access to services.[2] Some have joined efforts to stop prison expansion in California, while others have become active in other arenas of the struggle for social justice. Although people who have been incarcerated need time, even years, to heal and recover, Susan's life story demonstrates that a successful transition from the denigrating effects of prison life back to a healthy life often requires a form of self-reevaluation that is at once political, emotional, and spiritual. The practice of a politics of abolition can be part of this process of personal healing. Susan and many of the other women at NWOL have come to embody this vision of healing and transformation, which offers women a radically new perspective on themselves, their place in the world, and the possibility of a future without prisons.

NOTES

1. When we use the term *prison abolition* in this chapter, we include the abolition of the prison-industrial complex. Critical Resistance defines abolition as a political vision that seeks to eliminate the need for prisons, policing, and surveillance by creating sustainable alternatives to punishment and imprisonment.

2. All of Us or None is a national organizing initiative of prisoners, former prisoners, and felons that seeks to combat the many forms of discrimination that we face as the result of felony convictions. For more information on the organization, see www.allofusornone.org/about.html.

86

Booking It beyond the Big House

Jean Trounstine

Theresa hid behind a baseball cap and slouched low in her chair. "I liked the story," she said, eyes fleeing my face. I smiled. We both knew she was an unlikely person to be in the Middlesex Community College president's office, a former addict and alcoholic, recently arrested. But there she was, with a probation officer (PO), six other probationers, and the judge who'd sentenced them to the Changing Lives Through Literature (CLTL) women's seminar. Sitting around an oblong table, we had come together for our first session, and we'd just finished reading aloud Tillie Olsen's "I Stand Here Ironing."

Theresa continued. "The mother. She struggled to make ends meet."

I nodded.

Addie shook her head no. A waitress who'd dropped out of school in ninth grade, she had no support from the father of her child. "I don't agree. The mother was bad; she shouldn't have left Emily in the care of strangers." Addie crossed her arms.

"What was she to do?" Theresa said. "She's like a lot of moms in the hood. Okay, not black but white, and whatever, she needed a job!" She sat up straight, slapping her cap down on the table. "She did it to *help* her kid."

Addie squirmed, looked out the window.

"What do the rest of you think?" I asked. "There's no right or wrong here, just responses. Strong opinions are fine," I said, aiming my comment at Addie, but she had drifted away.

Devora, a woman with HIV began to talk slowly. Her arm was in a sling, and she was painfully thin. She'd been at Framingham Women's Prison, earned her GED, and taken part in the theater program I'd developed behind bars. Now she was out, but after a new arrest, had agreed to try CLTL, hoping to find "something to get me off the streets." She pointed out that Emily's mother had been deserted by her husband. "He left her a note, you know. He refused to 'share want' with her. Pretty lousy."

The judge added, "Don't forget, this was the Depression, before welfare. I don't mean to diminish her experience; but men were ashamed too, to be out of work."

Theresa turned to Addie and said, "I think the mother knows she's wrong. That's why she keeps going over and over it."

"Good point," said the judge. Addie was silent.

"You know, the daughter does come around." Jesse leaned in, looked from face to face. She was twenty-five and looked like any other college student—jeans and a sweatshirt—but she was unemployed and living in a local shelter with her three children. "Yeah, Emily gets left with a lady who lives downstairs and gets sick and sent away and all, but she does become a kind of star on stage. She turns out all right."

"She almost flunks out of school!" Addie said, exasperated.

"But she doesn't," said Bonnie. Bonnie, a forty-three-year-old single mother of two, was the oldest of the group. "She has a lot of strength. She knows she has to make it on her own." She looked across the table at Addie. "But you're right in a way. The mother became a better mother after Emily. She kind of learned on the other kids."

"See," Addie said, jutting her chin into the air.

"I'm beginning to agree with Addie. It's almost a kind of child abuse," the PO chimed in. "I'd bring her in."

"No way! This mother gives it up for her kid." Theresa was adamant. "She's a fighter." A few others nodded.

"Nina, what do you think?" I asked. Nina, a Latina with nine brothers and eight sisters, had never held a job or completed high school. "If my mother ever favored my sisters like that Susan, who's like, you know, the little blond perfect, what's her name, Shirley Temple . . . " She proceeded to go off on a string of Spanish, which made everyone laugh, and triumphantly sat back in her seat.

We continued the conversation, everyone pushing and pulling in a way I hadn't seen in many of my college classes, where less seemed to be at stake. Each person's past seemed to come pouring out through the characters. I found myself asking questions, intending to be provocative, hoping to have the members of the group challenge each other's thinking. Toward the end of the session, I said that the mother has to make choices that are heartbreaking.

A few women agreed, but Addie retorted, "She should've put the kid first. That's all there is to it."

I read aloud the last paragraphs, in which the mother says she can never "total" it all and prays that her daughter has "enough to live by" so that she is not like a dress on the ironing board, merely to be ironed. "Do you think the mother loves Emily?" I asked the room.

"She does her best," said Devora.

"Absolutely," the judge rang out.

"It's a faulty kind of love," said the PO. "But yes."

"Love, no love," Addie muttered. "It's too late for Emily."

Theresa looked over at her. "Maybe it made her stronger. Emily became a fighter—like her mom." I noticed Theresa had snapped her cap back on her head.

I handed out books for the next session. Bonnie flipped to the end to see how many pages she had to read. Jesse asked if she could keep the book, and when we said yes, she put her name on the inside cover. While the members of the group gathered up papers, they continued chatting. The mood was different now, lighter, easier. The tension was gone.

As I straightened up chairs, Addie popped her head into the room. "I didn't mean to be a pain."

"You weren't! Look at all the good discussion your comments prompted."

"My mother was like that mother in the story." She stared down for a moment. I waited.

"But you know what? I think it did make me stronger." She smiled, the first smile I'd seen from her. "And I actually might like this class. What's this book about?" She held up Anne Tyler's *Dinner at the Homesick Restaurant*.

"A family."

"Oh boy. You're not gonna hear the end of me."

As I shut the door behind us, somehow more sure of my footing, we both laughed, and then headed together toward the elevator.

. . .

Changing Lives Through Literature, a program originally for male probationers, was the 1991 brainchild of Judge Robert Kane and University of Massachusetts Dartmouth professor Robert Waxler. Corrections authorities typically talk about success only in terms of recidivism—how much, how often, and in what ways people return to crime—but Kane and Waxler were interested in the thinking behind the choices people made. Their idea was simple but profound: literature could be a road to insight, and insight could pave the way to change.

Literature discussion groups that put probationers on the same playing field as judges and POs had been unheard of in our criminal justice system. The belief that everyone's opinion about the story *mattered*, and that no one had the final say, democratized the conversation.

Joining with Judge Joseph Dever from the Lynn District Court and with probation officers from both Lynn and Lowell, we began the first program for women in 1992. We knew that some of the women, like Devora, would have served time, and others would come with long probation rap sheets. Many would have sentences for crimes such as possession of drugs, prostitution, assault and battery, shoplifting, and theft. A few would have had no previous experience with the system. Unlike their male counterparts, CLTL women would most likely not have support from partners; their drinking and drugging had often brought them abusive boyfriends who threatened them. They had lives of failed commitments, and most had ceased to believe in themselves. They blamed themselves for any scars on the family, for their poverty, and most of all, for crippling the lives of their children.

At Framingham Prison, I'd found that few had read books by female authors. The women were used to identifying with the male hero precisely because they didn't have a great deal of experience with readings about or by women. Some reported they didn't trust their own opinions. Others had never finished a book, yet almost all of them wanted their children to learn to read. With these thoughts in mind, I compiled our first CLTL syllabus with books all by female authors.

· · ·

When the women returned after two weeks, encouraged to bring notes and questions, they piled into the president's office, with chips, sodas, and books. I began with a "Go Round," asking each person simply to voice thoughts about *Homesick Restaurant,* asking "What mattered to you?" Because the book emphasizes relationships and focuses on several members of a family who see the world from different points of view, it had the potential to lead us in many directions.

Bonnie arrived late, her son having been in an accident. She talked about how hard it was to read while working two jobs, going to school, and raising her children. Not surprisingly, she had mixed reactions to Pearl Tull, the cold but feisty mother who raises three kids in an unsympathetic world.

"That's my family," exclaimed Addie. "I understand my mother more after reading this book. Just like Pearl, you couldn't love her but you couldn't hate her. She'd yell and scream, but you couldn't blame her, raising three kids, working a dead-end job."

Judge Dever mentioned that all the children had turned out pretty well—a doctor, a businessman, and a restaurant owner. Most of us hadn't considered that point.

We saw the women every two weeks. And between our meetings, they had to live their lives, attend other programs dictated by their probation terms, and deal with housing issues, jobs, sobriety, and relationships. We were requiring a lot of them by asking them to read books and get to meetings, not to mention to think deeply about the issues they encountered.

"Where is the hope in this book?" I asked the evening of Toni Morrison's *The Bluest Eye.* Nina sat twirling her dark hair around a pencil. It was her third class, but she had almost decided not to attend. Her therapist had contacted the PO and said that she thought this book might provoke too many issues for Nina, who was dealing with an abusive uncle. However, Nina had chosen to read the book, though she confessed it confused her and said that she had skipped all "the bad parts."

Now, she looked up and said, "There is no hope. It's awful what happens to Pecola."

Pecola, a young African American girl, believes that if she gets blue eyes, she will get access to a Shirley Temple world and all her pain and suffering will disappear. In a way, she does get these blue eyes, after Cholly, her father, has sexually molested her, and she has been teased mercilessly in school, gone to a town shaman, and lost her sanity. Morrison makes sure we know that such "gifts" do not assure happiness.

Bonnie agreed with this premise, saying that she hated the book "because it hurt." Her struggles with alcoholism and drugs had once landed her in prison. "A better place than home," she said, where she had dealt with her parents' insistent battles.

Theresa began to argue. "Claudia lives to tell the story, right? I think Claudia *is* the hope." Claudia, the survivor, is part of the African American family that takes in Pecola at one point in her troubled life. While a few people in the group admitted to difficulty with time frames and language, Theresa had read the book twice in two weeks "just to get it all." Theresa said her mother had been a domestic, and she understood the world Morrison describes. "Pecola's lost, but Claudia isn't."

"Can the rest of you identify with Claudia?" I asked.

Nina sat sullenly staring at the open book. She didn't remember who Claudia was. I was afraid we would lose her.

Years later, when another group was reading this book, one of the women would ask, "Do you think Cholly really believes rape is love?" At first there was stunned silence as we thought about her question. The men in the room—Judge Dever and a male PO from Lowell—exclaimed "No!" and like Nina years before, wanted to push the question aside. But the women wanted to explore what was in Cholly's mind. They wanted to talk at length about how and why Cholly might think that he was truly loving his daughter with his actions. They pondered his background, his losses, his social understandings as well as Pecola's, and we could tell that several of them were alive to their own abuse experience while they discussed this question. Without talking about themselves, they processed the ideas deeply on two levels, the level of the text and the level of self. They clearly understood that there was hope for them because there is hope for Claudia.

But this night, when we filed out of the room, Nina ran quickly to the elevator, clutching her cigarettes.

· · ·

The probationers began to think about making new choices in their lives. For example, some decided to go back to school. Others became more involved in their communities. As the women sought to understand how the characters in the books we read got through their struggles, a healing seemed to happen. While our discussions were in no way therapy, and in no way did we talk about our own lives as the primary source of material, the class allowed us to hear each other's perspectives, to share ideas, and to see that different opinions were valued. The women nodded at each other's comments, took cigarette breaks together, laughed, and shared their wounds without having to mention them.

Despite the fact that we worried we might lose her, Nina came back, and with the others delighted in Sandra Cisneros's *House on Mango Street,* the poetic tale of a Mexican American girl who grows up in a poor Chicano neighborhood in Chicago and dreams about having a home. Nina saw herself in Esperanza, whose name means "hope" in Spanish. She talked about her favorite part, in which Louie steals a yellow Cadillac and flies down the street, followed by cops, with Esperanza waving at him. She talked animatedly about Esperanza's ability to survive with so little.

Other texts we read during that first session gained mixed responses. Everyone disliked Sylvia Plath's *The Bell Jar,* despite a charged conversation about Esther, the young magazine writer, and her gradual mental decline. They loved Barbara Kingsolver's *Animal Dreams,* a story with Native American legends and social and environmental issues, which tells the tale of a woman who returns to her home town to take care of her father suffering from Alzheimer's.

At the end of the twelve weeks, Judge Dever held a graduation session at the beginning of the First Session in the Lynn District Court. All the graduates were recognized with diplomas, flowers, and books donated by the Library of America. The ceremony took place in front of the full court and in front of some of the women's family members, who'd come to recognize them, along with the judge, the POs, and me, in a half-hour ceremony before the regular day of court business began. "This is just the beginning for me," said Theresa after the graduation.

. . .

Since 1992, CLTL programs have spread throughout the state and throughout the country to include Arizona, California, Connecticut, Indiana, Kansas, Maine, New York, Rhode Island, Texas, and even to the United Kingdom. Some of the groups are all of one gender and some are mixed, but the basic concept—literature, discussion, and equalization of the playing field—remains at our program's core, fostering the democratic classroom. As Kim, a female graduate from Lynn-Lowell later wrote, "The judge, probation officer, and teacher . . . were all there for us . . . It was their belief in the program and us that helped me deal with a lot of shame. They respected me until I could learn to respect myself."

The most successful participants make sure they build community, and several have come back as mentors for two, three, and even four programs. Although I do not read the records of women before the classes begin, they often tell me about their lives. For example, Kim told me she had done prison time and had been strung out on drugs for longer than she wanted to remember. She could hold down a job but couldn't hold onto a good relationship. Kim had grown up in a tough town, and her comments during the CLTL classes made clear that her childhood had been rough, with a divorce and court involvement beginning in her teens.

After CLTL, Kim went on to college, got married, bought a house, became a stepmother, and had her own children. She struggled every inch of the way to stay clean, to keep perspective, to handle her emotions. I remember how surprised she was when Judge Dever actually listened to her discuss her reactions to Pearl in *Homesick Restaurant*, a woman Kim said she understood and admired in spite of her seeming coldness—and although Kim did not say so, a woman like herself. On the day of Kim's wedding, when she stood with all who had helped her on her path to success, she said she realized that learning doesn't always come in a rush—success after success. It is populated with ups and downs.

Changing Lives Through Literature allows participants an opportunity to rethink their lives, rewrite their tales, adding a new chapter to whatever came before. In a small room at a college, a community of learners contemplate who they are and what they might become. Through the power of story, they gain a second chance.

87

Being Out of Prison

Joanne Archibald

I went from prison to a halfway house, an awful place. It was designed for people who were going to be there for a couple of years, so you had a system of levels. I was never able to get past second level, so I wasn't able to get passes to stay out overnight or anything like that. The staff there was unbelievably petty and not supportive of me spending time with my son, David.

I had to go out and find a job, and every place I went, the first thing I had to do was hand them this slip they had to sign that said I was in the halfway house and that they had interviewed me. This didn't create a good first impression and made it hard to find jobs. Plus, I didn't really have a lot of job skills. I ended up getting a part-time, minimum-wage job at a health food store that wasn't enough to live on. I did take a class at the university, because I had been in college when I was arrested, and I wanted to continue my education. But the halfway house staff wouldn't allow me any library time to do the research paper. And they were so obstructive about everything. For example, I signed in when I came back to the house, but I forgot to write "p.m." after the time, so I lost my weekend privileges even though the staff person was right there watching me. That was the horrible mentality there. Also, the house was right next to an entrance ramp to the freeway, so there was nonstop traffic noise. It would have been better to stay in prison than go there, because I saw David less there.

When I first got out, I was lost. I really thought my life was ruined and kind of over. I didn't know how to start up again. Somebody found me an apartment, found me a used car. It seemed that, even in that short time, I got used to somebody making the decisions and taking care of things. Also, I was so depressed. Then I went on public aid, which didn't help at all, because then I was an ex-con and a welfare mother, feeling bad about myself for both reasons. I couldn't see a way out. I had this image—like for five years after I got out—of being in a well and trying to climb out and getting knocked back down. Getting almost near the top and then, any little thing that happened would become a big thing and knock me back down.

A lot of people helped me, and I don't know what I would've done without that, because I really felt like I didn't know how to do anything anymore. I remember being really freaked out by the phone because in prison, there were phones ringing all the time. The phone would just ring and ring until somebody answered it. But a prisoner could never touch a ringing phone. When I had my own phone again, I felt this big weird hesitation. I had to remind myself, "Okay, this is your phone, you need to answer this." For months I was afraid of the phone.

I had this feeling, "Nothing is mine anymore. They can take anything at any time." My property was not my property. I hadn't had privacy, and it was a long time before I was comfortable expressing what I really thought—even on paper—without worrying. I became my own censor. It took a long time to get over that.

It also took a long time to deal with the impact on my son and on our relationship. He was seven months old when I went in, and I was gone for a little over ten months. In a way, that was a short time, but it's . . . I wasn't there when he made his first steps. I think the things I missed the most were the little day-to-day things. For him, the feeling "my mom's not here" carried over. He had a low frustration tolerance. He would get really, really upset sometimes, way out of proportion to what the thing was.

I made a tape for him when I got locked up, of the songs I always sang to him, and Joan used to play it for him while I was gone. Really shortly after I got back, I was singing to him, and he said, "Don't sing." Many years later, when he was seven, and I was able to explain to him what had happened when he was little, he said to me, "Sing those songs you sang when I was a baby." He made me sing those songs every night for months and months. Now I saw why he hadn't wanted to hear them. For him, those songs were about me being gone. So when I was back, he didn't want to hear them anymore. Now that he had the words and we had actually talked about it, hearing the songs was helping him process some of those feelings that he had at the time.

Being locked up changed me in every way. Emotionally, I changed a lot because it started unlocking some really deep things I had never dealt with before. My worldview changed drastically, especially how I looked at politics. Before I was in prison, I didn't know anybody who had been to prison. I believed what I learned in civics class, that you are innocent until proven guilty and that there are laws that the criminals don't follow but that good guys do. I really got a whole different take on that idea after I was arrested. I was guilty, but the police who arrested me used some really illegal tactics. Then they got on the stand and lied. I'd thought I was pretty politically aware, but this really shocked me. I was immediately treated like I was guilty by the arresting officers, the people at the jail.

Being in prison and meeting the women there and seeing how very, very, very few of them needed to be in a place like that and how many other kinds of needs they had—so many emotional and mental health needs, including substance abuse, just all kinds of things that weren't being taken care of—it was so clear: prison isn't going to make things better for any of these people.

It really changed how I looked at government, how I looked at everything in life.

Before that, I guess I thought that certain people are more political and that that's good, and that they take care of it for all of us. After prison, I realized that you have to know about all this stuff. It's one of the things that I really encourage everybody to do. I think that's the most important thing. Now, through my work, I do a lot of public education about prison and the prison system. I give some information, but I always say, "You have to keep studying this and not just take the mainstream word for what's happening. Don't rely on big media because it's so not true." That was my biggest change: seeing that everybody needs to pay attention to politics, not just certain people who will take care of it for us.

The fact is, I'm still paying for those ten months. When I got out of prison, I had a lot of debts, deferred school loans that I had to start paying. One school loan that I somehow missed when arranging for the deferments had gone into default and was almost tripled by the time they got to me because it had gone to 30-some percent in default. So I had a lot of debts. Almost ten years later, I declared bankruptcy because I was getting in deeper and deeper. I had a job, but by the time I made all my payments, I didn't have enough to live on. I had to charge groceries and gas. So financially I am still paying for it, after all these years, with the bankruptcy, with a horrible credit rating. I have nothing.

It has taken years and a lot of counseling—time and energy—to fix the relationship with my son and for him to feel good about himself. I still have as part of my self-identity that I'm a convicted felon, and that's never going to go away. Because of that, I can never be a teacher. It doesn't matter how much time has passed. The financial aid forms you fill out to get aid for school ask if you've had a drug conviction. There are so many things that will always be denied me because of this mistake I made. You're paying and paying and paying, in some ways for the rest of your life.

CONTRIBUTORS

CASSANDRA ADAMS Formerly Incarcerated Woman; writer

MARY ALLEY Parenting coordinator at the Nebraska Correctional Center for Women, York, NE

ALTE Incarcerated/Formerly Incarcerated Woman; writer

JOANNE ARCHIBALD Formerly Incarcerated Woman; former Assistant Director of CLAIM, Chicago, IL; Associate Director, Beyondmedia

MARLEINE BASTIEN Executive Director, Fanm Ayisyen Nan Miyami (Haitian Women of Miami)

ALEXANDRA BELL Lower East Side Harm Reduction Center; Audre Lorde Project

JUNE BENSON Incarcerated/Formerly Incarcerated Woman; writer

AMOREL BEYOR Incarcerated/Formerly Incarcerated Woman; writer

ERLINE BIBBS Incarcerated Woman; organizer

ANDREA BIBLE CA Habeas Project; National Clearinghouse for the Defense of Battered Women

KATHY BOUDIN Formerly Incarcerated Woman; HIV, parenting, and education activist; Leslie Glass Fellow, Teachers College, Columbia University; coauthor of *Breaking the Walls of Silence: Women and AIDS in a Maximum-Security Prison*

IRIS BOWEN Incarcerated/Formerly Incarcerated Woman; education activist

MELISSA BURCH Director of Programs, A New Way of Life Re-Entry Project; formerly antiprison organizer in Louisiana

KIMBERLY BURKE Incarcerated Woman; writer

CELESTE "JAZZ" CARRINGTON On Death Row in California; writer

CYNTHIA CHANDLER Cofounder and Codirector, Justice Now

JUDITH CLARK Incarcerated Woman; Leslie Glass Fellow, doctoral candidate, Teachers College, Columbia University; poet; canine trainer; peer facilitator; chaplain; coauthor of *Breaking the Walls of Silence: Women and AIDS in a Maximum-Security Prison*

MAYRA COLLADO Incarcerated/Formerly Incarcerated Woman; writer; member of WORTH (Women on the Rise Telling HerStory)

SHAWNNA D. Incarcerated Woman; organizer

JUANITA DÍAZ-COTTO Associate Professor of Sociology, Women's Studies, and Latin American and Caribbean Area Studies at SUNY Binghamton; author of *Gender, Ethnicity, and the State: Latina and Latino Prison Politics*

GWEN D'ARCANGELIS Doctoral student, UCLA

ANNETTE WARREN DICKERSON Director of Education and Outreach, Center for Constitutional Rights

DARLENE DIXON Incarcerated/Formerly Incarcerated Woman; writer; activist

CAROLE E. Formerly Incarcerated Woman; writer; member of WORTH (Women on the Rise Telling HerStory)

SHEILA R. ENDERS Former MSW; Assistant Clinical Professor with the Department of Internal Medicine at the UC Davis Medical Center; author of *Simple Answers to Health Care Questions—Choice*

TANYA ERZEN Associate Professor, Ohio State University; author of *Straight to Jesus: Sexual and Christian Conversions in the Ex-Gay Movement*

BETH FALK Psychologist; community volunteer in Story Book Project at Bedford Hills prison, NY

LINDA FIELD Incarcerated Woman; antiviolence and disability rights activist; writer

MICHELLE FINE Distinguished Professor of Psychology, Women's Studies and Urban Education, The Graduate Center of the City University of New York; author/coauthor of ten books and numerous essays

PHILIP M. GENTY Clinical Professor of Law, Columbia Law School

CHRISTY HALL Cofounder of the Birth Attendants; doula; organizer; development coordinator

SANDY HAMILTON Incarcerated/Formerly Incarcerated Woman; writer

HOLLI HAMPTON Incarcerated/Formerly Incarcerated Woman; poet

LYNNE HANEY Associate Professor of Sociology; Associate Director, Center for the Study of Gender and Sexuality, NYU; author of *Offending Women: Gender, Punishment, and the Regulation of Desire*

TRACY LYNN HARDIN Incarcerated Woman; writer

MARGARET OOT HAYES MSN, RN, Assistant Professor of Nursing, St. Anselm's College

BEVERLY (CHOPPER) HENRY Incarcerated/Formerly Incarcerated Woman; writer

JOHANNA HOFFMAN former Justice Now staff attorney in private practice, San Francisco

DONNA HYLTON Incarcerated Woman; MFA; counselor; teacher; tutor

SUZANNE JABRO Founder, Get on the Bus; leader in restorative justice movement for more than thirty years

TIFFANY JACKSON Incarcerated/Formerly Incarcerated Woman; writer

KINNARI JIVANI Incarcerated Woman; poet

PAULA C. JOHNSON Professor of Law, College of Law, Syracuse University; author, *Inner Lives, Voices of African American Women in Prison,* coeditor of *Interrupted Life*

KELLY KESTER-SMITH President, YES! Communications

SHEENA M. KING Incarcerated/Formerly Incarcerated Woman; writer

MIMI LAVER Director of Legal Education, Director of Opening Doors: Improving the Legal System's Approach to Lesbian, Gay, Bisexual, Transgender, and Questioning (LGBTQ) Youth in Foster Care Project; Assistant Director of the Pennsylvania Permanency Barriers Project; Assistant Director of the National Child Welfare Resource Center on Legal and Judicial Issues at the American Bar Association Center on Children and the Law; author of *Opening Doors for LGBTQ Youth in Foster Care: A Guide for Lawyers and Judges*

LECHE Formerly Incarcerated Woman

ARLENE F. LEE Senior Associate, Center for the Study of Social Policy

ELIZABETH LESLIE Formerly Incarcerated Woman; writer; member of WORTH (Women on the Rise Telling HerStory)

JUNE MARTINEZ Incarcerated/Formerly Incarcerted Woman; writer

MIGDALIA MARTINEZ Formerly Incarcerated Woman; founder, Latinas Organizadas Viviendo; cofounder, College Bound program at Bedford Hills; harm reduction counselor; researcher; writer

LORRIE SUE MCCLARY Formerly Incarcerated Woman; writer

LAUREN MELODIA Education and Outreach Associate, Center for Constitutional Rights

MICHELE MOLINA Incarcerated Woman; poet; artist; spokesperson

STORMY OGDEN Formerly Incarcerated Woman; Kashaya Pomo and Yokuts from Tule River Indian Reservation; activist and advocate for Native women in prison; coauthor of *The American Indian in a White Man's Prison: A Story of Genocide*

NOELLE PALEY Graduate student, Center for Interdisciplinary Studies in Philosophy, Interpretation, and Culture, Binghamton University

JOSHUA PRICE Associate Professor, College of Community and Public Affairs, Binghamton University

MARTHA L. RAIMON J.D.; Senior Associate, Center for the Study of Social Policy, coeditor of *Interrupted Life*

TINA REYNOLDS Formerly Incarcerated Woman; cofounder, WORTH (Women on the Rise Telling HerStory) for women affected by the criminal justice system; coeditor of *Interrupted Life*

MELISSA RIVERA Associate Director of Research at the Center for Puerto Rican Studies at Hunter College, CUNY; Associate Director of the National Latino/a Education Research and Policy Project

ROSEMARIE A. ROBERTS Assistant Professor of Education, Connecticut College

ALFREDA ROBINSON-DAWKINS Formerly Incarcerated Woman; founder, National Women's Prison Project, Inc.

JASMIN RODRIGUEZ Incarcerated/Formerly Incarcerated Woman; poet

RACHEL ROTH Former Soros Justice Fellow; author of *Unlocking Reproductive Rights* (*forthcoming*); author of *Making Women Pay: The Hidden Costs of Fetal Rights*

SOPHIA SANCHEZ Formerly Incarcerated Woman; Former coordinator, Young Mothers United; program Coordinator, Center for Young Women's Development, San Francisco

LETICIA M. SAUCEDO Associate Professor, Boyd School of Law, University of Nevada; codirector of immigration clinic at Boyd

IRUM SHIEKH Filmmaker; scholar; expert on detention; films include *Hidden Internment: The Art Shibayama Story*

SETSU SHIGEMATSU Assistant Professor, Department of Media and Cultural Studies, University of California, Riverside

PAMELA SMART Incarcerated Woman; tutor; teacher; M.A.; pastoral program, Bedford Hills

BRENDA V. SMITH Professor, Washington College of Law at American University; Project Director, United States Department of Justice, National Institute of Corrections Cooperative Agreement on Addressing Prison Rape

EDALEEN SMITH Incarcerated Woman; organizer

KEMBA SMITH Formerly Incarcerated Woman, pardoned by President Clinton; founder, Kemba Smith Foundation

RICKIE SOLINGER Historian; curator; coeditor of *Interrupted Life*

ANN FOWELL STANFORD Professor, School for New Learning, DePaul University, Chicago; author of *Bodies in a Broken World: Women Novelists of Color and the Politics of Medicine*; leader of poetry workshops for women in Cook County Jail

NANCY STOLLER Professor of Community Studies and Sociology at UC Santa Cruz; organizer with several community based action-research and organizing projects addressing the impact of incarceration on individual and public health

AMY STOUT Formerly Incarcerated Woman; writer

JULIA SUDBURY Professor, Ethnic Studies, Mary S. Metz Chair, Mills College; editor of *Global Lockdown: Race, Gender, and the Prison-Industrial Complex*; author of numerous prison-related essays

TAMMICA SUMMERS Incarcerated Woman; essayist; poet

MEGAN SWEENEY Assistant Professor of English Language and Literature, and Afro-

American and African Studies, University of Michigan; author of *"The Underground Book Railroad": Cultures of Reading in Women's Prisons*

FREDA SWINNEY Formerly Incarcerated Woman; writer

TABITHA Incarcerated/Formerly Incarcerated woman; writer

RUBY C. TAPIA Associate Professor, Comparative Studies, Ohio State University, author of *Breeding Ghosts: Race, Death, and the Maternal in U.S. Visual Culture*; coeditor of *Interrupted Life*

ANDRÁS TAPOLCAI Writer; teacher

ROSTA TELFORT Affiliated with Fanm Ayisyen Nan Miyami (Haitan Women of Miami)

MARÍA ELENA TORRE Director, Institute for Participatory Action Research and Design, Graduate Center of the City University of New York

JEAN TROUNSTINE Professor of Humanities, Middlesex (MA) Community College; former writing teacher, theater director, Framingham Women's Prison; coeditor of *Changing Lives Through Literature*; author of *Shakespeare Behind Bars*

DEBORA UPEGUI Doctoral candidate, CUNY Graduate Center, immigration experiences and policies, Columbian and Dominican immigrants in New York

MARIA VENTURA Incarcerated Woman; poet

KEBBY WARNER Incarcerated/Formerly Incarcerated woman; writer; parents' rights activist

KAY WHITLOCK Former National Representative for LGBT Issues, American Friends Service Committee (AFSC); author of *In a Time of Broken Bones* and *Corrupting Justice: A Primer for LGBT Communities on Racism, Violence, Human Degradation and the Prison Industrial Complex*

CHERYL WILKINS/"MISSY" Associate Director, College Initiative Reentry Program; Educational Director, Women of Integrity; Facilitator, Network in the Community; advocate; speaker

PATRICIA ZIMMERMAN Formerly Incarcerated Woman; writer

INDEX

Italicized page numbers refer to illustrations.

Treatment of Prisoners, 47; Body of Principles for the Protection of All Persons under
Any Form of Detention or Imprisonment,
47; Convention against Torture and Other
Cruel, Inhuman or Degrading Treatment or
Punishment (CAT), 47, 54, 118–19; Convention on the Elimination of All Forms of Dis-
crimination against Women (CEDAW), 53,
230; Convention Relating to the Status of
Refugees, 288; Human Rights Commission
report, 9, 45–56; International Covenant on
Civil and Political Rights (ICCPR), 47, 54,
118–19, 229; Standard Minimum Rules for
the Treatment of Prisoners, 45–47, 49–50,
55, 118–19; Universal Declaration of Human
Rights, 47, 229, 351n1
University of Massachusetts, 421
University of Nevada, Las Vegas, 282
University of Southern California's Post-
Conviction Justice Project, 339
Upegui, Debora, 189
urban fiction, 181–84
Urquilla, Esmeralda, 318
U.S. Citizenship and Immigration Services
(USCIS), 17
U.S.-Mexico border, 17

Valencia, Delma, 318
Valley State Prison for Women (VSPW, Calif.),
69, 70, 231, 234, 323, 329
Vanzant, Iyanla, 186–87
Vera Institute, 79
Vietnam war protesters, 29–30
Violent Crime Control and Law Enforcement
Act, 188
violent crimes, 5, 32; and long-termers, 274,
294–99, 308–09; and participatory action
research (PAR), 194. See also murder/
murderers
Virginia, 378
Virginia Union University, 343
visas, 275, 277–78, 283
Visions, 197–201, 203, 204
visitation rights, 4, 41–42; and Adoption and
Safe Families Act (ASFA, 1997), 78, 83–85;
of asylum seekers/refugees, 282, 289–90; at
Bedford Hills Correctional Facility, 98, 100–
101; and college programs in prison, 192,
194; at Cook County Jail (Chicago), 166,
168, 257; and gender-responsive movement,
234, 336; Get on the Bus program, 67–70;

and incarcerated young mothers' bill of
rights, 318; at Nebraska Correctional Center
for Women (NCCW), 94–97; in *Out of Sight,
Not Out of Mind,* 74–76; and pen pals, 148–
49; personal narratives about, 58–59, 71–
72, 83–85, 91, 94–97, 148–49; poems about,
209–10; and prison sex, 114, 117–19, 139–
40, 143; at Sybil Brand Institute for Women
(SBI), 139–40, 143; and telephone justice,
347; in UN report, 52, 55–56
vocational training, 47, 54, 59. *See also* employment opportunities/skills
volunteers, 4, 65; and asylum seekers/refugees,
290; and battered women, 339–40; and elder
prisoners, 304; gender identity regulations
for, 153–55; for Get on the Bus (Calif.), 68;
and health care, 259–63; and intellectual life
of incarcerated persons, 163, 167, 188; for
Story Book Project, 98, 102; and Women of
Wisdom circle (CIW), 216–19

Walker, Alice, 189
wardens, 52, 94, 190, 239–40, 370
warehousing, 13, 18–19, 309
war on drugs, 9, 12, 14–15, 20, 22, 23nn14,15,
294, 415
war on terror, 20, 275–81
Washington State, 65, 69, 86–88; Correction
Center for Women, 86–88; King County's
Department of Adult and Juvenile Detention
(DAJD), 153–55
water-treatment plants, 277–78
Watterson, Kathryn, 140
Waving Goodbye Ritual, 299
Waxler, Robert, 421
websites, 191–93, 319, 418n2
"We Fall Down" (song), 123
"we" in jail, 165, 170, 171–72, 174
welfare: and Changing Lives Through Literature
(CLTL), 420; and children of incarcerated
parents, 41; cutbacks in, 12–13, 163, 377–
78; and gender-responsive movement, 335;
and indigenous women in California, 359;
and long-termers, 296; and reentry, 402, 406,
410, 426; welfare-to-work programs, 13, 406
West Virginia, 378
whites: and abolition of prison system, 29–30,
31; and citizenship, 212; and college programs in prison, 190, 194; in demographics
of prison system, 23n2, 24n17, 166; as drug
users, 15, 24n17, 269; and gender-responsive

TEXT
Minion Pro

DISPLAY
Minion Pro

COMPOSITOR
Integrated Composition Systems

INDEXER
Sharon Sweeney

PRINTER AND BINDER
Maple-Vail Book Manufacturing Group